Using C++

Using C++

Bruce Eckel

Osborne **McGraw-Hill**

Berkeley New York St. Louis San Francisco
Auckland Bogotá Hamburg London Madrid
Mexico City Milan Montreal New Delhi Panama City
Paris São Paulo Singapore Sydney
Tokyo Toronto

Osborne **McGraw-Hill**
2600 Tenth Street
Berkeley, California 94710
U.S.A.

For information on translations and book distributors outside of the U.S.A., please write to Osborne **McGraw-Hill** at the above address.

A complete list of trademarks appears on page 607.
Reprinted with coreections, April, 1990.

Using C++

34567890 DOC/DOC 99876543210

ISBN 0-07-881522-3

Acquisitions Editor: Jeff Pepper
Technical Reviewer: Ron Burk
Copy Editor: Leslie Tilley
Proofreaders: Barbara Conway, Julie Anjos
Word Processor: Judy Koplan
Composition: Bonnie Bozorg
Production Supervisor: Kevin Shafer

This book was produced using Ventura Publisher Version 2.

Dedication

Dedicated to our parents

Contents

Acknowledgments

There were several technical readers for this book. Foremost was Ron Burk of Burk Labs in Seattle. Ron's thorough knowledge and acid pen (ouch!) are greatly responsible for making this book accurate. John Carolan of Glockenspiel in Dublin also read many of the chapters and contributed comments. Bjarne Stroustrup read Chapter 11 and answered many questions about the language by electronic mail—questions I don't think I could have answered any other way. Other technical readers were Walter Bright (Zortech) and Brian McElhinney.

I received help with the style from my friend and editor at Micro Cornucopia Magazine, Gary Entsminger, and the staff at Osborne/McGraw-Hill, including acquisitions editor Jeff Pepper and associate editor Judith Brown.

Emotional support came primarily from Melinda. Comraderie was provided by Carl Haflinger, Mary Nerini, Marilyn Cvitanic, Tim Hohn, Cheri Singer and Sam, Mark Bennett Western, the Moelter Family, the Robbins Family, Allison Brody, Michael Wilk, Dave and Sue Renschler, Dave Mayer, Patrick Conley, Joseph McIssac, Brad Jerbic, Todd, Lynn, Jim and Brice. Larry Fogg contributed the occasional Fractal Thought Pattern.

A lot of the incentive for this book came from my friend Daniel Will-Harris, with whom I seem to have been competing in everything since the first day in junior high school, when we met. We now both have two computer books to our names. If he (and Toni, of course) get a screenplay produced, I could be in trouble. However, that bet about who would be tallest will always be my ace (you still owe me thousands of dollars for that one, DWH!).

Preface

It seems that the most creative and innovative software is developed by small teams of one or two people. As software projects have become larger and more sophisticated, development teams have grown larger in an attempt to cope with the complexity and deadlines. We have seen these teams, and the companies that manage them, lose the clarity of their vision about a project, or simply lose the ability to implement it in a timely manner. The project either fails to materialize, or the delivery date slips, and slips, and slips...

C++ is an object-oriented extension to the C programming language. An object-oriented language allows, among other things, the complexity of a program to be hidden. Most languages come with built-in data types and ways for you to use those data types (add them, pass them around, print them, and so on). C++ and other object-oriented languages allow you to *define your own data types and the ways to use those types.* This is a powerful ability, but it also opens up many new questions (How will you pass objects around? Will you add them? If so, how? How will an object handle errors?). Most users of a language don't need to think about these details (and users of predefined data types in C++ don't need to, either) but when you begin defining your own types each of these questions must be answered. This book serves as a guide to answering those questions.

C++ improves productivity. It does this not by imposing a structure that you must follow if you want the program to come out "right," but by creating a framework in which building an easy-to-read, robust, maintainable, extensible program is the most natural path. This is true whether one is experimenting or creating production code—in fact, you will find that much of the code you create while experimenting survives into production.

The size of the problem a team can manage is based on their abilities and the sophistication of their tools. One of the great benefits I see in C++ is that it puts the power needed to build large, complex projects back in the hands of the one- or two-person team. This means we may start seeing the kind of wild innovation that was so refreshing in the early days of the computer revolution (which I start counting from the time when computers got cheap enough that you weren't forced to do "serious" work on them all the time—people aren't creative when they have to be serious). C++ certainly isn't limited to small projects, however. The language provides a way to communicate interface specifications between members of a large programming team and to enforce the correctness of those interfaces at compile-time. In addition, the ability to easily create and maintain large libraries of useful tools will be a benefit to one-person projects as well as very large teams.

There are numerous advantages to using C++. Some of the reasons the language was designed are

■   To simplify the building and use of libraries.

■   To allow code re-use. If a library function doesn't suit your needs, you can easily modify a portion of it without understanding the whole thing—whether or not you have access to the source code.

■   To improve "maintainability" of code. Since the language supports object-oriented design, code is generally much easier to understand, fix, and modify (someone with a strong bent can still write bad code, however.) C++ fosters systems that can be designed for extensibility.

Many people who learn the language discover a more mysterious benefit. Once a program compiles, it often seems to "just work right the first time." Although there is no way to measure or verify this benefit, it is probably due to the stronger type checking C++ has over C, and the structure even the most avid hackers are seduced into using when creating new data types.

C++ is the first object-oriented language with efficiency as one of its primary goals. Inefficiency and lack of compile-time error checking has held object-oriented languages back from being practical in many production programming situations.

I see the language from an individual viewpoint. One of my favorite things about C++ is that it makes me think about programming in ways I've never considered before. Most commonly used procedural languages make you think about programming; C++ helps you think about problem-solving.

I've had the same experience with C++ as I had when I learned calculus. Before I learned calculus, algebra and trigonometry were interesting, but only marginally useful. I didn't remember them very well. When I learned calculus, a lot of things about algebra and trigonometry became very clear and I quickly learned their intricacies because I had to use them, without thinking about it, on a daily basis. The same thing happened with C++. C++, like calculus, added a new dimension to my thinking. From this new perspective, I could easily see the reasoning behind most of the features in my previous framework of thinking (which was C and Pascal). My knowledge of C has improved greatly since I started programming in C++ in 1987. Except for operator precedence—I've never found a way to make that stick.

If you can shake yourself free from the mindset of "fitting the problem to the computer," I think that you'll find the naturalness of "sending messages to objects" to be a very comfortable and powerful way of thinking about problems.

The Organization of this Book

This book assumes you already know another programming language. It would be easiest, of course, to assume that language is C. However, many people haven't had any incentive to learn C—their own programming language (probably BASIC or Pascal) has been satisfactory—until now. C++ offers enough real benefits over traditional languages that large numbers of programmers will want to learn it.

The book is divided into two parts. After introducing object-oriented languages, Part One (including Chapters 1-4) presents the syntax of ANSI C and C++, covering the features that are common between the two languages, describing the extensions that C++ adds to ANSI C, and especially flagging the places where they are different. This section focuses on more than just the syntax of the languages, however. When you begin writing larger programs in C++, you inevitably create many files that must be managed and compiled properly to build the project. Part One covers the proper construction of multifile projects, emphasizing header files and the **make** utility. All the programs in each chapter, in fact, are created with the **makefile**, which is placed at the end of each chapter.

Part Two covers object-oriented and advanced programming in C++. While Part One shows you what the language features *are,* Part Two shows you how to use them. Chapter 5 shows you how to "overload" operators and functions. Operator overloading means you can give an operator like + or − a special meaning when used with a new data type you create. Function overloading means you can create several meanings for the same function identifier, depending on the argument list.

Chapter 6 shows you how to create objects at run time, for situations when you don't know at compile-time how many objects you will need or what their lifetimes will be. Creating objects at run time is an extremely powerful feature of C++.

Chapter 7 demonstrates how code can be re-used in C++, both by using objects inside of other objects, and through the mechanism of *inheritance*. Chapter 8 shows you how to use inheritance to build extensible programs. Once you've built an extensible program, you or someone else can easily add features without ripping the existing code apart. The ability to build extensible programs will save programmers a lot of time (and software companies a lot of money).

Chapters 9-11 cover advanced topics. Chapter 9 considers the somewhat thorny problems of passing object arguments and returning object values. Much emphasis is placed on the copy-constructor **X(X&)**, which often causes new C++ programmers a lot of grief. Chapter 10 has several complete examples, which provide you with some projects to sink your teeth into. Finally, Chapter 11 covers the latest release of the C++ language from Bell Labs, AT&T release 2.0.

The book has three appendices, each of which is a programming project. Appendix A is a small graphics application that suggests a framework for building a CAD system in C++. Appendix B is a mathematical matrix manipulation package. Appendix C is a text windowing class. Appendices A and C use library functions specific to a certain compiler (Zortech C++), but these functions are hidden in the class methods and may easily be changed. All the rest of the examples in the book should compile under any C++ implementation.

Throughout the book, I've tried to use interesting examples. I have tried to avoid repeating the typical textbook examples in favor of programs that have either been useful or fascinating. One of the more difficult problems in teaching this language seems to be the order in which concepts are introduced. Great efforts have been made to ensure a concept is introduced before it is used in an example, or at least to tell you where a concept is explained, in the few cases where they are used prematurely.

A Note About Compilers

While I was writing this book, I used two different implementations of C++ on the PC: Glockenspiel C++ and Zortech C++ (I have also used AT&T **cfront**, Gnu C++, and Oregon Software C++ on the Sun 3, but not for this book). At the time, both products contained discrepancies with the C++

language. Between the two, however, I could find a way to compile all the examples of correct C++. By the time you read this, many or all of the discrepancies should be fixed. If you are doing serious development work, especially if you want to port it to other platforms, I highly recommend that you acquire more than one implementation of C++. Just because the compiler complains about something doesn't mean it's a bug; and just because code compiles on one implementation doesn't mean it is legal C++ or will work with other compilers. Someday problems like this may be fixed. Until then, you will get surprises unless you constantly test your code for portability.

Source Code Disk

For your convenience, you can get all the sources listed in this book on a 5-1/4″ DS/DD IBM PC-formatted diskette. Each chapter has its own subdirectory and the **makefile**, which is at the end of every chapter, so all you need to do to compile the code is move into the subdirectory and type **make**. There are some further examples; tools I used in the preparation of this book, programs I used to investigate compiler features, and (space allowing) anything else I could add that didn't make it into the book.

The listings in the book have all been compiled. After testing, the source code was automatically put into book format, so human hands didn't have a chance to introduce errors. Sometimes, however, logic errors are discovered, or a compiler bug that allows incorrect syntax to pass through unflagged is fixed. If you discover errors like this, please mail them to the publisher (the address is shown on the copyright page). They will be fixed in the book at the earliest possibility, and the source-code disk will be updated immediately. If you have trouble with a listing, chances are it will be fixed on the source-code disk.

The disk is available postpaid for $25 from

Revolution2

501 N. 36th Street, Suite 163

Seattle, WA 98103

Checks only, please. Foreign orders please add $7, and use a check in U.S. funds drawn on a U.S. bank or an international postal money order. See the form at the end of this preface for details.

My firm, Revolution2, offers C++ consulting and on-site training. For more information, write to the address given for source code disk orders. You can get the company's phone number from the *C Gazette,* where I am the C++ editor and columnist, by calling (213) 473-7414. This is also the number to call if you want a subscription to the magazine. I can be reached electronically on BIX as Beckel, on Compuserve as 72070,3256 or on the internet as 72070.3256@compuserve.com.

Source-Code Disk Order Form

Please send me_____ copies of *Using C++ Source Code Disk* (plus additional projects). I have enclosed a check for $25 for each disk. (Foreign orders please add $7 for shipping and handling, and use a check in US funds drawn on a US bank).

Name _____

Company _____

Address _____

City _____ State _____ Zip _____

Telephone _____

IBM PC Diskette size (check one)   5¼" _____   3½" _____

Send to:

Revolution2
501 N. 36th Street, Suite 163
Seattle, WA 98103

Please send me information on Revolution2 consulting & training _____

Please include any comments you wish the author to read.

Osborne/McGraw-Hill assumes NO responsibility for this offer. This is solely an offer of the author, Bruce Eckel, and not of Osborne/McGraw-Hill.

Introduction to Object-Oriented Languages

Part One

1 Introduction to Object-Oriented Languages

This chapter will lay the groundwork for the rest of the book. To learn C++ you will need some programming experience (described here). The rest of the chapter discusses the ideas behind object-oriented programming, especially as they apply to C++. If all the ideas don't make sense to you as you read them, *don't panic*. The object-oriented approach is a new way to think about programming. You may need to "un-learn" some old ideas before the object-oriented ideas drop into place; non-programmers often pick up object-oriented programming quicker than programmers do.

Basics and Conventions

You will find this book much easier to understand if you are proficient in a *procedural programming language* such as Pascal or C, and have experience creating and using data structures (**record** in Pascal, **struct** in C). In a traditional procedural language, like C or Pascal, functions are emphasized over data. Pieces of data move into a function, other pieces of data move out of the function. Traditional procedural languages are often modeled with *data flow diagrams*, which show data flowing through a system, in and out of functions. C++ and other object-oriented languages combine data structures and functions. The discussions in this book assume you have a fundamental understanding of a traditional procedural language and data structures.

This book covers many of the fundamentals of the C language; it is not, however, a complete reference. Many fine books on C are available. The definitive reference is *The C Programming Language, 2d ed.*, by Brian Kernighan and Dennis Ritchie. The second edition follows the ANSI C standard. (ANSI, the American National Standards Institute, is a standard-setting group.) Since many of the new features of ANSI C were taken from C++, non-ANSI C books will be more confusing than helpful.

Occasionally, references will be made to "Stroustrup." Bjarne Stroustrup created, and continues to evolve, C++. His book with Margaret Ellis, *The Annotated C++ Reference Manual* (ARM) (Addison-Wesley, 1990), is the base document for the ANSI C++ committee (X3J16). When an argument arises about the language, "The Book" is used to resolve the issue. If the experts cannot resolve it, they consult Bjarne himself

In this book, *italics* introduce a new word or concept or emphasize a word or phrase. Keywords, variable names, and function names are in **boldface**. The *programmer* is someone who creates a collection of related functions, which are made available to the *user* (or *client programmer*), who writes programs using these functions. The related functions are generally delivered as a *library*. The source code for the library may or may not be available to the user. The programmer must understand the internals of the library, but the user generally has no desire to. Thus, unlike books that describe "end user" applications, in this book the word "user" refers to someone who writes programs, but is a user of a library.

Programming in an object-oriented language means creating new types of data (called *classes*) and "teaching" those data types how to handle *messages*. You teach a class what to do with a message by creating a *method*. The user creates variables of a data type—*objects* or *instances*—and sends messages to those objects. You could think of this as "Send a message to an object, and let the object figure out what to do with it."

Why Use an Object-Oriented Language?

Object-oriented programming is a new way of thinking about problem solving with computers. Instead of trying to mold the problem into something familiar to the computer, the computer is adapted to the problem. In object-oriented programming, the problem is examined for independent "entities," which relate to other parts of the problem. These entities are chosen not for their "computerizability," but because they have some physical or conceptual boundary that divides them from the rest of the problem. The entities are then represented as objects in the computer program. The goal is to have a one-to-one correspondence between entities in the physical problem and objects in the program.

You may find you have trouble choosing objects because the process is *too* obvious. You are used to forcing problems into the arbitrary solution space of conventional computer programming. It can be a hard habit to break, but try to look at a problem in simple terms. For example, if you're creating a simulation of a parking lot, your objects will be cars, parking spaces, and toll booths. Objects for an oil field might be wells or blasts (for geological mapping). Shape objects can be used in a drawing program. Some statistical analysis programs might need matrix objects.

The Evolution of Object-Oriented Languages

It has been suggested that object-oriented programming is a direct result of the chaos that occurs when conventional languages are applied to very large problems (Jim Waldo, "A New Generation," Unix Review Vol. 6, No. 8, pp. 33-40). As languages develop, so does their ability to handle complexity. In the evolution of each language, there comes a point when programmers begin to have difficulty managing programs of a certain size and sophistication.

The first programming languages were designed to minimize the mistakes created in translating from programming concept to machine representation. These languages use English-like words, and allow the replacement of memory locations with names chosen by the programmer. This support for *mnemonic devices* to trigger mental association means the human spends more time on *semantics* (what the code means) and less time on *syntax* (how the words and phrases are assembled).

The Limits of Functional Languages

Complexity expands to fill available resources. Early programmers soon discovered difficulties in creating large, elaborate programs that worked correctly. Procedural languages were the next step in language evolution. The model used in traditional procedural languages is the *black box*. Each piece of a program is boxed off so the complexity of that piece is hidden. These "boxes" are functions (and, in Pascal, procedures). At the top level, the finished program is a collection of function calls.

The ideal black box doesn't make changes to data outside its boundaries—it doesn't introduce *side effects*. In practice, this constraint is too severe; black boxes do use data outside their boundaries. However, this introduces a weakness to the box since the data isn't completely under its control.

Programs written in early, non-procedural languages tended to be small. So, when the move was made to procedural languages, the code was not difficult to rewrite. Procedural languages, however, are powerful enough to write large and complicated programs, which cannot be cheaply abandoned. Unfortunately, the designers of traditional procedural languages made an unconscious assumption when using the model of the black box that goes something like this: "Maintenance shouldn't be necessary. Needs don't change. Once the code is working, debugged, and correct, it should be epoxied into its black box." This assumption works fine as long as project size is limited, but it can cause surprising disasters as complexity increases.

Programming languages are supposed to manage complexity. But, in the late sixties and early seventies, practitioners saw the limits of procedural languages in managing complexity. Then began the long, drawn-out complaint known as "The Software Crisis." The crisis sneaks up on people. There is no abrupt, chaotic edge when software suddenly becomes unmanageable. It just slowly becomes harder to change, harder to get the bugs out—and harder to find programmers willing to do maintenance work. Managers are frustrated and bewildered, because they know it is *possible* to fix the program, if only they can get someone to stick with it long enough. It is expensive to abandon old code, so people keep trying to save it rather than looking for new ways to program.

STRUCTURED DEVELOPMENT   In traditional procedural languages large programs can be difficult to modify and maintain. The reaction to this problem was to force structure into the programs from outside through a methodology called *structured development*. The techniques salvage traditional procedural languages for use in large projects. However, they require a great deal of forethought and planning so the project will assemble quickly and correctly, and be bug-free and easy to maintain. Because it is an attempt to salvage a particular group of languages and not an insight into the needs of programmers, structured development tends to sound better than it works.

People learn and create through experimentation, not planning. Programmers are no different, and they often have shorter attention spans than most during management planning meetings. Programmers need a system that supports experimentation and salvages as many experiments as possible, not one that requires an entire project to be planned out before any code can be written.

Many useful techniques came out of structured development, but it was not a "magic Band-Aid." The structured techniques were part of the natural progression of a scientific revolution. Whenever the traditional system is found to be flawed, an attempt is made to salvage it. The next step is the creation of a new system which accepts the limitations the old system attempted to deny. Object-oriented programming is one such system. It certainly isn't the final solution. Object-oriented techniques tend to emphasize and support design even more than do structured techniques. You could even think of object-oriented programming as "better structured development."

Support for Experiments and Structure

Using assembly language, the programmer could stop decoding numbers and instead think about words. Procedural languages hid the complexity of operations on data. Object-oriented languages hide the complexity of the program itself, as well as hiding the data.

An object-oriented language emphasizes data types and the intrinsic operations that can be performed on those data types. In object-oriented programming, data do not flow openly around a system, but are protected from accidental modification. *Messages,* rather than data, move around the system. Instead of the procedural approach—"invoke a function on a piece of data"—in an object-oriented language you "send a message to an object."

An object-oriented language supports experimentation in two ways.

■ Objects are neat, robust packages that don't break simply because other objects are around. The programmer can introduce new objects and code knowing that bugs in the new code will be isolated from the rest of the system.

■ New object types may be derived from old ones. This saves programmer time and supports quick explorations. It also localizes bugs to the code for the derived object type, since the original type is assumed to be working correctly.

The support for natural "packaging" of objects has another important effect. Programmers choose to structure a program in an object-oriented language because it helps them code, not because it has some unseen future benefit. Good style becomes the path of least resistance rather than a "cultural revolution." Planning is minimized and action is maximized.

The Process of Language Translation

To further describe object-oriented programming, some background in language translation is necessary. All computer languages are translated from something easy for a human to understand into something executed on a computer, called *machine instructions*. Traditionally, translators fall into two classes: *interpreters* and *compilers*.

How Interpreters Work

An interpreter translates *source code*, written in the programming language, to activities, which may comprise groups of machine instructions, and immediately executes those activities. BASIC is the most popular interpreted language. BASIC interpreters translate and execute one line at a time, and then forget the line has been translated. This makes them slow. More modern interpreters translate the entire program into an intermediate language, which is then executed by a much faster interpreter.

Interpreters have many advantages. The transition from writing code to executing code is almost immediate, and the source code is always available so the interpreter can be much more specific when an error occurs. The benefits often cited for interpreters are ease of interaction and rapid development.

However, interpreters usually have severe limitations when building large projects. The interpreter, or a reduced version, must always be in memory to execute the code, and even the fastest interpreter may introduce unacceptable speed restrictions. Most interpreters require that the complete source code be brought into the interpreter all at once. Not only does this introduce a space limitation, it can also cause more difficult bugs if the language doesn't provide a means to localize the effect of different pieces of code.

How Compilers Work

A compiler translates source code directly into machine instructions. This is an involved process, and usually takes several steps. The transition from writing code to executing code is significantly longer with a compiler.

Depending on the acumen of the compiler writer, programs generated by a compiler tend to require much less space to run, and run much more quickly. Although size and speed are probably the most often cited reasons for using a compiler, in many situations they aren't the most important ones. Some languages, such as C, are designed to allow pieces of a program to be compiled independently. These pieces are eventually combined into a final executable program by a program called the *linker*. This is called *separate compilation*.

Separate compilation has many benefits. A program that, taken all at once, would exceed the limits of the compiler or the compiling environment can be compiled in pieces. Programs can be built and tested one piece at a time. Once a piece is working, it can be saved and forgotten. Collections of tested and working pieces can be combined into libraries for use by other programmers. As each piece is created, the complexity of the other pieces is hidden. All these features support the creation of large programs.

Compiler debugging features have improved significantly. Early compilers only generated machine code, and the programmer inserted print statements to see what was going on. This is not always effective. Recent compilers can insert information about the source code into the executable program. This information is used by powerful *source-level debuggers* to show exactly what is happening in a program by tracing its progress through the source code.

Some compilers, such as Turbo C and Quick C, tackle the compilation speed problem by performing *in-memory compilation*. Most compilers work with files, reading and writing them in each step of the compilation process. In-memory compilers keep the program in RAM. For small programs this can seem as responsive as an interpreter. A compiler that works with files can handle larger files than an in-memory compiler.

The Compilation Process

If you are going to create large programs, you need to understand the steps and tools in the compilation process. Some packages use in-memory compilation. However, in this discussion, the compiler manipulates files.

Some languages (C and C++, in particular) start compilation by running a *preprocessor* on the source code. The preprocessor is a simple program that replaces patterns in the source code with other patterns the programmer has defined using *preprocessor directives*. Preprocessor directives are used to save typing and to increase the readability of the code. The preprocessed code is written to an intermediate file.

Compilers often do their work in two passes. The first pass *parses* the preprocessed code. That is, the compiler breaks the source code into small units and organizes it into a structure called a *tree*. In the expression **A + B** the elements **A**, **+**, and **B** are leaves on the parse tree. The parser then generates a second intermediate file containing the parse tree. A *global optimizer* is sometimes used between the first and second passes to produce smaller, faster code.

In the second pass, the *code generator* walks through the parse tree and generates either assembly-language code or machine code for the nodes of the tree. If the code generator creates assembly code, the assembler is run. The end result in both cases is an object module: a file with an extension of **.o** or **.obj**. A *peephole optimizer* is sometimes used in the second pass to look for pieces of code containing redundant assembly-language statements.

The use of the word "object" to describe chunks of machine code is an unfortunate artifact. The word came into use before anyone thought of object-oriented programming. "Object" is used in the same sense as "goal" when discussing compilation, while in object-oriented programming it means "a thing with boundaries."

The linker combines a list of object modules into an executable program, which can be loaded and run by the operating system. When a function in one object module makes a reference to a function or variable in another object module, the linker resolves these references. The linker brings in a special object module to perform start-up activities. The linker can also search through special files called *libraries*, which contain a collection of object modules in a single file. A library is created and maintained by a program called a *librarian*.

STATIC TYPE CHECKING The compiler performs *type checking* during the first pass. Type checking tests for the proper use of arguments in functions, and prevents many kinds of programming errors. Since type checking occurs during compilation rather than when the program is running, it is called *static type checking*.

Some object-oriented languages (notably Smalltalk) perform all type checking at run time. This is called *dynamic type checking*. Dynamic type checking is less restrictive during development, since you can send *any* message to *any* object—the object figures out, at run time, whether the message is an error. But it adds overhead to program execution and leaves the program open for run time errors that can only be detected through exhaustive testing.

C++ uses static type checking because the language cannot assume any particular run time support for bad messages. Static type checking notifies the programmer about misuse of types right away, and maximizes execution speed. As you learn C++ you will see that most of the language design decisions favor the same kind of high-speed, robust, production-oriented programming the C language is famous for.

(If you wish you can disable static type checking. You can also do your own dynamic type checking—you just need to write the code.)

Why You Need Objects

Now that some of the framework is in place, the specific problems with traditional programming languages and the solutions offered by C++ will be examined.

Creating Multiple Entities

When using a traditional procedural language, the programmer often creates functions that cannot easily be adapted to new situations. A common pitfall is the "one-function solution." Here, it is assumed that there is only one of something, and that fact is wired into the system. When a situation arises where there is more than one, the program must be redesigned. As an example, when displaying information, you can fall into the habit of programming as if the screen is the only way to talk to the end user. If a window system is used, however, your whole way of thinking must change—now there are many screens, each of which must be treated as a separate entity.

To manage multiple entities in a traditional procedural language, a data structure must be declared to hold all the information necessary for each entity. For instance, a window structure has an X,Y location, a size, foreground and background colors, a place to store data, and so on. Functions are defined to initialize, clean up, and manipulate the entities. It takes effort to think of the display as a single screen and then switch to thinking of multiple windows. If the code is written using the object-oriented features of C++, creating multiple entities is fairly simple: a data structure is declared for each entity, and functions are called with the address of a structure as a parameter. It is as easy to create one entity as to create many.

This system works fine, but there is a lot of room for bookkeeping errors. The user of the library must remember to initialize and clean up the structures. Sometimes the programmer forces the user to do this via direct manipulation of the structure, rather than through functions. This can be confusing, since there are usually structure elements that are used internally by the system, but are visible to the user. The visibility of structure elements presents another problem: the user's functions may also manipulate structure elements—sometimes intentionally, sometimes by accident. The user can inadvertently change structure elements, which can cause bizarre and untraceable results. Headaches from trying to use someone else's library are familiar to anyone who has tried it—your luck depends on the diligence of the person documenting the system.

Other languages provide various levels of support for the use of libraries. With some effort, the programmer can design systems that allow multiple entities in other languages. Stroustrup feels that library use is essential to building large projects, so he puts a lot of emphasis on that in C++, and tries to support a coding style that lends itself to the manipulation of multiple entities.

Data Abstraction

C++ supports multiple entities and libraries using *data abstraction*. Data abstraction means you can combine the data structure and the operations on that data structure together into a new *abstract data type*. An abstract data type behaves just like data types that are built into the language, except they aren't part of the language definition; they are something the programmer has created.

When you create a data structure in a traditional procedural language, you usually create functions to manipulate the structure. Those functions can only be used on that structure. Other functions won't know how to manipulate the structure since the structure isn't a built-in type. It makes sense, then, to bind into one unit the data structure and the functions that will manipulate it. In C++, this unit is called a *class* (also called a *user-defined type*). Variables, or *instances*, of that class are called *objects*.

As a user of a traditional functional language, you don't think about what goes on when you declare and use a built-in data type, or what the variable looks like inside. The functionality of a data type is built into the compiler, and it is complicated. An IEEE floating-point number, for example, contains an exponent, a mantissa, and a sign bit, all of which must be initialized properly. When you use floating-point numbers, the compiler calls special floating-point functions. To prevent errors, you don't have explicit control over the exponent, mantissa, or sign data—these are only manipulated by the special functions called by the compiler.

Abstract data typing works the same way. The data elements of a structure may be *private*, so the user cannot directly manipulate them. **Private** data elements may only be manipulated by special functions that are part of the class (*member functions*) or non-member functions that have been given special permission (*friend functions*). This prevents accidental modification of the data, and makes it much easier to track down bugs.

Each class has two special types of member function. One, called the *constructor*, takes care of initialization when a new object is created. The other, the *destructor*, automatically cleans up an object when it is no longer needed. In the case of a window object, a constructor might create space in memory and paint the window on the screen. The destructor would remove the window from the screen and free the memory. Constructors and destructors prevent the existence of objects that haven't been initialized properly, and thus remove another source of bugs.

Some languages, such as C, can define an *alias* for a structure or built-in type and use the alias as if it were a new type. In C, the keyword for this is **typedef**, which suggests abstract data typing. True abstract data typing differs from defining an alias. In abstract data typing, the programmer defines a data structure, the private elements and the functions that are used only with that structure, and the initialization and cleanup functions. The resulting abstract data type is treated by the compiler almost as if it were a built-in data type. The compiler ensures that the type is used properly and that only specific functions modify the data in the object.

Organizing Code

In C++, the *interface* description and the *implementation* of a class are separate. The interface describes what the class does; the implementation defines how the class works. Compilation—but not final linking—can occur with only the interface description. A different implementation can be created at a later date and linked in, without recompiling the rest of the project. This feature has a number of benefits. Bugs, and bug fixes, tend to be isolated; they don't ripple through the rest of the code. You can make improvements and modifications without worrying about destroying the correct behavior of some other part of the system.

Software engineers find the separation of interface and implementation very helpful. You can describe and compile a system to ensure it all fits together without writing an implementation. The compiler is, in effect, a "design checker." Once the interfaces are specified, the implementation proceeds with the knowledge that system integration has already occurred.

FINDING THE OBJECTS IN YOUR SYSTEM   Classes also support a logical breakdown of code components. The best way to define classes is to look for distinct elements in the problem description. An object in the computer program (the solution domain) should correspond as closely as possible to an object in the problem domain. This makes the program much simpler to describe to non-programmers. It also prevents the phenomenon often seen in programming where every solution looks like a computer, rather than like a weather system, a controller, a multimeter, or whatever. A solution that is a reflection of the problem domain is much easier to repair and modify, and thus cheaper to maintain.

C++ is intended to support library use. It guides the programmer toward a particular style of program organization. In addition, a particular interface is not just a suggestion to be used or discarded by the user. Although the structured approach relies on human organization to make sure the implementation doesn't stray from the specification, the C++ translator *enforces* the proper use of data types (classes). This feature supports the construction of very large projects; the specification language is the **class** declaration, and the compiler checks for accurate implementation and use.

The Advantages of Inheritance

In an object-oriented language, you can *inherit* the characteristics of one user-defined type (class) into another. When you inherit, you say, "This new class is an old one, plus a few additions and modifications," or, "with a few restrictions."

Effort

Inheritance is useful in two ways. One way is that it conserves coding effort. If you have a debugged, operational class that you or someone else has written, inheritance helps you reuse the code in the class. You don't need to fight through the source code and understand the implementation; you just make changes where you need them and reuse old code. If this weren't possible you might prefer to start from scratch rather than struggle to figure out how the code works.

Creating Extensible Programs

The second use for inheritance is more subtle and powerful. The object-oriented concept of *subclassing* helps the programmer organize a solution to make it easy to maintain and extend.

When a *derived class* inherits from a *base class*, the objects of the derived class still retain membership in the base class. By deriving many classes from the same base class, you can create a group of classes that have the same interface but different implementations. The main program manages a group of these objects. It can send any message to any object, but the effect will be different depending on the specific subclass.

For instance, suppose you are designing an air traffic control system. All objects on the display will be of **class plane**, but they will each have their own pattern on the screen. The base class in this system is **plane**, and the interface to **plane** says that "a **plane** object knows how to draw itself and move itself," even though a **plane** can't know how to perform these operations until it knows whether it's an airliner or a small private aircraft. The different types of **plane**s are derived from **plane**, and each is given methods to draw and move themselves. The air traffic control system handles **plane** objects, it sends messages to the objects telling them to draw and move themselves, and the objects figure out what to do with the messages.

Using identical interfaces with different implementations is called *polymorphism*. Like many C++ features, polymorphism improves program clarity. A program designed around polymorphism is easy to maintain and extend. To extend a polymorphic program, simply derive a new subclass from the same base **class** the other generic objects inherited. The new subclass can be managed by the same program without modification. And since the program is only a manager for a set of generic objects, bugs are automatically isolated in the objects themselves. Once a base class is debugged, any errors in a new derived class must be due to the new code in the derived class.

You can see an example of polymorphism in Appendix A. This is a program called MicroCAD, which creates and manipulates graphic objects on the screen of an IBM PC or compatible using a mouse (the framework can be adapted for any system). The program manages generic objects of the base class named **cadshape**. The **cadshape** class has an interface that includes methods to **draw( )** and **erase( )**. The **circle**, **square**, and **line** subclasses are all derived from **cadshape** and they have specific implementations of **draw( )** and **erase( )**. The program sends, for instance, the **draw( )** message to a **cadshape** object, ignorant of whether it is a **circle**, **square**, or **line**. The object figures out how to draw itself. The program never needs to know the specific type of the object, only that it is a **cadshape**.

To extend MicroCAD, derive a new subclass, for example, **triangle**, from **cadshape**, add "triangle" to the mouse menu, and implement the methods to **draw( )**, **erase( )**, and destroy a **triangle**. That's all there is to it—the program already knows how to send all possible messages to objects of type **triangle**, since **triangle** is just another **cadshape**.

LATE BINDING *Resolving* a function call is the process of inserting the address (or some other reference) of the function definition at the point where the function is called. When the program executes, the function is executed by performing an assembly-language call to that address. A typical compiled language resolves function calls at compile time.

A program designed around polymorphism manages a collection of base class objects. The precise result of a message sent to one of these objects cannot be determined at compile time, since only the base class, not the subclass, of the object is known. The specific function that is called must thus be determined at run time, rather than at compile time. The ability to delay function resolution until run time is called *late binding*. Late binding is an essential feature of an object-oriented language because it is the mechanism that implements polymorphism.

Using Overloading

The idea of an "intelligent object" deciding what to do with a message has one more aspect in C++. *Overloading* means one function name can be used in many different ways. As an example, suppose a class has a method called **print**. You can overload **print** so it will display the contents of an object when called without arguments, or display the object and some text when called with a string argument, or display some other kind of information when called with other arguments. Therefore, you can call **print** with a variety of different arguments, and, in effect, the object figures out what to do with the message.

Ordinary functions (not class methods) can also be overloaded in C++, providing a single function name and many argument lists. C++ also allows operators (**+**, **−**, **=**, and so on) to be overloaded so that mathematically oriented objects can be used with a familiar syntax. For example, Appendix B is a matrix class. Matrices may be added, subtracted, multiplied, and so on. The code looks just like the mathematical equations, so it's a better match to the problem being solved.

The Definition of
An Object-Oriented Language

Now that you've been introduced to all the concepts, you are ready for a complete definition.

■ An object-oriented language supports three key features: abstract data typing, inheritance, and polymorphism.

■ The primary activity in object-oriented programming is the creation of new abstract data types (**class**es). These data types can be created through inheritance and can have polymorphic characteristics.

■ The user of a **class** creates objects and sends messages to the objects. An object "figures out" what to do with a message.

■ Data abstraction and hiding reduce inter-module dependence. This means that modifying code in one section won't affect code in another section—changes are isolated, and don't propagate through the system.

■ Inheritance helps you reuse code. When used with polymorphism, inheritance helps you reuse program designs and create extensible programs. This isn't automatic; you must build it into the system.

How C++ Supports
Object-Oriented Programming

These features of C++ support object-oriented programming:

■ C++ supports abstract data typing with the **class** construct. Elements of the **class** (*members*) can be built-in data types, objects, or functions. Members can be **public** (available to everyone), **private** (only available to other members), or **protected** (available to **class** members and members of inherited classes). Combining like functions and data is called *encapsulation*. Removing some data from public view is called *data hiding*.

■ C++ supports inheritance. You can derive a new user-defined type from an old one, and make changes only where you need them. Inheritance promotes easy code re-use, and it is essential to implement polymorphism.

■ C++ supports polymorphism with the **virtual** keyword. When a **virtual** function is created in a base **class** it may be redefined in a derived **class**. When the function is called as a member of the base **class**, the proper code is called via late binding.

■ Function overloading provides support for the general idea of "send a message to an object, and let the object figure out what to do with it."

■ C++ supports object-oriented programming without losing the efficiency of C.

C++ Versus Smalltalk

Smalltalk and similar object-oriented languages are different from C++. They generally provide much more of an "environment" for programming. Many implementations of Smalltalk go so far as to replace the operating system. Often, all the function binding occurs at run time and there is no static type checking. Debugging is built into each object. Every object is derived from the same base **class** and the *activation record* (containing the primary information about each object) is the same size, so all objects can be manipulated by the debugger. For these reasons, Smalltalk and similar languages have a much different feel than C++, and a common claim from Smalltalk programmers is that C++ is not truly object-oriented.

C++ was designed to provide support for object-oriented programming, and to bring the benefits of that system into the mainstream development world. On the way, some compromises were made. In particular, Stroustrup was unwilling to give up the run time efficiency of C. For robust production code, static type checking was necessary. Finally, demanding that all objects be derived from the same base **class** is an impractical constraint on the programmer. Debugging à la Smalltalk isn't possible, so conventional compiled-language debuggers are used instead.

C++ combines the benefits of object-oriented programming with the practical speed of C. It was designed for and is used in real programming projects at AT&T, in switching systems and the next version of UNIX, among others. Whether it is "truly object oriented" is unimportant—what's important is that it increases your programming power.

Summary

If, after this brief and somewhat philosophical introduction to object-oriented programming, you don't feel you can dive in and instantly use all the features, fear not; you can still write working programs. One of the objectives of C++ is to retain the experience of the enormous number of C programmers (and, since Pascal is a cousin to C—at least in spirit—this extends to Pascal programmers). You can start using C++ by programming in your usual style, and then add features as you learn them. Don't worry, though, the features are enticing. Once you get an appetite for new ones you will want to keep trying them.

2 Using Predefined Classes

The user-defined data type, or class, distinguishes C++ from traditional procedural languages. A class is a new data type that is designed to solve a particular type of problem. Once a class is defined anyone can use it—without knowing the specifics of how it works or even how classes are created. This chapter will teach you enough of the basics of C and C++ that you can use a class written by someone else, without knowing how it was created. The coverage of C++ features that are similar to C features will continue in Chapters 3 and 4.

This chapter treats classes as if they are just another built-in data type available for use in programs. To avoid using concepts before they are defined, the process of writing your own classes is delayed until the end of Chapter 3. This may seem tedious to experienced C programmers, but leaping over the necessary basics would be confusing for programmers moving to C++ from other languages.

Unless otherwise noted, all descriptions in this book (up to Chapter 11) refer to the version of C++ that conforms to AT&T release 1.2. Chapter 11 describes many of the new features in AT&T release 2.0. All references to C, unless otherwise noted, mean ANSI C.

If you are experienced with Pascal or some other procedural language, this chapter will give you a background in the style of C used in C++. If you are familiar with the style of C described in the first edition of Kernighan & Ritchie (often called "K&R C"), you will find some new and different features in C++ as well as in ANSI C. If you are familiar with ANSI C, and in particular with function prototypes, you should skim through this chapter looking for features that are particular to C++.

Classes that someone else has created are often packaged into a library. This chapter uses the *streams* I/O library of classes, which comes with all C++ implementations. Streams are a very useful way to read from files and the keyboard, and to write to files and I/O devices including displays and printers. After the basics of building a program in C and C++ are covered, streams will be used to show how easy it is to use a predefined library of classes.

But first, to create a program you must understand the tools used to build applications.

Tools for Separate Compilation

Chapter 1 discussed the importance of separate compilation when building large projects. In C and C++, a program can be created in small, manageable, independently tested pieces. Programs created with separate compilation can be much larger than programs created by "one-file" languages. One-file languages require the entire program to be contained in a single file. BASIC and early versions of Turbo Pascal are examples of one-file languages.

Programming in a language that supports separate compilation is different from programming in a one-file language. To create a program with multiple files, functions in one file must access functions and data in other files. When compiling a file, the C or C++ compiler must know about the functions and data in the other files: their names and proper usage. The compiler can then ensure the functions and data are used correctly. This process of "telling the compiler" the names of external functions and data and what they should look like is called *declaration*. Once a function or variable is declared, the compiler knows how to check to make sure it is used properly.

At the end of the compilation process, the executable program is constructed from the *object modules* and libraries. Object modules are produced by the compiler from the source code. They are files with extensions of **.o** or **.obj**, and should not be confused with object-oriented programming "objects."

The linker must go through all the object modules and resolve all the external references, that is, make sure that all the external functions and data you claimed existed, via declarations during compilation, actually exist.

Declarations Versus Definitions

A *declaration* tells the compiler, "This piece of data or function exists somewhere else, and this is what it should look like." A *definition* tells the compiler, "Make this piece of data here" or "Make this function here." You can declare a piece of data or a function in many different places, but there must only be *one* definition in C and C++. When the linker is uniting all the object modules, it will complain if it finds more than one definition for the same function or piece of data. Almost all C and C++ programs require declarations. Before you can write your first program, you need to understand the proper way to write a declaration.

Function Declaration Syntax A function declaration in ANSI C and C++ gives the function name, the argument types passed to the function, and the return value of the function. For example, here is a declaration for a function called **func1** that takes two integer arguments (integers are denoted in C and C++ with the keyword **int**) and returns an integer:

int func1(int,int);

C programmers should note that this is different from function declarations in K&R C. The first keyword you see is the return value, all by itself: **int**. The arguments are enclosed in parentheses after the function name, in the order they are used. The semicolon indicates the end of a statement; in this case it tells the compiler, "That's all—there is no function definition here."

    C and C++ declarations attempt to mimic the form of the item's use. For example, if **A** is another integer, the above function might be used the following way:

A = func1(2,3);

Since **func1( )** returns an integer, the C or C++ compiler will check the use of **func1( )** to make sure **A** is an integer and that both arguments are integers.

In C and C++, arguments in function declarations may have names. The compiler ignores the names, but they can be helpful as mnemonic devices for the user. For example, we can declare **func1( )** in a different fashion that has the same meaning:

int func1(int length, int width);

Empty Argument Lists   There is a significant difference between C (both ANSI and K&R) and C++ for functions with empty argument lists. In C, the declaration

int func2( );

means "a function with any number and type of argument." In C++ it means, "a function with no arguments." If you declare a function with an empty argument list in C++, remember that it's different from what you may be used to in C.

Function Definitions   Function definitions look like function declarations except they have *bodies*. A body is a collection of statements enclosed in braces ({ }). Braces denote the beginning and ending of a block of code; they have the same purpose as the **begin** and **end** keywords in Pascal. To give **func1( )** a definition that is an empty body (a body containing no code), write this:

int func1(int length, int width) { }

Notice that in the function definition, the braces replace the semicolon. Since braces surround a statement or group of statements, you don't need a semicolon. Note that the arguments in the function definition must be given names. The arguments are used in the function body (the above case is a pathological exception) and there must be some way to reference them. Function definitions are explored later in the book.

Variable Declaration Syntax   The meaning attributed to the phrase "variable declaration" has historically been confusing and contradictory; it's important you understand the correct definition so you can read code properly. A variable declaration tells the compiler what a variable looks like. It says, "I know you haven't seen this name before, but I promise it exists someplace, and it's a variable of X type." In a function declaration you give a type (the return value), the function name, the argument list, and a semicolon. That's enough for the compiler to figure out that it's a declaration, and what the function should look like. By inference, a variable declaration *might* be a type followed by a name. For example,

int A;

could declare the variable **A** as an integer, using the above logic. Here's the conflict: there is enough information in the above code for the compiler to create space for an integer called **A**—and that's what happens. **Int A** can be both a declaration and a definition. To resolve this dilemma, a keyword was necessary in C and C++ to say, "This is only a declaration; it's defined elsewhere." The keyword is **extern**. It can mean the definition is external to the file, or comes later in the file.

   Declaring a variable means using the **extern** keyword before a description of the variable, like this:

extern int A;

The keyword **extern** can also apply to function declarations. It looks like this for **func1( )**:

extern int func1(int length, int width);

This statement is equivalent to the previous **func1( )** declarations. Since there is no function body, the compiler must treat it as a function declaration rather than a function definition. The **extern** keyword is superfluous and optional for function declarations. It is probably unfortunate that the designers of C did not require the use of **extern** for function declarations; it would have been more consistent and less confusing. This book will use the **extern** keyword for clarity when making function declarations.

Including Headers   Most libraries contain significant numbers of functions and variables. To save work and ensure consistency when making the external declarations for these items, C and C++ use a device called the *header* file. A header file is a file containing the external declarations for a library. The programmer who creates the library provides the header file. To declare the functions and external variables in the library, the user simply includes the header file.

Header files conventionally have filename extensions containing the letter "h." In C, a header file name looks like

headerfile.**h**

In C++, you can include plain C header files or you can include C++ header files, which can look like

headerfile.**h**

or

headerfile.**hxx**

or

headerfile.**hpp**

In the original UNIX version of C++ from AT&T, it was not considered necessary to differentiate between C header files and C++ header files. They are both essentially just files filled with text. Other implementors, however, found it useful to set C++ header files apart from C header files by the use of a special extension, usually ".**hpp**" or ".**hxx**." In this book, the **.hxx** extension will be used; the Glockenspiel and Zortech packages both allow it.

To include a header file, use the **#include** preprocessor directive. This tells the preprocessor to open the named header file and insert its contents where the **#include** statement appears. Files may be named in an **#include** statement in two ways: in double quotes("") or in angle brackets (**<>**). Filenames in double quotes, such as

#include "local.h"

tell the preprocessor to search the current directory for the file and report an error if the file does not exist. Filenames in angle brackets tell the preprocessor to look through a search path specified in the environment. Setting the search path varies between machines, operating systems, and C++ implementations.

To include the streams header file on MS-DOS, you say

#include <stream.hxx>

For UNIX, you say

#include <stream.h>

The preprocessor will find the streams header file (often in a subdirectory called INCLUDE) and insert it. Please note that **stream.hxx** is the name used for Glockenspiel C++. If you are using Zortech C++ you must either change the name in the program to **stream.hpp** or move to the INCLUDE subdirectory and copy **stream.hpp** to **stream.hxx**.

In C, a header file should not contain any function or data definitions because the header can be included in more than one file. At link time, the linker would then find multiple definitions and complain. In C++, there are two exceptions: **inline** functions and **const** constants (described later in the book) can both be safely placed in header files.

Linking

The linker collects object modules generated by the compiler into an executable program the operating system can load and run. It is the last phase of the compilation process. Linker characteristics vary from system to system. Generally, you just tell the linker the names of the object modules and libraries you want linked together, and the name of the executable file, and it goes to work. Some systems require you to invoke the linker yourself. With most C++ packages you invoke the linker through C++. In many situations, the linker is invoked for you, invisibly.

Many linkers won't search object files and libraries more than once, and they search through the list you give them from left to right. This means that the order of object files and libraries can be important. If you have a mysterious problem that doesn't show up until link time, one possibility is the order in which the files are given to the linker.

Using Libraries

Now that you know the basic terminology, you can understand how to use a library. To use a library

1. Include the library's header file.

2. Use the functions and variables in the library.

3. Link the library into the executable program.

These steps also apply when the object modules aren't combined into a library. Including a header file and linking the object modules are the basic steps for separate compilation in both C and C++.

How the Linker Searches a Library   When you make an external reference to a function or variable in C or C++, the linker, upon encountering this reference, can do one of two things. If it has not already encountered the definition for the function or variable, it adds it to its list of "unresolved references."   If the linker has already encountered the definition, the reference is resolved.

If the linker cannot find the definition in the list of object modules it searches the libraries. Libraries are indexed, so the linker doesn't need to look through all the object modules in the library—it just looks in the index. When the linker finds a definition in a library, the entire object module, not just the function definition, is linked into the executable program. Note that the whole library isn't linked, just the object module (otherwise programs would be unnecessarily large). If you want to minimize executable program size, you might consider putting a single function in each source code file when you build your own libraries. This requires more editing, but it can be helpful to the user.

Because the linker searches files in the order you give them, you can preempt the use of a library function by inserting a file with your own function, which uses the same name, into the list before the library name appears. Since the linker will resolve any references to this function by using your function before it searches the library, your function will be substituted for the library function.

Secret Additions   When an executable C or C++ program is created, certain items are secretly linked in. One of these is the *start-up module*, which contains initialization routines that must be run anytime a C or C++ program executes. These routines set up the stack and initialize certain variables in the program.

The linker always searches the *standard library* for the compiled versions of any "standard" functions that were called in the program. The streams functions, for example, are in the standard C++ library.

Because the standard library is always searched, you can use any function (or class, in C++) in the library by simply including the appropriate header file in your program. To use the streams functions, you just include the **stream.hxx** header file.

In non-ANSI implementations of C (and C++ C-code generators that use non-ANSI implementations of C), commonly used functions are not always contained in the library that is searched by default. Math functions, in particular, are often kept in a separate library. The library name must be added to the list of files handed to the linker.

Using Plain C Libraries   You are not restricted from using C library functions just because you are writing code in C++. A tremendous amount of work has been done for you in these functions, so they can save you a lot of time. You should hunt through your compiler manuals before writing new functions. Using these predefined C library functions is quite simple; just include the appropriate header file and use the function.

This book will use C library functions whenever possible. Only ANSI C library functions will be used, to increase the portability of the programs.

NOTE   Since ANSI C header files use function prototyping, their function declarations agree with C++. If, however, your C header files use the older K&R C "empty-argument-list" style for function declarations, you will have trouble because the C++ compiler takes these to mean "functions with no arguments." To correct the problem you must create new header files and either put the proper argument lists in the declarations or simply put ellipses (**...**) in the argument list, which means "any number and type of arguments."

Your First C++ Program

You now know enough of the basics to create and compile a program. The program will use the predefined C++ streams class that comes with all C++

packages. The streams class handles input and output for files, with the console, and with "standard" input and output (which may be redirected to files or devices). In this very simple program, a stream object will be used to print a message on the screen.

Using the Streams class

To declare the functions and external data in the streams class, include the header file with the statement

#include <stream.hxx>

On some Unix C++ implementations, the C++ header files use a **.h** extension, so the statement will look like

#include <stream.h>

From now on, the **.hxx** format will be used. If you are using Unix or some other system you may need to change the extension.

The first program uses the concept of *standard output*, which means "a general-purpose place to send output." You will see other examples using standard output in different ways, but here it will just go to the screen. The streams class automatically defines a variable (an object) called **cout** that accepts all data bound for standard output.

To send data to standard output, use the operator **<<**. C programmers know this operator as the *bitwise left shift*. C++ allows operators to be *overloaded*. When you overload an operator, you give it a new meaning that depends on the object the operator is used with. With streams, the operator **<<** means "send to." For example,

cout << "howdy!";

sends the string **"howdy!"** to the object called **cout**. Chapter 5, "Overloading Functions and Operators," covers operator overloading in detail.

Fundamentals of Program Structure

A C or C++ program is a collection of variables, function definitions, and function calls. When the program starts, it executes initialization code and calls a special function, **main( )**. You put the primary code for the program here. (All functions in this book are shown with parentheses after the function name).

A function definition consists of a return value type (which defaults to integer if none is specified), a function name, an argument list in parentheses, and the function code contained in braces. Here is a sample function definition:

int function( ) {

**   // function code here (this is a comment)**

}

The above function has an empty argument list and a body that contains only a comment.

There can be many sets of braces within a function definition, but there must always be at least one set surrounding the function body. Since **main( )** is a function it must follow these rules.

C and C++ are *free-form* languages. With few exceptions, the compiler ignores carriage returns and white space, so it must have some way to determine the end of a statement. In C and C++, statements are delimited by semicolons.

C comments start with **/*** and end with ***/**. They can include carriage returns. C++ uses C-style comments and adds a new type of comment: **//**. A **//** starts a comment that terminates with a carriage return. It is more convenient than **/* */** for one-line comments, and is used extensively in this book.

The "Hello, world!" Program

And now, finally, the first program:

```
// HELLO.CXX : Saying Hello with C++

#include <stream.hxx> // stream declarations

main() {
    cout << "Hello, World! I am " << 5 << " Today!\n";
}
```

The **cout** object is handed a series of arguments, which it prints out in left-to-right order. With streams, you can string together a series of arguments like this, which makes the class easy to use.

Text inside double quotes is called a *string*. The compiler creates space for strings and stores the ASCII equivalent for each character in this space. The string is terminated with a value of 0 to indicate the end of the string. Special characters that do not print are expressed with *escape sequences,* consisting of a backslash (****) followed by a special code. In the preceding program, the **\n** means *new line*. Your compiler manual or ANSI C guide gives a complete set of escape sequences. Others used in this book are **\t** (tab), **** (backslash), and **\b** (backspace). Notice that the entire phrase terminates with a semicolon.

String arguments and constant numbers are mixed in the **cout** statement. This is possible because the operator **<<** is overloaded. Because the **<<** operator can have a variety of meanings when used with **cout**, you can send **cout** a variety of different arguments, and it will "figure out" what to do with the message.

Running the Compiler

To compile the program, edit it into a plain text file called HELLO.CXX and invoke the compiler with HELLO.CXX as the argument. For simple, one-file programs like the preceding example, most compilers will take you all the way through the process. To run Glockenspiel C++, the command line is

ccxx hello.cxx

The Zortech C++ compiler looks at the filename extension to determine whether to use the C or C++ compiler, so a command line of

ztc hello.cxx

or

ztc hello

works equally well. The first form will be used in this book, since it is compatible with both packages.

Unix C++ packages vary. Plain "vanilla" **cfront** from AT&T uses a capital **CC** to run C++, but you should check your particular installation.

C++ Translation Strategies

Chapter 1 stated that all languages are implemented with translators. There are two types of translators for C++: *C-code generators* and *native-code* compilers (see the following section, "Native-Code C++ Compilers"). The activities you see when you invoke C++ depend on the approach used in your translator.

C-Code Generation   When Bjarne Stroustrup created C++, he realized that a large hurdle in its acceptance would be availability. To make it more readily available, he created a C-code generator that can be quickly ported to any platform having a C compiler. The C-code generator translates C++ into C and feeds it to the local C compiler. Most packages for Unix are derived from AT&T **cfront**, and thus are C-code generators. The Guidelines and Glockenspiel C++ packages for MS-DOS are also C-code generators derived from **cfront**.

C-code generators have several advantages. Because they are derived from the original AT&T sources, C++ programs tend to be transportable between different platforms running C-code generators. The debugged C-code generator can be quickly moved to another environment. For example, Glockenspiel C++ has a package available for OS/2 at this writing. When attempting to decipher the meaning of a C++ statement, it is possible (though often painful) to discern meaning from the generated C code.

C-code generators benefit from the libraries and tools developed for their companion C compiler. Guidelines and Glockenspiel C++, for example, use

Microsoft C to compile their output. This means that all the libraries commercially available for Microsoft C can be used with Guidelines and Glockenspiel C++ (although the header files may need modification if they use K&R-style declarations). Conversely, the output from the Zortech C++ native-code compiler often will not link with commercial libraries unless those libraries have been compiled with the Zortech C or C++ compiler.

C-code generators tend to be slower than native-code compilers because once the C-code generator finishes the C compiler must run. The maximum size and complexity of the source code file they can compile is usually less than for native-code compilers. (However, you can sometimes fix this by breaking the program into smaller files.) C-code generators are dependent upon the vagaries of their companion C compiler. For instance, Microsoft C truncates function and variable names after 32 characters. Since C++ tends to generate long variable names, this can sometimes cause problems. C-code generators also tend to be somewhat more expensive than native-code compilers, since the companies marketing them must pay royalties to AT&T.

Native-Code C++ Compilers   Native-code C++ compilers perform all the activities of the C-code generator and the C compiler combined. They tend to run much faster and compile larger source code files than C-code generators. Native-code compilers are built from scratch. This means the compiler-writer has control over the entire compilation process, and the system can be optimized for C++. It also means a much bigger job, and more opportunity for error.

Native-code compilers do not use AT&T sources, so they can be cheaper (no royalties to AT&T) and they don't inherit the bugs and limitations of the C-code generator. It is generally agreed that the native-code compiler is the more desirable implementation and that C-code generators are a temporary phase to speed acceptance.

At this writing, five native-code compilers are available. For Unix, Oregon Software C++ compiler (and source-level debugger) runs on Sun workstations. The Free Software Foundation distributes the GNU C++ compiler with source code for the compiler and libraries, but is only designed to run under Unix on Suns and other machines with large linear address spaces. On MS-DOS, Zortech C++ was created from Walter Bright's well-tested Datalight C compiler. It has been around long enough to be robust and supports features in AT&T release 2.0 (see Chapter 11). Borland's Turbo C++ is an excellent, very complete C++ 2.0

compiler for MS-DOS, along with tools including a superb debugger and profiler.

Terminology Both C-code generators and native-code compilers are a type of compiler: they take code in one form and produce code in another. This book will use the term "compiler" when discussing both C-code generators and native-code compilers. When a distinction is necessary, the more specific "C-code generator" or "native-code compiler" will be used.

make—*an Essential Tool* *For Separate Compilation*

There is one more tool you should understand before creating programs in C++. The **make** utility manages all the individual files in a project. **make** was developed on Unix. The C language was developed to write the Unix operating system, and as programs encompassed more and more files, the job of deciding which files should be recompiled because of changes became tedious and error-prone, so **make** was invented.

When you edit the files in a project, **make** ensures that only the source files that were changed, and other files affected by the modified files, are recompiled. By using **make**, you don't have to recompile all the files in your project every time you make a change. It also remembers all the commands to put your project together. Learning to use **make** will save you a lot of time and frustration.

Most C compilers come with a **make** program. *All* C++ packages either come with a **make**, or are used with a C compiler that has a **make**.

make *Activities*

When you type "**make**," the **make** program looks in the current directory for a file named MAKEFILE, which you have created if it's your project. This file contains rules describing *dependencies* between source code files. **make** looks at the dates on files; if a dependent file has an older date than a file it depends on, **make** executes the *rule* given after the dependency.

All comments in makefiles start with a **#** and continue to the end of the line. As a simple example, the makefile for the "hello" program might contain

 # a comment

hello.exe: hello.cxx

    ztc hello.cxx

This says that HELLO.EXE (the *target*) depends on HELLO.CXX. When HELLO.CXX has a more recent date than HELLO.EXE, the rule ZTC HELLO.CXX is executed. There may be multiple dependencies and multiple rules. All the rules must begin with a tab.

By creating groups of interdependent dependency-rule sets, you can modify source code files, type "make", and be certain that all the affected files will be recompiled correctly.

Macros A makefile may contain *macros*. Macros allow convenient string replacement. The makefiles in this book use a macro to invoke the C++ compiler. For example:

#Macro to invoke Glockenspiel C++

CPP = ccxx

hello.exe: hello.cxx

    $(CPP) hello.cxx

The **$** and parentheses expand the macro. To *expand* means to replace the macro call **$(CPP)** with the string **cxx**. With the above macro, if you want to change to a different compiler (Turbo C++, for instance), you just change the line

CPP = ccxx

to

CPP = tcc

You can also add compiler flags to the macro.

Makefiles in This Book

Makefiles will be used throughout the book at the end of chapters to compile all the programs in the chapter. Because implementations of **make** vary from system to system, only the most basic features will be used. You should be aware that there are many advanced shortcuts that can save a lot of time when using **make**. Your documentation will describe the further features of **make**.

More About Streams

So far you have seen only the most rudimentary aspect of the streams **class**. The output formatting available with streams includes number formatting in decimal, octal, and hex. Here's another example of the use of streams:

```
// STREAM2.HXX : more streams features
#include <stream.hxx>

main() {
  cout << "a number in decimal: " << dec(15) << "\n";
  cout << "in octal: " << oct(15) << "\n";
  cout << "in hex: " << hex(15) << "\n";
  cout << "a floating-point number: " << 3.14159 << "\n";
  cout << "non-printing char (escape): " << chr(27) << "\n";
  cout << "printf-style formatting: " <<
          form("this is a string: %s\n", "a string");
}
```

This example shows the streams **class** printing numbers in decimal, octal, hexadecimal, and floating-point formats. In addition, any character can be sent to a stream object using the **chr( )** function and the character's ASCII value. In the preceding program, an escape is sent to **cout**.

The last line in the example shows the **form( )** function, which has all the functionality of C's **printf( )**, the general-purpose output function in C. **form( )** and **printf( )** both take as arguments a *format string* and an indeterminate number of values, which can be strings, numbers, or variables. The format string contains percent (%) signs, followed by special characters. These are *format commands;* they indicate the function is to take the corresponding value and send it to the output. In the preceding example, **%s** means to expect a string, which is the first value after the format string. Other format commands include **%d**, for a decimal integer, **%c**, for a character, and **%f**, for a floating-point number. All C books and manuals have sections on **printf( )**.

String Concatenation

An important feature of the ANSI C preprocessor is *string concatenation*. This feature is used often in the C++ examples in this book. If two quoted strings are adjacent, and no punctuation comes between them, the compiler will paste the strings together as a single string. This is particularly useful when printing listings in books and magazines that have width restrictions.

```
// CONCAT.CXX : String Concatenation

#include <stream.hxx>

main() {
    cout << "This string is far too long to put on a single "
        "line but it can be broken up with no ill effects\n"
        "as long as there is no punctuation separating "
        "adjacent strings.\n";
}
```

Reading Input

The streams class provides the ability to read input. The object used for standard input is **cin. cin** normally expects input from the console, but input can be redirected from other sources. An example of redirection will be shown later in this chapter.

The streams operator used with **cin** is **>>**. This operator waits for the same kind of input as its argument. For example, if you give it an integer argument, it waits for an integer from the console. Here's an example program that converts number bases:

```
// NUMCONV.CXX : Converts decimal to octal & hex

#include <stream.hxx>

main() {
    int number;
    cout << "Enter a decimal number: ";
    cin >> number;
    cout << "value in octal = 0" << oct(number) << "\n";
    cout << "value in hex = 0x" << hex(number) << "\n";
}
```

Notice the declaration of the integer **number** at the beginning of **main( )**. Since the **extern** keyword isn't used, the compiler creates space for **number** at that point.

Simple File Manipulation

Standard I/O provides a very simple way to read and write files called *I/O redirection*. If a program takes input from standard input (**cin** for streams) and sends its output to standard output (**cout** for streams), that input and output can be redirected. Input can be taken from a file, and output can be sent to a file. To redirect I/O on the command line, use **<** to redirect input and **>** to redirect output. For example, if we have a fictitious program FICTION.EXE (or simply FICTION, in Unix) that reads from standard input and writes to standard output, you can redirect standard input from the file STUFF and redirect the output to the file SUCH with the command

fiction < stuff > such

Since the files are opened for you, the job is much easier.

As a useful example, suppose you want to record the number of times you perform an activity, but the program that records the incidents must be loaded and run many times, and the machine may be turned off. To keep a permanent record of the incidents you must store the data in a file. This file will be called INCIDENT.DAT and will initially contain the character **0**. For easy reading, it will always contain ASCII digits representing the number of incidents. The program to increment the number is very simple:

```
// INCR.CXX : Read a number, increment it and write it
#include <stream.hxx>

main() {
    int num;
    cin >> num;
    cout << num + 1;
}
```

To test the program, run it and type a number followed by a carriage return. The program should print a number one larger than the one you type.

The program can be called from inside another program using the ANSI C **system( )** function, which is declared in the header file **stdlib.h**:

```
// INCIDENT.CXX : Records an incident using INCR

#include <stdlib.h> // declare the system() function

main() {
    // other code here...
    system("incr < incident.dat > incident.dat");
}
```

To use the **system( )** function, give it a string that you would normally type at the operating system command prompt. The command executes and control returns to the program.

Notice that the file INCIDENT.DAT is read *and* written using I/O redirection. Since the single **>** is used, the file is overwritten. Although it works fine here, reading and writing the same file like this isn't always a safe thing to do—if you aren't careful you can end up with garbage in the file. If a double **>>** is used instead of a single **>**, the output is appended to the file (and the program wouldn't work the way it is supposed to).

This program shows you how easy it is to use plain C library functions in C++: just include the header file and call the function. The upward compatibility from C to C++ is a big advantage when you are learning the language.

Controlling Execution
In C and C++

This section covers the execution control statements in C++. You must be familiar with these statements before you can read C or C++ code. C++ uses all C execution control statements. These include **if-else, while, do-while, for,** and a selection statement called **switch**. C also allows the infamous **goto**, which will be avoided in this book.

True and False in C

An expression is *true* in C if it produces a non-zero integer value. An expression is *false* if it produces an integer zero. All conditional statements in C use the truth or falsehood of a conditional expression to determine the execution path. An example of a conditional expression is **A == B**. This uses the conditional operator **==** to see if the variable **A** is equivalent to the variable **B**. The expression returns 1 if the statement is true and 0 if it is false. Other conditional operators are **>, <, >=**. Chapter 3 covers conditional statements.

The if-else *Statement*

The **if-else** statement can exist in two forms: with or without the **else**. The two forms are

if(*expression*)

 statement

or

if(*expression*)

   statement

else

   statement

The *expression* indicates a statement that evaluates to true or false. The *statement* means either a simple statement terminated by a semicolon or a compound statement, which is a group of simple statements enclosed in braces. Anytime the word "statement" is used, it is always implied that the statement can be simple or compound.

Pascal programmers should notice that the "then" is implied in C and C++, which are terse languages. The "then" is left out because it isn't essential.

```
// IFTHEN.CXX : Demonstration of if and
// if-else conditionals

#include <stream.hxx>

main() {
    int i;
    cout << "type a number and a carriage return\n";
    cin >> i;
    if ( i > 5 )
        cout << "the number was greater than 5 \n";
    else
        if ( i < 5 )
            cout << "the number was less than 5 \n";
        else
            cout << "the number must be equal to 5 \n";

    cout << "type a number and a carriage return\n";
    cin >> i;
    if ( i < 10 )
        if ( i > 5 )  // "if" is just another type of statement
            cout << "5 < i < 10 \n";
        else
            cout << "i <= 5 \n";
    else // matches "if ( i < 10 ) "
        cout << "i >= 10 \n";
}
```

Indentation makes C and C++ code easier to read. Since C and C++ are "free-form" languages, the extra spaces, tabs, and carriage returns do not affect the resulting program. It is conventional to indent the body of a control flow statement so the reader may easily determine where it begins and ends.

The while *Statement*

while, **do-while**, and **for** control looping. A statement repeats until the controlling expression evaluates to false. The form for a **while** loop is

while(*expression*)

  statement

The *expression* is evaluated once at the beginning of the loop, and again before each further iteration of the statement.

This example stays in the body of the **while** loop until the secret number is typed or a CTRL-C is pressed (in Unix or MS-DOS).

```
// GUESS.CXX : Guess a number

#include <stream.hxx>

main() {
    int secret = 15;
    int guess = 0;
    // "!=" is the "not-equal" conditional:
    while ( guess != secret ) { // compound statement
        cout << "guess the number: ";
        cin >> guess;
    }
    cout << "You got it!\n";
}
```

The do-while *Statement*

The form for **do-while** is

do

   statement

while(*expression*);

The **do-while** is different from **while** because the statement always executes at least once, even if the expression evaluates to false the first time. In a simple **while**, if the conditional is false the first time the statement never executes.

If a **do-while** is used in the GUESS program, the variable **guess** does not need to be given an initial dummy value since it will be initialized by the **cin** statement before it is tested.

```
// GUESS2.CXX : The guess program using do-while

#include <stream.hxx>

main() {
    int secret = 15;
    int guess; // no initialization needed this time
    do {
        cout << "guess the number: ";
        cin >> guess;
    }   while ( guess != secret );
    cout << "You got it!\n";
}
```

The **for** *Statement*

A **for** loop performs initialization before the first iteration, conditional testing, and some form of "stepping" at the end of each iteration. The form of the **for** loop is

for(*initialization; expression; step*)

   statement

Any of the expressions *initialization, expression,* or *step* may be empty. The *initialization* code executes once at the very beginning. The *expression* is tested before each iteration—if it evaluates to false at the beginning, the statement never executes. At the end of each loop, the *step* is executed.

for loops are usually used for "counting" tasks.

```
// CHARLIST.CXX : Display all the ASCII characters.
// Demonstrates "for."

#include <stream.hxx>

main() {
    for( int i = 0; i < 128; i = i + 1 )
        if (i != 26 )  // ANSI Terminal/ANSI.SYS Clear screen
            cout << " value: " << i <<
                    " character: " << chr(i) << "\n";
}
```

You may notice that the variable **i** is defined at the point where it is used, instead of at the beginning of the block denoted by the opening brace ({). Traditional procedural languages require that all variables be defined at the beginning of the block so when the compiler creates a block it can allocate space for those variables.

Declaring all variables at the beginning of the block requires the programmer to write in a particular way because of the implementation details of the language. Most people don't know all the variables they are going to use before they write the code, so they must keep jumping back to the beginning of the block to insert new variables, which is awkward and causes errors. It is confusing to read the code because each block starts with a clump of variable declarations, and the variables might not be used until much later in the block.

In C++ (*not* in C) you can spread your variable declarations throughout the block. Whenever you need a new variable, you can define it right where you use it. This allows a more natural coding style and makes code easier to understand. C++ compilers collect all the variable declarations in the block and secretly place them at the beginning of the block.

The break *and* continue *Keywords*

Inside the body of any of the looping constructs, you can control the flow of the loop using **break** and **continue**. **break** quits the loop without executing the rest of the statements in the loop. **continue** stops the execution of the current iteration and goes back to the beginning of the loop to begin a new iteration.

As an example of the use of **break** and **continue**, here is a program that is a very simple menu system:

```cpp
// MENU.CXX : simple menu program demonstrating
// the use of "break" and "continue"

#include <stream.hxx>

main() {
    char c; // to hold response
    while(1) {
        cout << "MAIN MENU:\n";
        cout << "l for left, r for right, q to quit: ";
        cin >> c;
        if ( c == 'q')
            break; // out of "while(1)"
        if ( c == 'l') {
            cout << "LEFT MENU:\n";
            cout << "select a or b: ";
            cin >> c;
            if ( c == 'a' ) {
                cout << "you chose 'a'\n";
                continue; // back to main menu
            }
            if ( c == 'b' ) {
                cout << "you chose 'b'\n";
                continue; // back to main menu
            }
            else {
                cout << "you didn't choose a or b!\n";
                continue; // back to main menu
            }
        }
```

```
if ( c == 'r' ) {
    cout << "RIGHT MENU:\n";
    cout << "select c or d: ";
    cin >> c;
    if ( c == 'c' ) {
        cout << "you chose 'c'\n";
        continue; // back to main menu
    }
    if ( c == 'd' ) {
        cout << "you chose 'd'\n";
        continue; // back to main menu
    }
    else {
        cout << "you didn't choose c or d!\n";
        continue; // back to main menu
    }
}
cout << "you must type l or r or q!\n";
}
cout << "quitting menu...\n";
}
```

If the user selects "q" in the main menu, the **break** keyword is used to quit, otherwise the program just continues to execute indefinitely. After each of the submenu selections, the **continue** keyword is used to pop back up to the beginning of the **while** loop. Notice the **char** declaration. A **char** is a data type designed to hold characters.

The **while(1)** statement is the equivalent of saying "do this loop forever." The **break** statement allows you to break out of this infinite **while** loop when the user types a "q".

The switch *Statement*

A **switch** statement selects from among pieces of code based on the value of an integral expression. Its form is

```
switch(selector) {

  case integral-value1 : statement; break;

  case integral-value2 : statement; break;

  case integral-value3 : statement; break;

  case integral-value4 : statement; break;

  case integral-value5 : statement; break;

       (...)

  default: statement;

}
```

Selector is an expression that produces an integral value. The **switch** compares the result of *selector* to each *integral-value*. If it finds a match, the corresponding *statement* (simple or compound) executes. If no match is found, the **default** *statement* executes.

You will notice in the preceding definition that each **case** ends with a **break**, which causes execution to jump to the end of the **switch** body. This is the conventional way to build a **switch** statement, but it is not required. If the **break** statement is missing, the code for the following **case** statements executes until a **break** is encountered. Although you don't usually want this happening, it can be useful to an experienced C programmer.

The **switch** statement is a very clean way to implement *multi-way selection* (selecting from among a number of different execution paths), but it requires a *selector* that can be evaluated to an integral value. If you want to use, for instance, a string as a selector, it won't work in a **switch** statement. For a string selector, you must use instead a series of **if** statements and compare the string inside the conditional.

Menus often lend themselves neatly to a **switch**.

```
// MENU2.CXX : a menu using a switch statement

#include <stream.hxx>

main() {
    char response; // the user's response
    int quit = 0;  // flag for quitting
```

```
while ( quit == 0 ) {
    cout << "Select a, b, c or q to quit: ";
    cin >> response;
    switch(response) {
        case 'a' : cout << "you chose 'a'\n";
                    break;
        case 'b' : cout << "you chose 'b'\n";
                    break;
        case 'c' : cout << "you chose 'c'\n";
                    break;
        case 'q' : cout << "quitting menu...\n";
                    quit = 1;
                    break;
        default  : cout << "you must use a,b,c, or q!\n";
    }
  }
}
```

Introduction to C and C++ Operators

You can think of operators as a special type of function—C++ operator overloading treats operators precisely that way. An operator takes one or more arguments and creates a new value. The arguments are admittedly given in a different form than ordinary function calls, but the effect is the same.

Several operators have been used so far and you should be reasonably comfortable with them from your previous programming experience. The concepts of addition, **+**, subtraction and unary minus, -, multiplication, *, division, /, and assignment, =, all work much the same in any programming language. The full set of operators will be enumerated in Chapter 3.

Operator Precedence

Operator precedence defines the order in which expressions evaluate when several different operators are present. C and C++ have specific rules to determine the order of evaluation. The easiest to remember is that multiplication and division happen before addition and subtraction. After that, if an expression isn't transparent to you it probably won't be for anyone reading the code, so you should use parentheses to make explicit the order of evaluation. For example,

A = X + Y - 2/2 + Z;

has a very different meaning from the same statement with a particular grouping of parentheses:

A = X + (Y - 2)/(2 + Z);

Auto-Increment and Auto-Decrement

C—and therefore C++—is full of shortcuts. Shortcuts can make code much easier to type, but sometimes much harder to read. Perhaps the designers thought it would be easier to understand a tricky piece of code if your eyes didn't have to scan as large an area of print. Two of the nicer shortcuts in C are the *auto-increment* and *auto-decrement* operators. These are often used in loops, which usually contain some variable that is incremented or decremented each time through the loop.

The auto-decrement operator is — and means "decrease by one unit." The auto-increment operator is **++** and means "increase by one unit." If **A** is an **int**, for example, the expression **++A** is equivalent to **(A = A + 1)**. Auto-increment and auto-decrement operators produce the value of the variable as a result. If the operator appears before the variable, as in **++A**, the operation is performed and the value is produced. If the operator appears after the variable (**A++**), the value is produced, then the operation is performed. For example:

```
// AUTOINC.CXX : Shows use of auto-increment
// and auto-decrement operators.

#include <stream.hxx>
```

```
main() {
    int i = 0;
    int j = 0;
    cout << ++i << "\n"; // pre-increment
    cout << j++ << "\n"; // post-increment
    cout << --i << "\n"; // pre-decrement
    cout << j-- << "\n"; // post decrement
}
```

If you've been wondering about the name "C++," now you understand. It implies "one step beyond C."

Using Standard I/O For Easy File Handling

The streams class contains functions to read and write files (see Chapter 10). Often, however, it is easiest to read from **cin** and write to **cout**. The program can be tested by typing at the console and, when it is working, files can be manipulated via redirection on the command line (in Unix and MS-DOS).

Simple cat Program

So far, all the messages you've seen are sent via operator overloading to stream objects. In C++, a message is usually sent to an object by calling a *member function* for that object. A member function looks like a regular function: it has a name, argument list, and return value. However, it must always be connected to an object; it can never be called by itself. A member function is always selected for a particular object via the dot (.) member selection operator.

The streams **class** has several non-operator member functions. One of these is **get( )**, which can be used to fetch a single character (or a string, if it is called differently). The following program uses **get( )** to read characters from the **cin** object. The program uses the complementary member function **put( )** to send characters the **cout** object. Characters are read from standard input and written to standard output.

```
// CAT.CXX : Demonstrates member function calls
// and simple file i/o.
#include <stream.hxx>

main() {
   char c;
   while ( cin.get(c) )
      cout.put(c);
}
```

Notice that **get( )** returns a value, which is tested to determine when the end of the input is reached. As long as the return value is non-zero (true), the **while** loop continues.

To use **cat**, simply redirect a file into it. The results will appear on the screen:

cat < infile

If you redirect the output file you've created a simple "copy" program:

cat < infile > outfile

Pass-by-Reference   C programmers may find the preceding program puzzling. According to plain C syntax, the character variable **c** looks like it is *passed by value* to the member function **get( )**. Yet **c** is used in the **put( )** member function as if **get( )** had modified the value of **c**, which is impossible if it was passed by value! What goes on here?

C++ has added another kind of argument passing: *pass-by-reference*. If a function argument has been defined as pass-by-reference, the compiler takes the address of the variable when the function is called. The argument of the stream function **get( )** is defined as pass-by-reference, so the program works correctly. Chapter 4 describes passing by reference in more detail. The first part of the chapter describes addresses, which you must understand before references make any sense.

Handling Spaces in Input

To read and use more than one character at a time from standard input, you will need to use a *buffer*. A buffer is a data storage area used to hold and manipulate a group of data items with identical types. In C and C++, you can create a buffer to hold text with an *array* of characters. Arrays in C and C++ are denoted with the bracket operator ([ ]). To define an array, give the data type, a name for the array, and the size in brackets. For an array of characters (a character buffer) called **buf**, the declaration could be

char buf[100]; // space for 100 contiguous characters

To read an entire word instead of a character, use **cin** and the **>>** operator, but send the input to a character buffer instead of sending just a single character. The operator **>>** is overloaded so you can use it with a number of different types of arguments. The idea is the same in each case: you want to get some input. You need different *kinds* of input, but you don't have to worry about it because the language takes care of the differentiation for you.

Here's a program to read and echo a word:

```
// READWORD.CXX : Read and echo a word from standard input

#include <stream.hxx>

main() {
    char buf[100];
    cout << "type a word: ";
    cin >> buf;
    cout << "the word you typed is: " << buf << "\n";
}
```

You will notice the program works fine if you type a word, but if you type more than one word it only takes the first one. The **>>** operator is word-oriented; it looks for white space, which it doesn't copy into the buffer, to break up the input. You must type a carriage return before any of the input is read.

To read and manipulate anything more than a simple character or word using streams, it is best to use the **get( )** function. **get( )** doesn't discard white space, and it can be used with a single character, as shown in the CAT.CXX program, or with a character buffer (**get( )** is an overloaded function). When used with a character buffer, **get( )** needs to know the maximum number of characters it should read (usually the size of the buffer) and, optionally, the terminating character it should look for before it stops reading input.

This terminating character that **get( )** looks for (the *delimiter*) defaults to a new-line character (**\n**). You don't need to change the delimiter if you just want to read the input one line at a time. To change the delimiter, add the character you want to be the delimiter in single quotes at the end of the argument list. When **get( )** matches the delimiter with the terminating character, the terminating character isn't copied into the character buffer—it is left on the input stream. This means you must read the terminating character and throw it away, otherwise the next time you try to fill your character buffer using **get( )**, the function will immediately read the terminating character and stop.

Here's a program that reads input one line at a time using **get( )**:

```
// GETLINE.CXX : Stream input by lines

#include <stream.hxx>

main() {
    char buf[100];
    char trash;
    while( cin.get(buf,100) ) { // get chars until '\n'
        cin.get(trash); // throw away the terminator
        cout << buf << "\n"; // add the '\n' at the end
    }
}
```

The **get( )** function reads input and places it into **buf** until either 100 characters are read, or a **\n** is found. **get( )** puts the zero byte, which is required for all strings in C, at the end of the string in **buf**. The character **trash** is only used for throwing away the line terminator. Because the new-line character was never put in **buf**, you must send a new-line out when you print the line. Try redirecting the contents of a text file into another file using GETLINE.

Examining Header Files   As your knowledge of C++ increases, you will find the best way to discover the capabilities of the streams **class**, or any **class**, is to look at the header file where the **class** is defined. The header file will contain the **class** definition. (The **class** definition will be more completely explained in Chapter 3.) The **class** definition contains some **private** elements, which you don't have access to, and a list of **public** elements, usually functions, which you as the user of the class may utilize. Although there isn't necessarily a description of the functions in the **class** definition, the function names are often descriptive and the **class** definition acts as a sort of "table of contents." It isn't as good as a language with built-in documentation features, but it will give you direction.

Header files for predefined classes like streams are usually located in a subdirectory, often called INCLUDE, under the installation directory for your C++ package or associated C package, if you use a C-code generator. On Unix, you must ask your system administrator where the C++ INCLUDE files are located.

Utility Programs Using Streams And Standard I/O

Now that you've had an introduction to streams and know how to manipulate files with I/O redirection, you can write some simple programs. This section contains examples of useful utilities.

Pipes

Notice that in Unix and MS-DOS, you can also use *pipes* on the command line for I/O redirection. Pipes feed the output of one program into the input of another program if both programs use standard I/O. If **prog1** *writes* to standard I/O and **prog2** *reads* from standard I/O, you can pipe the output of **prog1** into the input of **prog2** with the command

prog1 | prog2

where | is the pipe symbol. If all programs that follow use standard I/O, you can chain them together like this:

prog1 | prog2 | prog3 | prog4

Text Analysis Program

The following program counts the number of words and lines in a file and checks to make sure no line is greater than **maxwidth**. It uses two functions from the ANSI C library, both of which are declared in the header file **string.h**. **strlen( )** finds the length of a string, not including the zero byte that terminates all strings. **strtok( )** is used to count the number of words in a line; it breaks the line up into chunks that are separated by any of the characters in the second argument. For this program, a word is separated by white space, which is a space or tab. The first time you call **strtok( )**, you hand it the character buffer, and each subsequent time you hand it a zero, which tells it to use the same buffer it used for the last call (moving ahead each time **strtok( )** is called). When it can't find any more words in the line, **strtok( )** returns zero.

```
// TEXTCHEK.CXX : Counts words and lines in a text file.
// Checks to see that no line is wider than maxwidth

#include <stream.hxx>
#include <string.h> // ANSI C strlen() & strtok() declarations

main() {
    const int maxwidth = 64;  // const means "you can't change it"
    int linecount = 0;
    int wordcount = 0;
    char buf[100], trash;
    while ( cin.get(buf,100) ) {
```

```
        cin.get(trash); // discard terminator
        linecount++; // we just read a whole line
        if ( strtok(buf," \t") ) {
            wordcount++;  // count the first word
            while ( strtok(0," \t") )
                wordcount++; // count the rest of the words
        }
        if ( strlen(buf) > maxwidth )
            cout << "line " << linecount << "is too long.\n";
    }
    cout << "number of lines: " << linecount << "\n";
    cout << "number of words: " << wordcount << "\n";
}
```

Notice the use of auto-increment to count lines and words. Since the value produced by auto-incrementing the variable is ignored, it doesn't matter whether you put the increment first or last.

To count words, **strtok( )** is set up for the first call by handing it the text buffer **buf**. If it finds a word, the word is counted. If there are more words, they are counted.

The keyword **const** is used to prevent **maxwidth** from being changed. **const** was invented for C++ and later added to ANSI C. It has two purposes: the compiler will generate an error message if you ever try to change the value, and an optimizer can use the fact that a variable is **const** to create better code. It is always a good idea to make a variable **const** if you know it should never change.

Notice the way **buf**, **c**, and **trash** are all declared with a single **char**. You can declare all types of data this way, just by separating the variable names with commas.

Expanding Tabs

Some text processing systems cannot handle tabs in files, but word processing programs often insert them. Here's a program that replaces tabs with spaces.

```
// DETAB.CXX : Replace tabs with spaces

#include <stream.hxx>

main() {
    const int tabsize = 8;
    char c;
    while( cin.get(c) ) {
        if ( c == '\t') {
            for(int i = 0; i < tabsize; i++)
                cout << " ";
        }
        else
            cout.put(c);
    }
}
```

When a tab is found, the spaces are counted out using a **for** loop. The **for** loop allows you to easily change the number of spaces per tab.

Makefile for Chapter Examples

Here is the makefile for all the examples shown in this chapter:

```
# MAKEFILE for the examples in chapter 2
# Requires modification for Unix

# for Zortech C++:
CPP = ztc
# for Glockenspiel C++:
#CPP = ccxx

all:    hello.exe stream2.exe concat.exe numconv.exe \
        incr.exe incident.exe ifthen.exe guess.exe \
        guess2.exe charlist.exe menu.exe menu2.exe \
        autoinc.exe cat.exe readword.exe getline.exe \
        textchek.exe detab.exe
```

```
hello.exe: hello.cxx
        $(CPP) hello.cxx

stream2.exe : stream2.cxx
        $(CPP) stream2.cxx

concat.exe : concat.cxx
        $(CPP) concat.cxx

numconv.exe : numconv.cxx
        $(CPP) numconv.cxx

incr.exe : incr.cxx
        $(CPP) incr.cxx

incident.exe: incident.cxx incr.exe
        $(CPP) incident.cxx

ifthen.exe : ifthen.cxx
        $(CPP) ifthen.cxx

guess.exe : guess.cxx
        $(CPP) guess.cxx

guess2.exe : guess2.cxx
        $(CPP) guess2.cxx

charlist.exe : charlist.cxx
        $(CPP) charlist.cxx

menu.exe : menu.cxx
        $(CPP) menu.cxx

menu2.exe : menu2.cxx
        $(CPP) menu2.cxx

autoinc.exe : autoinc.cxx
        $(CPP) autoinc.cxx

cat.exe : cat.cxx
        $(CPP) cat.cxx

readword.exe : readword.cxx
```

```
        $(CPP) readword.cxx
getline.exe : getline.cxx
        $(CPP) getline.cxx

textchek.exe : textchek.cxx
        $(CPP) textchek.cxx

detab.exe : detab.cxx
        $(CPP) detab.cxx
```

The **make** program looks at the first target (item to be made) in the **makefile** unless you specify one on the command line, such as

make textchek.exe

Thus, if you want to make all the files in a subdirectory by typing "make," the first target should be a dummy name that depends on all the other targets in the file. In the above **makefile**, and all the ones in this book, the dummy target is called **all**.

When a line is too long in a **makefile**, you can continue it on the next line by using a backslash (\). White space is ignored here, so you can format for readability.

Summary

This chapter covered the basic tools you need to create programs, and the general form of C and C++ programs. It also demonstrated how to use predefined **classes** by including the header file to define the **class** and sending messages to objects.

The next chapter will show you how to write your own classes in C++. First, built-in data types, operators, and functions for C and C++ are introduced, followed by classes and other class-like items (structures, enumerated data types, and unions). Finally, some debugging hints are presented. Chapter 4 is the last of the chapters devoted to issues common to C and C++. It covers the concept of addresses, which are manipulated with *pointers* in C and C++, and *references* in C++. The remainder of the book covers subjects unique to C++ and object-oriented programming.

3 *Creating Classes With C++*

Chapter 2 introduced enough of the C and C++ languages so you can use predefined classes. This chapter teaches you how to define your own classes in C++. Chapter 4 will discuss the very important subject of addresses in C and C++.

This chapter begins by discussing the different types of data built into C and C++. Before you can define your own data types, you must understand how to create methods for those data types. Methods take the form of functions in C++. This chapter shows you how to create functions and demonstrates the extensions C++ has added for functions. Finally, you will see how to package data elements and functions together into a built-in, abstract data type: the **class**.

Keep in mind that this is intended to be an introduction and guide, not a reference manual. The final word for C is the ANSI C draft (which is tedious to read, and not recommended unless you are inclined toward that kind of thing) and the second edition of Kernighan and Ritchie (K&R). The final word on C++ is *The Annotated C++ Reference Manual* (which will be folded into the ANSI C++ specification).

Introduction to C++ Data

Data types can be built-in or abstract. A *built-in data type* is one the compiler intrinsically understands, one that "comes with the compiler." All built-in data types are identical in C and C++. An *abstract data type* is one created by the programmer as a class. The compiler knows how to handle built-in types when it starts up; it "learns" how to handle abstract data types by reading header files containing class declarations. Unless otherwise specified, all the descriptions here are based on ANSI C.

Basic Built-in Types

The ANSI C specification doesn't say how many bits each of the built-in types must contain. Instead, it stipulates the minimum and maximum values the built-in type must be able to hold. In machines based on binary, this maximum value can be directly translated into bits. If a machine uses, for instance, binary-coded decimal (BCD) to represent numbers, the amount of space in the machine required to hold the maximum numbers for each data type will be different than in a machine based on binary. The minimum and maximum values that can be stored in the various data types are defined in the system header files **limits.h** and **float.h**.

C and C++ have four basic built-in data types, which will be described here for binary-based machines. A **char** is for character storage and uses a minimum of 1 byte of storage. An **int** stores an integral number and uses a minimum of 2 bytes of storage. The **float** and **double** types store floating-point numbers, often in IEEE floating-point format. **float** is for single-precision floating point and **double** is for double precision floating point.

You can define and initialize variables at the same time. Here's how to define variables using the four basic data types:

```
// BASIC.CXX : Defining the four basic data
// types in C & C++

main( ) {
// Definition without initialization:
    char protein;
    int carbohydrates;
    float fiber;
    double fat;
    // Definition & initialization at the same time:
    char pizza = 'A', pop = 'Z';
    int DongDings = 100, Twinkles = 150, HeeHos = 200;
    float chocolate = 3.14159;
    double fudge_ripple = 6e-4; // exponential notation
}
```

The first part of the program defines variables of the four basic data types without initializing them. If you don't initialize a variable, its contents are undefined (although some compilers will initialize to 0). The second part of the program defines and initializes variables at the same time. Notice the use of exponential notation in the constant **6e-4**, meaning, "6 times 10 to the minus fourth power."

Specifiers

Specifiers modify the meanings of the basic built-in types, and expand the built-in types to a much larger set. There are four specifiers: **long, short, signed**, and **unsigned**.

The **long** and **short** specifiers modify the maximum and minimum values a data type will hold. A plain **int** must be at least the size of a **short**. The size hierarchy for integral types is **short int, int, long int**. All the sizes could conceivably be the same, as long as they satisfy the minimum and maximum value requirements. On a machine with a 64-bit word, for instance, all the data types might be 64 bits.

The size hierarchy for floating point numbers is **float, double**, and **long double. long float** is not allowed in ANSI C. There are no **short** floating-point numbers.

The **signed** and **unsigned** specifiers tell the compiler how to use the sign bit with integral types and characters (floating-point numbers always contain a sign). An **unsigned** number does not keep track of the sign and can store positive numbers twice as large as the positive numbers that can be stored in a **signed** number. The default is **signed** and is only necessary with **char**; **char** may or may not default to **signed**. By specifying **signed char**, you force the sign bit to be used.

The following example shows the size of the data in bytes using the **sizeof( )** operator, introduced later in this chapter:

```
// SPECIFY.CXX : Demonstrates the use of specifiers

#include <stream.hxx>

main( ) {
    char c;
    unsigned char cu;
    int i;
    unsigned int iu;
```

```
        short int is;
        short iis; // same as short int
        unsigned short int isu;
        unsigned short iisu;
        long int il;
        long iil;  // same as long int
        unsigned long int ilu;
        unsigned long iilu;
        float f;
        double d;
        long double ld;
        cout << "sizeof(char) = " << sizeof(c) << "\n";
        cout << "sizeof(unsigned char) = " << sizeof(cu) << "\n";
        cout << "sizeof(int) = " << sizeof(i) << "\n";
        cout << "sizeof(unsigned int) = " << sizeof(iu) << "\n";
        cout << "sizeof(short) = " << sizeof(is) << "\n";
        cout << "sizeof(unsigned short) = " << sizeof(isu) << "\n";
        cout << "sizeof(long) = " << sizeof(il) << "\n";
        cout << "sizeof(unsigned long) = " << sizeof(ilu) << "\n";
        cout << "sizeof(float) = " << sizeof(f) << "\n";
        cout << "sizeof(double) = " << sizeof(d) << "\n";
        cout << "sizeof(long double) = " << sizeof(ld) << "\n";
}
```

When you are modifying an **int** with **short** or **long**, the keyword **int** is optional, as the preceding shows.

Scoping

Scoping rules tell you where a variable is valid, where it is created, and where it gets destroyed, or *goes out of scope*. The scope of a variable extends from the point where it is defined to the first closing brace matching the closest opening brace before the variable is declared. Here's an illustration:

```
// SCOPE.CXX : How variables are scoped.

main( ) {
    int scp1;
    // scp1 visible here
    {
        // scp1 still visible here
        //......
        int scp2;
        // scp2 visible here
        //......
        {
            // scp1 & scp2 still visible here
            //...
            int scp3;
            // scp1, scp2 & scp3 visible here
            // ...
        } // <-- scp3 destroyed here
        // scp3 not available here
        // scp2 & scp3 still visible here
        // ...
    } // <-- scp2 destroyed here
    // scp3 & scp2 not available here
    // scp1 still visible here
    //...
} // <-- scp1 destroyed here
```

This example shows when variables are visible, and when they are unavailable (go out of scope). A variable can only be used when inside of its scope. Scopes can be *nested*, indicated by matched pairs of braces inside other pairs of braces. Nesting means you can access a variable in a scope that encloses the scope you are in. In the preceding example, the variable **scp1** is available inside all of the other scopes, while **scp3** is only available in the innermost scope.

Defining Data on the Fly

There is a significant difference between C and C++ when defining variables. Both languages require that variables be defined before they are used, but C requires all the variables to be defined at the beginning of a scope. When reading C code, a block of variable definitions is often the first thing you see when entering a scope. These variable definitions don't usually mean much to the reader because they appear apart from the context in which they are used.

C++ allows you to define variables anywhere in the scope, so you can define a variable right before you use it. This makes the code much easier to write and reduces the errors caused by having to jump back and forth within a scope. It makes the code easier to understand because you see the variable definition in the context of its use. This is especially important when you are defining and initializing a variable at the same time—the meaning of the initialization value can be seen by the way the variable is used.

Here's an example showing on-the-fly data definitions:

```
// ONTHEFLY.CXX : On-the-fly data definitions

main( ) {
    //...
    { // begin a new scope
        int q = 0; // plain C requires definitions here
        //...
        for(int i = 0; i < 100; i++) { // define at point of use
            q++; // a silly activity
            // notice q comes from a larger scope
            int p = 12; // definition at the end of the scope
        }
        int p = 1;  // A different p
    } // end scope containing q & outer p
}
```

In the innermost scope, **p** is defined right before the scope ends, so it is really a useless gesture (but it shows you can define a variable *anywhere*). The **p** in the outer scope is in the same situation.

The definition of **i** in the **for** loop is rather tricky. You might think that **i** is only valid within the scope bounded by the opening brace that appears after the **for**. The variable **i** is actually valid from the point where it is defined to the end of the scope that *encloses* the **for** loop. This is consistent with C, where the variable **i** must be defined at the beginning of the scope enclosing the **for** if it is to be used by the **for**.

Specifying Storage Allocation

When creating data, you have a number of options to specify the lifetime of the data, how the data will be allocated, and how the data will be treated by the compiler.

Global Variables

Global variables are defined outside of all function bodies and are available to all parts of the program (even code in other files). Global variables are unaffected by scopes and are always available; that is, the *lifetime* of a global variable lasts until the program ends. If the existence of a global variable in one file is declared using the **extern** keyword in another file, the data is available for use by the second file. Here's an example of the use of global variables:

```
// GLOBAL.CXX : Demonstration of global data.

int global;

main( ) {
    global = 12;
}
```

This file accesses **global** as an **extern**:

```
// GLOBAL2.CXX : accessing external global data

extern int global;  // the linker resolves the reference

void foo( ) {
    global = 47;
}
```

Space for the variable **global** is created by the definition in **global.cxx**, and that same variable is accessed by the code in **global2.cxx**. Since the code in **global2.cxx** is compiled separately from the code in **global.cxx**, the compiler must be informed that the variable exists elsewhere by the declaration

extern int global;

Local Variables

Local variables occur within a scope; they are "local" to a function. They are often called "automatic" variables because they automatically come into being when the scope is entered and go away when the scope closes. The keyword **auto** makes this explicit, but local variables default to **auto** so it is never necessary to declare something as an **auto**.

register VARIABLES   A *register* variable is a type of local variable. The **register** keyword tells the compiler "make accesses to this variable as fast as possible." Increasing the access speed is implementation-dependent, but, as the name suggests, it is often done by placing the variable in a register. There is no guarantee that the variable will be placed in a register or even that the access speed will increase; it is a hint to the compiler.

There are restrictions to the use of **register** variables. You cannot take or compute the address of a **register** variable. A **register** variable can only be declared within a block, you cannot have global or **static register** variables. You can use a **register** variable as a formal argument in a function, that is, in the argument list.

static

The **static** keyword has three distinct meanings. Normally, variables defined local to a function disappear at the end of the function scope. When you call the function again, space for the variables is created anew and the data is reinitialized. If you want the data to be persistent—to be *static*—you can define that variable as **static** and give it an initial value. The initialization is only performed when the program begins to execute, and the data retains its value between function calls. This way, a function can "remember" some piece of information between function calls.

You may wonder why global data isn't used instead. The beauty of static data is that it is unavailable outside the scope of the function, so it can't be inadvertently changed. This localizes errors. Here's an example of the use of static data:

```
// STATIC.CXX: Using static data in a function

#include <stream.hxx>

void func( ) {
    static int i = 0;
    cout << "i = " << ++i << "\n";
}

main( ) {
    for(int x = 0; x < 10; x++)
        func( );
}
```

Each time **func( )** is called in the **for** loop, it prints a different value. If the keyword **static** is not used, the value printed will always be 1.

The second meaning of **static** is related to the first in the "unavailable outside a certain scope" sense. When **static** is applied to a function name or to a variable that is outside of all functions, it means "this name is unavailable outside of this file." The function name or variable is *local to the file* or *has file scope*. As a demonstration, compiling and linking the following two files will cause a linker error.

```
// FILESTAT.CXX : file scope demonstration
// compiling and linking this file with FSTAT2.CXX
// will cause a linker error

static int fs; // file scope: only available in this file

main( ) {
    fs = 1;
}
```

Even though the variable **fs** is claimed to exist as an **extern** in the following file, the linker won't find it because it has been declared **static** in FILESTAT.CXX.

```
// FSTAT2.CXX : Trying to reference fs
extern int fs;

void func( ) {
   fs = 100;
}
```

The **static** specifier may also be used inside a class. This discussion will be delayed until after classes have been described later in the chapter.

extern

The **extern** keyword was briefly described in Chapter 2. It tells the compiler that a piece of data or a function exists, even if the compiler hasn't yet seen it in the file currently being compiled. This piece of data or function may exist in some other file (as was described in Chapter 2) or farther on in the current file. This is an example of the latter:

```
// FORWARD.CXX : Forward function & data declarations
#include <stream.hxx>
extern int i; // not actually external, but the compiler
            // must be told it exists somewhere
extern void foo( );

main( ) {
   i = 0;
   foo( );
}

int i;
void foo( ) {
   i++;
   cout << i;
}
```

When the compiler encounters the declaration **extern int i;** it knows that the definition for **i** must exist somewhere as a global variable. This definition can be in the current file, later on, or in a separate file. When the compiler reaches the definition of **i**, no other declaration is visible, so it knows it has found the same **i** that was declared earlier in the file. If you were to define **i** as **static**, you would be telling the compiler **i** is defined globally (via the **extern**), but that it also has file scope (via the **static**), so the compiler will generate an error.

LINKAGE   To understand the behavior of C and C++ programs, you need to know about *linkage*. Linkage describes the space created in memory to represent an identifier as it is seen by the linker. An identifier is represented by space in memory to hold a variable or a compiled function body. There are two types of linkage: *internal linkage* and *external linkage*.

Internal linkage means that space is created to represent the identifier only for the file being compiled. Other files may use the same identifier with internal linkage or for a global variable, and no conflicts will be found by the linker—separate space will be created for each identifier. Internal linkage is specified by the keyword **static** in C and C++.

External linkage means that a single space is created to represent the identifier for all files being compiled. The space is created *once*, and the linker must resolve all other references to that space. Global variables and function names have external linkage, and these can be accessed from other files by declaring them with the keyword **extern**. Variables defined outside all functions (with the exception of **const** in C++) and function definitions default to external linkage. You can specifically force them to have internal linkage using the **static** keyword. You can explicitly state that an identifier has external linkage by defining it with the **extern** keyword. Defining a variable or function with **extern** is not necessary in C, but it is sometimes necessary for **const** in C++.

Automatic (local) variables exist only temporarily, on the stack, while a function is being called. The linker doesn't know about automatic variables, and they have no linkage.

Constants

In pre-ANSI C, if you wanted to make a constant, you had to use the preprocessor, like this:

#define PI 3.14159

Everywhere you used **PI**, the value was substituted by the preprocessor. (You can still use this method in C and C++.)

Using the preprocessor to create constants places control of those constants outside the scope of the compiler. No type checking can be performed on the name **PI** and you can't take the address of **PI** (so you can't pass a pointer or a reference to **PI**). **PI** cannot be a variable of a user-defined type. Symbolic debuggers will be completely ignorant of **PI** since the preprocessor removes all information about the name. The meaning of **PI** lasts from the point where it is defined to the end of the file; the preprocessor doesn't recognize scoping.

C++ introduced the concept of a *named constant*, which is just like a variable except its value cannot be changed. The modifier **const** tells the compiler that an identifier represents a constant. Any data type, built-in or user-defined, may be modified by **const**. If you define something as **const** and then attempt to modify it, the compiler will generate an error.

As with **short** and **long**, if you use the **const** modifier alone, it defaults to **int**.

const x = 10; // means: const int x = 10;

In ANSI C and C++, you can use a named constant in an argument list, even if the argument it fills is a pointer or a reference—you can take the address of a **const**. A **const** has a scope, just like a regular variable, so you can "hide" a **const** inside a function and be sure that the name will not affect the rest of the program. You cannot create a **const** inside a **class** definition.

The **const** was taken from C++ and incorporated into ANSI C, albeit quite differently. In ANSI C, a **const** is treated by the compiler as a variable with a special tag attached that says "don't change me." When you define a **const** in ANSI C, the compiler creates space for it, so if you define more than one **const** with the same name in two different files (or put the definition in a header file), the linker will generate error messages about conflicts. The intended use of **const** in ANSI C is quite different from its intended use in C++.

DIFFERENCES IN const   In C++, **const** was intended to replace the use of **#define** in most situations requiring a constant value with an associated name. In C++, **const** is *meant* to go into header files, and be used in places where you would normally use a **#define** name. For instance, C++ lets you use a **const** in declarations such as arrays:

const sz = 100;

int buf[sz]; // not allowed in ANSI C !

In ANSI C, a **const** cannot be used in any expression where the compiler is expecting a constant expression.

A **const** must have an initializer in C++. ANSI C doesn't require an initializer; if none is given it initializes the **const** to 0.

In C++, a **const** doesn't necessarily create space—in ANSI C a **const** *always* creates space. Whether or not space is reserved for a **const** in C++ depends on how it is used. In general, if a **const** is used simply to replace a name with a value (just as you would use **#define**), then space doesn't have to be created for the **const**. If no space is created (this depends on the complexity of the data type and the sophistication of the compiler), the values may be folded into the code for greater efficiency—*after* type checking, not before, as with **#define**. If, however, you take an address of a **const** (even unknowingly, by passing it to a function that takes a reference argument) *or* you define it as **extern**, then space is created for the **const**.

In C++, a **const** that is outside of all functions is implied to have file scope (it is invisible outside the file). That is, it defaults to internal linkage. This is very different from all other identifiers in C++ (and from **const** in ANSI C!), which default to external linkage. Thus, if you declare a **const** of the same name in two different files and you don't take the address or define that name as **extern**, the ideal compiler won't allocate space for the **const**, but simply will fold it into the code (although, admittedly, this is very difficult for complicated types). Because **const** has implied file scope, you can put it in header files (in C++ only) with no conflicts at link time.

Since a **const** in C++ defaults to internal linkage, you can't just define a **const** in one file and reference it as an **extern** in another file. To give a **const** external linkage so it can be referenced from another file, you must explicitly define it as **extern**, like this:

extern const x = 1;

Notice that by giving it an initializer, you force space to be created for the **const**—the compiler no longer has the option of doing constant folding. The initialization establishes this as a definition, not a declaration. The declaration

extern const x;

in C++ means that the definition exists elsewhere. (Again, this is not necessarily true in ANSI C.) You can now see why C++ requires a **const** definition to have an initializer: the initializer distinguishes a declaration from a definition. (In ANSI C it's always a definition, so no initializer is necessary.)

CONSTANT VALUES   In C++, a **const** must always have an initialization value (in ANSI C, this is not true). Constant values can be expressed as decimal, octal, hexadecimal, or floating-point numbers (sadly, binary numbers were not considered important), or as characters.

In the absence of any other clues, the compiler assumes a constant value is a decimal number. The numbers **0**, **47**, and **1101** are all treated as decimal numbers.

A constant value with a leading **0** is treated as an octal number (base 8). Base 8 numbers can only contain digits **0 to 7**; the compiler flags other digits as an error. A legitimate octal number is **017** (15 in base 10).

A constant value with a leading **0x** is treated as a hexadecimal number (base 16). Base 16 numbers contain the digits **0 to 9** and **a** through **f** or **A** through **F**. A legitimate hexadecimal number is **0x1fe** (510 in base 10).

Floating-point numbers can contain decimal points and exponential powers (represented by **e**, which means "10 to the power"). Both the decimal point and the **e** are optional. If you assign a floating-point value or variable to a floating-point variable, the compiler will take the constant value and convert it to a floating-point number (this process is called *implicit type conversion*). However, it is a good idea to use either a decimal point or an **e** to remind the reader you are using a floating-point number; some older compilers also need the hint.

Legitimate floating-point constant values are **1e4**, **1.0001**, **47.0**, **0.0** and **-1.159e-77**. You can add *suffixes* to force the type of floating-point number: **f** or **F** forces a **float**, L or l forces a **long double**, otherwise the number will be a **double**.

Character constants are characters surrounded by single quotes, as **'A'**, **'0'**, **' '**. Notice there is a big difference between the character **'0'** (ASCII 96) and the value 0. Special characters are represented with the "backslash escape" **\n** (new-line), **\t** (tab), **** (backslash), "**\r** (carriage return), **\"** (double quote), **\'** (single quote), and so on. You can also express **char** constants in octal **\17** or hexadecimal, **\xff**.

volatile

Whereas the qualifier **const** tells the compiler "this never changes" (which allows the compiler to perform extra optimizations), the qualifier **volatile** tells the compiler "you never know when this will change," and *prevents* the compiler from performing any optimizations. The keyword was designed to be used when reading some value outside the control of the system, such as a register in a piece of communication hardware. A **volatile** variable is always read whenever its value is required, even if it was just read the line before. (Note that **volatile** came from ANSI C, and migrated to C++ release 2.0—although your C++ release 1.2 may support it.)

C and C++ Operators
And Their Use

Operators were briefly introduced in Chapter 2. This section covers all the operators in C and C++.

All operators produce a value from their operands. This value is produced without modifying the operands, except with assignment and increment and decrement operators. Modifying an operand is called a *side effect*. The most common use for operators that modify their operands is to generate the side effect, but you should keep in mind that the value produced is available for your use just as in operators without side effects.

Assignment

Assignment is performed with the operator **=**. It means "take the right-hand side (often called the *rvalue*) and copy it into the left-hand side (often called the *lvalue*). An rvalue is any constant, variable, or expression that can produce a value, but an lvalue must be a distinct, named variable—that is, there must be a physical space to store the rvalue. For instance, you can assign a constant value to a variable (**A = 4;**), but you cannot assign anything to a constant value—it cannot be an lvalue (you can't say **4 = A;**).

Mathematical Operators

The basic mathematical operators are the same as the ones available in most programming languages: addition (+), subtraction (-), division (/), multiplication (∗) and modulus (%, which produces the remainder from integer division). Integer division truncates the result (it doesn't round off). The modulus operator cannot be used with floating-point numbers.

C and C++ also introduce a shorthand notation to perform an operation and an assignment at the same time. This is denoted by an operator followed by an equal sign, and is consistent with all the operators in the language (whenever it makes sense). For example, to add 4 to the variable **x** and assign the result to **x**, you would say "**x += 4;**".

This example shows the use of the mathematical operators:

```
// MATHOPS.CXX : mathematical operators

#include <stream.hxx>
// A macro to display a string and a value.
#define print(str, var) cout << str " = " << var << "\n"

main( ) {
    int i, j, k;
    float u,v,w;  // applies to doubles, too

    cout << "enter an integer: ";
    cin >> j;
    cout << "enter another integer: ";
    cin >> k;
    print("j",j);  print("k",k);
    i = j + k; print("j + k",i);
    i = j - k; print("j - k",i);
    i = k / j; print("k / j",i);
    i = k * j; print("k * j",i);
    i = k % j; print("k % j",i);
    // the following only works with integers:
    j %= k; print("j %= k", j);

    cout << "enter a floating-point number: ";
    cin >> v;
    cout << "enter another floating-point number: ";
    cin >> w;
    print("v",v); print("w",w);
```

```
    u = v + w; print("v + w", u);
    u = v - w; print("v - w", u);
    u = v * w; print("v * w", u);
    u = v / w; print("v / w", u);

    // the following works for ints, chars, and doubles too:
    u += v; print("u += v", u);
    u -= v; print("u -= v", u);
    u *= v; print("u *= v", u);
    u /= v; print("u /= v", u);
}
```

The rvalues of all the assignments can, of course, be much more complex.

PREPROCESSOR MACROS Notice the use of the macro **print( )** in the preceding example to save typing (and typing errors). The arguments in the parenthesized list following the macro name are substituted in all the code following the closing parenthesis. The preprocessor removes the name **print** and substitutes the code wherever the macro is called, so the compiler cannot generate any error messages using the macro name, and it doesn't do any type checking on the arguments. The latter can be beneficial, as shown in the debugging macro at the end of the chapter.

OPERATORS ARE LIKE FUNCTION CALLS There are two differences between the use of an operator and an ordinary function call. The first is that the syntax is different: an operator is often called by placing it between or sometimes after the arguments. The second difference is that the compiler determines what function to call. For instance, if you are using the operator **+** with floating-point arguments, the compiler calls the function to perform floating-point addition (this call is sometimes the action of inserting in-line code, or a floating-point coprocessor instruction). If you use the operator **+** with a floating-point number and an integer, the compiler calls a special function to turn the **int** into a **float**, and then calls the floating-point addition code.

It is important to be aware that operators are a different kind of function call because in C++ you can define your own functions for the compiler to call when it encounters operators used with your abstract data types. This feature is called *operator overloading* and is described in Chapter 5.

Relational Operators

Relational operators are used to establish a relationship between the values of the operands. They produce a value of 1 if the relationship is true and a value of 0 if the relationship is false. The relational operators are **<** (less than), **>** (greater than), **<=** (less than or equal to), **>=** (greater than or equal to) , **==** (equivalent), and **!=** (not equivalent). They can be used with all built-in data types in C and C++. In C++ they can be given special definitions for user-defined data types.

Logical Operators

The logical operators AND (**&&**) and OR (**| |**) produce a true (1) or false (0) based on the logical relationship of their arguments. Remember that in C and C++, a statement is true if it has a non-zero value, and false if it has a value of zero.

This example uses the relational and logical operators:

```
// BOOLEAN.CXX : Relational and logical operators.

#include <stream.hxx>

main( ) {
    int i,j;
    cout << "enter an integer: ";
    cin >> i;
    cout << "enter another integer: ";
    cin >> j;
    cout << "i > j is " << (i > j) << "\n";
    cout << "i < j is " << (i < j) << "\n";
    cout << "i >= j is " << (i >= j) << "\n";
    cout << "i <= j is " << (i <= j) << "\n";
    cout << "i == j is " << (i == j) << "\n";
    cout << "i != j is " << (i != j) << "\n";
    cout << "i && j is " << (i && j) << "\n";
    cout << "i || j is " << (i || j) << "\n";
    cout << " (i < 10) && (j < 10) is "
            << ((i < 10) && (j < 10))  << "\n";
}
```

You can replace the definition for **int** with **float** or **double** in this program. Be aware, however, that the comparison of a floating-point number with the value of zero is very strict: a number that is the tiniest fraction different from another number is still not equal. A number that is the tiniest bit above zero is still true.

Bitwise Operators

The bitwise operators allow you to manipulate individual bits in a number, thus they only work with integral numbers. Bitwise operators perform Boolean algebra on the corresponding bits in the two arguments to produce the result.

The bitwise AND operator (**&**) produces a 1 in the output bit if both input bits are 1; otherwise it produces a 0. The bitwise OR operator (**|**) produces a 1 in the output bit if either input bit is a 1 and only produces a 0 if both input bits are 0. The bitwise EXCLUSIVE OR, or XOR (**^**), produces a 1 in the output bit if one or the other input bit is a 1, but not if both are. The bitwise NOT (**~**, also called the *ones complement operator*) is a *unary* operator—it only takes one argument (all other bitwise operators are binary operators). Bitwise NOT produces the opposite of the input bit—a 1 if the input bit is 0, a 0 if the input bit is 1.

Bitwise operators may also be combined with the equal sign to unite the operation and assignment: **&=**, **|=** and **^=** are all legitimate (since **~** is a unary operator it cannot be combined with the **=** sign).

Shift Operators

The shift operators also manipulate bits. The right-shift operator, **>>**, shifts the operand to its left *right* by the number of bits specified after the operator. The left-shift operator, **<<**, shifts the operand to its left *left* by the number of bits specified after the operator. These are shifts, not rotates. (A rotate command is usually available in assembly language, but since you can build your own rotate command, presumably the designers of C felt justified in leaving "rotate" off—aiming, as they said, for a minimal language.)

If the value after the shift operator is greater than the number of bits in the left-hand operand, the result is undefined. If the left-hand operand is unsigned, the right shift is a *logical shift*, so the upper bits will be filled with zeros. If the left-hand operand is signed, the right shift may or may not be logical.

Shifts can be combined with the equal sign (**<<=** and **>>=**). The lvalue is replaced by the lvalue shifted by the rvalue.

Here's an example that demonstrates the use of all the operators involving bits:

```
// BITWISE.CXX: demonstration of bit manipulation

#include <stream.hxx>

// A macro to print a new-line (saves typing and mistakes):
#define NL cout << "\n"
// Notice the trailing ';' is omitted — this forces the
// programmer to use it and maintain consistent syntax

// This function takes a single byte and displays it
// bit-by-bit.  The (1 << i) produces a one in each
// successive bit position; in binary: 00000001, 00000010, etc.
// If this bit bitwise ANDed with val is nonzero, it means
// there was a one in that position in val.
void print_binary(unsigned char val) {
    for(int i = 7; i >= 0; i—)
      if( val & (1 << i) )
        cout << "1";
      else
        cout << "0";
}

// generally, you don't want signs when you are working with
// bytes, so you use an unsigned char.
main( ) {
    // an int must be used instead of a char here because the
    // "cin >>" statement will otherwise treat the first digit
    // as a character.  By assigning a and b to getval, the value
    // is converted to a single byte (by truncating it).
    unsigned int getval;
    unsigned char a,b;
    cout << "enter a number between 0 and 255: ";
    cin >> getval; a = getval;
    cout << "a in binary: "; print_binary(a); cout << "\n";
    cout << "enter another number between 0 and 255: ";
```

```
    cin >> getval; b = getval;
    cout << "b in binary: "; print_binary(b); NL;
    cout << "a | b = "; print_binary(a | b); NL;
    cout << "a & b = "; print_binary(a & b); NL;
    cout << "a ^ b = "; print_binary(a ^ b); NL;
    cout << "~a = "; print_binary(~a); NL;
    cout << "~b = "; print_binary(~b); NL;
    unsigned char c = 0x5A; // interesting bit pattern
    cout << "c in binary: "; print_binary(c); NL;
    a |= c;
    cout << "a |= c; a = "; print_binary(a); NL;
    b &= c;
    cout << "b &= c; b = "; print_binary(b); NL;
    b ^= a;
    cout << "b ^= a; b = "; print_binary(b); NL;
}
```

Here are functions to perform left and right rotations:

```
// ROLROR.CXX : Perform left and right rotations

unsigned char ROL(unsigned char val) {
    int highbit;
    if ( val & 0x80 ) // 0x80 is the high bit only
        highbit = 1;
    else
        highbit = 0;
    val <<= 1;  // left shift (bottom bit becomes 0)
    val |= highbit; // rotate the high bit onto the bottom
    return val; // this becomes the function value
}

unsigned char ROR(unsigned char val) {
    int lowbit;
    if ( val & 1 ) // check the low bit
        lowbit = 1;
    else
        lowbit = 0;
    val >>= 1; // right shift by one position
    val |= (lowbit << 7); // rotate the low bit onto the top
    return val;
}
```

Try using these functions in the BITWISE program. Notice the definitions (or at least declarations) of **ROL( )** and **ROR( )** must be seen by the compiler in BITWISE.CXX before the functions are used.

The bitwise functions are generally extremely efficient to use because they translate directly into assembly language statements. Sometimes a single C statement will generate a single line of assembly code.

Unary Operators

Bitwise NOT isn't the only operator that takes a single argument. Its companion, the logical NOT (!), will take a true value (non-zero) and produce a false value (zero). The unary minus (-) and unary plus (+) are the same operators as binary minus and plus—the compiler figures out which usage is intended by the way you write the expression. For instance, the statement

x = -a;

has an obvious meaning. The compiler can figure out

x = a * -b;

but the reader might get confused, so it is safer to say

x = a * (-b);

The unary minus produces the negative of the value. Unary plus is provided for symmetry with unary minus, although it doesn't do much.

The increment and decrement operators (**++** and **--**) were introduced in Chapter 2. These are the only operators other than those involving assignment that have side effects. The increment operator increases the variable by one unit ("unit" can have different meanings according to the data type—see Chapter 4, "Pointers and References") and the decrement operator decreases the variable by one unit. The value produced depends on whether the operator is used as a *prefix* or *postfix* operator (before or after the variable). Used as a prefix, the operator changes the variable and produces the changed value. As a postfix, the operator produces the unchanged value and *then* the variable is modified.

The last unary operators are the *address-of* (**&**), *dereference* (*****) and cast operators in C and C++, and **new** and **delete** in C++. Address-of and dereference are used with pointers. Casting is described in "Casting Operators," later in this chapter, and **new** and **delete** are described in Chapter 6.

The Conditional Operator

The conditional operator is unusual because it has three operands. It is truly an operator because it produces a value, unlike the ordinary **if-else** statement. It consists of three expressions: if the first expression (followed by a **?**) evaluates as true, the expression following the **?** is evaluated and its result becomes the value produced by the operator. If the first expression is false, the third expression (following a **:**) is executed and its result becomes the value produced by the operator.

The conditional operator can be used for its side effects or for the value it produces. Here's a code fragment that demonstrates both:

A = --B ? B : (B = -99);

Here, **A** is assigned to the value of **B** if the result of decrementing **B** is non-zero. If **B** became 0, **A** and **B** are both assigned to -99. **B** is always decremented, but it is only assigned to -99 if the decrement causes **B** to become 0. A similar statement can be used without the **A =** just for its side effects:

--B ? B : (B = -99);

Here the second **B** is superfluous, since the value produced by the operator is unused. An expression is required between the **?** and **:**. In this case the expression could simply be a constant, which might make the code run a bit faster.

The Comma Operator

The comma is not restricted to separating variable names in multiple definitions (as in "**int i, j, k;**"). When it is used as an operator to separate expressions, it produces only the value of the last expression. All the rest of the expressions in the comma-separated list are only evaluated for their side effects. This code fragment increments a list of variables and uses the last one as the rvalue:

A = (B++,C++,D++,E++);

The parentheses are critical here. Without them, the statement will be evaluated as

(A = B++), C++, D++, E++;

Common Pitfalls
When Using Operators

As the preceding illustrated, one of the pitfalls of using operators can be trying to get away with not using parentheses when you are even the least bit uncertain how an expression will be evaluated. (Consult your C manual for the order of expression evaluation.)

Another extremely common error looks like this:

```
// PITFALL.CXX : operator mistakes

main( ) {
    int a = 1, b = 1;
    while( a = b ) {
        // ....
    }
}
```

This statement will always evaluate to true when **b** is non-zero. The variable **a** is assigned to the value of **b**, and the value of **b** is also produced by the operator **=**. Generally you want to use the equivalence operator **==** inside a conditional statement, not assignment. This one traps a lot of programmers.

A similar problem is using bitwise instead of logical AND and OR. Bitwise AND and OR use one character (**&** or **|**) while logical AND and OR use two (**&&** or **||**). Just as with **=** and **==**, it's easy to just type one character instead of two.

Casting Operators

The word *cast* in C is used in the sense of "casting in a mold." C will automatically change one type of data into another if it makes sense to the compiler. For instance, if you assign an integral value to a floating-point variable, the compiler will secretly call a function to convert the **int** to a **float**. Casting allows you to make this type of conversion explicit, or to force it when it wouldn't normally happen.

To perform a cast, put the desired data type, including all modifiers, inside parentheses to the left of the item to be cast. This item can be a variable, constant, the value produced by an expression, or the return value of a function. Here's an example:

int B = 200;

A = (unsigned long int)B;

You can even define casting operators for user-defined data types.

Casting is very powerful, but it can cause headaches because in some situations it forces the compiler to treat data as if it were, for instance, larger than it really is—and this can trample over other data. However, this usually occurs when casting pointers, not when making simple casts like the one shown above.

C++ adds a new kind of cast, which follows the "function-call" syntax used with constructors (defined later in this chapter). This syntax puts the parentheses around the argument, like a function call, rather than around the data type, like this:

float A = float(200);

sizeof—an Operator by Itself

The **sizeof( )** operator stands alone because it satisfies an unusual need: it gives you information about the amount of memory allocated for data items. As described earlier in this chapter, **sizeof( )** tells you the number of bytes used by any particular variable. It can also be used to give the size of a data type, with no variable name:

printf("sizeof(double) = %d\n", sizeof(double));

sizeof( ) can also give you the sizes of user-defined data types. This will be used later in the book.

Creating Functions in C and C++

Most modern languages have an ability to create subroutines or subprograms, and C and C++ are no exception. In C and C++, a subprogram is called a *function*. All functions have return values (although that value can be "nothing"), so functions in C are very similar to functions in Pascal. (The Pascal *procedure* is the specialized case of a function with no return value.)

Function Prototyping

Function prototyping is another improvement invented in C++; it has since propagated back into ANSI C. You have been seeing function prototyping in this book described as "telling the compiler that a function exists, and how it should be called." Now it's time for more details.

In pre-ANSI C, you could call a function with any number or type of arguments, and the compiler wouldn't complain. Everything seemed fine until you ran the program. You got mysterious results (or worse, the program crashed) with no hints as to why. The lack of help with argument passing and the enigmatic bugs that resulted is probably one reason why C was dubbed a "high-level assembly language."

C programmers just got used to it. When Stroustrup designed C++, he decided that something had to be done about the problem, so he added *function prototyping*. With function prototyping you always use a template when declaring and defining a function. When the function is called, the compiler uses the template to ensure the proper arguments are passed in, and that the return value is treated correctly. If the programmer makes a mistake when calling the function, the mistake is caught at compile time.

TELLING THE COMPILER HOW ARGUMENTS ARE PASSED   In a function prototype, the argument list (which follows the name and is enclosed in parentheses) contains the types of arguments that must be passed to the function and (optionally for the declaration) the names of the arguments. The order of the arguments must match in the declaration, definition, and function call. Here's an example of a function prototype in a declaration:

int translate(float x, float y, float z);

You cannot use the same form when defining variables in function argument lists as you do in ordinary variable definitions, as in **float x, y, z**. You must indicate the type of each argument. In a function declaration, the form

int translate(float, float, float);

is also acceptable, since the compiler doesn't do anything but check for types when the function is called.

In the function definition, names are required because the arguments must be referenced inside the function.

int translate(float x, float y, float z) {

x = y = z;

// ...

}

The only exception to this rule occurs in C++: an argument may be unnamed in the argument list of the function definition. Since it is unnamed, you cannot use it in the function body, of course. The reason unnamed arguments are allowed is to give the programmer a way to "reserve space in the argument list." The function must still be called with the proper arguments, but if the programmer wants to *use* the argument in the future, it can be done without modifying any of the other code. This option of ignoring an argument in the list is possible if you leave the name in, but you will get an obnoxious warning message about the value being unused every time you compile the function. The warning is eliminated if you remove the name.

ANSI C and C++ have two other ways to declare an argument list. If you have an empty argument list, you can declare it as **foo( );** in C++. Remember, this only means an empty argument list in C++. In ANSI C it means "an indeterminate number of arguments." In both ANSI C and C++, the declaration **foo(void);** means an empty argument list. The **void** keyword means "nothing" in this case. (It can also mean "no type" when applied to certain variables.)

The other option for argument lists occurs when you don't know how many arguments or what type of arguments you will have; this is called a *variadic* function. This "uncertain argument list" is represented by ellipses (**...**). Defining a variadic function is significantly more complicated than defining a plain function. You can use a variadic function declaration for a function that has a fixed set of arguments if, for some reason, you want to disable the error checks of function prototyping.

RETURNING ARGUMENTS FROM A FUNCTION   A function prototype also specifies the return value of a function. The type of this value precedes the function name. If no type is given, the return value type defaults to **int** (as do most things in C). If you want to specify that no value is returned, as in a Pascal procedure, the **void** keyword is used. This will generate an error if you try to return a value from the function. Here are some complete function prototypes:

foo1( ); // **returns an int, takes no arguments**

foo2(void); // **like foo1( ) in C++ but not in ANSI C!**

float foo3(float, int, char, double); // **returns a float**

void foo4(void); // **takes no arguments, returns nothing**

At this point, you may wonder how a return value is specified in the function definition. This is done with the **return** statement. **return** causes an exit from the function back to the point where it was called. If an argument to **return** is given, that argument becomes the return value of the function. You can have more than one **return** statement in a function definition.

```
// RETURN.CXX : Use of "return"

#include <stream.hxx>

char cfunc(int i) {
    if(i == 0)
        return 'a';
    if(i == 1)
        return 'g';
```

```
    if(i == 5)
        return 'z';
    return 'c';
}

main( ) {
    cout << "type an integer: ";
    int val;
    cin >> val;
    cout << cfunc(val) << "\n";
}
```

The code in **cfunc( )** acts like an **if-else** statement. The **else** is unnecessary because the first **if** that evaluates true causes an exit of the function via the **return** statement. Notice that a function declaration is avoided because the function is defined before it is used in **main( )**, so the compiler knows about it. Arguments and return values are covered in detail in Chapter 9.

Using the C Function Library

All the functions in your local C function library are available while you are programming in C++. You should look hard at the function library before defining your own function—chances are someone has solved the problem for you, and probably given it a lot more thought (as well as debugging it).

A word of caution, though: many compilers include a lot of extra functions that make life easier and are very tempting to use, but are not part of the ANSI C library. If you are certain you will never want to move the application to another platform (and who can be certain of that?), go ahead—use those functions and make your life easier. If you want your application to be portable, you should restrict yourself to ANSI C functions. Keep a guide to ANSI C handy, and refer to that when looking for a function rather than your C or C++ guide. If you must perform platform-specific activities, try to isolate that code in one spot so it can easily be changed when porting to another platform. Platform-specific activities can often be encapsulated in a **class**—this is the ideal solution.

The formula for using a library function is as follows: first, find the function in your guidebook (many guidebooks will index the function by category as well as alphabetically). The description of the function should include a section that demonstrates the syntax of the code. The top of this section usually has at least one **#include** line, showing you the header file containing the function prototype. Duplicate this **#include** line in your file so the function will be properly declared. Now you can call the function in the same way it is shown in the syntax section. If you make a mistake, the compiler will discover it by comparing your function call to the function prototype in the header, and tell you about your error. The linker searches the standard library by default, so that's all you need to do: include the header file, and call the function.

Creating Your Own Libraries With the Librarian

You can collect your own functions together into a library, or add new functions to the library the linker searches by default (you should back up the old one before doing this). Most packages come with a librarian, which manages groups of object modules. Each librarian has its own commands, but general idea is this: if you want to create a library, make a header file containing the function prototypes for all the functions in your library. Put this header file somewhere in the preprocessor's search path, either in the local directory (so it can be found by **#include "header"**) or in the include directory (so it can be found by **#include <header>**). Now take all the object modules and hand them to the librarian along with a name for the finished library (most librarians require a common extension, such as .LIB). Place the finished library in the same spot the other libraries reside so the linker can find it. When you use your library, you will have to add something to the command line to tell the linker to search the library for the functions you call. All the details must be found in your manual, since they vary from system to system.

Unique Features of C++ Functions

C++ functions have a number of improvements over C functions, which are designed to make them easier to program and use.

inline *Functions*

The preprocessor macro function introduced earlier in this chapter for the MATHOPS program saves typing, improves readability, reduces errors, and eliminates the overhead of a function call. Preprocessor macro functions are popular in C, but they have the drawback that they aren't "real" functions, so the usual error checking doesn't occur during compilation.

C++ encourages (sometimes even requires) the use of small functions. The programmer concerned with speed, however, might opt to use preprocessor macros rather than functions to eliminate the overhead of a function call. To eliminate the cost of calls to small functions, C++ has *inline* functions. These functions are specified with the **inline** keyword, like this:

inline int one( ) { return 1; }

Notice the definition accompanies the **inline** keyword. When the compiler encounters an **inline** definition, it doesn't generate code as it does with an ordinary function definition. Instead, it remembers the code for the function. When a call to an **inline** function is made (a call to an **inline** looks like a call to any other function), the compiler checks for proper usage as it does with any function call, then substitutes the code for the function call. Thus, the efficiency of preprocessor macros is combined with the error checking of ordinary functions.

The **inline** function is another tough nut when it comes to terminology. Because the body of the function doesn't actually reserve any space for the function code, it is tempting to call it a declaration rather than a definition. Indeed, you cannot "declare" an inline function in the usual sense. In the "declaration"

inline int one( );

the **inline** keyword has no effect—it does the compiler no good to know that a function is an **inline** if it doesn't have the code to substitute when it encounters a function call. **inline** functions must be contained in header files, or otherwise occur before they are used, just like ordinary function declarations. However, there is nothing else that could be called a definition other than the place where the function body is—so definition it is.

SAVING SPACE   Because an **inline** function duplicates the code every place it is called, you might think that it automatically increases code space. But for small functions (which **inline**s were designed for) this isn't necessarily true. Keep in mind that a function call requires code to pass arguments and to handle the return value; this code isn't present for an **inline**. If your **inline** function turns out to be smaller than the amount of code necessary for arguments and the return value, you are actually *saving* space. In addition, if the **inline** function is never called, no code is ever generated. With an ordinary function, code for that function is there whether you call it or not. The **inline** keyword is actually just a hint to the compiler. The compiler may ignore the **inline** and simply generate code for the function.

inline *ABUSE*   A big advantage to **inline** functions is that they save a lot of typing—your function is declared and defined in one place. However, the code is often clearer to the reader, as well. The result is often an abuse of **inline** functions; they are used because they are easier and clearer rather than because they are faster. This abuse is most rampant in—of all places—articles and books on programming in C++. As you will see, some projects in this book push the boundaries of good sense when using **inline**s.

You may wonder what the problem is. The C++ compiler must remember the definition for the **inline** function, rather than simply compiling it and moving on as with an ordinary function. **inline** functions can take up a lot more space than the other items a compiler must remember—enough space, in fact, to crash some implementations of C++ on a machine with limited memory (MS-DOS machines, for example).

The speed benefits of **inline** functions tend to diminish as the function grows in size. At some point the overhead of the function call becomes small compared to the execution of the function body, and the benefit may be lost.

C++ Function Overloading

C++ introduces the concept of *function overloading*. This means you can call the same function name in a variety of ways, depending on your needs. An overloaded **print( )** function might be able to handle **float**s, **int**s, and strings.

print(3.14);

print(47);

print("this is a string");

Here, the function name **print** is overloaded with several meanings.

The most useful place to overload functions is in **class** definitions, as you will see later. You can also overload ordinary functions by using the **overload** keyword in release 1.2 and earlier. The keyword is still available, but obsolete, in release 2.0. The **overload** keyword is placed before any of the function declarations.

overload print; // warn C++ we are overloading this name

void print(float);

void print(int);

void print(char ∗); // for strings; see Chapter 4

In the last declaration, you see a new type of argument: **char** ∗. The asterisk (∗) indicates that this argument isn't an actual argument, but instead a pointer to the argument. Pointers are discussed in detail in Chapter 4, but they are such an integral part of C and C++ that a brief introduction is necessary here. A pointer is a variable that holds the *address* of another variable. Because you don't know how long a string is at compile time, the compiler can't know how to pass the string to the **print( )** function. If we tell **print( )** "where the string lives" by passing the address, the function can figure out for itself where to get the characters in the string and how long the string is (at run time, instead of compile time).

DISTINGUISHING OVERLOADED FUNCTIONS For the compiler to tell the difference between one use of the function and another, each time the function is overloaded it must be given a unique set of arguments. These can even be the same arguments, as long as the order is different

```
// OVERLOAD.CXX: same parameters, different order
#include <stdio.h>

overload print;  //not necessary with 2.0
void print(int x, char c) {
    puts("first function : int, char");
}

void print(char c, int x) {
    puts("second function : char, int");
}

main( ) {
    int i = 0;
    char c = 'x';
    print(i,c);
    print(c,i);
}
```

Overloading for functions and operators is covered in detail in Chapter 5. Improvements to overloading are described in Chapter 11.

IS OVERLOADING OBJECT-ORIENTED?   Object-oriented programming can be perceived as one more step in the long process of shifting the petty details of managing a program from the programmer onto the computer. The motto might be: "let the programmer think more about the design, and let the computer handle more of the implementation." If you use this rather generous interpretation, then any construct that allows the programmer to fire off a message and let the system figure out what to do with the message is an object-oriented feature. Function overloading allows you to use the same message name with different arguments and the compiler will figure out how to handle it. You don't have to remember as many message names—you do less work, the computer does more work, so it's object-oriented, right?

It depends. Object-oriented programming was developed in an interpreted environment, where all messages are resolved during program execution. Resolving messages at compile time rather than run time is not considered an object-oriented feature if you come from this background. Resolving all messages at run time introduces a lot of overhead to the system. In addition, the type checking (and error detection) the compiler can do on messages is removed. Both these drawbacks are counter to the design philosophy of C++.

Whether function overloading is object-oriented really depends on where you draw the boundary. If you are willing to be casual and say, "I write the code and the computer takes care of it. I don't care how," then function overloading is object-oriented. If you insist that all messages must be resolved at run time, then function overloading (as well as many other implementation details of C++) isn't object-oriented.

Default Arguments

C++ functions may have *default arguments*, which are substituted by the compiler if you don't supply your own. Default arguments are specified when the function is declared.

void foo(int i = 0);

You can now call the function as **foo( );** (which is the same as **foo(0)**) or as **foo(47);**. Default arguments seem like function overloading to the client programmer. Note that the variable name **i** is optional in the declaration, even with default arguments.

You can have more than one default argument in a list, but all the default arguments must be at the end of the list, like this:

void foo2(int q, int r, int u = 4, int v = 5, int w = 6);

The class: Defining Boundaries

Now you know enough about data types, operators, and functions to understand the creation of the central construct for object-oriented programming in C++: the *class*. Predefined classes were used in the last chapter, and now you can start defining your own classes.

A class is a way to package associated pieces of data together with functions to be used with that data. It allows data and functions to be hidden, if desired, from the general purview. When you create a class, you are creating a new type of data (an abstract data type) and the operations that can be performed on that data. It is a data type just as a **float** is a data type. When you add two **float**s, the compiler knows what to do. A class definition "teaches" the compiler what to do with your new data type.

A class definition consists of the **class** keyword, followed by the name of the class followed by a body, enclosed in braces, followed by a semicolon. (Remember the semicolon—leaving it off causes strange errors.) The class body contains variable definitions and function declarations. These variables and functions are intimately tied to the class and may only be used in association with an object belonging to that class. Although the variable definitions look like the ordinary definitions of local variables inside a function, no space is allocated for them until a variable (object) of the class type is created. When this happens, all the space for the variables is allocated at once, in a clump.

The variables and functions (collectively called *members*) of a **class** are normally hidden from the outside world—the user cannot access them. These variables and functions are called *private*. The privacy can be made explicit using the **private** keyword; members in a class default to **private**. To allow the client programmer access to members, use the **public** keyword.

Here's a simple class definition:

```
class nurtz {
  int i;  // default to private
public:  // everything past here is public
  void set(int v) { i = v; } // inline function
  int read( ) { return i; } // inline function
};
```

class nurtz has three members: the data item **i** and two functions. The value of **i** can only be changed by calling the member function **set( )** and can only be read by calling the member function **read( )**. **set( )** and **read( )** are sometimes called *access functions*, since their sole purpose is to provide access to the private data. It is important to remember that only member functions (and **friend** functions, described later) may read or change the values of private variables.

As you can see, **set( )** and **read( )** are **inline** functions, but the **inline** keyword isn't used. Because a **class** is so unique, the compiler doesn't need any hints to know that a function is **inline**. You can also **overload** functions inside a class without using the **overload** keyword.

To create and use some variables (objects) of **class nurtz**, you define them just as you define any other variables.

nurtz A, B, C;

To use the objects, you call member functions using a dot.

A.set(2);

int q = A.read( );

Member functions aren't like ordinary functions—they can only be called in association with an object. (**Static** member functions in release 2.0 are an exception—see chapter 11.)

Thinking About Objects

You can think of an object as an entity with an *internal state* and *external operations*. The external operations in C++ are member functions. The functions that execute the messages in an object-oriented language are called *methods*, and *messages* are the actual function calls. The concept of *state* means an object remembers things about itself when you aren't using it. An ordinary C function (one without any static variables) is *stateless* because it always starts at the same point whenever you use it. Since an object has a state, however, you can have a function that does something different each time you call it. For example:

```
// STATE.CXX : a state-transition class
#include <stream.hxx>

// See "enum" defined later in this chapter for a better
// way to do this:
#define idle  0
#define pre_wash  1
#define spin1 2
#define wash  3
#define spin2 4
#define rinse  5
```

```
#define spin3  6

class washing_machine {
    int current_cycle;
  public:
    void start( ) { current_cycle = idle; }
    void next( ) {
      switch(current_cycle) {
        case idle : current_cycle = pre_wash; break;
        case pre_wash  : current_cycle = spin1; break;
        case spin1 : current_cycle = wash; break;
        case wash: current_cycle = spin2; break;
        case spin2 : current_cycle = rinse; break;
        case rinse: current_cycle = spin3; break;
        case spin3 : current_cycle = idle; break;
      }
      cout << "current_cycle = " << current_cycle
        << "\n";
    }
};

main( ) {
  washing_machine WM;
  WM.start( );
  for (int i = 0; i < 7; i++)
    WM.next( );
}
```

The **state** variable **WM** shows a washing machine going through all its
cycles, one for each time you call **next( )**.

DESIGN BENEFITS   One of the design benefits of C++ is that it separates
the *interface* from the *implementation*. The interface in C++ is the **class**
definition. The interface says, "here's what an object looks like, and here
are the methods for the object." It doesn't specify (except in the case of
inline functions) how the methods work. The implementation shows *how*
the methods work, and consists of all the member function definitions.
While the interface must be present everywhere the class is used, the
implementation can only exist in one spot. If, at some point in the future,
the programmer wishes to improve the implementation, it can be done

without disturbing the interface or the code that was compiled using the interface. The implementation can be changed, and the whole system relinked (only the implementation code must be recompiled). Assuming the interface is well planned, code changes are very isolated, which prevents the propagation of bugs.

In a similar vein, you can design and code the interface and delay writing the implementation code. The interface can be used as if the implementation code exists ("only the linker knows for sure"). This means you can make the equivalent of a rough sketch of your system and check to see that everything fits together properly by compiling but not linking all the modules that use the interface.

Declaration versus Definition

Although ANSI has established a clear picture of declaration and definition for C, with the C++ **class** it again grows fuzzy. It can be argued that a class description reserves no storage space (except in the case of static members) and is really just a model of a new data type and not an actual variable, so it should be called a declaration. However, a class description certainly contains more information and is more complex than a declaration in C.

This book will follow a suggestion by Stroustrup. A **class** name without a description of the class, such as

class foobar;

will be called a *name declaration*. A name declaration followed by a body, such as

class foobar {

  int i;

  //...

};

is a **class** declaration.

Constructors and Destructors— Initialization and Cleanup

When you define an instance of a built-in type (such as an **int**), the compiler creates space for that variable. If you choose to assign a value when space is reserved for the variable, the compiler does that too. In effect, the compiler *constructs* the variable for you. When a variable of a built-in type goes out of scope, the compiler causes the space for that variable to be freed; it cleans up the variable by *destroying* it.

C++ is designed to make user-defined types (classes) as indistinguishable from built-in types as possible. This means the compiler needs a function to call when the variable is created (a constructor) and a function to call when the variable goes out of scope (a destructor). If the programmer doesn't supply constructors (there can be more than one) and a destructor (there can only be one) for a class, the compiler assumes the simplest actions.

The constructor is a member function with the same name as the class. Except in unusual cases (see "Assignment to **this**" in Chapter 7), the constructor assumes that the space has been allocated for all the variables in the object's structure when it is called.

Here's an example of a constructor:

```
// CONSTRUC.CXX : a class with constructors
#include <stream.hxx>

class thizbin {
    int i, j, k;
  public:
    thizbin( ) { i = j = k = 0; }  // constructor
    thizbin(int q) { i = j = k = q; } // overloaded constructor
    thizbin(int u, int v, int w) {
        i = u;
        j = v;
        k = w;
    }  // more overloading
    void print(char * msg) {
        cout << msg << ": \n";
        cout << "i = " << i << "\n";
        cout << "j = " << j << "\n";
        cout << "k = " << k << "\n";
    }
```

```
};

main( ) {
    thizbin A;  // calls constructor with no arguments
    thizbin B(47); // calls constructor with 1 argument
    thizbin C(9,11,47); // calls constructor with 3 arguments
    A.print("A — no argument constructor");
    B.print("B — 1 argument constructor");
    C.print("C — 3 argument constructor");
}
```

class thizbin has three overloaded constructors, one that takes no arguments (used in the definition of **A**), one that takes one **int** (used for **B**), and one that takes three **int**s (used for **C**). The **print( )** method displays the **private** values of the objects after they are initialized.

The name of the destructor is the **class** name with a tilde (~) attached at the beginning. For the preceding example, the destructor name would be **~thizbin( )**. The destructor never takes any arguments; it is only called by the compiler and cannot be called explicitly by the programmer (except in Release 2.0).

While you will almost always want to perform various types of initialization on an object, the "default destructor" (doing nothing) is often sufficient and you may not need to define a destructor. However, if your object initializes some hardware (for instance, puts a window up on the screen) or changes some global value, you may need to undo the effect of the object (close the window) when the object is destroyed. For this, you need a destructor.

As an example, this program keeps track of the number of objects in existence by modifying a global variable:

```
// OBJCOUNT.CXX : Counts objects in existence

#include <stream.hxx>

int count = 0;

class obj {
    public:
    obj( ) {
        count++;
        cout << "number of objects: " << count << "\n";
    }
```

```
  ~obj( ) {
    count--;
    cout << "number of objects: " << count << "\n";
  }
};

main( ) {
  obj A, B, C, D, E;
  {
    obj F;
  }
  {
    obj G;
  }
}
```

As the objects are created, they increase the count, and as they go out of scope they decrease the count. Notice that after the first group of variables is created, **F** is created, then destroyed, and **G** is created, then destroyed, then the rest of the variables are destroyed. When the closing brace of a scope is encountered, destructors are called for each variable in the scope.

static class *MEMBERS* Every time you define an object that belongs to a particular class, all the data elements in that class are duplicated for the variable. It is possible, however, to define a variable in a class such that only one instance of the variable is created for all the objects ever defined for that class. Each object has access to this one piece of data, but the data is shared among all the objects instead of being duplicated for each object. To achieve this effect, declare the variable **static** (a third meaning of the keyword **static**).

static member variables are often used to allow communication between objects. For example:

```
// STATVAR.CXX : Static member variable in a class

#include <stream.hxx>

class comm {
  static i;  // compiler initializes it to zero
```

```
  public:
    comm( ) { i++; }
    ~comm( ) { i—; }
    void look_around( ) {
      if( i > 1 )
        cout << "there are other objects of this class\n";
      else
        cout << "there are no other objects of this class\n";
    }
};

main( ) {
  comm A;
  A.look_around( );
  {
    comm B;
    B.look_around( );
  } // B destroyed here
  A.look_around( );
} // A destroyed here
```

This example also shows another need for the destructor; it is used to keep track of information about objects. For a more sophisticated example of this, look at the examples using reference counting in Chapter 9 and Appendix B.

All static members are initialized by the compiler to 0. You should never initialize a **class static** variable as you do a function **static** variable. That is, *do not* do this:

class bad {

  static int i = 33; // a no-no

};

The compiler may accept this, but it will create space for the static variable in every file that includes the **class** declaration. At link time, you will get an error. Of course, if you know the class will only be included in one place, you can get away with this declaration, but it is not a good practice.

C++ Release 2.0 has a more sophisticated way to initialize static members. This is shown in Chapter 11.

The Header File

When you create a class, you are creating a new data type. Generally, you want this type to be easily accessible to yourself and others. In addition, you want to separate the class declaration from the the definition of the class member functions so the implementation can be changed without forcing recompilation of the entire system. These ends are achieved by putting the class declaration in a header file.

Function Collections
And Separate Compilation

Instead of putting the class declaration, the definition of the member functions, and the **main( )** function in the same file, it is best to isolate the class declaration in a header file that is included in every file in which the class is used. The definitions of the class member functions are also separated into their own file. The member functions are debugged and compiled once, and are then available as an object module (or in a library, if the librarian is used) for anyone who wants to use the class. The user of the class simply includes the header file, creates objects of that class, and links in the object module or library.

The concept of a collection of associated functions combined into the same object module or library, and a header file containing all the declarations for the functions, is very standard when building large projects in C. It is *de rigueur* in C++: you could throw any function into a collection in C, but the class in C++ determines which functions are associated by dint of their common access to the private data in the class. Any member function for a class *must* be declared in the class definition; you cannot put it in some separate header file. The use of function libraries was encouraged in C and institutionalized in C++.

IMPORTANCE OF COMMON HEADER FILES   When using a function from a library, C allows you the option of ignoring the header file and simply declaring the function by hand. You may want the compiler to speed up just a bit by avoiding the task of opening and including the file. For example, here's an extremely lazy declaration of the C function **printf( )**.

printf(...);

It says, "**printf( )** has some number of arguments, and they all have some type, but just take whatever arguments you see and accept them." By using this kind of declaration, you suspend all error checking on the arguments.

This practice can cause subtle problems. If you declare functions by hand in each different file, you may make a mistake that is accepted by the compiler in a particular file. The program will link correctly, but the use of the function in that one file will be faulty. This is a tough error to find and can be easily avoided. If you place all your function declarations in a header file and include that file everywhere the function is used (and especially where the function is defined) you ensure a consistent declaration across the whole system. You also ensure that the declaration and the definition match—by including the header in the definition file.

However, C does not enforce this practice. It is very easy, for instance, to leave the header file out of the function definition file. The novice programmer tends to be confused by (and ignore) the proper use of header files. But if a class is declared in a header file in C++, you *must* include the header file everywhere a class is used or a class member function is defined. The compiler will treat it as an error otherwise. By enforcing the proper use of header files, the language ensures consistency in libraries, and reduces bugs by forcing the same interface to be used everywhere.

All the problems are not solved by proper use of header files, though. When you overload ordinary (non-member) functions, the *order* of overloading is important. If you use the same function names in separate header files, you can change the order of overloading without knowing it, simply by including the files in a different order. The compiler won't complain, but the linker will—it can be very mystifying. This problem (further detailed in Chapter 5) exists in all C++ compilers that follow AT&T releases up through 1.2. It has been solved by a change in the language called "type-safe linkage" (see Chapter 11).

Preventing Redeclaration of Classes

When you put a **class** declaration in a header file, it is possible for the file to be included more than once in a complicated program. The **streams class** is a good example. Any time a class performs I/O (especially in **inline** functions) it may include the **streams class**. If the file you are working on uses more than one kind of **class**, you run the risk of including the **streams** header more than once and redeclaring **streams**.

The compiler considers the redeclaration of a class to be an error, since it would otherwise allow you to use the same name for different classes. To prevent this error when multiple header files are included, you need to build some intelligence into your header files using the preprocessor (the **streams class** already has this "intelligence").

***THE PREPROCESSOR DIRECTIVES* #define, #ifdef, *AND* #endif**   Earlier in this chapter, you saw **#define** can be used to create *preprocessor macros* that look similar to function definitions. **#define** can also be used to set flags. You have two choices: you can simply tell the preprocessor that the flag is defined, without specifying a value, as in

#define FLAG

or you can give it a value (which is the pre-ANSI C way to define a constant).

#define PI 3.14159

In either case, the label can now be tested by the preprocessor to see if it has been defined.

#ifdef FLAG

This will yield a true result, and the code following the **#ifdef** will be included in the package sent to the compiler. This inclusion stops when the preprocessor encounters the statement

#endif

or

#endif FLAG

Any text after the **#endif** on the same line is ignored in C++ (although it isn't legal ANSI C), and may be used as comments. To be safe, it is better to comment the text after an **#endif**. The **#ifdef** and **#endif** pairs may be nested within each other.

The complement of **#define** is **#undef** (short for "undefine"), which will make an **#ifdef** statement using the same variable yield a false result. **#undef** will also cause the preprocessor to stop using a macro. The complement of **#ifdef** is **#ifndef**, which will yield a true if the label has *not* been defined (this is the one used in header files).

There are other useful features in the preprocessor (especially the ANSI preprocessor). You should check your local guide for the full set. Macros can be very useful for debugging, as will be shown later in this chapter.

A STANDARD FOR EACH CLASS HEADER FILE   In each header file that contains a class, you should first check to see if the file has already been included in this particular code file. You do this by checking a preprocessor flag. If the flag isn't set, the file wasn't included and you should set the flag (so the class can't be redeclared) and declare the class. If the flag was set, the class has already been declared so you should just ignore the code declaring the class. Here's how the header file should look:

#ifndef CLASS_FLAG

#define CLASS_FLAG

// Class declaration here...

#endif // CLASS_FLAG

As you can see, the first time the header file is included, the **class** declaration will be included by the preprocessor, but all subsequent times the **class** declaration will be ignored. The name **CLASS_FLAG** can be any unique name, but a reliable standard to follow is to take the name of the header file and replace periods with underscores. Here's an example:

```
// SIMPLE.HXX : Simple class which prevents redefinition
// Notice it doesn't matter if comments are outside of
// the #ifndef clause; they are ignored anyway.

#ifndef SIMPLE_HXX
#define SIMPLE_HXX

class simple {
    int i,j,k;
```

```
public:
    simple( ) { i = j = k = 0; }
};

#endif // SIMPLE_HXX
```

Although the **SIMPLE_HXX** after the **#endif** is ignored by the prepro-cessor, it is useful for documentation.

A PITFALL   Sometimes you can get by without including a header file for a library function, but it is a very bad habit to fall into and can cause subtle errors. Zortech C++ contains a feature called *autoprototyping* that supports the use of an external function without previously declaring it. If you don't declare a function before you use it, the autoprototyping feature will create a function prototype based on the first use of the function. If subsequent function calls don't conform to the prototype, you get an error message. This can serve as a reminder that you didn't include the proper header file in some cases. In the following example, the **stdio.h** file is not included, so Zortech C++ creates a function prototype based on the first use. The prototype is wrong, since it requires an exact number of arguments and **printf( )** has a variadic argument list (an arbitrary number of arguments). This means the second time **printf( )** is called with a different number of arguments, an error message is generated, so you are reminded that you forgot to include the header file.

```
// REMINDER.CXX : Zortech Autoprototyping will sometimes remind
// you to include a header file.

// #include <stdio.h>  // error generated without this.

main( ) {
    printf("The first use is autoprototyped\n");
    printf("The second generates an error, %s\n",
            "Since the prototype is wrong!");
}
```

Autoprototyping can cause bugs that are very tough to trace and hark back to the days before function prototyping. For instance, the ANSI C **fabs( )** library function takes a **double** argument and returns a **double** result (which is the absolute value of the argument). If you forget to include the **math.h** header file, the **cfront**-derived C-code generators and any other compiler without autoprototyping will generate a warning message, complaining that you used a function that wasn't declared. (They will still go ahead and finish the compile, however, and the program will generate bad answers—ignore warning messages at your own risk.) Zortech C++ won't say anything. The following program prints the wrong answer but gives no complaint. It's easy to see here, but if **fabs( )** is embedded in some complicated class (as it is in **class matrix** in Appendix B), you will simply start seeing wrong answers and not know why.

```
// BADFABS.CXX : A pitfall due to Zortech C++ Autoprototyping

#include <stdio.h>
//#include <math.h>  // No prototype — Zortech doesn't complain

main( ) {
    float f = 0.5;
    float fa = fabs(f);
    printf("fa = fabs(f) : %f\n", fa);  // prints garbage
}
```

In this case, autoprototyping has disabled the type checking that function prototyping was designed to provide. It should probably be changed to an optional feature in Zortech C++, not a default. If you begin to suspect that you aren't including a header file with Zortech C++, try turning off the autoprototyping feature with the **-p** flag, or use strict prototyping with the **-r** flag. You can also set the environment variable CFLAGS to **-r** or **- p**. Note that this problem was fixed in Zortech C++ 2.0.

PORTABLE INCLUSION OF HEADER FILES   Because there is no standard way to name header files, you can run into problems when you try to move code from one compiler to another. Do you say **#include "header.h"** or **#include "header.hpp"** or **#include "header.hxx"**? This book has taken the approach of using the **.hxx** extension, which, with a little work, is acceptable with all compilers. You can name files that are part of your source code anything you want, since the file always comes with the source code. The only problem occurs when a library is part of all C++ installations (like the **streams** library) and the header file is named differently between implementations. In this situation, you can either rely on a predefined preprocessor macro that many compilers use to identify themselves, or you can define your own preprocessor flags to easily switch between header filenames.

As an example of the first approach, the Zortech compiler defines the flag __ZTC__, which you could use if you wanted to differentiate between Zortech and Glockenspiel header-naming conventions.

```
#ifdef __ZTC__
#include <stream.hpp>
#else
#include <stream.hxx>
#endif
```

If you wanted compatibility between Unix and MS-DOS, you can take the second approach and define your own preprocessor flags: UNIX and MSDOS.

```
#ifdef MSDOS
#include <stream.hxx>
#endif
#ifdef UNIX
#include <stream.h>
#endif
```

In this case, compatibility between Zortech and Glockenspiel on MS-DOS is achieved by copying the Zortech header file **stream.hpp** to **stream.hxx** in Zortech's INCLUDE directory. (This also works for Turbo C++.)

Since the files that come as part of C++ are (so far) few, you can decide to take the "copy the header to a file with a common extension" approach for all the operating systems, and then create any new header files with that common extension. If everyone does it, it will make life much easier. (**.hxx** is probably the best choice for an extension, at this point.)

Defining class *Member Functions*

All the member function definitions so far have been **inline**. In the general case, functions will be defined in a separate code file. This section shows the specifics of defining member functions.

The Scope Resolution Operator ::

To define a member function, you must first tell the compiler that the function you are defining is associated with a particular class. This is accomplished using the *scope resolution operator* (**::**). For example:

```
// SCOPERES.CXX : Defining a non-inline member function
#include <stream.hxx>

class example {
   int i, j, k;
  public:
   example( ); // declare the function
   void print( ); // ditto
};

example::example( ) { // the constructor
   i = 12;
   j = 100;
   k = 47;
}

void example::print( ) {
   cout << "i = " << i;
   cout << ", j = " << j;
   cout << ", k = " << k << "\n";
}

main( ) {
   example test;
   test.print( );
}
```

As you can see, the member function is associated with the **class** name by attaching the **class** name, followed by the scope resolution operator. The functions will now be compiled as normal functions instead of **inline** functions.

The scope resolution operator can be used anytime you aren't sure which definition the compiler will use. You can also use scope resolution to select a definition other than the normal default. For instance, if you create a **class** in which you define your own **puts( )** function (**puts( )** is an ANSI C library function that puts a string to standard output), you can select the global **puts( )** as follows:

```
// DISPLAY.CXX : A class with its own puts( ) function

#include <stdio.h>  // contains the puts( ) declaration

class display {
  public:
    void puts(char *); // declare the function
};

void display::puts(char * msg) {
    ::puts("this is my puts function");
    ::puts(msg);
}

main( ) {
    display A;
    A.puts("calling A.puts( )");
}
```

If, inside of **display::puts( )**, the **puts( )** function was called without the scope resolution operator, the compiler would call **display::puts( )** instead of the library function **puts( )**. If the scope resolution operator is used with no name preceding it, it means, "use the global name."

Calling Other Member Functions

As the preceding example implies, you can call member functions from inside other member functions. It was stated before that a member function can never be called unless it is associated with an object, so this might look a bit confusing at first. If you are defining a member function, that function is already associated with an object (the "current object," also referred to with the keyword **this**). A member function can simply be called using its name inside another member function (no object name and dot are necessary inside a member function). This is illustrated in an example that creates a "smart array" (one that checks boundaries). The array was briefly introduced in Chapter 2.

```cpp
// SMART.CXX : An array that checks boundaries
#include <stdio.h>  // for puts( ) declaration
#include <stdlib.h> // for exit() declaration

const int size = 10;

class array {
    int a[size];
    void check_index(int index); // private function
public:
    array(int initval = 0); // default argument value
    void setval(int index, int value);
    int readval(int index);
};

// constructor:
array::array(int intval) { // don't duplicate the default value!
    for (int i = 0; i < size; i++ )
        setval(i, intval);  // call another member function
}

void array::check_index(int index) {
    if ( index < 0 || index >= size ) { // logical OR
        puts("array error: setval index out of bounds");
        exit(1);  // ANSI C library function; quits program
    }
}

void array::setval(int index, int value) {
    check_index(index);
    a[index] = value;
}

int array::readval(int index) {
```

```
        check_index(index);
        return a[index];
}

main( ) {
    array A, B(47);
    int x = B.readval(10); // out of bounds — see what happens
}
```

check_index( ) is a **private** member function, which can only be called by other member functions. Whenever the user wants to set or read a value, **check_index( )** is called first to make sure the array boundaries are not exceeded.

You can see that C tries to make the definition of a variable mimic its use (but this doesn't always succeed). For an array, the definition might be

int values[100];

To use the array, you write

int y = values[4];

to read element 4, or

values[99] = 128;

to assign to element 99. Remember that elements are counted from zero, so if you define an array with 100 elements you must start at element 0 and stop at element 99.

friend: *Access to* private *Elements of Another* class

There are times when the program design just won't work out right. You can't always make everything fit neatly into one class; sometimes other functions must have access to private elements of your class for everything to work together harmoniously. You could make some elements **public**, but this is a bad idea unless you really want the client programmer to change the data.

The solution in C++ is to create **friend** functions. **friend** functions are functions that aren't class members—although they can be members of some other class. In fact, an entire class can be declared a **friend**. A **friend** has the same access privileges as a member function, but it isn't associated with an object of the host class. (So you can't call member functions of the host class without associating the functions with objects.) The host class has control over granting **friend** privileges to other functions, so you always know who has the ability to change your private data. It's much easier to trace bugs that way.

As an example, suppose you have two different classes, both of which keep some kind of internal time—a **watch** and a **microwave_oven**—and you want to be able to synchronize the clocks in the two separate classes.

```
// FRIENDLY.CXX : Demonstration of friend functions
// The synchronize( ) function has arguments from both watch
// and microwave_oven.  The first time synchronize( ) is declared
// as a friend in watch, the compiler won't know that
// microwave_oven exists unless we declare its name first:
class microwave_oven;

class watch {
    int time;  // a measure of time
    int alarm;  // when the alarm goes off
    int date;  // other things a watch should know
public:
    // constructor sets starting state:
    watch( ) { time = alarm = date = 0; }
    void tick( ) { time++; } // very simple transition
    // declare a friend function:
    // (see text for meaning of '&')
    friend void synchronize(watch &, microwave_oven &);
};

class microwave_oven {
    int time;
    int start_time;
    int stop_time;
    int intensity;
```

```
public:
   microwave_oven( ) {
      time = 0;
      start_time = stop_time = 0;
      intensity = 0;
   }
   void tick( ) { time++; } // different transition
   friend void synchronize(watch &, microwave_oven &);
};

void synchronize(watch & objA, microwave_oven & objB) {
   objA.time = objB.time = 15;  // set both to a common state
}

main( ) {
   watch  que_hora;
   microwave_oven  nuker;
   que_hora.tick( );
   que_hora.tick( );
   nuker.tick( );
   synchronize(que_hora,nuker);
}
```

Since **synchronize( )** is a **friend** function to both **watch** and **micro-wave_oven**, it has access to the private elements of both. In a non-**friend** function, the references to **objA.i** and **objB.i** would be illegal.

REFERENCES   Something new has been introduced in this example: the '**&**' in the argument list for **synchronize( )**. Normally, when you pass an argument to a function, the variable you specify in the argument list is copied and handed to the function. If you change something in the copy, it has no effect on the original. When the function ends, the copy goes out of scope and the original is untouched. If you want to change the original variable, you must tell the function where the original variable lives instead of making a copy of the original variable. As described earlier in this chapter (in "C++ Function Overloading"), a *pointer* is one way to tell a function where the original variable lives. In that example, the address of a string was being passed to a function called **print(char *)**; and it was necessary to use the address because the compiler couldn't know how long the string was. A reference, specified by the operator **&**, is the second way to pass an address. It is a much nicer way to pass an address to a function, and it is only available in C++.

A reference quietly takes the address of an object. Inside the function, the reference lets you treat the name as if it were a real variable, and not just the address of a variable.

As you can see in the definition for **synchronize( )**, the elements of **objA** and **objB** are selected using the dot, just as if **objA** and **objB** were objects, and not addresses of objects. The compiler takes care of everything else. (References are described in detail in Chapter 4.)

Notice that **synchronize( )** can reach right in and modify the **private** elements of both **objA** and **objB**. This is only true because **synchronize( )** was declared a **friend** of both classes. An alternative solution is to declare an entire class as a friend, and make **synchronize( )** one of the member functions.

```cpp
// FRIEND2.CXX : Making an entire class a friend

class watch {
    int time;  // a measure of time
    int alarm;  // when the alarm goes off
    int date;   // other things a watch should know
public:
    // constructor sets starting state:
    watch( ) { time = alarm = date = 0; }
    void tick( ) { time++; } // very simple transition
    // Allow all members of microwave_oven access to private
    // elements of watch:
    friend class microwave_oven;
};

class microwave_oven {
    int time;
    int start_time;
    int stop_time;
    int intensity;
public:
    microwave_oven( ) {
        time = 0;
        start_time = stop_time = 0;
        intensity = 0;
    }
    void tick( ) { time++; } // different transition
```

```
       void synchronize(watch & WA) {
          time = WA.time = 15;  // set both to a common state
       }
    };

    main( ) {
       watch  que_hora;
       microwave_oven  nuker;
       que_hora.tick( );
       que_hora.tick( );
       nuker.tick( );
       nuker.synchronize(que_hora);
    }
```

This program is identical to FRIENDLY.CXX except **synchronize( )** is a member function of **microwave_oven**. Notice that **synchronize( )** only takes one argument here, since a member function already knows about the object it is called for. Also notice that the name declaration for **microwave_oven** is unnecessary before **class watch**, since it is included in the **friend** declaration.

Often, the choice of whether to use member functions or non-member functions comes down to your preference for the way the syntax should look.

Other class-like Items

There are several other constructs in C++ that have declarations similar to the class. Each of these constructs have a different purpose. They include the "plain" structure **struct**, the enumerated data type **enum**, and the space-saving **union**.

struct: a class with All Elements Public

The data structure keyword **struct** was developed for C so a programmer could group together several pieces of data and treat them as a single data item. As you can imagine, the **struct** is an early attempt at abstract data typing (without the associated member functions). In C, you must create non-member functions that take your **struct** as an argument. There is no concept of private data, so any function (not just the ones you define) can change the elements of a **struct**.

C++ will accept any **struct** you can declare in C (so it's upward compatible). However, C++ expands the definition of a **struct** so it is just like a class, except a class defaults to **private** while a **struct** defaults to **public**. Any **struct** you define in C++ can have member functions, constructors, and a destructor. Although the **struct** is an artifact from C, sometimes it is used to emphasize that all elements are public. You can make a class in C++ work just like a **struct** in C++ by putting "**public:**" at the beginning of your class. Notice that a **struct** in ANSI C doesn't have constructors, destructors, or member functions.

As you can see from this example, all the elements in a **struct** are **public**.

```
// STRUCT.CXX : demonstration of structures vs classes

class CL {
    int i, j, k;
public:
    CL(int init = 0 ) { i = j = k = init; }
};

struct ST {
    int i, j, k;
    // don't need to say "public."  Everything is public!
    ST (int init = 0 ) { i = j = k = init; }
};

main( ) {
    CL A(10);
    ST B(11);
    B.i = 44; // this is OK
// A.i = 44; // this will cause an error!
}
```

Clarifying Programs with enum

An enumerated data type is a way of attaching names to numbers, thereby giving more meaning to anyone reading the code. The **enum** keyword (from

C) automatically enumerates any list of words you give it by assigning them values of 0, 1, 2, and so on. You can declare **enum** variables (which are always **int**s). The declaration of an **enum** looks similar to a class declaration, but an **enum** cannot have any member functions.

An enumerated data type is very useful when you want to keep track of some sort of feature.

```
// ENUM.CXX : Keeping track of shapes.

enum shape_type {
   circle,
   square,
   rectangle
}; // must end with a semicolon like a class

main( ) {
   shape_type shape = circle;
   // activities here....
   // now do something based on what the shape is:
   switch(shape) {
      case circle: /* circle stuff */ break;
      case square: /* square stuff */ break;
      case rectangle: /* rectangle stuff */ break;
   }
}
```

shape is a variable of the **shape_type** enumerated data type, and its value can be compared with the value in the enumeration. Since **shape** is really just an **int**, however, you are not restricted from giving it any value an **int** can hold (including a negative number). You can also compare an **int** variable with a value in the enumeration.

If you don't like the way the compiler assigns values, you can do it yourself, like this:

enum shape_type { circle = 10, square = 20, rectangle = 50 };

If you give values to some names and not to others, the compiler will use the next integral value. For example:

enum snap { crackle = 25, pop };

The compiler gives **pop** the value 26.

You can see how much more readable the code is when you use enumerated data types.

Saving Memory with union

Sometimes a program will handle different types of data using the same variable. In this situation, you have two choices: you can create a **class** or **struct** containing all the possible different types you might need to store, or you can use a **union**. A **union** piles all the data into a single space; it figures out the amount of space necessary for the largest item you've put in the **union** and makes that the size of the **union**. Unions are used when memory must be saved.

Anytime you place a value in a **union**, the value always starts in the same place at the beginning of the **union**, but only uses as much space as is necessary. Thus, you create a "super-variable," capable of holding any of the **union** variables. All the addresses of the **union** variables are the same (in a **class** or **struct**, the addresses are different).

Here's a simple use of a **union**. Try removing various elements and see what effect it has on the size of the union. Notice that it makes no sense to declare more than one instance of a single data type in a union (unless you're just doing it to use a different name).

```
// UNION.CXX : The size and simple use of a union
#include <stream.hxx>

union packed { // declaration similar to a class
    char i;
    short j;
    int k;
    long l;
    float f;
    double d;  // the union will be the size of a double,
               // since it's the largest element
}; // semicolon ends a union, like a class
```

```
main( ) {
    cout << "sizeof(packed) = " << sizeof(packed) << "\n";
    packed X;
    X.i = 'c';
    X.d = 3.14159;
}
```

The compiler performs the proper assignment according to the **union** member you select.

Once you perform an assignment, the compiler doesn't care what you do with the **union**. In the preceding example, you could assign a floating-point value to **X** with

X.f = 2.222;

and then send it to the output as if it were an **int**.

cout << X.i;

This would produce complete garbage.

C++ allows a **union** to have a constructor, destructor, and member functions just like a class.

```
// UNION2.CXX: Unions with constructors and member functions

union U {
    int i;
    float f;
    U(int a) { i = a; }
    U(float b) { f = b;}
    ~U( ) { f = 0; }
    int read_int( ) { return i; }
    float read_float( ) { return f; }
};

main( ) {
    U X(12), Y(1.9F);
    X.i = 44;
    X.read_int( );
    Y.read_float( );
}
```

Although the member functions civilize access to the **union** somewhat, there is still no way to prevent the user from selecting the wrong element once the **union** has been initialized. A "safe" **union** can be encapsulated in a **class** like this. (Notice how the **enum** clarifies the code.)

```
// SUPERVAR.CXX : A super-variable
#include <stream.hxx>

class super_var {
  enum {
    character,
    integer,
    floating_point
  } vartype; // define an instance of the enum
  union { // anonymous union
    char c;
    int i;
    float f;
  };
public:
  super_var(char ch) {
    vartype = character;
    c = ch;
  }
  super_var(int ii) {
    vartype = integer;
    i = ii;
  }
  super_var(float ff) {
    vartype = floating_point;
    f = ff;
  }
  void print( ) {
    switch (vartype) {
      case character:
        cout << "character: " << chr(c) << "\n";
        break;
      case integer:
        cout << "integer: " << i <<  "\n";
        break;
      case floating_point:
        cout << "float: " << f << "\n";
```

```
        break;
      }
    }
};

main( ) {
  super_var A((char)'c'), B(12), C(1.44F);
  A.print( );
  B.print( );
  C.print( );
}
```

In this code, the **enum** has no type name. This is acceptable if you are going to immediately define instances of the **enum**, as is done here. There is no need to refer to the **enum**'s type in the future, so the type is optional.

The **union** has no type name and no variable name. This is called an *anonymous union*, and creates space for the **union** but doesn't require accessing the **union** elements with a variable name and the dot operator. For instance, if your anonymous **union** is

union { int i, float f };

you access members by saying

i = 12;

f = 1.22;

just like other variables. The only difference is that both variables have the same address.

Debugging Hints

When you're writing your own classes, you can use the features of C++ to your advantage and build in debugging tools. In particular, each class should have a function called **dump( )** (or some similar name) that will display the contents of an object. This way you can **dump( )** your objects at various points in your program to trace their progress. If you build the **dump( )** function in from the start, you won't have as much mental resistance to running a trace.

This class has a built-in **dump( )** function.

```
// DEBUG1.CXX : A class with a dump( ) function
// (It isn't supposed to do anything, just act as
// an example).
#include <stream.hxx>

class debuggable {
    int counter; // some sort of internal counter
    float a, b;  // data the user is aware of
public:
    debuggable (float x = 0.0, float y = 0.0) {
        a = x; b = y; counter = 2;
    }
    void set_a(float x) { a = x; counter++; }
    float read_a( ) { return a; counter++; }
    void set_b(float y) { b = y; counter++; }
    float read_b( ) { return b; counter++; }
    void dump(char * msg = " ") {
        cout << msg << ":\n";
        cout << "a = " << a << "\n";
        cout << "b = " << b << "\n";
        cout << "counter = " << counter << "\n";
    }
};

main( ) {
    debuggable U, V(3.14), W(1.1,2.2);
    U.set_a(99);
    U.dump("After 1 set_a");
    U.read_b( );
    U.dump("After 1 read_b");
    // other operations ...
    V.dump("V");
    W.dump( ); // string argument is optional
}
```

Because the argument **msg** is given a default value of an empty string, providing a message when you call **dump( )** is optional. In this program, the variable **counter** is normally completely hidden from the user's view, and no functions are provided to access it. **counter** is a variable to keep track of some sort of internal information. When debugging, this information may be essential. It is best to provide as much information as possible, as well as optional messages, in the **dump( )** function.

Debugging Flags

If you hard-wire your debugging code into a program, you can run into problems. You start to get too much information, which makes the bugs difficult to isolate. When you think you've found the bug, you start tearing out debugging code, only to find you need to put it back in again. These problems can be solved using two types of flags: preprocessor debugging flags and run time debugging flags.

PREPROCESSOR DEBUGGING FLAGS   By using the preprocessor to define (with **#define**) one or more debugging flags (preferably in a header file), you can test a flag using an **#ifdef** statement to conditionally include debugging code. When you think your debugging is finished, you can simply undefine (with **#undef**) the flag(s) and the code will automatically be removed. The size of your executable file will also be reduced.

It is best to decide on names for debugging flags before you begin building your project so the names will be consistent. Preprocessor flags are often distinguished from variables by writing them in capital letters. A common flag name is simply DEBUG (but be careful you don't use NDEBUG, which is reserved in ANSI C). The sequence of statements might be

#define DEBUG // probably in a header file

//....

#ifdef DEBUG // check to see if flag is defined

/* debugging code here */

#endif // DEBUG

Many C and C++ implementations will even let you use **#define** and **#undef** on flags from the compiler command line, so you can recompile code and insert debugging information with a single command (preferably via the makefile). Check your manual for details.

RUN TIME DEBUGGING FLAGS In some situations it is more convenient to turn debugging flags on and off during program execution. (It is much more elegant to turn flags on and off when the program starts up, using the command line. See Chapter 4 for details of using the command line.) Large programs can be tedious to recompile just to insert debugging code.

You can create integer flags and use the fact that non-zero values are true to increase the readability of your code. For instance:

int debug = 0; // default off

//...

cout << "turn debugger on? (y/n): ";

cin >> reply;

if (reply == 'y') debug++; // turn flag on

//...

if(debug) {

  // debugging code here

}

Notice that the variable is in lowercase letters to remind the reader it isn't a preprocessor flag.

Turning a Variable Name into a String

When writing debugging code it is tedious to write print expressions consisting of a string containing the variable name followed by the variable. Fortunately, ANSI C has introduced the "string-ize" operator #. When you put a # before an argument in a preprocessor macro, that argument is turned into a string by putting quotes around it. This, combined with the fact that strings with no intervening punctuation are concatenated into a single string, makes possible a very convenient macro for printing the values of variables during debugging:

#define PR(x) cout << #x " = " << x << "\n";

If you print the variable **A** by calling the macro **PR(A)**, it will have the same effect as the code

cout << "A = " << A << "\n";

The ANSI C assert( ) Macro

The **assert( )** macro is very convenient in debugging. When you use **assert( )**, you give it an argument that is an expression you are "asserting to be true." The preprocessor generates code that will test the assertion. If the assertion isn't true, the program will stop after issuing an error message telling you what the assertion was and that it failed. Here's a small example:

```
// ASSERT.CXX : Use of the assert( ) debugging macro
#include <assert.h>  // contains the macro
#include <stdio.h>
#include <stdlib.h>

main( ) {
    int i = 100;
    assert(i != 100);
}
```

The ANSI C library header file **assert.h** contains the macro for assertion. When you are finished debugging, you can remove the code generated by the macro simply by placing the line

#define NDEBUG

in the program before the inclusion of **assert.h**, or by defining **NDEBUG** on the compiler command line.

Debugging Techniques Combined

By combining the techniques discussed in this section, a framework appears that you can follow when writing your own debugging code. Keep in mind that if you want to isolate certain types of debugging code, you can create variables **debug1**, **debug2**, and so forth, and preprocessor flags **DEBUG1, DEBUG2**....

NOTE: The following example shows the use of command line flags, which are not formally introduced until the next chapter. Although this may be somewhat confusing, it is better to see the right way to do something rather than learning a method that will later need to be unlearned. A much cleaner way to implement command line flags is shown in Chapter 10.

The flags on the command line are accessed through the arguments to **main( )**, which are called **argc** and **argv**.

```
// DEBUG2.CXX : Framework for writing debug code
#include <stream.hxx>
#define DEBUG
#include <stdlib.h>

main( int argc, char * argv[ ]) {
   int debug = 0;
   if ( argc > 1 ) { // if more than one argument
     if (*argv[1] == 'd')
        debug++; // set the debug flag
     else {
        cout << "usage: debug2  OR  debug2 d\n"
           "optional flag turns debugger on.";
        exit(1);  // quit program
     }
   }
   // ....
#ifdef DEBUG
   if(debug)
     cout << "debugger on\n";
#endif // DEBUG
   // ...
}
```

If you type on the command line

debug2

nothing will happen, but if you type

debug2 d

the "debugger" will be turned on. When you want to remove the debugging code at some later date to reduce the size of the executable program, simply change the **#define DEBUG** to a **#undef DEBUG**. (Or better yet, do it from the compiler command line.)

makefile *for Chapter Examples*

Here is the **makefile** for the chapter examples. This **makefile** uses a feature of **make**, called *rules* (or *inference rules*). A rule is the way to teach **make** how to convert a file with one type of extension (**.cxx**) into a file with another type of extension (**.obj** or **.exe**). This eliminates the redundancy you saw in the **makefile** for Chapter 2, which created a long **makefile** and invited typing errors. Once you teach **make** the rules for producing one kind of file from another, all you have to do is tell **make** which files depend on which other files. When **make** finds a file with a date earlier than the file it depends on (which means the source file has been changed and not yet recompiled), it uses the rule to create a new file.

This **makefile** also uses a *built-in macro*, of which there are several in **make**. Calling a built-in macro is just like calling a regular macro, except you leave out the parentheses. One built-in macro used here is **$***, which means "the file to be produced" (also called the target file) without the file extension. The target without the extension is called the *base name*.

Here's the first rule used in the **makefile**:

```
.cxx.exe :
    $(CPP) $*.cxx
```

It says, "to take a file with an extension of **.cxx** and create a file with an extension of **.exe**, run C++ on the base name with an extension of **.cxx**."

Notice that there is no space between **.cxx** and **.exe**, and that the command must be preceded with a tab. The second rule is similar, and creates a **.obj** file from a **.cxx** file.

You will notice in the "master dependency list," **all**, that most of the dependencies are on **.exe** files, so the first rule will be used. One dependency, ROLROR.OBJ, will use the second rule. In all cases, if **make** cannot find the appropriate **.cxx** file in the current directory, it will complain that it "cannot create" that **.cxx** file.

There are two programs that depend on more than one file. These programs are GLOBAL.EXE and FILESTAT.EXE. When **make** encounters these names in the **all** list, it checks for other dependencies before executing the rules. The dependencies exist, so **make** uses those *instead* of the rules. The commands use another built-in macro: **$∗∗**, which means "the full list of dependencies" (in this case, all the **.obj** files). This macro is available on several versions of **make** on the PC, including Zortech and Microsoft, but isn't part of most Unix **makes.** If you are using Unix, simply replace the **$∗∗** with the list of dependencies. When **make** goes to create GLOBAL.EXE or FILESTAT.EXE, it first uses the default rule to create the .obj files from the **.cxx** files, and then runs the linker on all the **.obj** files in the dependency list.

By learning to use rules and built-in macros, you will create a smaller, more error-free **makefile**.

```
# MAKEFILE for examples in Chapter 3
# Zortech:
CPP = ztc
# Glockenspiel:
#CPP = ccxx

.cxx.exe:
        $(CPP) $*.cxx

.cxx.obj:
        $(CPP) -c $*.cxx

all: basic.exe specify.exe scope.exe onthefly.exe \
     static.exe global.exe \
     forward.exe mathops.exe boolean.exe bitwise.exe \
     rolror.obj pitfall.exe return.exe overload.exe state.exe \
     construc.exe objcount.exe statvar.exe \
     scoperes.exe display.exe smart.exe friendly.exe \
```

```
        friend2.exe struct.exe enum.exe union.exe union2.exe \
        supervar.exe debug1.exe assert.exe debug2.exe badfabs.exe

# This should generate warnings/errors:
reminder.exe : reminder.cxx

global.exe : global.obj global2.obj
        $(CPP) $**

# running "make filestat.exe" should cause a linker error:
filestat.exe : filestat.obj fstat2.obj
        $(CPP) $**
```

4 *Pointers and References*

Many high-level languages (even BASIC) have the ability to take the address of a variable and manipulate addresses at run time. In perhaps no other languages is it so essential to understand how this works than C and C++. This chapter covers the ins and outs of manipulating addresses in C and C++.

Addresses Are Just Like Mailboxes

All data and code in a programming language is stored in memory while a program is running. Each memory cell can be individually selected by using its address (like the address on your mailbox). The fact that variables and code live in memory opens up a new way to refer to them: by their *starting address*—the address of the first byte of the variable or piece of code.

When writing code, you refer to starting addresses with symbolic names—the identifiers you give your variables or functions. The compiler uses symbolic names for functions, global variables, and **static** variables. The names are often modified during translation, but some form of the name exists all the way through into the object modules. Only at link time are the names resolved into addresses. At this time all information about the names is removed and doesn't exist in the executable file. (Although it's usually possible to tell the compiler and linker to leave special information for use by a symbolic debugger, this is unavailable to the executing program.) This means that if you want to perform an operation on a variable or function without knowing all the details about that variable or function at compile time, you must use its address.

Local (automatic) variables are created on the stack and are referred to via their starting address on the stack. Local variables may also be used via their addresses.

Pointers

There exists a special type of variable that is designed to manipulate addresses. It is called a "pointer," and is denoted by the unary operator *. This is different than the binary multiplication operator *. Operators, like overloaded functions, are called according to the context in which they are used. A pointer is really an additional data type—it has its own rules, and can be manipulated with all the operators available for the "ordinary" data types **char**, **int**, **float**, and **double**.

Pointers allow you to select and manipulate the addresses of variables and functions at run time. Some programs aren't possible without this flexibility. Pointers have four primary uses: in arrays, as function arguments, for direct memory access, and in dynamic memory allocation.

Use of Pointers in Arrays

An array has a single name but refers to a block of variables (all of the same type). To select any of the variables in the block, you can *index* into the array using the bracket operator, [ ], or you can use pointer arithmetic. The name of the array by itself is the starting address of the block of variables.

Arrays were previously introduced when creating character buffers. You define an array of ten characters like this:

char array[10];

Notice the use of the bracket operator in the definition. Remember that in C and C++, the definition of a variable attempts to mimic the use of the variable. So to produce an element in the array, use the bracket operator in the same way:

char c = array[9];

This produces the value of the tenth element in the array (since you start counting at zero this is the last element). Array indexing can also be used as an lvalue. The statement

array[0] = 'A';

sets the first element of the array to the character value **'A'** (ASCII 65). The starting address is produced by simply saying **array**. You are not restricted to constants inside the brackets. Generally, arrays are used to choose elements at run time, so expressions are valid within arrays

c = array[2*i];

There is no bounds checking on arrays specified in C or C++. The compiler may perform compile time checking and/or add code to impose run time range constraints, but most do not. This means that just because you declare an array to be ten elements you are not prevented from selecting the one-hundredth element of the array.

c = array[100]; // who knows what this will be?

You may also create multi-dimensional arrays.

float TWO_D[10][5]; // a two-dimensional array

float THREE_D[10][15][12]; // a three-dimensional array

// etc...

STRINGS: A SPECIAL TYPE OF ARRAY The compiler treats quoted text strings specially. When you use a string, as in the function **puts( )**, which sends a string to the console,

puts("This is a string");

the compiler takes the characters inside the double quotes, turns them into their equivalent ASCII numbers, adds a zero byte (to indicate the end of the string), and stashes the whole thing away in memory somewhere. Then it places the starting address of that memory in the argument list. This means that whenever you create or use a string like **"A String"**, what you are really talking about is the starting address of that string.

You can treat a string as an array:

char ∗ ca = "A String Is Really An Array";

You can select elements of the array by using brackets: **ca[0]** produces **'A'**, **ca[2]** produces **'S'**, and so on. Examples of the use of string pointers will be seen through the rest of this book.

Functions That Modify Their Arguments

An important use for pointers is as function arguments, when you want to affect the function argument rather than simply copy its contents into a local variable inside the function. In this discussion, the variable that is outside the scope of the function and originates the function argument either by being copied into the function or by having its address taken will be called the *outside variable*. In a function with ordinary arguments, such as

int ordinary_args(int j) {

   //...

   j = 10;

}

the variable **j** is a local variable. When you call it by saying **ordinary_args(x);**, a local variable **j** is created and the contents of **x**, the outside variable, are copied into **j**. When **j** is assigned the value **10**, as shown, only the local variable is affected. When the function ends, the local variable goes out of scope. The value of the outside variable **x** is unchanged through all this.

Often, you want to change the value of the outside variable. You can pass the value back as the return value of the function and assign the outside variable to the new value. This is the preferred method, since it clarifies what is going on, but it only works for one variable. What if you want a function to change more than one outside variable, or you're already using the return value of the function for something (like an error code)?

The answer is to pass the address of the outside variable. Since the function now knows where the outside variable lives (rather than simply getting a copy of its contents), it can go out and manipulate the outside variable directly. In the above example, the function definition becomes

int pointer_args(int ∗ j) {

   // ...

   ∗j = 10;

}

The ∗ in the argument list says "this argument is a *pointer* to an integer, rather than an integer." The **∗j** says "what the pointer points to." Using the ∗ here is called *dereferencing* the pointer. If you use **j** by itself, as in

printf("%ld", (unsigned long)j); // print the pointer as a long

you get the contents of the pointer, which is some address in memory. To get at what the pointer points to, you must dereference the pointer with a ∗. So **∗j = 10;** says, "set the value (not the pointer) to 10."

Direct Memory Access

There are numerous reasons why you may want to access memory directly. For example, video memory in a personal computer can be changed more quickly via direct access than by calling operating system functions. Some computers are designed with *memory-mapped I/O,* in which hardware devices are located in the memory space—pointers allow you to access these devices. Sometimes a pointer is simply the most expedient way to access portions of memory.

Dynamic Memory Allocation

There are situations where you don't know the quantity or type of object until run time, or you don't want the objects to be subject to normal scoping rules. Normally, you define and use all your objects at compile time, but the concept of *dynamic memory allocation* (covered in Chapter 6) allows you to create and destroy objects at run time. Dynamic memory allocation is an important part of programming in C and C++, since it frees you from the normal limitations of having to know everything at compile time.

When you create an object dynamically (using the **new** keyword), you get an address back (which you assign to a pointer), and you must access the object through the pointer. When you destroy a dynamic object (using the **delete** keyword), you must give the address of the object to **delete**.

Using Pointers and Addresses

A pointer is just like any other variable—it contains a value, and that value can be manipulated by operators, passed as a function argument, used as an index in a **for** loop, and so on. The only difference is that the value is treated as an *address,* and so the pointer always *points* somewhere, even if that somewhere is nonsense. Because the pointer contains an address, its contents are always treated as a positive integral value (so you can't assign a pointer to a floating-point value).

The distinction between the definition of an ordinary variable and the definition of a pointer is the *. The * means "what's in the box at this address." Thus, when you define a pointer, as in

int * ip;

the definition says "an **int** is in the box at the address contained in **ip**." Remember that C and C++ variable definitions attempt to mimic their use. When you use a pointer by dereferencing it, such as

*ip = 2;

it says: "change the contents of the box at the address contained in **ip** to 2."

When you create a pointer, it doesn't point to anything intelligent unless you first initialize it. To initialize a pointer, you must set it to an address. You have several choices when doing this.

■ If you know what the address is, (for instance, if you want to point to some piece of hardware, or video memory) assign the pointer to a specific number.

■ If you are working with a string, or inside a function dealing with a pointer argument, the address is handed to you.

■ The address of a function or array is simply the name of the function without the argument list, or the name of the array without the brackets.

■ If you are using dynamic memory allocation, the keyword **new** returns the starting address of the object you create.

■ If you want to use the address of an existing variable, you must use the "address-of" operator, **&**. This is a unary operator that produces the address of whatever variable it precedes. If you want to create a pointer and initialize it to the address of another variable, you say

int A = 47; // define an ordinary int

int * ap; // define an int pointer

ap = &A; // set the int pointer to the address of the int

int * aap = &A; // create and initialize simultaneously

■ If you want to pass an address to be used as a pointer argument for the function **pointer_args( )**, you say **pointer_args(&A);**. Note that since a pointer name without the * also produces the address, you can say **pointer_args(ap);** as well, if **ap** is defined as in the preceding code fragment.

Pointer Arithmetic

When you use operators on pointers, the arithmetic comes out a bit differently. In fact, the way pointer arithmetic is performed depends on the type of pointer involved. To see why this is, imagine you have an array of **char**, and a pointer to the start of that array (element 0). If you want to look at element 1, you need the address of the next **char** in the array. Since a **char** is 1 byte long, element 1 lives at the starting address plus 1.

Now imagine you have an array of **double** and a pointer to element 0. An IEEE **double** is 8 bytes long, so element 1 lives at the starting address plus 8 bytes.

Fortunately, you don't have to figure this out every time you calculate an address. Pointer arithmetic is automatic, as this example shows.

```
// PTRARITH.CXX : Demonstration of pointer arithmetic
#include <stream.hxx>

main( ) {
  char A = 'a';
  char * cp = &A;  // create and initialize a char pointer
  double d = 1.119;
  double * dp = &d; // create and initialize a double pointer

  cout << "Addition & Subtraction: \n";
  char * cp2 = cp + 1;
  double * dp2 = dp + 1;
  cout << "cp2 = cp +1; dp2 = dp + 1;\n";
  cout << "cp2 - cp = " << cp2 - cp << "\n";
  cout << "dp2 - dp = " << dp2 - dp << "\n";
  cout << "(int)cp2 - (int)cp = " << (int)cp2 - (int)cp << "\n";
  cout << "(int)dp2 - (int)dp = " << (int)dp2 - (int)dp << "\n";
  cout << "increment & decrement:\n";
  cout << "cp2 = cp; dp2 = dp; cp2--;cp2--;  dp2++; dp2++;\n";
  cp2 = cp; dp2 = dp;
  cp2--;cp2--;
  dp2++; dp2++;
  cout << "cp - cp2 = " << cp - cp2 << "\n";
  cout << "dp2 - dp = " << dp2 - dp << "\n";
  cout << "(int)cp - (int)cp2 = " << (int)cp - (int)cp2 << "\n";
  cout << "(int)dp2 - (int)dp = " << (int)dp2 - (int)dp << "\n";
}
```

This example demonstrates pointer arithmetic by showing you the result of pointer calculations. For comparison, calculations are made with both **char** pointers and **double** pointers. The results are printed both in terms of pointers and in bytes. The result of the pointer calculation can be printed directly, but to see the result in bytes you must first cast the pointers to integer values.

The use of *casting* is very important here. The **(int)** cast tells the compiler, "I know this is actually some other type, but treat it like an **int** for this operation." When you run the program, you will see that pointer arithmetic always takes the size of the pointer into account. If you add 1 to a **double** pointer, for instance, the pointer is incremented by 8 bytes, which is the size of a **double**. However, if you subtract two pointers that point to adjacent **double** locations (as shown in the program), you don't get 8, the size of the **double**; you get 1, the number of **double** variables between two adjacent **double** addresses. A pointer is really another kind of built-in data type and it has its own kind of arithmetic.

To see the actual integer values of the pointers, you must cast the pointer to an **int** so that integer operations instead of pointer operations are performed on the pointer.

The program also demonstrates that the increment and decrement operators use pointer arithmetic. Modify the program and try other operators and other types of pointers.

Variable Pointers

Any data type (built-in or user-defined) can have a pointer, and the way you define a pointer is always the same: the name of the data type, an asterisk, and the variable name. Here's a program with many kinds of pointers to variables, including an object pointer.

```
// VARPTRS.CXX : Different kinds of pointers to variables

class CLS { }; // an empty class definition

main( ) {
    int A;
    int * ap = &A;
    unsigned char B;
    unsigned char * bp = &B;  // pointer must be same type
    long double C;
    long double * cp = &C;
    CLS D;
    CLS * dp = &D;
    // Note pointers don't have to be initialized when
    // you create them:
    CLS * ep; // this points somewhere random...
}
```

You can even take the address of a constant.

```
// CONSTPTR.CXX : Taking the address of a constant

main( ) {
   const int X = 100;
   const int * XP = &X;
}
```

Notice that you can't assign a non-constant pointer to the address of a constant. The language won't allow this because you could then change the contents of the **const** variable. The variable that is constant depends on where the modifier **const** is placed in the definition. Thus,

const int * XP;

means that **XP** points to a constant integer, so **XP** can be changed but ∗**XP** cannot. In contrast,

int * const XPC;

means **XPC** is a constant that points to an integer value that can be changed, so ∗**XPC** can be modified, while **XPC** cannot.

It is often helpful to use constant pointers to ensure that a variable cannot be changed. This is especially true when passing pointers to functions; you may want to pass a pointer but not want the outside variable to change.

```
// CONSTARG.CXX : Passing a pointer to a constant argument

struct sam {
   int i;
   float j;
   double k;
};

void func(const sam * arg) {
   if(arg->i == 0 ) { // reading values is OK
      // ...
   }
   // arg->k = 1.23;  // writing values is an error
}
```

```
main( ) {
    sam A;
    A.i = 1;
    A.j = 1.1;
    A.k = 2.2;
    func(&A);
}
```

Since **sam** is a **struct**, all its members are **public**, so anyone can change them. In **main( )**, elements of the variable **sam A** are changed, with no error message from the compiler. However, in the definition of **func**, the argument is **const**, so the compiler will generate an error if you try to do anything but read the argument, or call member functions. If you un-comment the line that changes **private** data

// **arg->k = 1.23;**

you will get an error message from the compiler.

Void Pointers

A variable can reside in any part of data memory (not necessarily program memory—processors that use a "Harvard architecture" separate program and data memory). Because a **char** can have the same address as a **long**, you might come to the conclusion that a pointer to a **char** is the same size as a pointer to a **long**. While this is indeed true in many architectures, it is not always the case. If you assume it to be true, the code you write will not be portable.

For example, consider a machine that uses a 32-bit word. Its addressing may be designed to use 32-bit boundaries, so a **long** fits nicely inside a single word, and the ordinary address works nicely as a pointer. However, a **char** might be implemented in 8 bits on such a machine, which means that four **char**s would fit inside a word. This means a **char** pointer might require some extra information to locate a particular byte inside a word. Thus, the **char** pointer might be a different size than a **long** pointer.

The *concept* of a pointer as "a variable containing the address of another variable" has intriguing possibilities. If you always knew how big a pointer was, you wouldn't have to determine the pointer type at compile time, so you could pass an address of any type to a function. The function could then cast that address to a pointer of the proper type (based on some other piece of information) and perform operations on the result. This way, you could create functions that operate on a number of different data types.

C++ invented the **void** pointer for this purpose. The use of the keyword **void** to describe a pointer is different from its use to describe function argument lists and return values (which mean "nothing"). A **void** pointer means a pointer to any type of data. Thus a function such as

funcv(void ∗ vp) {

   //...

}

can take a pointer to any piece of data. If you have **int i** and **float f**, the function calls **funcv(&i)** and **funcv(&f)** are both valid. The definition of a **void** ∗ guarantees that it is at least as large as the largest typed pointer implemented, so it can contain a pointer of any type.

Of course, inside the function call you will need to know exactly what kind of data type was passed (you could pass a flag or check an outside variable). Once you know what data type the void pointer references, you must cast the pointer to a pointer of that type so it's treated properly. For instance, here's a function called **print( )** that takes a character, an integer, or a floating point number:

```
// PRINTV.CXX : A Print Function Using Void Pointers
#include <stream.hxx>

enum numtype { floating, character, integer };

void print( void ∗ number, numtype type ) {
   switch(type) {
     case floating:
       cout << "float : " << ∗( (float ∗)number ) << "\n";
       break;
     case character:
       cout << "character : " << chr(∗( (char ∗)number)) << "\n";
       break;
     case integer:
       cout << "integer : " << ∗( (int ∗)number ) << "\n";
       break;
   }
}
```

```
main( ) {
   int i = 47;
   float f = 6.28;
   char c = 'Z';
   print( &i, integer);
   print( &f, floating);
   print( &c, character);
}
```

Notice that after the **void** pointer is cast to the correct type of pointer (**(float *)**, **(int *)**, or **(char *)**) it must be dereferenced with the * operator so the value at the address is produced. If it wasn't dereferenced, the address in the pointer would be produced instead.

If you recall the section on function overloading in the last chapter, you might think it makes more sense to simply overload the function and let the compiler figure out which one you are calling. This, however, means you must know the data type at compile time. The preceding function lets you delay the specific knowledge of the data type until run time.

Chapters 7 and 8 contain a much better solution to this type of problem, using simple inheritance in Chapter 7 and virtual functions in Chapter 8.

Array Pointers

Anytime you need to manipulate a group of identical variables, and especially when you need to calculate which variable to select from the block at run time, you can use an array. You can create an array of multiple dimensions for any type of variable, even a user-defined type.

In C and C++, whenever you calculate the address of a variable at run time, you are using a pointer. It turns out that an array is really another type of pointer. In fact, arrays and pointers are almost interchangeable.

```
// ARRAYPTR.CXX : A pointer to the starting address of
// an array can be treated like the array itself.
#include <stream.hxx>

// The translator initializes global arrays for you:
int c[ ] = { 1,2,3,4,5,6,7,8,9,10 };
```

```
main( ) {
    // int * c is the same as int c[ ], if c isn't external:
    for(int i = 0; i < 10; i++)
        cout << "c[" << i << "] = " << c[i] << "\n";
    int * cp = c;
    for(i = 0; i < 10; i++, cp++)
        cout << "i = " << i << ", *cp = " << *cp << "\n";

    int a[10];  // allocates space for 10 integers
    int *b = a;  // b & a are now equivalent
    for(i = 0; i < 10; i++)
        b[i] = i * 10;  // put some values in
    for(i = 0; i < 10; i++)
        cout << "a[" << i << "] = " << a[i] << "\n";
        // the same value comes out of a[i] as was
        // installed with b[i] !
}
```

Once the pointer **cp** is assigned to the starting address of **c**, you can index into the array with **cp** just as you can with **c**. The same is shown for the pointer **b** and the starting address of **a**. Notice that array names and pointers are *not* identical. A pointer is a variable that holds a value, while an array name is an identifier that is used with brackets to manipulate an array element, and by itself to produce the starting address of an array. You *cannot* modify an array name. For the preceding code, the expressions

a++;

and

c = cp;

are illegal.

How to Count When Using Arrays

A common pitfall when using arrays is the so-called "off by one" error. Since you define an array of, for example, ten elements as **array[10]**, it is easy to think that you index the array all the way up to and including 10. However, the first element of the array is right at the starting address: the name of the array plus zero offset, **array[0]**. Thus you must count a ten-element array from zero to nine.

Arrays are actually indexed at run time by taking the starting address and adding the number of bytes necessary to produce the address of the desired element. Since pointer arithmetic is used in C and C++, you don't have to worry about counting the bytes in the data type; it's taken care of for you. For instance, **array[0]** is equivalent to *(**array + 0**), and **array[1]** is the same as *(**array + 1**). Here's an example that emphasizes how arrays are indexed:

```
// INDEX.CXX : Demonstration of array indexing
#include <stream.hxx>

main( ) {
    int x[10];
    for(int i = 0; i < 10; i++)
        x[i] = 100 - i * i; // for interesting numbers

    // Three different ways of selecting the zeroth element:
    cout << "x[0] = " << x[0] << "\n";
    cout << "*(x + 0) = " << *(x+0) << "\n";
    cout << "*x = " << *x << "\n";

    // print the array using pointer addition:
    for(i = 0; i < 10; i++)
        cout << "*(x + " << i << ") = " << *(x + i) << "\n";
}
```

If you study this code, you'll convince yourself that indexes must start at zero.

Initialization of Aggregates

In ARRAYPTR.CXX you see an interesting definition.

int c[ ] = { 1,2,3,4,5,6,7,8,9,10 };

This creates a global array *and* initializes all the array elements to the values inside the braces. This is called *aggregate initialization* and it's a very convenient feature, since the compiler saves you a lot of typing and

potential errors. There's a limitation to aggregate initialization, however—
it only works with global and **static** variables in many implementations
of C and C++. C++ and ANSI C allow **auto** aggregate initialization, but at
this writing no C++ compiler actually performs it. With a global variable,
the compiler causes the initialization to occur once, when the code is loaded.
If an automatic aggregate is initialized, it means that every time the scope
is entered (in a function, every time the function was called), some special
code must initialize the variables.

You can use aggregate initialization for more than just arrays. Here are
some other alternatives:

```
// AGREGATE.CXX : Aggregate initialization examples for
// a compiler with no auto aggregate initialization.
#include <stream.hxx>

struct simple {
    int i, j, k;
};

simple A = { 100, 200, 300 };

struct {  // no type name needed on the structure ...
    int i;
    char * name;
    float f;
} array_of_struct[ ] = { // ... since an instance is defined
    1, "first", 1.1,
    2, "second", 2.2,
    3, "third", 3.3,
    4, "fourth", 4.4
};

void function( ) {
    // statics work too, since they are not automatics (i.e.
    // they are not made on the stack:
    static simple B[ ] = { 1,2,3, 4,5,6, 7,8,9 };
}

// You can't use aggregate initialization on a class with
// private members, but you can declare an array of objects.
class X {
```

```
        int i;
        char * name;
        float f;
public:
    X( ) { i = 0; name = " "; f = 0.0; } // empty arg list
    X(int ii, char * nm, float ff) {
        i = ii; name = nm; f = ff;
    }
};

main( ) {
    // notice you can declare an array of objects ONLY if
    // the class has a constructor with no arguments:
    X arr[10];

    for(int p = 0; p < 4; p++) {
        cout << "array_of_struct[" << p << "].i = "
            << array_of_struct[p].i << "\n";
        cout << "array_of_struct[" << p << "].name = "
            << array_of_struct[p].name << "\n";
        cout << "array_of_struct[" << p << "].f = "
            << array_of_struct[p].f << "\n";
    }
}
```

The first example shows the aggregate initialization of an instance of **struct simple**. The initialization values are copied into the array elements in the order in which they appear: **i** gets 100, **j** gets 200, **k** gets 300. The second example shows a **struct** with no type name. The type name is unnecessary here because the name is never used; an instance of the **struct** is immediately created. The instance in this case is an array. Each set of three items in the initialization list is used as an element of the array.

The third example shows how **static** variables within a function can also use aggregate initialization, even on a C or C++ compiler that doesn't support **auto** aggregate initialization. This is true because a **static** has the same lifetime as a global, so it is initialized only once, when a program starts. The last example shows how you can define an array of objects. You can perform aggregate initialization for objects only if they have no **private** member data or functions (in which case it looks like a **struct**). You can only define an array of objects if the **class** has a constructor with no arguments.

STRINGS AS AGGREGATES Strings are another form of aggregate initialization. A *string literal* is really just an array of characters, initialized to the ASCII values of the letters inside the quotes. However, a string literal is significantly different from normal arrays—there is no analog in other data types to the way quoted strings are handled by the compiler. For one thing, a quoted string is not always a constant; you may be able to modify the characters in a quoted string at run time (ANSI C doesn't allow this). Also, you can perform what looks like aggregate initialization of an automatic string array. For instance, you can do the following:

void localstring( ) {

    char * hello = "hello, world!\n";

    cout << hello[4]; // you can treat it like an array!

    //...

}

Although you are using pointer notation to define the array, the end result acts like an array. The difference is the string is actually **static**, so if you modify the string (not a portable activity) it will hold your changes between function calls. The following example illustrates this, and tests to see if your compiler allows modification of string literals:

```
// STATCSTR.CXX : Strings are actually static arrays.
#include <string.h>  // prototype for strlen( )
#include <stream.hxx>

int StringHolder( ) {
    static int i = 0; // to count through the string
    char * st = "This is a static string\n";
    if (i < strlen(st)) { // counts chars in the string
        st[i] = 'X';
        i++;  // point to next character
        cout << st;  // print the string
        return 1;  // indicate there's still some string left
    } else
        return 0; // indicate there's no string left
}
```

```
main( ) {
   while( StringHolder( ) )
     ; // do it until there's none left
}
```

Each function call in this example will write over another character in the string.

SIMILARITIES BETWEEN ARRAYS AND POINTERS   With strings the global definitions **char cha[ ] = "string";** and **char * chp = "string";** have the same effect. A string is created and its starting address is used for **cha** or **chp**. An **int** pointer (or any other data type except **string**) cannot be initialized to an array of **int** values like this. At this writing, the construct **cha[ ]** was only allowed globally in C++, but the pointer form has the same effect.

Notice that there is a significant difference between **char cha[ ]** and **char * chp**. The latter is a pointer variable, so you can modify it—**chp = cha** and **chp++** are both legal. However, **cha[ ]** is an array and not a pointer. When you say **cha**, you produce the starting address of the array, but **cha** is *not* a variable, so you cannot say **cha = chp** or **cha++**. If you create an array in one file, and declare the array as an **extern** pointer in another file, you will have problems because there is no external pointer variable.

String literals are only initialized once, when the program starts up. In contrast, single constant variables may be initialized, but sometimes the compiler builds their values right into the code—this is called *constant folding*. After start-up, the act of "initializing" a local string pointer simply means copying its starting address to the pointer.

An example may clarify this. Suppose you create a character array inside a function body, like this:

function( ) {

char * A = "This is a string";

putchar(A[6]);

}

Notice pointer notation is used to define **A**. If you were to say **char A[17]**, the compiler would make local space for an array of 17 characters, and then (on C++ compilers used for this book, and many C compilers) complain because you asked it to initialize that local array every time the function is called.

When you use the pointer notation as shown previously, here's what happens. When the program starts up, space is created in a special area for constants, and the ASCII characters for "This is a string" are copied into that space, followed by a zero byte to indicate the end of the string. Then, every time **function( )** is called, local space is allocated for **char ∗ A**, and the starting address of the string is copied into the pointer **A**. Similarly, if you make a call to a function that takes a string argument, such as **puts( )**,

puts("hello");

it is equivalent to making a global pointer or array,

char ∗ cp = "hello";

char cp2[ ] = "hello";

and passing the starting address (via the pointer) as the argument of **puts()**.

puts(cp);

puts(cp2);

It is often useful to imagine these activities when you are trying to figure out how the language is translating your code.

STRING EXAMPLES   Because strings are so important, it is helpful to see a few working examples. The first example centers some lines of text on the screen (assuming an 80-column display). To do this, the number of characters is counted by looking for the zero byte that terminates each string. (This is just for a demonstration—if you want to count the characters in a string you should use the ANSI C library function **strlen( )**.)

```
// CENTER.CXX : centers text on display.
#include <stream.hxx>

const width = 80; // width of screen
char str1[ ] = "This is the first line of text";
char *str2 = "second line";
char str3[ ] = "This is the third and last line of text";

void center(char * string) {
    char * cp = string;
    for(int len = 0; *cp != 0; cp++, len++)
        ; // empty statement -- all the work is done in the "if"
    // at this point, len contains the number of chars in
    // the string
    for(int col = 0; col < (width - len)/2; col++)
        cout << " ";
    cout << string << "\n";
}

main( ) {
    center(str1);
    center(str2);
    center(str3);
    center("that's all, folks!");
}
```

In the function **center( )**, the first **for** loop does all the work with the initialization and stepping, so the body of the loop is empty. Notice that the comma operator is used in the stepping section, so two operations are performed instead of just one. Before the initialization clause, the character pointer **cp** is created and initialized to the pointer argument. Then **cp** and the integer **i** are incremented until the variable that **cp** points to is 0 (which means the end of the string). At this point, the count in **i** is the number of characters in the string.

Code like this (combining two operations into a clause with the comma operator) is sometimes considered to be "too clever." You will, however, encounter it when you are reading other people's code (which is a very good way to learn programming).

Here's a program that is more fun. It consists of two functions, **encrypt()** and **decrypt( )**. **encrypt( )** takes a string to be coded and an encryption key (a second string), and replaces the string with an encrypted value. **decrypt( )** reverses the process.

```
// ENCRYPT.CXX : Captain Midnight Secret Decoder Ring
#include <stream.hxx>

void encrypt(char * msg, char * key) {
    unsigned char ckey = 0;
    for(char * cp = key; *cp != 0; cp++)
        ckey += *cp;  // generate a number from the key
    for(cp = msg; *cp != 0; cp++)
        *cp += ckey;  // use the number to encrypt the msg
}

void decrypt(char * msg, char * key) {
    unsigned char ckey = 0;
    for(char * cp = key; *cp != 0; cp++)
        ckey += *cp;  // generate a number from the key
    for(cp = msg; *cp != 0; cp++)
        *cp -= ckey;  // use the number to decrypt the msg
}

char * msg = "this is the message";
main( ) {
    cout << msg << "\n";
    encrypt(msg, "mom");
    cout << msg << "\n";
    decrypt(msg, "mom");
    cout << msg << "\n";
}
```

The encryption process is trivial. An encryption key is generated by summing up all the numerical values of the characters in the **key** string. The encryption key is then added to each character in the **msg** string to generate an encrypted message. The process is reversed for decryption.

You can also stash the text in an object and create methods to encrypt and decrypt the information. Here is a program using classes that has the same effect:

```
// ENCODE.HXX : A Class to hold a text string, encrypt and
// decrypt it.
#ifndef ENCODE_HXX
#define ENCODE_HXX
class encode {
   char * encrypted_string;
   unsigned char make_key(char *);
public:
   encode(char * msg, char * key);  // install a message
   char * decode(char * key);  // decode it and read it back
};
#endif // ENCODE_HXX
```

The following file contains the methods for **encode** and a program to test the **class**. You should remove the **#define TEST** for normal use—for example, when you're linking with a file that contains a **main( )**.

```
// ENCODE.CXX : Methods for the encryption/decryption class
#define TEST
#include <stream.hxx>
#include "encode.hxx"

// private function to create a key from a string:
unsigned char encode::make_key(char * keystring) {
   unsigned char ckey = 0;
   for(char * cp = keystring; *cp != 0; cp++)
      ckey += *cp;  // generate a number from the key
   return ckey;
}

encode::encode(char * msg, char * key) {
   unsigned char ckey = make_key(key);
   encrypted_string = msg;  // save the pointer to the message
   for(char * cp = encrypted_string; *cp != 0; cp++)
      *cp += ckey;  // use the key to encrypt the msg
}

char * encode::decode(char * key) {
   unsigned char ckey = make_key(key);
   for(char * cp = encrypted_string; *cp != 0; cp++)
      *cp -= ckey;  // use the key to decrypt the string
   return encrypted_string;
}
```

```
#ifdef TEST

main( ) {
    encode hidden_message("This is a test string", "key string");
    cout << hidden_message.decode("key string") << "\n";
}

#endif // TEST
```

The process of creating a key now has its own **private** function. Encrypting a message is built into the constructor. Because the encryption and decryption schemes are hidden inside the methods, you can modify them without changing the interface.

To construct the object, the **encode** class simply stashes the address of the string argument in its private pointer. This means it is using the space of the global string to hold its data. You may not want to rely on the creation of global text strings to hold your data. For instance, if you are working with a string, you may want to stash an encrypted copy away in the object, and then go on working with your string. To do this, you must use the **new** operator to create space for the string and then copy the string. Chapter 6 contains examples of this.

Arrays of Pointers

In C and C++ you are not restricted to making simple arrays and simple pointers. You can combine the two into a very useful construct—an array of pointers. An array of pointers is exactly what it sounds like. You have an array, and the elements in that array contain the addresses of other data objects, which can be pointers themselves. (Yes, you can have an array of pointers to pointers to pointers to....) The most common place you will see an array of pointers is in the command-line arguments for **main( )**.

main(int argc, char * argv[ ]) {

   //...

}

This use of the empty brackets in an argument declaration is different from that in a global or **static** definition. In a global or **static** definition, the empty brackets in **int A[ ] = { 1, 2, 3 };** mean "create enough space for this array," but in an argument list (or **extern** declaration), the empty brackets cause a pointer to be created. Since pointers can always be dereferenced using the bracket operator instead of the asterisk, you can also say (and this is quite common)

main(int argc, char ** argv) {

   // ...

}

When a C or C++ program starts up, **argc** and **argv** are initialized by the start-up code. **argc** is the number of arguments, and **argv** is an array of pointers to the argument strings. The start-up code counts the arguments (including the command itself, so a command line with no arguments has an **argc** of 1) and places the count in **argc**. Then it takes each space-delimited argument, builds a string from it, and places the pointers to the strings in the array **argv[ ]**. Since you never know how big this array is until the program starts up, you can use the count in **argc** to know when to stop pulling string pointers out of **argv**. The ANSI C standard requires that the last **argv** be NULL, so you can also check the value of **argv** to find the end of the list if your compiler supports this feature.

You index into the array of pointers just like an ordinary array. However, the result is a pointer, not a character, so you must treat it appropriately. This example takes command-line arguments and concatenates them (you might use this in a shell script in UNIX or batch file in MS-DOS to generate potential names for your company from pieces of names):

```
// NAMECAT.CXX : Concatenates the command line together
#include <stream.hxx>

main(int argc, char * argv[ ]) {
   char namebuf[200];  // to hold the concatenated string
   char * np = namebuf; // to put characters in namebuf
   for(int i = 1; i < argc; i++) {
      for(char * cp = argv[i]; *cp !=0; cp++)
         *np++ = *cp;
   }
   *np = 0;  // zero byte terminates a string
   cout << namebuf << "\n";
}
```

The program first creates a local character buffer, **namebuf**, to hold the finished string. Then the program defines a pointer and assigns it to the starting address of the buffer. The pointer is used to stuff characters into the buffer.

The outer **for** loop simply steps through the command-line arguments until there are no more left (until **i** is not less than **argc**). For each of these arguments, the inner **for** loop is executed: the character pointer **cp** is assigned to the starting address of the command-line argument, and the pointer is stepped through all the characters in the argument. For each step, the character in the argument is stuffed into the output buffer **namebuf**. The command-line argument ends (as all strings do) with a zero byte. This is tested with the expression in the **for** loop: *cp != 0.

In the statement that performs the actual stuffing of the character into the output buffer, *np++ = *cp;, the increment applies to the *pointer,* not to the variable pointed to. This statement says, "Put the value **cp** points to into the slot **np** points to, and then move **np** to the next slot." If you say (*np)++;, it means, "Add 1 to the character **np** points to."

If you don't put the statement *np = 0; after all the strings have been copied, your command-line arguments will print OK, but will be followed by unpredictable garbage—**cout** will just keep printing until it finds a zero byte. Other examples are shown at the beginning of Chapter 10.

The Size of a Pointer (Memory Models)

While the size of a built-in data type depends on the variable to be stored, the size of a pointer only depends on one thing—the size of the address (since that's all you store in the pointer). On many computers, the size of a pointer only depends on the type of data that is pointed to. These are called *linear address space* machines.

The Intel 80x86 microprocessors (including the 8088, 8086, 80286, and 80386) upon which the IBM PC family is based, use a *segmented addressing* scheme, which breaks the address into two pieces, a *segment* and an *offset*. The segment can be thought of as selecting the city where the address is located, and the offset chooses the specific apartment within the city. Where a linear addressing scheme generates unique addresses for an apartment in Vienna and one in Denver, a segmented scheme might have the same offset for both apartments.

The size of a pointer in an 80x86 processor varies depending on the *memory model* selected during compilation. The memory model tells the compiler how large your code and data will be. Some programs are very small and don't need very much data space. For these, the segment for the *program counter* (a "hardware pointer" built into the processor; it points to the next instruction to be executed) and the segments for all the data pointers in the program *never change*. This program spends its whole life in the same small town, so the pointers can be the size of the offsets (which is the only part that changes).

Some programs, however, contain a large amount of code (more than fits in one segment), and their data pointers must range all over the map, just like a program on a linear address space machine. These programs must calculate segment addresses as well as offset addresses for both the program counter and all the data pointers, so pointers are larger. On the PC, the memory model selected is a combination of the size the program will be and the size the data will be.

Novice programmers and programmers familiar with linear address processors find the 80x86 frustrating (it is unquestionably a nemesis to programmers). Their solutions range from ignoring the problem to always using the largest memory model and pretending they are on a linear address space machine. (Indeed, the 80386 processor has a linear address mode.)

Ignoring the problem is a good way to start, and compilers support this by choosing a default memory model. You will run into problems, however, when you try to address an absolute location (some piece of hardware, perhaps, or a special area in memory) outside your program's segment area. Also, if you want to manage a large amount of data (more than 64K bytes on the PC) you will need a different memory model.

You may wonder why you can't just use the largest memory model. You can, but there's a price. If all your data is in one segment, the pointer is the size of the offset and the calculations are straightforward when you change a pointer (increment it, for instance). However, if your data ranges all over the map, your pointer is the size of the segment *and* the offset, and both must be calculated every time you change the pointer. This can slow your program significantly.

Far Pointers

One of the problems with using various memory models is you don't always know the exact model you will be using when you are writing code. A program designed, for instance, for a small data space may someday need to access a large data space. You may also encounter situations where you want to keep all your pointers small and fast but you must access some absolute location in memory (video memory on the PC, for instance).

Many C and C++ implementations on 80x86 allow you to override the default pointer size for specific variables by using the non-portable, implementation-specific **near** and **far** keywords. The **near** keyword forces an offset-only pointer when the pointers would normally default to segment plus offset; **near** is generally used to increase speed. The **far** keyword forces a segment plus offset pointer when the pointers would normally default to offset-only. If you know you are addressing a specific location or you will always be pointing to a chunk of data larger than 64K, you should declare your pointer **far**. A **far** pointer always does the right thing, regardless of the memory model used.

Example Showing Pointer Sizes

If you are on an 80x86 machine, you should try compiling and running the following program with the various memory models available with your compiler. For each different memory model, it will show you the size of various different pointers—the "default" pointer, which is affected by the memory model, and the **near** and **far** pointers, which are not affected by the memory model. The program uses the "stringize" preprocessor directive **#**, applied to its argument **PP**, so the name as well as the size of the pointer can be printed automatically.

```
// PTRSIZE.CXX : The sizes of pointers with various memory
// models on a segmented-addressing processor (won't compile
// with linear-addressing processors).
#include <stdio.h>  // for printf( )

// A macro to display the name and size of a pointer:
#define SIZE(PP) printf("sizeof(" #PP ")= %d\n", sizeof(PP))

main( ) {
    char * byte_ptr;  // points to the smallest kind of data
    long double * longd_ptr; // the biggest kind of data

    char far * far_byte_ptr;
    long double far * far_longd_ptr;
```

```
    char near * near_byte_ptr;
    long double near * near_longd_ptr;

    SIZE(byte_ptr);
    SIZE(longd_ptr);
    SIZE(far_byte_ptr);
    SIZE(far_longd_ptr);
    SIZE(near_byte_ptr);
    SIZE(near_longd_ptr);
}
```

Consult your manual for the specifics of compiling with various memory models and building **near** and **far** pointers to absolute locations. This is not a straightforward topic.

Function Addresses

Once a function is compiled and loaded into the computer to be executed, it occupies a chunk of memory. That memory, and thus the function itself, has an address. C has never been a language to bar entry where others fear to tread. You can use function addresses just as you can use variable addresses, with pointers. The declaration and use of function pointers looks a bit opaque at first, but it follows the format of the rest of the language.

Defining a Function Pointer

To define a pointer to a function, you say

void (*func_ptr)( );

When you are looking at a complex definition like this, the best way to attack it is to start in the *middle* and work your way out. "Starting in the middle" means starting at the variable name, which is **func_ptr**. "Working your way out" means looking to the right for the nearest item (nothing in this case; the right parenthesis stops you short), then looking to the left (a pointer denoted by the asterisk), then looking to the right (an empty argument list indicating a function), then looking to the left (**void**, which indicates the function has no return value). This right-left-right motion works with most declarations.

To review, "start in the middle" ("**func_ptr** is a ..."), go to the right (nothing there — you're stopped by the right parenthesis), go to the left and find the * ("... pointer to a ..."), go to the right and find the empty argument list ("... function ..."), go to the left and find the **void** ("**func_ptr** is a pointer to a function returning **void**").

You may wonder why ∗**func_ptr** requires parentheses. If you didn't use them, the compiler would see

void ∗func_ptr( );

You would be declaring a function rather than defining a variable. You can think of the compiler as going through the same process you do when it figures out what a declaration or definition is supposed to be. It needs those parentheses to "bump up against" so it goes back to the left and finds the ∗, instead of continuing to the right and finding the empty argument list.

Complicated Declarations And Definitions

Once you figure out how the C and C++ declaration syntax works, you can create much more complicated items. For instance:

```
// DECL.CXX: Some complicated definitions

/* 1. */    void * (*(*fp1)(int))[10];

/* 2. */    float (*(*fp2)(int,int,float))(int);

/* 3. */    typedef double (*(*(*fp3)( ))[10])( );
            fp3 A;

/* 4. */    (*(*f4( ))[10])( );
```

Walk through each one and figure it out. Number 1 says, "**fp1** is a pointer to a function taking an integer argument and returning a pointer to an array of ten **void** pointers (pointers with unspecified type)."

Number 2 says, "**fp2** is a pointer to a function taking three arguments (**int**, **int**, and **float**) and returning a pointer to a function taking an integer argument and returning a float."

If you are creating a lot of complicated definitions, you might want to use a **typedef**. Number 3 shows how a **typedef** saves typing the complicated description every time. It says, "An **fp3** is a pointer to a function returning a pointer to an array of ten pointers to functions taking no arguments and returning **double**s." Then it says, "**A** is one of these **fp3** types." You can also use **typedef** to build complicated descriptions from simple ones.

Number 4 is a function declaration instead of a variable definition. It says "**f4** is a function returning a pointer to an array of ten pointers to functions returning **int**s." The outer functions each return an **int** by implication, since C and C++ default to **int** if a data type isn't specified.

You will rarely, if ever, need such complicated declarations and definitions as these. However, if you go through the exercise of figuring them out you will not be even mildly disturbed by the slightly complicated ones you will encounter in real life.

Using a Function Pointer

Once you define a pointer to a function, you must assign it to a function address before you can use it. Just as the address of an array **arr[10]** is produced by the array name without the brackets (**arr**), the address of a function **func( )** is produced by the function name without the argument list (**func**). To call the function, you dereference the pointer in the same way that you declared it (remember that C and C++ always try to make definitions look the same as the way they are used). The following example shows how a pointer to a function is defined and used.

```
// PTRFUNC.CXX : Defining and using a pointer to a function
#include <stdio.h>

void func( ) {
    puts("func( ) called...");
}

main( ) {
    void (*fp)( );  // define a function pointer
    fp = func;  // initialize it
```

```
(*fp)( );    // dereference it to call the function

void (*fp2)( ) = func;  // define and init at the same time
(*fp2)( );
}
```

After the pointer to function **fp** is defined, it is assigned to the address of a function **func( )** using **fp = func;**—notice the argument list is missing on the function name. The second case shows simultaneous definition and initialization.

An Array of Pointers to Functions

One of the more interesting constructs you can create is an array of pointers to functions. To select a function, you just index into the array and dereference the pointer. This supports the concept of *table-driven code*— instead of using conditionals or **case** statements, you select functions to execute based on a state variable or combination of state variables. This kind of design can be very useful if you often add or delete functions from the table.

The following example creates some dummy functions using a preprocessor macro, then creates an array of pointers to those functions using automatic aggregate initialization. As you can see, it is very easy to add or remove functions from the table (and thus, functionality from the program).

```
// FUNCTABL.CXX : Using an array of pointers to functions
#include <stdio.h>

// A macro to define dummy functions:
#define DF(N) void N( ) { puts("function " #N " called..."); }

DF(A); DF(B); DF(C); DF(D); DF(E); DF(F); DF(G);

void (*func_table[ ])( )  = { A, B, C, D, E, F, G };
```

```
main( ) {
   while(1) {
      puts("press a key from 'a' to 'g' or q to quit");
      char c = getchar( ); getchar( ); // second one for CR
      if ( c == 'q' ) break; // ... out of while(1)
      if ( c < 'a' || c > 'g' ) continue;
      (*func_table[c - 'a'])( );
   }
}
```

A problem occurs when you add or remove functions from the list in this program. To keep from running off the end of the function table, you must change the bounds checking. A neater solution is to encapsulate the array inside a **class**. The following program adds the functions to the list at run time rather than at compile time. You can imagine how this **class** could be useful when creating some sort of interpreter or list processing program.

```
// DYNAFUNC.HXX : Class that holds an array of pointers
// to functions.  The functions are inserted into the array
// at run time.
#ifndef DYNAFUNC_HXX
#define DYNAFUNC_HXX
const int size = 100;  // max size of array

class function_holder {
   int func_count; // number of functions in array
   void (*function_ptr[size])( ); // array
   void error(char * msg1, char * msg2 = " ");
public:
   function_holder( );
   void add_function( void (*fp)( ) );
   void remove_function( int fnum );
   int last_function( ) { return func_count; }
   void run(int fnum);
   void run_all( );
};
#endif // DYNAFUNC_HXX
```

Here are the methods for **function_holder,** and a built-in test program that is removed by deleting the **#define TEST**.

```
// DYNAFUNC.CXX : function_holder methods
// remove the following line when you're done testing
#define TEST
#include <stdio.h>
#include "dynafunc.hxx"
 #include <stdlib.h>

void function_holder::error(char * msg1, char * msg2) {
   fprintf(stderr,"function_holder error: %s %s\n",msg1,msg2);
   exit(1);
}

function_holder::function_holder( ) {
   func_count = 0;
   for(int i = 0; i < size; i++)
     function_ptr[i] = NULL;
}

// The argument is a pointer to a function returning nothing
void function_holder::add_function( void (*fp)( ) ) {
   if ( func_count >= size )
     error("add_function: no more space in array");
   function_ptr[func_count++] = fp;
}

void function_holder::remove_function( int fnum ) {
   if ( fnum < 0 || fnum >= size )
     error("remove_function: index out of bounds");
   // move up all the function definitions by one:
   for(int i = fnum; i < func_count; i++)
     function_ptr[i] = function_ptr[i + 1];
   function_ptr[func_count] = NULL;
   func_count—; // we just removed a function from the list
}

void function_holder::run(int fnum) {
   if ( fnum < 0 || fnum >= size )
     error("run: index out of bounds");
   (*function_ptr[fnum])( );  // call the function
}
```

```
void function_holder::run_all( ) {
  for (int i = 0; i < func_count; i++)
    (*function_ptr[i])( );
}

#ifdef TEST

#define FDEF(NM) void NM( ) { puts("this is function " #NM); }

FDEF(f1); FDEF(f2); FDEF(f3); FDEF(foo); FDEF(bar); FDEF(fred);

main( ) {
  function_holder machine;
  machine.add_function(f1);
  machine.add_function(f2);
  machine.add_function(f3);
  machine.add_function(foo);
  machine.add_function(bar);
  machine.add_function(fred);
  machine.run_all( );
  machine.remove_function(3);
  machine.run_all( );
}
#endif // TEST
```

The method **add_function( )** assumes that **func_count** indexes the first empty element in the array. All functions are added to the end. The method **remove_function( )** moves up all the functions after the one to be removed. This deletes the function from the list and automatically reclaims the space previously used by that function. The methods **run( )** and **run_all( )** call functions in the list. The preprocessor macro **FDEF( )** allows quick creation of dummy functions for testing.

IMPROVEMENTS TO function_holder   There are a number of improvements you can make to the class. The functions don't take arguments or return values—you can easily modify the array definition to accept arguments, but the argument list is always fixed. What if you use a variadic argument list, which allows you to pass any number or kind of arguments? You would then have to write code to ensure the proper arguments are passed *before* the function is called, or use the macros for handling variable argument lists (in **stdarg.h**) to manage the arguments *inside* the function.

You may want to add a method to change the sequence of the functions or insert a new function in the middle of the list, so you can dynamically alter the order in which the functions are called. Finally, you may not want to be limited by the **const size**, which establishes the maximum size of the array at compile time. What if you don't know how big the array will be? You can create a dynamically sized array by using the **new** keyword in the constructor (see Chapter 6). You can also create new **function_holder** objects at run time using **new**.

Examples of Pointer Use

To give you a better feeling for the use of pointers, this section presents several examples of pointer use.

Character Statistics in a File

The first program takes standard input, which you can redirect from a file, and counts all the various kinds of characters, including tabs and spaces. After the file ends, it displays the statistics showing the number of occurrences of each kind of character.

```
// STATS.CXX : Statistics on a character file
#include <stream.hxx>
// limits.h contains the definition of CHAR_MAX, which
// is the maximum value a char can hold:
#include <limits.h>

main( ) {
    // one place for each character:
    int stat_array[CHAR_MAX + 1];
    char c;
    for(int i = 0; i <= CHAR_MAX; i++)
        stat_array[i] = 0;  // initialize array
    while(cin.get(c))  // do for all chars in input
        stat_array[c]++;  // use char as index; increment count
```

```
    for(i = 0; i <= CHAR_MAX; i++)
        if(stat_array[i] != 0)
            cout << "number of char #" << i <<", '" <<
                 chr(i) << "' : " << stat_array[i] << "\n";
}
```

Each time a character is read, it is used as an array index into **stat_array[ ]**. The array variable corresponding to the character count is selected and incremented in a single statement.

stat_array[c]++;

Passing Arguments of Unknown Size

There are many situations in C and C++ where you want to pass a piece of data to a function, but there is no way to know at compile time how big the piece of data is. The most common example of this is a string, which is really an array of characters.

In this situation, you have no choice but to pass a pointer. Since a pointer is a fixed size depending only on the pointer type, it is not affected by the size of the data it points to. Thus, there is no ambiguity at compile time. Of course, when the program is running and the function is called, you must somehow divine how big the piece of data really is. With strings, this is done by looking for the zero byte at the end of the string. If you are passing an array of some other type, you can either place some sort of terminator flag at the end of the array, or you can pass an extra argument to indicate how long the array is. (Both these approaches are taken with the command line.)

Here are two functions that show both approaches:

```
// PASSARRY.CXX : How to pass arrays
#include <stream.hxx>

void printa(const int x[ ], int size) {  //2nd arg = array size
    for(int i = 0; i < size; i++)
        cout << "x[" << i << "] = " << x[i] << "\n";
}
```

```
void printb(const int y[ ]) { // array has terminator flag
    int i = 0;
    while(y[i] != -1)  // you have to use some sort of end flag,
                       // which puts a restriction on your data
        cout << "y[" << i << "] = " << y[i++] << "\n";
}

int z[ ] = { 1, 3, 47, 74, 99, 212, 77, 11, 9, -1 };

main( ) {
    printa(z, sizeof(z)/sizeof(z[0]));
    printb(z);
}
```

The number of elements in the array is calculated with a useful trick. The expression **sizeof(z)/sizeof(z[0])** yields the size of the entire array in bytes, divided by the size of an individual element. On a PC, the size of the array is 20, since there are ten elements and each **int** element is 2 bytes, so you get 10 (you get 10 on any machine). By performing this calculation, you can change the size of the array without modifying the rest of the program. This trick can be used for any data type.

Notice that the arrays are passed as pointers, which means the functions **printa( )** and **printb( )** could change them. To prevent this, and to show anyone reading the code that it won't happen, the arguments are declared as **const**.

Functions That Modify
Outside Variables

If you can manage it, the "cleanest" way for a function to affect its environment is via a return value. There are times, however, when this approach is unsatisfactory and you must modify outside variables. (Another alternative is for the function to modify a global variable. But this is generally considered to be hostile toward efforts to create maintainable code.) The only way to modify an outside variable is to pass its address to the function.

There are a number of instances where this approach was taken with the ANSI C library. One of these is the math function **frexp( )**, which takes a floating-point number and breaks it into an integer exponent (to be used as a power of 2) and a mantissa with an absolute value between 0.5 and

1.0. Since there are two values to return, the designers chose to return the mantissa through the normal return mechanism. The exponent is returned through an integer pointer argument. The prototype for the library function is

double frexp(double val, int * exponent);

where **exponent** is the address where you want the integer exponent delivered. This function will be used shortly.

To write a function that modifies an outside variable, you must dereference the argument pointer inside the function body. For instance,

```
// MODIFY.CXX : A function that modifies an outside variable

void addten(int * val){
    *val += 10;
}

main( ) {
    int X = 37;
    addten(&X);  // you must explicitly take the address of
                 // a variable for a pointer argument
}
```

When you create a function that modifies an outside variable and install that function in a library with a header file, you must ensure that the user knows it requires a pointer argument, so the user will take the address of an argument instead of just blindly handing the variable to the function. With old C, this error would pass through with no complaint, causing endless headaches. Function prototyping causes warning messages if the user gets it wrong.

Forcing the user to be concerned about how function parameters are passed ("let the user beware") is not in the spirit of C++, which might be thought of as "don't bother the user with details the compiler can handle." C++ has a construct called a "reference" to solve this problem (described in "The Reference Feature," later in this chapter).

You should be aware that you aren't limited to returning only one variable. If you want to affect more than one variable and you don't want to modify the function arguments, you can package all your variables together into a **struct** and return a **struct**.

```
// RETSTRUC.CXX : Returning a structure to modify more than
// one variable in the environment.
#include <stdio.h>

struct X {
    int i;
    float j;
    long k;
};

X gary(int ii, float jj, long kk) {
    X local;
    local.i = ii;
    local.j = jj;
    local.k = kk;
    return local;  // return all values packaged in a struct
}

main( ) {
    X a;
    a = gary(99, 2.15, 3000);
    printf("a.i = %d, a.j = %f, a.k = %d\n", a.i, a.j, a.k);
}
```

Returning a **struct** has its limitations, which are outlined in Chapter 9.

Passing struct *and Object Pointers*

You often need to write functions that take structures (in C and C++) or objects (in C++) as arguments. You can do this two ways: by value, in which a local copy of the structure or object is made inside the function, or by passing an address, via either a pointer or a reference. It is generally more efficient to pass an address than to pass a value, especially because structures and objects tend to be larger than built-in types.

When you pass a pointer to a structure or object, you must dereference that pointer in a special way, using the *structure pointer operator* (->). You may wonder why a special dereferencing operator is necessary for structures and objects. The * operator refers to the *entire structure,* so you can't select individual members using *. The following example demonstrates what happens when * is applied to a structure.

```
// DEREFSTR.CXX : What happens when you dereference an
// entire structure using the *, instead of individual
// elements using ->
#include <stdio.h>

struct x {
    int i, j, k;
    float f;
};

#define PR(z) printf(#z " = %d\n", z)

main( ) {
    x A, B;
    x *xpa = &A, *xpb = &B;
    A.i = A.j = A.k = 0; A.f = 0.0;
    B.i = B.j = B.k = 91; B.f = 1.99;
    *xpa = *xpb;  // dereferencing the whole structure
    PR(A.i);
    PR(A.j);
    PR(A.k);
    printf("A.f = %f\n", A.f);
}
```

You will see that the entire structure is copied from **B** to **A**.

The next example shows how to select individual members of a structure or a class using the structure pointer operator.

```
// PTRSTRUC.CXX : Selecting members when you have a pointer
// to a structure or object.
#include <stdio.h>

struct A {
    char c;
    int i;
    float f;
};

class B {
    char c;
    int i;
    float f;
public:
```

```
    B(char cc = 0, int ii = 0, float ff = 0.0) {
        c = cc; i = ii; f = ff;
    }
    void print(char * msg = " ") {
        printf("%s: c = %c, i = %d, f = %f\n", msg, c, i, f);
    }
};

main( ) {
    A u;  // make a structure
    A * up = &u;  // make a pointer to the structure
    B v((char)'c',88);  // make an object
    B * vp = &v;  // make a pointer to the object
    up->i = 100;  // select a member of the structure
    vp->print("vp"); // call a member function of the object
    // notice that B->i = 100; is illegal since i is private
}
```

The expression **up->i = 100;** selects the member **i** of the structure variable **u** that **up** points to. The expression **vp- >print("vp");** calls the member function **print( )** of the object **v** that **vp** points to. Notice that selecting a function is the same as selecting a variable; you simply need to add the argument list to call the function. If you didn't include the argument list, you would produce the starting address of the function.

Examining the Contents of a float

The next example demonstrates a more sophisticated use of pointers. An IEEE floating-point number consists of an exponent, a mantissa, and a sign bit, all packed together into 4 bytes for a **float** and 8 bytes for a **double**. A **float** uses 1 bit for the sign, 7 bits for the exponent, and 24 bits for the mantissa. The high bit of the mantissa is not actually stored in the **float**—there will always be a 1 in the high bit, so it doesn't need to be stored.

If your system uses IEEE floating point, it is very educational to look at the contents of these bytes to see how a number is constructed. The following program will print the exponent and mantissa of a **float** and the bit pattern of the internal floating-point representation, broken up into its individual parts. The program works on a PC or a machine with similar byte ordering; you may have to modify the byte ordering to make it work on your particular machine.

```
// SEEFLOAT.CXX : Examine the bit pattern of a float
#include <math.h>
#include <stdio.h>
 #include <stdlib.h>

// this function displays the bit number bitnum in byte
// as a '1' or a '0'.
void display_bit(const unsigned char * byte, int bitnum) {
    printf("%c", *byte & (1 << bitnum) ? '1' : '0');
}

main(int argc, char * argv[ ]) {
    if ( argc < 2 ) {
        fprintf(stderr, "usage: seefloat number\n");
        exit(1);
    }
    float f = atof(argv[1]); // 1st arg is float value
    int exponent;
    // display the exponent and mantissa:
    double mantissa = frexp(f, &exponent);
    printf("exponent in base 2 = %d\n", exponent);
    printf("mantissa = %f\n", mantissa);
    // Now display the binary representation:
    printf("Binary representation:\n");
    // cast the starting address of the floating point number
    // into a byte pointer:
    unsigned char * bytewise = (unsigned char *)&f;
    // Now use the byte pointer as an array, and pick out the
    // bytes one by one.  Notice the byte ordering in a
    // floating-point number is very machine dependent; yours
    // may work differently.  On the PC, the starting address + 3
    // is the high byte and they count down from there.
    printf("sign: ");
    // The address of the third element is given to display_bit( ):
    display_bit(&(bytewise[3]), 7);
    printf("\n");
    printf("exponent: ");
    for(int i = 6; i >= 0; i—)
        display_bit(&(bytewise[3]), i);
    // the last bit of the exponent is in the next byte:
    display_bit(&(bytewise[2]), 7);
    printf("\n");
    printf("mantissa: 1");  // high bit is always 1
```

```
// display the rest of the byte:
for(i = 6; i >= 0; i—)
    display_bit(&(bytewise[2]), i);
// display the other 2 bytes in their entirety:
for(int j = 1; j >= 0; j—)
    for(i = 7; i >= 0; i—)
        display_bit(&(bytewise[j]), i);
printf("\n");
printf("all: ");
for(j = 3; j >= 0; j—) {
    for(i = 7; i >= 0; i—)
        display_bit(&(bytewise[j]), i);
    printf(" ");
}
}
```

A number of new features have been introduced here. First, the floating-point number is plucked off the command line. If the command-line argument isn't there, the program sends an error message to standard error using **fprintf( )**, which sends output somewhere other than standard output, and then exits. The **exit( )** function sets the error value that the program returns.

The floating-point number is converted from the command-line argument (a string) with the ANSI C library function **atof( )**, which means "ASCII to float." It takes an ASCII string and returns a floating-point **double**. Since the result of the function is going to a **float**, the compiler performs an automatic type conversion from **double** to **float**.

The ANSI C library function **frexp( )** (mentioned earlier) is used to print one version of the exponent and mantissa, and the function **display_bit()** is used to display the individual bits of the floating-point number. You hand **display_bit( )** a pointer to a byte, and the number of the bit you wish to display.

A pointer called **bytewise** is created to point to individual bytes. **bytewise** is assigned to the starting address of the floating-point number. Since it is a character pointer, you can select each of the bytes in the floating-point number by treating **bytewise** as an array. Since **display_bit( )** must be given an address and not a value, the address of the array element must be taken, which produces expressions like **&(bytewise[3])**.

When you are experimenting with this program, try numbers whose patterns you recognize in base 2, such as 1, 2, 8, 15, 31, 255. Notice that the exponent is in an "offset binary format"—an exponent of 0 is represented with 01111111, an exponent of 1 is 10000000, and so on. This allows the representation of negative exponents.

The Reference Feature

When building function libraries, a good design philosophy is to make the use of a function as transparent as possible for the user. Generally, a user will want to hunt through a function library (or **class** library, in C++), grab a function, and use it without spending a lot of time figuring out how it works.

Functions in C and C++ that take addresses as arguments or return addresses force the user to be concerned with the implementation mechanics of a solution. The evolution of programming languages has been away from forcing the user to cope with details and towards allowing the user to spend more time thinking about the "big picture." In this spirit, C++ contains a feature called the *reference,* which allows the programmer to take responsibility for the way arguments are passed to functions. References were *not* added to ANSI C or any other version of C.

An example will illustrate. If a function in C or C++ takes a pointer argument,

void func(const datatype * x);

and you want to call it for a variable **A**, you are responsible for passing the address of **A** to **func( )**. You must explicitly take the address, using the "address-of" operator (**&**), like this:

func(&A);

Forcing the user to take the address of a variable doesn't add much to the semantics of the program. Because of this, it's easy to forget.

If a function returns an address, you can write code that makes the function call part of an lvalue. For example, if you have a **class** called **matrix,** and a member function **float * val(int,int)** that returns a pointer to a floating-point element of the matrix, you can assign to that element

```
matrix m;
//...
*(m.val(3,5)) = 1.19;
```

You can also use matrix elements in expressions.

```
float f = *(m.val(1,1)) - *(m.val(3,4));
```

Again, the use of pointers doesn't add to the meaning of the expressions. The pointers talk about *how* a value is produced or a variable is changed, not *what* the program does. If anything, dereferencing the pointers makes the code harder to read.

Using References in C++

Since references are solely a feature of C++, the rest of this chapter only refers to C++.

A reference in C++ is like a pointer because it contains an address, and like an ordinary variable because you don't have to dereference it. If a function takes a reference argument,

```
void funcr(int & x);
```

then you simply call the function the same way you call it if you are passing by value: **funcr(A);**. The fact that you are taking an address is invisible (this isn't a panacea; see the comments later in this chapter). In the matrix example, if the member function is redefined to return a reference to a floating-point number instead of a pointer, its prototype will be **float & valr(int, int);**. Now, to use it, you say,

```
m.valr(2,3) = 2.159;
```

```
float ff = m.valr(1,1) + m.valr(4,7);
```

Since the notation is cleaner, the user can focus on *what* the program does rather than *how* it is accomplished.

Void references (**void&**) are not allowed.

Reference Syntax

The only place you will notice references is in the function argument list. You can pass arguments by reference, and return a reference to a variable. Everywhere else in a function body the argument looks like an ordinary variable, that is, as if you had passed it by value. In fact, one of the bonuses of using references is that you can switch back and forth between pass-by-value and pass-by-reference by simply changing the argument list. Here's an example showing passing and returning by value, by pointer, and by reference:

```
// PASSING.CXX : Demonstration of passing arguments and
// returning values by value, by pointer, and by reference.
#include <stdio.h>

class demo {
    int i, j, k;
public:
    demo(int u = 0, int v = 0, int w = 0 ) {
        i = u; j = v; k = w;
    }
    demo byvalue(demo X); // pass in and out by value
    demo * bypointer(demo * X); // pass in and out by pointer
    demo & byreference(demo & X);  // pass in and out by reference
    void print(char * msg = " ") {
        printf("%s: i = %d j = %d k = %d\n", msg, i, j, k );
    }
};

// Notice the private data in X can be changed because this is
// a member function.  A copy of X is created local to the
// function, and the return value is copied out.
demo demo::byvalue(demo X) {
    X.i = X.j = X.k = 999;
    return X; // return an object
}

// In both the bypointer( ) and byreference( ) functions, the
// address of the modified argument is returned because, here,
// it is the only "safe" object, because it's an outside
// variable.  You shouldn't return the address of a local
// variable.
```

```
demo * demo::bypointer(demo * X) {
    X->i = X->j = X->k = 888;
    return X;  // X is actually a pointer in this function
}

// Now notice that using X when it is passed by reference is
// exactly the same as when it is passed by value:
demo & demo::byreference(demo & X) {
    X.i = X.j = X.k = 777;
    return X;  // return a reference
}

main( ) {
    demo A, B;
    A.byvalue(B).print("result of byvalue( )");
    A.bypointer(&B)->print("result of bypointer( )");
    A.byreference(B).print("result of byreference( )");
}
```

In each case, the member function **print( )** is being called for the return value of the function, which is either an object or the address of an object. Notice the calling syntax is identical when values are used and when references are used. Although passing and returning objects by value happens automatically here, it is a non-trivial subject. (Chapter 9 is devoted to this topic.)

Why References Are Essential

References often cause a lot of confusion, and people approach them differently. Someone without a strong background in C will often begin using references everywhere except where pointers are essential. C programmers who learn C++ will often avoid references, thinking of them as just another way to pass an address. Since pointers can do the job, they use pointers.

There is a situation where references are essential, and for which they were introduced to C++. To understand the necessity, a sneak preview of operator overloading is necessary. (Operator overloading is covered in Chapter 5.)

When you overload an operator, you create a function that is exactly the same as any other function, except for its name. The name of the function always consists of the keyword **operator**, followed by the character(s) used for the operator. For instance, addition for a class **foo** might look like **foo foo::operator+(foo)**. The rest of the function is the same (although there are limitations on the number of arguments—you don't add to more than one thing at a time). The compiler secretly calls the overloaded function when it sees the appropriate data types being used with that operator. Here's a simple example of a class with an overloaded addition operator:

```
// OPERPLUS.CXX : Class with an overloaded + operator
#include <stdio.h>

class plus {
    int i;
public:
    plus(int x = 0) { i = x; }
    plus operator+(plus arg) { return plus(i + arg.i); }
    void print(char * msg = " ") {
        printf("%s: i = %d\n", msg, i);
    }
};

main( ) {
    plus A(13), B(34);
    plus C = A + B;
    C.print("C = A + B");
}
```

The **operator+( )** takes a single argument, which is the value to the right of the **+**. Remember this function is invoked for the object on the left of the **+**. The **operator+( )** function creates a new **plus** object by calling the **plus** constructor. The argument to the **plus** constructor is the sum of the private data parts of the two objects. The **plus** constructor creates a new (temporary) **plus** object, which is copied out of the function as the return value of the operator.

Everything works fine in the preceding example; all the objects are passed and returned by value. However, there are many occasions when you need to pass the address of an object. For example, objects may be too large to pass by value without destroying the efficiency of the program. Suppose you take the program and modify it to use pointers.

```
// OPERPL2.CXX : Trying to use pointers in operator overloading
#include <stdio.h>

class plus {
    int i;
public:
    plus(int x = 0) { i = x; }
    plus operator+(plus * arg) { return plus(i + arg- >i); }
    void print(char * msg = " ") {
        printf("%s: i = %d\n", msg, i);
    }
};

main( ) {
    plus A(13), B(34);
    plus C = A + &B;
    C.print("C = A + B");
}
```

This program works, but the syntax **A + &B** lands somewhere between confusing and horrendous. As a last ditch effort, you could attempt to at least make the syntax homogeneous, **&A + &B**. This *might* work with a **friend operator+( )** function instead of a member—but it doesn't. The C++ compiler must have some way of determining that you want to call the **operator+( )** for a particular class. If you say **&A + &B**, the compiler's best guess is that you are adding two pointers.

References allow you to pass addresses to overloaded operator functions, and still retain the clean notation of **A + B**. Here's how **class plus** works using references:

```
// OPERPL3.CXX : Using references for operator overloading
// when you need to pass an address instead of a value.
#include <stdio.h>

class plus {
    int i;
public:
```

```
    plus(int x = 0) { i = x; }
    plus operator+(plus & arg) { return plus(i + arg.i); }
    void print(char * msg = " ") {
        printf("%s: i = %d\n", msg, i);
    }
};

main( ) {
    plus A(13), B(34);
    plus C = A + B;   // The syntax is as clean as pass-by-value
    C.print("C = A + B");
}
```

With references, you can use operator overloading and still pass addresses when using large objects.

Once references were added for operator overloading, they were seen to improve the syntax for function arguments. Many people prefer references over pointers for function arguments.

Independent References

References are designed for argument passing and return values, but the language strives to be consistent in all its aspects. Even though it is not a good practice, you can create independent references that are not associated with function arguments. While a pointer doesn't have to point to anything in particular when it is created, a reference must *always* be initialized. An independent reference can only be initialized to an existing variable of the correct type, or to a constant. The syntax for creating an independent reference is

int A;

int & ar = A;

As is always the case with references, the address of **A** is automatically taken. At this point, you have two ways to refer to the same variable, both of which look and act exactly the same. You might think this sounds messy. It is; and you should think very hard before you decide you must use an independent reference. Remember they were included for syntactic completeness, not necessarily because they are a good idea.

You can even do equally questionable things like casting a variable of one data type into a reference of another data type.

float f;

int & x = (int &)f;

You cannot create arrays of references. Object-oriented programming often deals with collections of objects, so the array is a useful tool. The fact you can't use it with references is one more reason to avoid independent reference variables, and use pointers instead.

Notice that the subject here is "independent references" and *not* "independent reference variables." A reference is quite different from a pointer. A pointer is a variable—it can be reassigned to other addresses. A reference, however, must be intialized when it is created, and it can never refer to a different variable. When you say,

int X = 10, Y = 100;

int & xr = X;

xr = Y;

You don't cause **xr** to refer to **Y**. Since the compiler always dereferences the address for you, the preceding code will copy the value in **Y** into **X**.

Notice that you can also create references to constant values.

int & aa = 47;

The compiler creates a temporary variable, copies the constant value into it, and uses the address of the temporary variable in the reference. This means that any function that takes a reference argument can also take a constant argument (although the results are unpredictable if the function modifies an outside variable).

*What It Means
To Return an Address*

If you return an address from a function via either a reference or a pointer, you are giving the user a memory address. The user can read the value at the address, and if you haven't declared the pointer type to be **const**, the user can also write the value. By returning an address, you are giving the user permission to read and, for non-**const** pointer types, write to private data. This is a significant design decision.

DON'T DO THIS   You must be certain never to return the address of a local variable. Syntactically, this is a completely acceptable thing to do:

```
// RETLOCAL.CXX : Some compilers don't complain if
// you return the address of a local variable.
#include <stdio.h>

int * fred( ) {
   int A = 100;
   return &A;
}

int * bob( ) {
   int B = 200;
   return &B;
}

main( ) {
   int * x = fred( );
   bob( );
   printf("fred( ) = %d\n", *x);
}
```

Not only does the compiler accept the function **fred( )**, but it actually does what you want some of the time! For instance, in this test (using Zortech C++ on the PC), if the call to **bob( )** is not made, the value of **∗x** is 100. However, if **bob( )** is called, the value of **∗x** becomes 200.

Here's what happens. When **fred( )** is called, local space is created on the stack for the variable **A**, and the value 100 is stored there. **fred( )** returns the address of this local variable. If another function with local variables is called, those local variables will write over the space where **A** used to be, so the value at the old address of **A** gets changed. Since **x** still points to that variable, the value at **∗x** gets changed. Since **bob( )** is a function that is identical to **fred( )**, and its local variable **B** sits right in the space where **A** was, assigning **B** to 200 will also change **∗x** to 200. This, of course, is very dependent on the order the functions are called and the machine architecture, so you should never depend on it acting in any particular fashion.

You may see some code where, at first glance, it might appear that addresses of local variables are being returned. For example:

```
// RETSTAT.CXX : Functions which appear to be returning
// addresses to local variables.

char * Tim( ) {
    char * ts = "This looks like a local variable";
    return ts;
}

int & Cheri( ) {
    static int X = 200;  // this has local visibility
    return X;
}
```

In both cases the variables are actually **static**; so while they have local visibility they have global lifetime. Thus it is generally safe and acceptable to return their addresses. The only real trick here is remembering that a quoted string constant creates a **static** variable, even though it isn't explicitly declared **static**. So even though it might look wrong it is OK.

DANGERS OF RETURNING REFERENCES AND POINTERS   If you return a pointer from a function, the user can assign it to a pointer variable and instantly have unchecked access to the private data elements in your class. This includes the ability to index off the end of arrays, as shown here:

```
// RETPTR.CXX: Problems with returning pointers from functions
#include <stdio.h>
#include <stdlib.h>
const size = 100;

class vec {
    int v[size];
    void error(char * msg = " ") {
        fprintf(stderr,"vec error: %s\n", msg);
        exit(1);
    }
public:
    int * operator[ ](int index) {
```

```
      if(index < 0 || index >= size)
        error("index out of range");
      return &(v[index]);
   }
};

main( ) {
   vec vector;
   *vector[5] = 88;  // the way it's supposed to be used, ugly
                     // syntax and all.
   int * x = vector[0];
   x++;  // now we can point to the next element
   *x = 47;  // and change that.
   x[1000] = 4;  // Bad news — the user has control over
                 // private elements of the class, and can index
                 // off the end of the vector.
}
```

In **class vec**, the overloaded **operator[ ]( )** function allows you to index into the **vec** array. Since it returns a pointer, you must dereference the pointer to access the array element; this obfuscates the code. You can also easily take the pointer returned by **operator[ ]( )** and use it to index off the end of the array, as shown in the last statement.

Since a reference is bound to one address when it is created, and the address can't be changed, it is more difficult to gain control of private data. Returning a reference is thus the preferred method when you must return an address from a function.

Of course, it isn't impossible to mess around in the private data when you return a reference, as shown here:

```
// RETREF.CXX: returning a reference from a function
#include <stdio.h>
#include <stdlib.h>
const size = 15;

class vec2 {
   int v[size];
   void error(char * msg = " ") {
      fprintf(stderr,"vec2 error: %s\n", msg);
      exit(1);
   }
public:
   vec2(int ival = 0);
```

```
        int & operator[ ](int index) {
           if(index < 0 || index >= size)
              error("index out of range");
           return v[index];
        }
        void print(char * msg = " ");
};

vec2::vec2(int ival) {
   for (int i = 0; i < size; i++)
      v[i] = ival;
}

void vec2::print(char * msg) {
   if (*msg) // "" contains only the zero byte terminator
      printf("%s:\n",msg);
   for (int i = 0; i < size; i++)
      printf("%d  ", v[i]);
   printf("\n");
}

main( ) {
   vec2 vector(7);
   vector[7] = 88;  // Much more readable syntax

   int & x = vector[0];
   // You can't index using x, and there's no pointer to
   // increment.  In fact, x is glued to vector[0].
   // The user can change the value at vector[0], but you've
   // explicitly given permission to do that:
   x = 100;
   vector.print("vector after vector[0] = 100");
   // Of course, there always seems to be a way around these
   // things.  However, it's much more obscure and harder to
   // use than x[1] is in RETPTR.CXX.
   *(&x + 1) = 99;  // changing vector[1]
   vector.print("vector after *(&x + 1) = 99");
}
```

This example is very similar to the previous example, but **operator[ ]( )** returns a reference instead of a pointer. The reference means you get the much more readable syntax of

vector[7] = 88; // no dereferencing necessary!

Finally, the example shows that it's still possible to abuse references, but it is much harder. You can explicitly prevent the user from modifying the contents of the reference by returning a reference to a **const**. If you only want to allow the user to read a value, return a **const** reference.

Pointers and References to Objects

When you pass a pointer or reference to an object as a function argument, you select members (either data or functions) using the structure pointer operator for pointers, and the structure member operator for references.

```
// SELECT.CXX : Selecting members for address arguments
#include <stdio.h>

class PrintMe {
  char * phrase;
public:
  PrintMe(char * msg = " ") {
    phrase = msg;
  }
  void print(char * msg2 = " ") {
    printf("%s: %s\n", msg2, phrase);
  }
};

void ByPointer(PrintMe * P) {
  // arrow selects function from pointer:
  P->print("inside ByPointer");
}

void ByReference(PrintMe & P) {
  // dot selects function from reference:
  P.print("inside ByReference");
}

main( ) {
  PrintMe One("This is phrase 1"),
          Two("This is phrase 2");
  ByPointer(&One);
```

```
    ByReference(Two);
}
```

Both **ByPointer( )** and **ByReference( )** can only select **public** data or function elements. To select **private** elements, the functions must be declared as **friend** functions inside the **class** definition.

When to Use References

When it was necessary or beneficial to pass an address to a function or return an address from a function in C, there was no choice—you used a pointer. In C++, you often have a choice about how to pass and return addresses. This section examines some of the trade-offs.

Although it is syntactically possible to use independent references (just as it is possible to return addresses of local variables), it is rarely a good idea, and will not be considered further in this book.

Advantages of References

Here are some of the advantages of using references in C++:

■ References have the advantage of notational cleanliness. When you are trying to understand the meaning of a piece of code, you don't have to fight through the details of how parameters are passed. A good example is the **matrix** class shown in Appendix B. It is possible to write equations using **matrix** objects that look and act very similar to the mathematical equations describing the desired matrix manipulation. This means the user can concentrate on the meaning of the equations rather than their implementation.

■ References put the responsibility for argument passing on the programmer who writes the functions, not on the individual who uses them. This makes the language do more of the bookkeeping work, and the user less.

■ References are a necessary complement to operator overloading, as shown earlier.

■ References are a necessary complement to operator overloading, as shown earlier.

The efficiency of passing an address varies depending on the machine (some machines have special instructions that make passing by value more efficient). You can easily compare passing by value to passing by reference, since the only part you need to change is the argument list.

Problems with References

Although references are notationally cleaner and put the responsibility of knowing how parameters are passed on the programmer, there are some situations where they can hide bugs. For instance, the **streams** function **get( )** can be called with a character argument: **cin.get(c);**. Because a reference hides the type of argument passing that the function uses, you can't tell from looking at the function call whether **c** is passed by value or passed by reference. If you are trying to track down a problem associated with the variable **c**, you will probably read right past **cin.get(c);** and think that **c** is passed by value, so it wasn't modified by the function call (when, in fact, it was).

This is a valid complaint—a function has side effects that aren't apparent from its calling syntax. There are a number of reasons you shouldn't abandon references, however.

■ The problem exists primarily with built-in data types, in which all the "data elements" are public. That is, anyone can change an **int**. To make the method of argument passing explicit so the user knows a variable may be changed, you can use a pointer instead of a reference when passing built-in data types. In fact, passing an argument by value is usually very efficient for built-in types, so the only reason you would pass an address instead of a value for a built-in type is if the function modifies the argument. Therefore, while you shouldn't abandon references completely, you probably shouldn't use them for built-in types.

■ User-defined types have data-hiding mechanisms to protect their data from being unknowingly modified. Since you can force all modifications of internal data to be performed through member functions or **friend** functions, "unseen side effects" are much easier to monitor. You can even put statements in member functions to notify you if private data is changed.

■ User-defined types are often large enough that it is more efficient to pass an address than to pass by value (passing by value copies the entire object, and not just an address). However, the efficiency depends on the particular system you are using. Some computers are optimized to manipulate large chunks of data—with a machine like that, it might be more efficient to pass by value than to pass an address and dereference the address every time an element is used.

Guidelines for Passing Arguments

"So," you may ask, "how should I pass arguments?" The answer, in the spirit of C, is, "Anyway you want to." However, here are a few guidelines that may help you make the decision:

■ If a function does not modify an argument that is a built-in data type or a "small" user-defined type, pass arguments by value. The meaning of "small" depends on your system.

■ If a function modifies an argument that is a built-in type, pass a pointer. This makes it explicit to anyone reading the code that the built-in type is being modified.

■ If a function modifies an argument that is a user-defined type, pass a reference. Any function that modifies private data in an object must either be a member function or a **friend** function. This means the **class** has control over the functions that can modify its private data. Just because you hand the address of an object to a function doesn't mean the function can secretly change the private data in the object. Thus, the clue that a C pointer gives ("this function modifies an outside variable") is not as useful with user-defined types in C++, since the modifications can be traced directly through functions that have permission to change private data. When debugging, you should instead ask, "Who has permission to modify this object?" The answer is conveniently located in the class itself, instead of being scattered about in random functions. Since references reduce effort and confusion on the part of the user, they should be used for objects.

■ To pass "non-small" objects that are not modified, pass references to constants, on the premise that it is more efficient. The meaning of "non-small" is often obvious for a particular class, but it must be tested for your particular implementation. Testing is easy since it only involves adding and/or removing the **&** in the argument list. Since the argument is never modified, it is again clearer to the user if a reference is passed.

Here's an example that shows the various types of parameter passing suggested in the above list:

```
// PASSARGS.CXX : Demonstration of argument-passing guidelines

// Built in types:

int F1(int x);  // function doesn't modify outside variable
int F2(int * x);  // function modifies outside variable

// Small User-defined Types:

class XX {
    int i;
public:
    //...
    friend int F4(XX &); // explicit permission to change
        // private data
};

int F3(XX arg); // function doesn't modify outside variable
int F4(XX & arg); // function modifies outside variable by
        // directly manipulating its private data
int F5(XX & arg); // function modifies outside variable by
        // calling a member function, since this was not
        // declared "friend"

// Large User-defined Types:
const size = 50;
```

```
class big {
    int * data[size][size];  // 50 x 50 matrix
public:
    // ....
    friend int F7(big &);  // explicit permission to change
        // private data
};

int F6(const big & arg);  // function doesn't modify outside var
int F7(big & arg);  // function modifies outside var by
        // directly manipulating it's private data
int F8(big & arg);  // function modifies outside var by calling
                // member functions
```

Makefile for Chapter Examples

Here is the makefile for all the examples in this chapter:

```
# makefile for examples in chapter 4
# Zortech:
CPP = ztc
# Glockenspiel:
#CPP = ccxx

.cxx.exe:
        $(CPP) $*.cxx

.cxx.obj:
        $(CPP) -c $*.cxx
```

```
all:      ptrarith.exe varptrs.exe constptr.exe constarg.exe \
          printv.exe arrayptr.exe index.exe agregate.exe \
          statcstr.exe center.exe encrypt.exe encode.exe \
          namecat.exe ptrsize.exe decl.obj ptrfunc.exe \
          functabl.exe dynafunc.exe stats.exe passarry.exe \
          modify.exe retstruc.exe derefstr.exe ptrstruc.exe \
          seefloat.exe passing.exe operplus.exe operpl2.exe \
          operpl3.exe retlocal.exe retstat.obj retptr.exe \
          retref.exe select.exe passargs.obj

encode.exe : encode.cxx encode.hxx
dynafunc.exe : dynafunc.cxx dynafunc.hxx
```

Object-Oriented Programming with C++

Part Two

5 *Overloading Functions and Operators*

Language development seems to be a history of "necessary conveniences." Perhaps some of the first programmers, working in machine code, thought of assembly language as an overblown solution to the programming problem. Perhaps assembly language programmers thought of the first interpreters and compilers as slow, filled with arbitrary features, and not worth the effort (it certainly seems worthwhile now). Some programmers of early languages probably found concepts like data structures, functions, and separate compilation unnecessary and confusing. However, once you get used to any of these features, they go from curious inventions of computer scientists to indispensable features of any civilized computer language.

There is a faction in the C++ community that believes the language should follow C's "minimalist" philosophy; and there is the complementary faction that feels there aren't enough features to do proper object-oriented programming. The two factions, and those in the middle, make up the synthesis of conflicting impulses that seem to characterize "life" in a project. Many of these people feel that the ability to change the meaning of an operator is both confusing and superfluous. As discussed in Chapter 4, operator overloading was also the feature that "forced" the addition of references to C++; without operator overloading, references are a convenient but not essential feature. By getting rid of operator overloading, you get rid of references too, and remove a lot of complexity and confusion. Wouldn't this be better?

From the standpoint of a traditional procedural language, it probably *would* be better. However, C++ is striking out in a new direction. Although it is possible to create and maintain large projects and libraries with languages like C, they don't really have the features to support this kind of activity. These languages were really designed to solve one computer problem at a time. When the problem was solved, a few changes might be made, but long-term maintenance and significant program modifications are not supported.

Instead of asking, "How do we solve the problem of writing this computer program?" C++ asks, "How do we solve the problem of programming, and of thinking about programming? How do we support the creation of programs that are cheap to maintain and easy to modify? How do we avoid throwing away old code?" These questions go in a new direction and require a new approach.

The approach taken by C++ and other object-oriented languages is *extensibility*. Instead of making a program more complex as the problems get more complex (and further away from a model that is easily represented by the computer language), extensibility allows you to change the model of the computer language to fit your problem. Once you adapt the language to your problem, the solution can be expressed in a clean and concise manner. This means your program will be easy to understand and easy to change.

Extensibility has received some bad press due to languages like Forth, which is completely extensible, without bounds or restrictions. While Forth is a brilliant language and a fascinating experiment, its lack of boundaries often produces programs that may only be understood by their authors.

Like Forth, C++ allows you to essentially create a new language by extending the old one. The difference is that the new language elements (classes) you create in C++ must conform to a strict set of rules enforced by the C++ compiler. Your classes must, syntactically, fit seamlessly into the old language.

All data types have certain operations that may be performed upon them. The operations allowed for a user-defined type may be ordinary member functions; most of the examples up to this point have taken this approach. An operator, however, is another way of expressing functionality, and for some data types it is more natural to use an operator than a member function. To completely integrate a new user-defined data type into the language, you must have the ability to give operators a special meaning for that data type.

The Syntax of Operator Overloading

To overload an operator (as with function overloading, *overload* means "give it an additional meaning"), you simply define a function for the compiler to call when that operator is used with the appropriate data types. Whenever the compiler sees those data types used with the operator, it calls the function. You can have multiple functions overloading a single operator, but they must all take different arguments (so the compiler can differentiate between them).

The function definition syntax for operator overloading is different than for normal functions. The function name is the keyword **operator** followed by the operator itself, followed by the argument list and the function body. Thus, using the non-operator @ to represent the selected operator, the syntax is

returntype **operator**@(*argumentlist*) { *functionbody* }

for a **friend** function, and

*returntype classname::***operator**@(*argument*) { *functionbody* }

for a class member. A **friend** function has one argument for a unary operator, and two arguments for a binary operator, while a member function has no arguments for a unary operator and one argument for a binary operator. This is true because a member function is automatically dealing with one variable already, the object it was called for. The reasons for choosing member functions over **friend** functions will be discussed later in the chapter.

Examples of Operator Overloading

This section contains two examples of operator overloading. The most common situation in which operator overloading is useful is when you are dealing with a mathematically oriented object, as shown in the first example. Often, however, a particular operator may lend itself well to non-mathematical functionality, as demonstrated in the second example.

A Mathematical Class

The following class shows an exhaustive example of all the operators. A simple class called **point** is created to hold coordinates of a point in space, and all the operators are defined for **point** so you can see how to create each type of operator.

```
// POINT.HXX : Declaration of a class to represent a point in
// space.  Demonstrates operator overloading.
#ifndef POINT_HXX
#define POINT_HXX

class point {
protected:
    float x, y;
public:
    point(float xx = 0, float yy = 0) {
        x = xx; y = yy;
    }
    point operator=(point); // assignment
    float magnitude( );  // vector equivalents
    float angle( );
    point operator+(point); // add two points
    // see POINT.CXX for an explanation of this:
#ifndef __ZTC__
    point operator+( ); // unary plus
#endif // __ZTC__
    point operator-(point); // subtract two points
    point operator-( ); // unary minus
    point operator*(float); // multiply a point by a scalar
    point operator/(float); // divide a point by a scalar
    point operator%(point); // non-traditional modulus
    point operator+=(point); // same operators with '='
    point operator-=(point);
    point operator*=(float);
    point operator/=(float);
    point operator%=(point);
    point operator++( ); // increment
```

```
        point operator—( ); // decrement
        point operator[ ](float); // rotate the vector
        point operator<<(float); // shift the vector along the x- coord
        point operator>>(float); // shift the vector along the y- coord
        point operator<<=(float); // shift and assign
        point operator>>=(float);
        int operator<(point);  // relational comparison of points
        int operator>(point); // returns 1 if true, 0 if false
        int operator<=(point);
        int operator>=(point);
        int operator==(point);
        int operator!=(point);
        int operator!( );      // 1 if a point is zero
        int operator&&(point); // 0 if either is zero
        int operator||(point); // 0 only if both are zero
        float operator&(point); // cross-product (magnitude only)
        float operator|(point); // dot-product
        float operator^(point); // angle between two vectors
        point operator&=(point); // multiply point by cp magnitude
        point operator|=(point); // multiply point by dp magnitude
        point operator^=(point); // multiply point by angle
        void print(char * msg = " ");
};
#endif // POINT_HXX
```

Each operator that takes a **point** as an argument, or returns a **point**, passes or returns the object by value. The meaning of the preprocessor flag **__ZTC__** will be explained later when the methods for **class point** are described.

USING this   Many of the methods for **point** have rather strange looking **return** statements, such as

return *this;

The keyword **this** is unique to C++. It means "the starting address of the object for which this function was called." The starting address is the same as the address of the first variable in the class structure. Before looking at the methods for **point**, here is a small program that illustrates the meaning of **this**.

```
// THIS.CXX : Illustration of the "this" keyword
#include <stdio.h>

class charles {
    int i;
    float f;
public:
    long L;  // public data
    char C;
    charles(int ii = 0, float ff = 0.0,
            long ll = 0, char cc = 0 ) {
        i = ii;
        f = ff;
        L = ll;
        C = cc;
    }
    void test_this( ) {
        void * vp = this;
        printf("i = %d\n", *( (int *)vp ) );
        ( (int *)vp )++; // move past the int
        printf("f = %f\n", *( (float *)vp ) );
        ( (float *)vp )++; // move past the float
        printf("L = %ld\n", *( (long *)vp ) );
        ( (long *)vp )++; // move past the long
        printf("C = %c\n", *( (char *)vp ) );
    }
};

main( ) {
    charles X(1957, 7.865, 100000, 'X');
    X.test_this( );
}
```

The member function **test_this( )** creates a **void** pointer **vp** and gives it the value of **this**, the address of the current object. This is often the address of the first element in the structure, **i**. To test this premise, **vp** is cast to an **int** pointer and dereferenced with the expression *((**int** *)**vp**). The result is handed to **printf( )**. To point **vp** to the next element in the structure, it is again cast to an **int** pointer, and then incremented, in the statement ((**int** *)**vp**)++;. The pointer is now, presumably, pointing to the element **f**. This premise is tested by casting it to a **float** *, dereferencing it, and printing the result. The same type of actions are performed for **L** and **C**. This isn't terribly useful information, since it's much easier to access the elements by name. However, it *is* interesting.

The order of elements within a section with the same access (**public, private, protected**) is the same order that you define them. However, there is no guarantee that the *sections* will appear in the order you defined them. The **private** section may appear after the **public** section, even if you defined it first. Thus, the program above may not work as expected. The element **L** will appear before **C**, and **i** will appear before **f**, but **L** and **C** *may* appear before **i** and **f**. It is generally not a good idea to plan on the elements being ordered in any particular fashion.

Since **this** is a pointer to the beginning of the class structure, you can select structure elements using the arrow operator ->. Of course, you don't have to do this inside a member function, which is the only place you have access to **this**—you just refer to the elements by name.

If you want to refer to the entire structure of the object you are in, you say, "*this." Remember the dereference operator * produces the contents at the address contained in the pointer. Since **this** points to an entire structure, *this *is* the structure.

It is important to return a copy of the result of an operation when you overload an operator, because operators can generally be used in complicated expressions and are not necessarily used alone as are ordinary function calls. Thus the expression **A + B + C** relies on the result of the operation **A + B** being passed to the second operation and added to **C**. In the case of **operator+( )**, you don't usually modify the operands when you are adding two values together (although you can do anything you want when you overload an operator). If you look at the code for **operator+( )**, you see a brand new **point** is created and returned. In the case of **operator+=( )**, however, the lvalue is modified and becomes the result. You should return a copy of the result when you do any kind of assignment. Assignment, too, can be used in a complex statement as the other operators are.

X = A + (Y = 1);

Here are the methods for **point**:

```
// POINT.CXX : Methods for class to represent point in space.
// Notice that not all these definitions make sense; they just
// show you how to overload operators.
#include "point.hxx"
#include <math.h>
```

```
#include <stdio.h>
// Used to determine zero:
const float tiny = 0.0001;

point point::operator=(point rv) {
    x = rv.x; // copy the rvalue
    y = rv.y;
    return *this;  // return a copy of this object
}

float point::magnitude( ) {
    return sqrt(x*x + y*y);
}

float point::angle( ) {
    return atan2(y,x);
}

point point::operator+(point p) {
    return point(x + p.x, y + p.y);
}

// Here's how to solve the problem of a feature that doesn't
// exist on a particular compiler.  Zortech C++ versions 1.07
// and earlier don't allow you to overload unary operator+( )
// (this is a bug).  Since the compiler has a special #define
// to identify itself, you can use it to remove the offending
// code:
#ifndef __ZTC__
point point::operator+( ) {
    return *this;  // unary + normally doesn't do anything.
}
#endif // __ZTC__

point point::operator-(point p) {
    return point(x - p.x, y - p.y);
}

point point::operator-( ) {
    return point(-x, -y);
}
```

```
point point::operator*(float f) {
   return point(x * f, y * f);
}

point point::operator/(float f) {
   return point(x / f, y / f);
}

point point::operator%(point p) {
   // fmod( ) is the "floating point remainder" function
   return point(fmod(x, p.x), fmod(y, p.y));
}

point point::operator+=(point p) {
   x += p.x;
   y += p.y;
   return *this;
}

point point::operator-=(point p) {
   x -= p.x;
   y -= p.y;
   return *this;
}

point point::operator*=(float f) {
   x *= f;
   y *= f;
   return *this;
}

point point::operator/=(float f) {
   x /= f;
   y /= f;
   return *this;
}

point point::operator%=(point p) {
   x = floor(x / p.x);
   y = floor(y / p.y);
   return *this;
}
```

```cpp
point point::operator++( ) {
    x += 1.0;
    y += 1.0;
    return *this;
}

point point::operator--( ) {
    x -= 1.0;
    y -= 1.0;
    return *this;
}

point point::operator[ ](float f) {
    float new_x = magnitude( ) * cos(angle( ) * f);
    float new_y = magnitude( ) * sin(angle( ) * f);
    return point(new_x, new_y);
}

point point::operator<<(float f) {
    return point(x + f, y);
}

point point::operator>>(float f) {
    return point(x, y + f);
}

point point::operator<<=(float f) {
    x += f;
    return *this;
}

point point::operator>>=(float f) {
    y += f;
    return *this;
}

int point::operator<(point p) {
    if ( x < p.x && y < p.y )
        return 1;
    return 0;
}
```

```
int point::operator>(point p) {
   if ( x > p.x && y > p.y )
      return 1;
   return 0;
}

int point::operator<=(point p) {
   if ( x <= p.x && y <= p.y )
      return 1;
   return 0;
}

int point::operator>=(point p) {
   if ( x >= p.x && y >= p.y )
      return 1;
   return 0;
}

int point::operator==(point p) {
   if ( x == p.x && y == p.y )
      return 1;
   return 0;
}

int point::operator!=(point p) {
   if ( x != p.x && y != p.y )
      return 1;
   return 0;
}

int point::operator!( ) {
   if ( fabs(x) < tiny && fabs(y) < tiny )
      return 1;
   return 0;
}

int point::operator&&(point p) {
   if ( fabs(x) < tiny && fabs(y) < tiny )
      return 0;
   if ( fabs(p.x) < tiny && fabs(p.y) < tiny )
      return 0;
```

```
        return 1;
}

int point::operator||(point p) {
    if ( fabs(x) < tiny && fabs(y) < tiny &&
            fabs(p.x) < tiny && fabs(p.y) < tiny )
        return 0;
    return 1;
}

float point::operator&(point p) {
    return magnitude( ) * p.magnitude( ) *
            sin(point::operator^(p));
}

float point::operator|(point p) {
    return magnitude( ) * p.magnitude( ) *
            cos(point::operator^(p));
}

float point::operator^(point p) {
    return fabs(angle( ) - p.angle( ));
}

point point::operator&=(point p) {
    float cross =  magnitude( ) * p.magnitude( ) *
        sin(point::operator^(p));
    x *= cross;
    y *= cross;
    return *this;
}

point point::operator|=(point p) {
    float dot = magnitude( ) * p.magnitude( ) *
            cos(point::operator^(p));
    x *= dot;
    y *= dot;
    return *this;
}

point point::operator^=(point p) {
    float arc =  fabs(angle( ) - p.angle( ));
```

```
    x *= arc;
    y *= arc;
    return *this;
}

void point::print(char * msg) {
    if (*msg)
        printf("%s : ", msg);
    printf("x = %f, y = %f\n", x, y);
}
```

Many of the methods use ANSI C math library functions, contained in **math.h**. The description of **__ZTC__** is contained in a comment in the preceding listing. Each operator shown here is overloaded only once, but you can overload any operator several times, as long as the argument is different for each overload.

When you compile this code with Glockenspiel C++, you will notice numerous warning messages, complaining about "bitcopy" and claiming that an equal operator was defined. These will go away if you either remove the overloading of **operator=( )** (the function is identical to the default, so it doesn't matter) or define a copy-constructor **point(point &)**. The copy-constructor is described completely in Chapter 9.

All the methods in this class pass and return by value, which is generally efficient for a class this size. This becomes a problem with complicated classes (ones containing pointers) as shown in Chapter 9.

Remember that you are making important design decisions when you overload an operator. You should ask yourself whether you are making life easier or harder for the user. For example, in the preceding code, the operator **&** was overloaded to mean "cross- product." Will this be meaningful to someone using the class, or to someone reading the code in which the class is used?

CREATING TEMPORARY OBJECTS A number of the methods in **class point** use an unfamiliar form in their **return** statements. For instance, in **operator[ ]**, the **return** statement is:

return point(new_x, new_y);

What does it mean when you use a class name with an argument list like this? When the compiler sees a construct like this it treats it as a constructor call for a *temporary object,* which is an object with no name and usually a very brief lifetime. In the above example, space is created inside the function **operator[ ]** to hold a **point** object, and the constructor **point::point(float,float)** is called to initialize that object. Finally, the temporary **point** object is copied to the outside of the function via the **return** mechanism, and the temporary **point** object goes out of scope.

You can create your own temporary objects any place where a non-temporary object can be used. For instance, if there is a function **fp(point)** that takes a **point** object as an argument, you would normally hand it an initialized point, like this:

point A(1.1,2.2);

fp(A);

but you can also create a temporary for the express purpose of handing it to the function as an argument, like this:

fp(point(1.1,2.2));

Using temporary objects can make your code briefer, more efficient and easier to read.

IDIOSYNCRASIES IN OPERATOR OVERLOADING   There are certain operators that don't work *quite* the way they do in C, or in C++, if the operator isn't overloaded. When you overload **operator++( )** and **operator --( )**, the compiler can't tell prefix from postfix. In C and C++, the non-overloaded operators **&&** (logical AND) and **I I** (logical OR) have the "short- circuit" feature—if the truth or falsehood of the expression containing **&&** or **I I** can be determined at some point early in the expression, the entire expression isn't evaluated. For instance:

int cond1( ), cond2( );

if(cond1( ) && cond2( ))

   // ...

if(cond2( ) I I cond1( ))

   // ...

In the first **if** statement, if **cond1( )** evaluates to zero (false), then there is no point in evaluating **cond2( )**, because you already know the expression will be false. In the second **if** statement, if **cond2( )** is true, then you know the whole expression is true, so **cond1( )** is not evaluated. C and C++ "short-circuit" the expression when its truth or falsehood can be determined. However, if you overload **operator&&( )** or **operator||( )**, short-circuiting is not performed in expressions using those overloaded operators—the entire expression is *always* evaluated.

Here are a few exercises for **class point**:

```
// POINT.CXX : A few tests for the point class
#include "point.hxx"
#include <stdio.h>

main( ) {
    point A, B(1.1, 2.2), C(3.3, 4.4), D(5.5, 6.6);
    B.print("B");
    C.print("C");
    D.print("D");
    A = B + C - D;
    A.print("A = B + C - D");
    A += (B << 8.2) + (D >> 4.1);
    A.print("A += (B << 8.2) + (D >> 4.1)");
    printf("magnitude of A = %f, angle of A = %f\n",
            A.magnitude( ), A.angle( ));
    printf("Angle C ^ D = %f\n", C ^ D);
}
```

When designing the external operations for a class, remember that all the user usually sees is those operations. If the operations don't contribute to readable code, then you should think hard before you do it that way. This is especially true for operator overloading.

Esoteric Operator Overloading

The **point class** shows the overloading of the more common operators. C++ doesn't stop there, however—you can overload operators you wouldn't normally think of redefining, like the "address-of" operator, **&**, the pointer dereference operator, *****, and even the function-call parentheses. The class shown here has an element **index** before the array **vv[ ]**, so if you try to access the array directly using **this**, you will get **index** instead. (As mentioned before, it is a bad idea to rely on the implementation-dependent ordering of the elements in a **class** structure.) Both the **&** and the * select the starting address of **vv[ ]** instead of **index**, though of course you can return anything you want.

One reason overloading the function call is valuable is it allows you to use an operator syntax with multiple arguments. This also allows many different kinds of overloading. The example shown here simply sets an array element to a value.

```
// VECTOR.HXX: esoteric operator overloading
#ifndef VECTOR_HXX
#define VECTOR_HXX

const size = 20;

class vector {
    int index;
    float vv[size];
    void error(char * msg);
public:
    vector(float initval = 0.0);
    float & operator[ ](int index);
    // use the "address-of" operator to return the start
    // of the floating-point array
    const float * operator&( ) { return vv; }
    float operator*( ) { return vv[0]; }
    // Here's a strange one.  You can overload the "function call"
    // operator.  The function shown here sets element el to the
    // value f, and returns the new value.  Notice it is the only
    // overloaded operator that allows an argument list of more
    // than one for a member function (more than two for a
    // friend).
    float operator( )(int el, float f);
    void print(char * msg = " ");
};
#endif // VECTOR_HXX
```

Here are the methods for **class vector**:

```
// VECTOR.CXX: Methods for class vector
#include <stdio.h>
#include "vector.hxx"
 #include <stdlib.h>

void vector::error(char * msg) {
   fprintf(stderr, "vector error: %s\n", msg);
   exit(1);
}

vector::vector(float initval) {
   for(int i = 0; i < size; i++)
      vv[i] = initval;
}

float & vector::operator[ ](int index) {
   if(index < 0 || index >= size)
      error("operator out of range");
   return vv[index];
}

float vector::operator( )(int el, float f) {
   if(el < 0 || el >= size)
      error("operator out of range");
   vv[el] = f;
   return f;
}

void vector::print(char * msg) {
   if (*msg)
      printf("%s:\n", msg);
   for(int i = 0; i < size; i++) {
      printf("%6.6f ", vv[i]);
      if ( i % 5 == 4) // linefeed every 5
         printf("\n");
   }
   printf("\n\n");
}
```

This program exercises the overloaded operators in **vector**:

```
// VECTEST.CXX: Test for class vector.
#include "vector.hxx"
#include <stdio.h>

main( ) {
    vector V(1.1);
    V.print("V");
    for(int i = 0; i < size; i++)
        V[i] = (float)(i * 1.5);
    V[0] = 33.119;
    V.print("V after V[i] = (float)(i * 1.5); V[0] = 33.119;");
    const float * startval = &V;
    printf("*startval = %f\n", *startval);
    V(4, 999.99);
    V.print("V after V(4, 999.99)");
    printf("*V = %f\n", *V);
}
```

You will notice in **class vector** that the overloaded indexing brackets, **operator[ ]( )**, specifically allow the result to be used as an lvalue (that is, you can change the selected value in the **vector**). As noted in Chapter 4, this is an important design decision—if you don't want to allow the user to change the value, you should explicitly say so by declaring the return value **const**.

C++ release 2.0, (described in Chapter 11) allows overloading of the *member selection operator, ->*. This is sometimes called "smart pointers."

operator=( ) *IS UNIQUE*   You should be aware that all operators are not treated equally in C++. Although the definition for **operator=( )** looks much the same as the other definitions, because it deals with *assignment* the compiler treats **operator=( )** differently when the class is inherited into another class. (Inheritance is covered in Chapter 7.) While all other operators automatically inherit from an old class to a new one, **operator=( )** doesn't. This makes sense, because you often add data members to a new class. The old version of **operator=( )** only knows about the data members from the base class, so it will only copy those elements. The assignment will happen, but it will be wrong. This is too easy a trap to fall into, and it's very difficult to track down the problem, so the compiler does it for you by forcing you to redefine **operator=( )** whenever you inherit a class (that is, assuming it has been defined in the base class). Constructors and destructors also do not inherit.

Creating Your Own
Type Conversion Operators

In Chapter 3, an example was presented (file BADFABS.CXX) that caused problems because of the Zortech C++ autoprototyping function. Briefly, the example was

float f = 0.5;

float fa = fabs(f);

The result was garbage when the **math.h** header file was not included. Zortech C++ made no complaint. What is really going on here?

If **math.h** is not included, the first time Zortech C++ sees the function call **fabs( )**, it creates the prototype according to the way it is used.

float fabs(float);

However, the actual prototype in **math.h** is

double fabs(double);

What happens when **math.h** is included? The compiler sees that **fabs( )** is being given a **float** argument instead of the **double** it requires, so it silently does an *implicit type conversion* (also called *promotion*). It converts the **float** to a **double** by calling the special type conversion operation that can be explicitly called with the cast, denoted **(double)**. There is a cast for all the built-in data types, pointers, and references. Thus the explicit call to **fabs( )** is **fabs((double)f)**. In C++, you can also use the constructor form of type conversion—**double(f)**.

Since **fabs( )** returns a **double** and it is assigned to a **float**, the compiler must also perform a type conversion on the result. The explicit statement becomes

float fa = (float)fabs((double)f);

If the compiler knows the correct function prototype, it can silently call the casting operators for you. When **math.h** wasn't included in this example, it didn't cast the argument or the result, so the result was garbage.

Implicit type conversion even happens when you assign to a constant, for example:

double d = 'c';

Here, the right-hand side is an ASCII character, which the compiler treats as an integer constant. The compiler takes the ASCII value and promotes it to a **double** through the implicit application of the **(double)** operator.

Type Conversion For User-Defined Types

C++ gives you the ability to make a user-defined type look and act almost exactly like a built-in type. This extends to casting—you can define a casting operator so your new type can be converted to some other type, either built-in or user-defined. When the compiler sees your type being used where the other type is required (and it has no way to use your type directly), it quietly calls your casting operator. Here's an example:

```
// CASTING.CXX : Type conversion for user-defined types
#include <stdio.h>

class number {
   float f;
public:
   number(float x = 0.0) { f = x; }
   operator int( ) {  // return value established by function name
      return (int)f;
   }
};

class number2 {
   int i;
public:
   number2(int x = 0) { i = x; }
   operator number( ) {  // cast to another built-in type
      return number((float)i);
   }
};
```

```
void brian(number X) { }

main( ) {
    number n(9.7);
    number2 n2(25);
    int x = n;  // implicit call to number::operator int( )
    n = n2; // implicit call to number2::operator number( )
    brian(n2); // implicit call to number2::operator number( )
}
```

In this example, two possible implicit type conversions are specified. In **class number, operator int( )** is a way to make an **int** from a **number**. Note that you don't need to designate the return value on a type conversion operator—the name of the operator is the same as the return value. In **class number2, operator number( )** is a way to make a **number** from a **number2**. The statement

int x = n;

causes the compiler to call the first type conversion operator, and the statement

n = n2;

causes the compiler to call the second type conversion operator.

In the preceding listing, the conversion is performed by calling a function in the argument's class. You can also make the destination class perform the type conversion by creating constructors that take a single argument of the other user-defined type. The source class must either give explicit access privileges to the destination class (by declaring the destination class constructor to be a **friend**) or provide adequate access functions so the destination object's constructor can read the necessary data. Both of these alternatives are shown in the following example:

```
// CONSTCNV.CXX : Single-argument constructors to perform
// type conversion.  Two different alternatives are shown
// to allow the destination object access to the source
// object's private data.

class micah;  // declare the class
```

```
class shani {
   float f1, f2;
public:
   shani(float x1 = 0.0, float x2 = 0.0) {
      f1 = x1;  f2 = x2;
   }
   shani(micah &);  // type-conversion constructor
   float f_one( ) { return f1; }  // access functions
   float f_two( ) { return f2; }
};

class micah {  // define the class
   int i1, i2;
public:
   micah(int y1 = 0, int y2 = 0) {
      i1 = y1;  i2 = y2;
   }
   micah(shani &);  // type-conversion constructor
   friend shani::shani(micah &);  // allow access to private data
};

// This constructor has permission to read the private data in
// micah, since it's a friend function:
shani::shani(micah & m) {
   f1 = m.i1;  // implicit (float) cast
   f2 = m.i2;
}

// This constructor uses the access functions in shani to read
// the private data.  It isn't a friend, so it must get the data
// some other way than by directly reading the elements:
micah::micah(shani & s) {
   i1 = (int)s.f_one( );
   i2 = (int)s.f_two( );
}

void f1(shani s) { }
void f2(micah m) { }
```

```
main( ) {
    shani S;
    micah M;
    M = S;  // micah::micah(shani &) called
    S = M;  // shani::shani(micah &) called
    f1(M);  // shani::shani(micah &) called
    f2(S);  // micah::micah(shani &) called
}
```

In this example, you see a **class** *name declaration* at the beginning of the file. Since **shani** uses **micah** in the argument list for the type-conversion constructor, the compiler must know that **micah** is a legal class name. **class shani** has the access functions **f_one( )** and **f_two( )**, which provide the constructor **micah::micah(shani &)** with enough information to make a **micah** from a **shani**. **class micah**, however, does not contain these access functions. For the constructor **shani::shani(micah &)** to have enough information to make a **shani** from a **micah**, it must be given **friend** status in **micah** so it can access **private** data in **micah**.

CHOOSING BETWEEN CASTING OPERATORS AND CONSTRUCTOR COVERSION
As you can see from the two examples, the compiler doesn't seem to care whether you've defined a casting operator or a constructor to perform the type conversion—if a conversion path exists, it will perform the implicit type conversion whenever it can. So how do you decide which form of type conversion to use?

The compiler sees them both the same way—as a function to call implicitly to perform the type conversion when the need arises. The decision about which one to use is often made for you—if you own the class that needs to be converted, you can write a casting operator for it. If you don't own it and you can extract enough information, you can write a type-conversion constructor for the destination class. Also, you must use the casting operator when converting a user-defined type to a built-in type, since you can't define a constructor for a built-in type.

It is important that you don't use both a constructor and a casting operator for the same type conversion, since this introduces an ambiguity in how the conversion should be performed. The compiler generates an error message if you try to do both.

Dangers of Too Much Type Conversion

Automatic type conversion is very convenient and can greatly reduce the number of function definitions you need to write. For instance, with no automatic type conversions, you must have two overloaded versions of **Daniel( )**:

void Daniel(book);

void Daniel(play);

However, if there is a type conversion function **book::operator play( )** or **play::play(book)**, then you only need the single version of **Daniel( )**.

void Daniel(play);

Now if you call **Daniel( )** with a **play**, the function matches exactly, and if you use a **book** as an argument, the compiler automatically converts it to a **play**.

Because it saves work and makes life more convenient, you may be tempted to go a bit wild with automatic type conversion operators. This can get you in trouble in two ways.

One is that if you have two ways to perform the same type conversion, the compiler cannot resolve the ambiguity. The following program uses two ways to get from **lucy** to **ricky**:

```
// DUALCONV.CXX : Two ways to perform the same type conversion.
// The translator should generate an error message.

// Declare the class so ricky can use the name:
class lucy;

class ricky {
    double straight;
public:
```

```
    ricky(double f = 0.0) { straight = f; }
    ricky(lucy);  // type conversion from lucy to ricky
};

class lucy {
    double whacky;
public:
    lucy(double f = 0.0) { whacky = f; }
    // a second way to convert lucy to ricky:
    operator ricky( ) { return ricky(wacky); }
};

void ethel(ricky) { }

main( ) {
    lucy L;
    ethel(L);  // which implicit type conversion is used?
}
```

The compiler should generate an error message. This type of problem is straightforward, since you get an error message the instant you try to create the second form of type conversion in the new class.

The second and a more insidious problem occurs when you can convert to more than one type from a single **class**. If an overloaded function can take more than one argument that has an automatic type conversion, you'll have trouble. Here's an example:

```
// AMBIG.CXX : Too much automatic type conversion
// causes ambiguity.

class ricky;
class lucy;

class fred {
    short bald;
public:
    fred(int i = 0) { bald = i; }
    operator ricky( );
```

```
    operator lucy( );
};

overload ethel;  // tells the translator it's OK there is more
                 // than one argument list for this function name
void ethel(ricky);
void ethel(lucy);

main( ) {
  fred F;
  ethel(F);  // should we make a ricky or a lucy from a fred?
}
```

The design problem here is that you don't see the difficulty right away. The class works fine until some poor unfortunate overloads a function to take arguments of both **ricky** and **lucy**. The problem is compounded because the user may not own the original code, and thus may have no control over the situation. If the designer of the class doesn't exercise restraint when creating implicit type conversions, the user can get stuck with the results. The only way to repair the problem is for the user to modify the header file—by commenting out the undesirable automatic type conversion the remaining conversion becomes unambiguous. Modifying the header file when you don't own the source code is risky and should only be undertaken after you know it won't damage the rest of the system.

Design Guidelines for Type Conversion

Murray[1] has suggested guidelines for type conversion:

■ *Don't create more than one implicit type conversion from each user-defined type unless you absolutely must.* This will eliminate the problem shown in the preceding listing. This doesn't mean you are limited to the number of types you can convert to. It just means that only one conversion should be allowed *implicitly*. Here's an example that shows multiple conversions, with only a single implicit conversion.

---

1 Murray, R.B., "Building Well-Behaved Type Relationships in C++," Usenix C++ Conference Proceedings, October 1988.

```
// MULTCONV.CXX : Multiple type conversions, but only a single
// implicit conversion.  This design of this class will prevent
// future problems.

class craig;
class charles;
class john;

class todd {
    long i;
public:
    todd(int x = 0) { i = x; }
    operator craig( );  // single implicit type conversion.
    // The rest of the conversion functions cannot be called
    // secretly by the compiler; they must be called explicitly
    // by the user:
    charles To_charles( );  // make a charles from a todd
    john To_john( );        // make a john from a todd
};
```

■ *A conversion operator should always take a more complex type and generate a simpler type.* If a type is a logical extension of another type, the conversion operator should take the extension and create the simpler type from it. Since extensions usually proliferate from simpler types, choosing to go from the simpler type to one particular extension may cause trouble if you want to treat all the extensions in a similar fashion in a later application. The following example shows the proper "direction" for conversion operators:

```
// SIMPLIFY.CXX : Conversion operators should always simplify
// more complex types.
#include <stdio.h>

class price {
    unsigned long base;      // in pennies
    unsigned long sales_tax;
public:
    void set_base(unsigned long b) { base = b;}
    void set_tax(unsigned long st) { sales_tax = st; }
    void print(char * msg = " ") {
```

```
        if(*msg) { printf("%s :\n", msg); }
        printf("price = $ %ld.%ld\n", base/100, base%100);
        printf("tax = $ %ld.%ld\n", sales_tax/100, sales_tax%100);
        printf("total = $ %ld.%ld\n", (base + sales_tax)/100,
                            (base + sales_tax)%100 );
    }
    unsigned long base_price( ) {return base;} // access functions
    unsigned long tax( ) {return sales_tax;}
};

class non_deductible {
    char * name;
    price cost;
public:
    non_deductible(char * nm, unsigned long p, unsigned long st) {
        name = nm; // OK if using a constant character string
        cost.set_base(p); // there's an easier design for this type
        cost.set_tax(st); // of programming. See Chapter 7.
    }
    void print( ) {
        printf("non_deductible, ");
        cost.print(name);
    }
    // Automatic type conversion from more complicated type to
    // simpler type:
    operator price( ) { return cost; }
};

class deductible {
    char * name;
    char * category;
    int percent_deductible;
    price cost;
public:
    deductible(char * nm, char * ct, unsigned long p,
            unsigned long st, int percent) {
        name = nm;
        category = ct;
        cost.set_base(p);
        cost.set_tax(st);
        percent_deductible = percent;
    }
```

```
    void print( ) {
       printf("deductible category %s, ", category);
       cost.print(name);
       printf("percent deductible: %d\n", percent_deductible);
    }
    // Automatic type conversion from more complicated type to
    // simpler type:
    operator price( ) { return cost; }
};

// And finally, a class to add up all the prices:
class price_total {
    unsigned long sum;
public:
    price_total( ) { sum = 0; }
    void print( ) {
       printf("total is: $ %ld.%ld\n", sum/100, sum%100);
    }
    void add(price p) {
       sum += p.base_price( );
       sum += p.tax( );
    }
};

main( ) {
    non_deductible Refrigerator("Refrigerator", 74595, 5623);
    deductible stamps("Stamps", "postage", 24000, 0, 100);
    deductible mag1("Byte", "publications", 2000, 0, 100);
    deductible mag2("Micro Cornucopia",
                    "publications", 1800, 0, 100);
    non_deductible Dinner("Food", 2253, 180);
    price_total total;
    total.print( );
    Refrigerator.print( );
    total.add(Refrigerator);
    total.print( );
    stamps.print( );
    total.add(stamps);
    total.print( );
    mag1.print( );
    total.add(mag1);
    total.print( );
```

```
mag2.print( );
total.add(mag2);
total.print( );
Dinner.print( );
total.add(Dinner);
total.print( );
}
```

In this listing, both the **non_deductible** and **deductible** classes have implicit type conversion operators to produce the simpler type **price**. **class price_total** has a method called **add( )** that takes as an argument a **price**. Because of the implicit type conversion operators, you can **add( )** both **deductible** and **non_deductible** objects without the necessity of overloading **add( )**. The **%ld** in the **printf( )** format string indicates that the number to be printed is a **long int**.

■ *It is acceptable to provide mutual conversions between two classes.* Not all classes are logical extensions. Murray gives the example that the numbers represented by **double** include all numbers in a class called **rational,** so mutual conversion between **double** and **rational** makes sense. A function overloaded to take either a **double** or a **rational** will match either argument exactly; if the function only takes one type of argument, the type conversion will be called automatically for the other type of argument. Thus there is no ambiguity with mutual conversions.

■ *Don't use implicit type conversion unless it's necessary.* If implicit type conversion is used arbitrarily, it can cause problems for future users of your class.

Example: Creating Your Own Stream Functions

One of the most immediately useful applications for overloading is the creation of stream output functions for your user-defined type. Then you can say

MyType X;

cout << X;

This works very nicely, especially when you are debugging.

The **operator<<( )** has already been overloaded for the streams **class**, but you can easily overload it for your new class. The following example is a vector of X-Y pairs with both a stream input function and a stream output function.

```
// XYVEC.HXX : Vector of x-y pairs with stream output function
#ifndef XYVEC_HXX
#define XYVEC_HXX

#include <stream.hxx>
const size = 20;

class XYvec {
    float X[size];
    float Y[size];
    void error(char * msg);
public:
    XYvec(float xinit = 0, float xstep = 0,
          float yinit = 0, float ystep = 0);
    // modify values by overloading the function call operator:
    void operator( )(int index, float xval, float yval);
    // Stream input and output:
    friend ostream& operator<<(ostream &s, XYvec& v);
    friend istream& operator>>(istream &s, XYvec& v);
};
#endif // XYVEC_HXX
```

You'll notice that the header file **xyvec.hxx** must include the **stream.hxx** header file because of the declarations for **operator<<( )** and **operator>>( )**. The **xinit** and **xstep** in the constructor are initialization and step values. The first element in the X vector is set to the initialization value, the second is set to the first value plus the step value, and so on. The same is true for **yinit** and **ystep** for the Y vector.

Here are the methods for **XYvec:**

```
// XYVEC.CXX : Methods for X-Y pair vector
#include "xyvec.hxx"
#include <stdlib.h>

void XYvec::error(char * msg) {
    cerr << "XYvec error: " << msg << "\n";
    exit(1);
}

XYvec::XYvec(float xinit, float xstep,
                float yinit,float ystep) {
    for(int i = 0; i < size; i++) {
        X[i] = xinit + i * xstep;
        Y[i] = yinit + i * ystep;
    }
}

void XYvec::operator( )(int index, float xval, float yval) {
    if(index < 0 || index >= size)
        error("index out of range");
    X[index] = xval;
    Y[index] = yval;
}

ostream& operator<<(ostream &s, XYvec& v) {
    s << "\t   X\t\t   Y\n";
    for(int i = 0; i < size; i++)
        s << form("\t%-6.6f\t%-6.6f\n", v.X[i], v.Y[i]);
    return s;
}

istream& operator>>(istream &s, XYvec& v) {
    float val;
    int index = 0;
    while(!s.bad( ) && !s.eof( )) {
        s >> val;
        v.X[index] = val;
        if(s.bad( ) || s.eof( )) break;
        s >> val;
        v.Y[index++] = val;
        if(index == size) break;
    }
    return s;
}
```

The function-call operator ( ) is overloaded to allow you to set the X-Y values of a particular pair. It is useful as the only operator that can take an arbitrary number of arguments.

Because of the design of streams, an overloaded **operator<<( )** or **operator>>( )** must be a **friend** function, and it must take as arguments a stream object (either **istream** or **ostream**, depending on the operator) followed by an object of your user-defined type. The function must return the same stream object it takes as an argument. It is important that the stream object be passed into and out of the function, so you can have expressions of the form, such as

cout << "arg1: " << arg1 << "arg2" << arg2; // ...

In effect, each argument is added to the stream, and then the stream is passed down the line.

Here is a small program to test **class XYvec**:

```
// XYTEST.CXX : Test program for class XYvec
#include "xyvec.hxx"

main( ) {
    XYvec A(3.14, 0.47, 2.59, .939);
    A(4, 77.77, 111.9); // change pair #4
    cout << "A =\n" << A; // print it
    XYvec B;
    cin >> B;
    cout << "B =\n" << B;
}
```

To test the input function, redirect the output to a file, edit the first two lines out of the file, then run the program and redirect the file as input.

Selecting Friend or Member Functions for Operator Overloading

In many situations you get equivalent results by using either a **friend** function or a member function when you overload an operator. A **friend** function simply contains an extra argument. The **friend** function must have *both* objects passed to it, while the member function needs only a single argument. Why are both alternatives available? If you use a member function and an argument of a different type, the member function only allows the new type to be on the right-hand side of the operator. That is, **A + 2** may be legal, but **2 + A** is not. A **friend** function allows both combinations. These variations are shown in the following example:

```
// FRIEND.CXX : Why everybody need friends

class integer {
    int i;
public:
    // Notice there's no constructor for an int, so no
    // implicit type conversion can happen.
    void set(int ii = 0) { i = ii; }
    // operator overloading with a member functions:
    integer operator+(int);
    integer operator+(integer);
};

integer integer::operator+(int x) {
    // tedious without a constructor:
    integer result;
    result.set(i + x);
    return result;
}

integer integer::operator+(integer x) {
    integer result;
    result.set(i + x.i);
    return result;
}

class integer2 {
    int i;
public:
    void set(int ii = 0) { i = ii; }
    // Operator overloading with a friend functions.  Note
    // you need a function for each possible combination:
    friend integer2 operator+(integer2, integer2);
    friend integer2 operator+(integer2, int);
```

```
        friend integer2 operator+(int, integer2);
};

integer2 operator+(integer2 x, integer2 y) {
    integer2 result;
    result.set(x.i + y.i);
    return result;
}

integer2 operator+(integer2 x, int a) {
    integer2 result;
    result.set(x.i + a);
    return result;
}

integer2 operator+(int a, integer2 x) {
    integer2 result;
    result.set(x.i + a);
    return result;
}

main( ) {
    integer A; A.set(10);
    integer B;
    integer C; C.set(20);
    B = A + 4;  // This is legal for class integer
    B = A + C;  // This is legal for class integer
//  B = 4 + A;  // This isn't legal for class integer
    integer2 D; D.set(100);
    integer2 E;
    integer2 F; F.set(200);
    E = D + 40;  // This is legal for class integer2
    E = D + F;  // This is legal for class integer2
    E = 40 + D;  // This is also legal for integer2
}
```

In **class integer,** there are two overloaded versions of **operator+( ):**
one which takes an **int** argument, and one which takes an **integer**
argument. This, as demonstrated in **main( )**, means that you can add an
integer to an **int,** and an **integer** to an **integer,** but you can't add an **int**
to an **integer**.

In **class integer2**, the **operator+( )** is defined as a **friend** function. This means that **integer2** allows the combination that **integer** wouldn't: an **int** plus an **integer2**. Thus, a **friend** function allows a more natural syntax.

In the preceding example, you can see how tedious it gets when you have to redefine the same function (**operator+(integer2, int)** and **operator+(int, integer2)**.) Implicit type conversion can eliminate *both* definitions, as shown in this example:

```
// SUCCINCT.CXX : Implicit type conversion can eliminate
// repetitive coding.

class integer3 {
    int i;
public:
    // By creating a constructor which takes an int, the
    // compiler can perform implicit type conversion...
    integer3(int ii = 0) { i = ii; }
    // ...so only one operator+( ) definition is required:
    friend integer3 operator+(integer3, integer3);
};

integer3 operator+(integer3 x, integer3 y) {
    return integer3(x.i + y.i);
}

main( ) {
    integer3 A(10), B(20), C;
    C = A + B;  // legal
    C = A + 4;  // also legal
    C = 4 + A;  // also legal
}
```

To summarize: use a member function for notational convenience if you have no other compelling needs. Also use a member function if you want to force a particular syntax. (Using a member function **operator=(int)** prevents the user from saying **1 = A**.) If your syntax requires that the arguments be order-independent, use a **friend** (and, possibly, an implicit type conversion operator to reduce coding).

Function Overloading

Operator overloading is only one example of the general idea of function overloading. Function overloading means you can create many different functions, all with the same name but with different argument lists. The most common type of function overloading is seen in class constructors—more than one constructor is usually required for a class to handle different types of initialization. Inside a class, function overloading happens automatically. The programmer doesn't need to do anything except define more than one function with the same name, for example:

```
// WIDGET.CXX : Member functions are automatically, safely
// overloaded.

class widget {
    int i;
public:
    widget( ) { i = 0; }
    widget(int j) { i = j; }
    widget(double d) { i = (int)d; }
};
```

Here we see the constructor for **widget** has been automatically overloaded.

Functions that aren't associated with a class (non-member functions) may also be overloaded, but the compiler must be specifically told that the name will be overloaded beforehand. In compilers that conform to AT&T release 1.2 and earlier, this is accomplished by using the **overload** keyword. Here's an example of its use:

```
// FROB.CXX : Non-member function overloading

overload frob; // get ready!
int frob(int); // overload declarations
double frob(int, int);
void frob( );
```

```
main ( ) {
        frob(1);
        frob(1,2);
        frob( );
}
```

In compilers that conform to AT&T release 2.0, the line

overload frob;

is unnecessary.

A compiler can differentiate one overloaded function call from another by the function arguments. However, the linker just sees a name, not an accompanying argument list, so the name of an overloaded function with one argument list must be different than the function with a different argument list. So the linker can differentiate between one type of overloaded function and another, the compiler "mangles" the names—it adds characters to the names. If you want to see how this works, you can use the fact that most implementations of C++ have some way to look at the names.

■ Some Unix C-code generators leave **.cc** files behind that contain the translated C source code; others require a flag to leave the file behind.

■ Using the **!c** flag with Glockenspiel C++ causes the **.c** file containing C source code to be left behind.

■ Zortech C++ is a native-code compiler, and doesn't generate intermediate C code. To look at names, you must compile the file with the **-g** flag, and then run the utility program **objtoasm** on the result (redirect the output of **objtoasm** into a file). The assembly-language output of **objtoasm** will contain the names. For the preceding example, it would be

ztc -g -c frob

objtoasm frob > frob.asm

When you look at the names for **frob.cxx**, you will see something like this, which was generated with Zortech C++:

_frob

_frobFI_I_

frobF

You can see how the function names have been mangled to provide unique names; the linker won't see any conflicts. Notice, however, that the *first* instance of **frob** wasn't mangled. Instead, it looks like a plain C function name—the name from the source code with a prefixed underscore. This was designed into AT&T C++ releases 1.2 and earlier so the C++ code could call plain C functions without problem. Non-overloaded functions are turned into plain C names. When a function is overloaded, the first name is turned into a plain C name and the rest are mangled.

This design can cause trouble if declarations ever get mixed around. If you have a plain C **frob** (in a separate C file) and two C++ **frob**s, it is very important which **frob** is declared first—it will always be turned into the plain C name. In the preceding example, **int frob(int)** is the plain C name, but if you have some other file and you declare **void frob( )** first, the linker will quietly cause the plain C **frob** to be called for **int frob(int)** calls in the first file, while calling it for **void frob( )** in the second file. As you can imagine, this can cause some pretty subtle bugs.

The real trouble occurs with header files. If you are overloading a function name that is declared in two separate header files and you switch the order of inclusion of the header files in various definition files, the name mangling will happen differently. This is a particular problem when you are overloading a library function like **sin( )** for a user-defined type. If the header containing *your* declaration comes first, then the C library **sin( )** function will be mangled, which isn't what you want at all.

AT&T release 2.0 solves the problem using an approach called *type-safe linkage*. Type-safe linkage mangles *all* names. It uses a consistent algorithm depending only on the arguments and return value, so it doesn't matter in what order the functions are declared. C++ 2.0 contains an escape mechanism to allow plain C naming. See Chapter 11 for more about release 2.0.

If you don't have access to C++ with type-safe linkage, you can solve part of the problem by prefixing the declaration of overloaded functions with the **overload** keyword for each declaration. This forces all the names to be mangled. It doesn't solve the problem of including a plain C header file containing a function name you've just overloaded, though. You'll still need to be careful about that until you get 2.0.

Makefile for Chapter Examples

Here is the **makefile** for all the examples in this chapter:

```
# makefile for examples in chapter 5
# Zortech:
CPP = ztc
# Glockenspiel:
#CPP = ccxx

.cxx.exe:
          $(CPP) $*.cxx

.cxx.obj:
          $(CPP) -c $*.cxx

all:    this.exe vectest.exe pointtst.exe casting.exe \
        constcnv.exe dualconv.exe multconv.obj simplify.exe \
        xytest.exe friend.exe succinct.exe widget.obj frob.obj

errors: ambig.exe

vectest.exe : vectest.obj vector.obj
          $(CPP) $**

pointtst.exe : pointtst.obj point.obj
          $(CPP) $**

xytest.exe : xytest.obj xyvec.obj
          $(CPP) $**


vectest.obj : vector.hxx vectest.cxx
vector.obj : vector.hxx vector.cxx
point.obj : point.cxx point.hxx
pointtst.obj : pointtst.cxx point.hxx
xyvec.obj : xyvec.cxx xyvec.hxx
xytest.obj : xytest.cxx xyvec.hxx
```

6 Creating Objects at Run Time

One of the most important ways human beings interact is through language. Not only does language enable people to interact, it shapes those interactions and even the thoughts behind them. If you understand the limitations of your language, you can understand some of the limitations in your thinking and creativity.

Many popular computer languages have built-in biases towards particular ways of thinking, design, and programming. Since these languages are often learned first, new programmers close down the scope of their creativity and think in terms of "the correct way." As a result, there are entire classes of problems they are unable to solve.

The bias that will be examined here can be broadly cast as the idea that "you always know all the facts when you write the program." As you will see in later chapters, this bias actually extends to program design ("you always know all the problems the program must solve when you design it"), but this chapter will focus on the way variables are treated in other languages, how that affects your programming, and the improvements in C++ that free the way you think about certain types of problems.

The Bias of Some Popular Languages

Many popular languages, such as Fortran, Pascal, and C, lean toward the idea that you always know how many variables you will need when the program is running, and when they will be created and destroyed (their scope). When you encounter a problem that relies on some other constraint to determine how many variables you need and when they will be created and destroyed, you either can't solve the problem or you solve it the hard way and end up with an inflexible design.

For instance, consider the game of Life. Life is a computer simulation that models the population patterns of a simple creature living on a two-dimensional grid. The rules for the creature's existence are very simple. If there are a certain number of creatures adjacent to an empty spot on the grid, a new creature is born. If a creature has too many neighbors, or too few neighbors, it dies. By changing the initial conditions and the rules, you can generate all sorts of fascinating patterns.

In the Life simulation, objects (creatures) are constantly appearing and disappearing. The quantity and lifetime of the objects are not dictated by some fixed design inside the computer program. Instead, they depend on the number of other objects around the object. This is an example of a *simulation problem*. Most simulation problems are much more complicated than Life. Although Life has been programmed in many languages, a "real" simulation problem is much more manageable when written in an object-oriented language.

As another example of a situation where you don't know the number or lifetime of variables, consider the MicroCAD program in Appendix A. Here, the number of shapes and how long the shapes remain on the screen is up to the user.

It is clear that the arbitrary restriction of having to know the quantity, point of creation, and lifetime of an object excludes a lot of interesting problems. The way you may have learned to think as a result of a particular programming language can prevent you from even conceiving of some very interesting solutions.

To be fair, C and Pascal *do* have a method to create space for variables at run time. (Fortran, however, has none.) This feature, dynamic memory allocation, allows the programmer to grab chunks of memory to be used as variables. As you will see, the support for creating variables at run time in C++ is much more complete; creating an object at run time is as easy as creating one at compile time.

Languages like LISP and Smalltalk took the opposite approach. In these languages, all variables are created dynamically. The lifetimes of these variables are not determined by normal scoping rules. Since variables are not destroyed based on their scope, they can proliferate to the point of filling up memory. When the memory is full, these languages run a *garbage-collection* routine to free the space occupied by unused variables.

Languages with garbage collectors free the programmer from concerns about the lifetime of a variable, which is good. They are limited, however, in the kinds of problems they can solve—you wouldn't want a critical real-time process interrupted because the system just happened to run out of memory at that point.

Dynamic Object Creation

C++ takes the middle ground between languages that support dynamic memory allocation and languages in which all variables are dynamically allocated. In this book, the C++ approach will be called *dynamic object creation*. While C++ supports objects with scoped lifetimes (*stack-based objects*), it also supports objects with arbitrary lifetimes (*heap-based objects*). C++ is different than Pascal or C because it doesn't just allocate memory for an object, it *initializes* the object. Thus, when you use dynamic object creation in C++, you get back a live, initialized object, not just a chunk of memory big enough to hold an object. (When you dynamically allocate a built-in type, however, no initialization is performed, so the term "dynamic memory allocation" will still be used when built-in types are involved).

Because C++ supports both objects with scoped lifetimes and objects with arbitrary lifetimes, you are forced to know more about what is going on in a program, and to choose between stack-based and heap-based objects. This language design decision is often considered repugnant to users of more "pure" object-oriented languages (ones that contain garbage collectors). As you will see, however, it gives you the choice of optimizing your program for speed and real-time applications if you want. If you don't need a garbage collector or if it would make your application unusable, you aren't automatically saddled with a garbage collector. If you want to create an application that works best with garbage collection, you can build a garbage collector. (Admittedly, however, this is no small task.)

The Stack

To understand dynamic object creation, you need some background. When you define an object at compile time by saying

```
void Fogg( ) {
  int obj = 100;
  // ...

}
```

the compiler generates code to create enough space on the stack for an **int** and to put the integer value 100 in that space. Whenever the variable **obj** is used, code is generated to find that slot on the stack.

This activity takes place anytime **Fogg( )** is called. Thus, the memory is always created when the function is called, regardless of where the stack pointer is at the time. Functions in C and C++ that only use local variables do not depend on the state of the program when the function is called. Because of this, such functions are said to be *reentrant*—you can call them anytime, even in the middle of a call to the same function.

C and C++ also support *recursive* functions. You can design a function that calls itself, for instance:

```
// DAVE.CXX : A recursive function
#include <stdio.h>

const stupid = 100;

void Dave(int pun) {
  if (pun != stupid)
    Dave(++pun);
  else
    printf("stop! %d puns is enough!\n", pun);
}

main( ) {
  Dave(0);
}
```

A more useful example is the recursive scanner shown in the TAWK example in Chapter 10.

When a scope closes (with a]), the compiler generates code to move the stack pointer up past all the local variables that have been created. Thus, when a local variable goes out of scope, the memory for it is automatically freed. In C++, the destructor is called (if one exists) before the stack pointer is moved. C++ does more than just free the space occupied by the variable, it de-initializes the variable.

The Free Store

You can think of the stack pointer as moving down from the top of the memory available for use by the program (although the actual direction depends on your implementation). When a function is called that has local variables, the stack pointer moves down. (Actually, the return address is also stored on the stack when a call is executed, so the pointer always moves down for a function call.)

At the "other end" of the memory set aside for your program is the *free store,* also called the *heap.* When you request a chunk of memory, it comes from the free store, and when you release a chunk of memory it returns to the free store.

In ANSI C, the library functions **malloc( )**, **calloc( )**, and **realloc( )** are used to allocate free store, and **free( )** is used to release the allocated memory back to the free store. In Pascal, the predefined subprograms **new( )** and **dispose( )** manage the free store. In C++ the concept of dynamic memory allocation has been extended and built into the core of the language. Not only do the C++ keywords **new** and **delete** allocate and deallocate free store, **new** also calls the constructor and **delete** calls the destructor. Thus, calling **new** is almost exactly like creating a local variable, and calling **delete** is almost exactly the same as when the local variable goes out of scope. This is the reason the term "dynamic object creation" was chosen rather than "dynamic memory allocation." A lot more is going on than just memory allocation.

You may have noticed the phrase "almost exactly" in the above paragraph. Where is the difference? **new** and **delete** handle pointers, rather than the objects themselves. **new** returns a pointer to the initialized object, and **delete** takes a pointer to an object previously created on the free store using **new**. Except that you are manipulating an address instead of an entire object, you can treat objects created on the free store just as if they were local variables. Here's a simple example comparing a local object to one created on the free store. The example uses a class called **tracker**, which shows you when constructors and destructors are called.

```
// TRACKER.HXX : A class to track construction & destruction
#ifndef TRACKER_HXX
#define TRACKER_HXX
#include <stdio.h>

class tracker {
    int i;
public:
    tracker(int x = 0) {
        printf("constructor called with argument %d\n", x);
        i = x;
    }
    ~tracker( ) {
        printf("destructor called for object w/ i = %d\n", i);
    }
    void print( ) { printf("tracker::print( ); i = %d\n", i); }
};
#endif // TRACKER_HXX
```

Now you can create objects either on the stack (as local variables) or on the free store.

```
// FREESTOR.CXX : Local objects vs. dynamic object creation
#include "tracker.hxx"

void Toni( ) {
    tracker local(10);  // create a local object
    tracker * free = new tracker(20); // free store object
    local.print( ); // calling a member function for a variable
    free->print( ); // calling a member function for a pointer
}

main( ) {
    Toni( );
}

// Notice the destructor is called only once, for the local
// object!  The pointer "free" goes out of scope, but the
// object it points to is still valid!
```

It is very important to notice that the destructor is only called for the stack-based object, as it goes out of scope. Remember that *you* are responsible for destroying any objects you create on the free store. If you don't destroy them, the pointer may go out of scope (as the preceding example shows, when **Toni( )** ends) but the object hangs around on the free store. This is the worst situation—the object is there, but you can't get to it since the pointer has gone out of scope, so you can't destroy it. It's important that you destroy an object before you lose track of it, like this:

```
// DELETE.CXX : How to destroy an object on the free store
#include "tracker.hxx"

void JayP( ) {
   tracker * free = new tracker(20);
   free->print( ); // calling a member function for a pointer
   delete free; // delete must be handed the starting address
             // of the object created by "new."
}

main( ) {
   JayP( );
}
```

Life: A Framework for Simulation and Modeling

Many systems that simulate or model real-world processes require that information units representing elements of the process be created and destroyed at run time. The creation and destruction of these units is governed by some criterion that relates directly to the process, rather than scopes in the source code. Dynamic object creation in C++ is ideal for solving these kinds of problems.

This section presents a version of the famous Life program, but with a new twist. Because it is designed and implemented in an object-oriented manner, it is very easy for you to change the rules for the simulation. For instance, you might want to endow each element (called a **LifeUnit** in the program) with a life span, so a **LifeUnit** that is too young or too old cannot bear children. You could allow a **LifeUnit** to be mobile, or groups of **LifeUnit**s to band together into tribes. Because the main system simply asks a **LifeUnit** if it will live to the next generation, the "rule" for Life is focused in one place and can easily be changed. You can also add new kinds of rules: whether a **LifeUnit** will move, catch bubonic plague, win a million dollars, get married, buy a dog, and so on. The rules can be tested at various times in the life span ("**LifeUnit** fails driver's license test"), or for various other reasons ("**LifeUnit** overfeeds goldfish, **LifeUnit** flushes goldfish and buys hamster"). Because of the object-oriented nature of the design, you aren't limited when you want to extend the simulation.

There is nothing particularly sacred or inspired about the way this program was designed. It is an approach that seems to work, but it may have some limitations for the particular type of system you want to model. For instance, your idea of a **LifeUnit** may be much broader; you might want to model other animals as well as man, and limit their activities according to what type of animal they are ("a dog cannot buy a newspaper"). For this kind of problem you will want to use inheritance and **virtual** functions (see Chapters 7 and 8), so both people and dogs will be inherited from **LifeUnit** and will have some things in common but other abilities will be different. While you may need to change the design to fit your problem, you will benefit by studying it.

To maximize portability between systems, the program uses the ANSI terminal escape sequences to move the cursor. And, although this works, it slows the display. You may want to customize the display code (isolated in the **LifeUnit** functions **draw( )** and **erase( )**) to use whatever high-speed library functions your local platform provides.

NOTE Another approach to screen management in this book would have been to use a class to represent the screen. This way, reusable code could have been created, non-portable features could have been isolated, and the code would be easier to port. Unfortunately, you would have had to learn about classes before you learned about the basics of C and C++ programming—it's a "chicken-or-the-egg" type of problem.

While reading the code, you will notice that the variable names are different than you've seen so far in this book. For this example, the Smalltalk naming convention is used. Smalltalk variable names do not include underscores, so Smalltalk programmers often simply run the words together, capitalizing the first letter in each word.

A CLASS TO REPRESENT A SINGLE LIVING ENTITY   There are two classes in the Life program. The **LifeUnit** class represents an individual entity, and the **LifeField** is a two-dimensional array where all the **Life-Unit**s live. Each **LifeUnit** knows the **LifeField** where it lives and its location in the field, so if you ask a **LifeUnit** whether it will live into the next generation, it can look around to see how many neighbors it will have. A **LifeUnit** can **draw( )** and **erase( )** itself, and you can ask it if it will be **Alive( )** in the next generation.

The header file for the **LifeUnit** class also declares a non-member function **Fertile( )**, which is used with the address of an empty cell to see if a new **LifeUnit** will appear in the next generation.

```
// LIFEUNIT.HXX : an object for the "life" simulation
#ifndef LIFEUNIT_HXX
#define LIFEUNIT_HXX
#include <stdio.h>

// Character to indicate a LifeUnit is alive:
const char LifeChar = 'X';
// A happy face on the PC:
// const char LifeChar = '\x01';

class LifeField;  // forward declaration

class LifeUnit {
    // A LifeUnit knows what grid it lives on, and its location:
    LifeField * LF;
    int LRow, LCol;  // location of unit on screen
public:
    void draw( ) {
        // ANSI Terminal control Commands to put special character
        // at the coordinates.  An '\x1b' in a string produces an
        // "escape."  The \x precedes a hexidecimal number.
        printf("\x1b[%d;%dH%c", LRow, LCol, LifeChar);
    }
    void erase( ) {
        // Put a space where the X was:
        printf("\x1b[%d;%dH ", LRow, LCol);
    }
    LifeUnit(int Row_loc, int Col_loc, LifeField * L) {
        LRow = Row_loc; LCol = Col_loc;
        LF = L;  // Remember what grid you live on!
        draw( );
    }
    // Clean things up before the object goes away:
    ~LifeUnit( ) { erase( ); }
    // See if all the conditions are fullfilled so you can live
    // through the next lifecycle.
    int Alive( );  // returns 1 if alive, 0 if dead
};
```

```
// returns 1 if pregnant:
int Fertile(int Row, int Col, LifeField & LF);
// Helper function for Alive( ) and Fertile( ):
int NeighborAlive(int nr, int nc, LifeField & LF);

#endif // LIFEUNIT_HXX
```

The methods for **LifeUnit** include the rules for life. In this case, **Alive( )** and **Fertile( )** simply check to see how many neighbors the **LifeUnit** has, but you can easily add a more complicated algorithm. Also, if you want (for instance) to make the **LifeUnit** infertile during certain periods of life, you can easily add another state variable in the private data, and change the **draw( )** function so it prints different characters depending on the state of the variable.

```
// LIFEUNIT.CXX : The Rules for life.  Each LifeUnit figures
// out whether it survives into the next generation.
#include "lifefld.hxx"

const MinimumNeighbors = 2;
const MaximumNeighbors = 3;
const MinimumParents = 3;
const MaximumParents = 3;

// Checks to see if the specified cell is currently occupied
int NeighborAlive(int nr, int nc, LifeField & LF) {
    if( LF.InRange(nr, nc) ) {
        if ( LF(nr, nc) ) // if non-NULL pointer
            return 1;
        else
            return 0;
    }
    return 0;
}

// Counts the number of units surrounding R, C:
int SurroundingUnits(int R, int C, LifeField &LF) {
    return
        NeighborAlive(R -1, C, LF) +
        NeighborAlive(R +1, C, LF) +
        NeighborAlive(R, C + 1, LF) +
        NeighborAlive(R, C - 1, LF) +
```

```
      NeighborAlive(R -1, C - 1, LF) +
      NeighborAlive(R +1, C - 1, LF) +
      NeighborAlive(R -1, C + 1, LF) +
      NeighborAlive(R +1, C + 1, LF);
}


// Modify the following two functions to create more complicated
// rules for the simulation.

// Alive( ) determines whether the LifeUnit stays alive into the
// next generation by checking all around to see how many other
// units are alive.
int LifeUnit::Alive( ) {
    int Neighbors = SurroundingUnits(LRow, LCol, *LF);
    if( Neighbors >= MinimumNeighbors &&
        Neighbors <= MaximumNeighbors)
       return 1; // alive
    return 0; // died of loneliness or overpopulation
}


// Fertile( ) determines if the conditions are right (presumably
// in an empty cell) for new life.  It happens to use the same
// rules as Alive( ), but that can easily be changed.
int Fertile(int Row, int Col, LifeField & LF) {
    int Neighbors = SurroundingUnits(Row, Col, LF);
    if( Neighbors >= MinimumParents &&
        Neighbors <= MaximumParents)
       return 1; // Pregnant
    return 0; // too few parents, or overcrowding
}
```

A FIELD WHERE LIFEUNITS LIVE **LifeField** is simply a two-dimensional array the size of an ANSI terminal that holds pointers to **LifeUnit**s. If an array element is NULL, it contains no element. If it is non-NULL, there is a living **LifeUnit** associated with that space.

Generally, the next state of a simulation depends on the current state and some number of previous states. In this example, the next state only depends on the current state, but you can change that simply by increasing the constant **history**. This value establishes the number of states by creating an array for each count of **history**. In this example, **history** is 2—one array for the current state and one for the next state. Every time the system is stepped forward, the current state is examined and the next state is created. If **history** is 3, you would create the next state based on the current state and the previous state.

Since the matrices are constantly being recycled, you must make sure you are indexing the proper state. This can be done by thinking of the matrices as being wrapped around into a loop, and using the modulus operator (%) to generate the index. To calculate the index of the next state, you say

int NextField = (CurrentField + 1) % history;

This makes **NextField** count 0, 1, 2, ..., **history** - 1. To calculate the index of the **n** previous states, you say

(CurrentField + history - n) % history;

Here is the header file for **LifeField**:

```
// LIFEFLD.HXX : A class to hold a field of LifeUnits
#ifndef LIFEFLD_HXX
#define LIFEFLD_HXX
#include "lifeunit.hxx"
#include <stdlib.h>

// This simple simulation assumes a standard ANSI terminal
// Must have a buffer around field
const rowmin = 1;
const rows = 25;
const rowmax = rows - 2;
const colmin = 1;
const cols = 80;
const colmax = cols - 2;
// You can have any amount of history in your simulation.
// This example just looks back one space:
const history = 2;

class LifeField {
    LifeUnit * Field[history][rows][cols];
    // The system cycles through arrays.  The current time
    // step is given by the following variable:
    int CurrentField; // to select Field[0], Field[1], etc.
    void error(char * msg1 = " ", char * msg2 = " ") {
```

```
            fprintf(stderr,"LifeField error: %s %s\n", msg1, msg2);
            exit(1);
        }
        void RangeTest(int r, int c, char * msg = " ") {
            if ( r <= rowmin || r >= rowmax )
                error(msg, "rows out of range");
            if ( c <= colmin || c >= colmax )
                error(msg, "cols out of range");
        }
public:
    LifeField( ); // initialize all pointers to zero
    // select a pointer (null pointer means there is no
    // LifeUnit in that location).  For more sophisticated
    // simulations, you can use the pointer to interrogate
    // the LifeUnit at that location.
    const LifeUnit * operator( ) (int r, int c) {
        RangeTest(r, c, "operator( )");
        return Field[CurrentField][r][c];
    }
    // Add a new LifeUnit to the field:
    void birth(int r, int c, LifeUnit *lu) {
        RangeTest(r, c, "birth( )");
        Field[CurrentField][r][c] = lu;
    }
    // Remove a LifeUnit from the field:
    void death(int r, int c) {
        RangeTest(r, c, "death( )");
        Field[CurrentField][r][c] = NULL;
    }
    // returns 0 if out of range, 1 otherwise:
    int InRange(int r, int c);
    void Randomize(int factor);  // randomly put down LifeUnits
    // The higher the factor, the sparser the randomization
    int NextGeneration( ); // returns nonzero if LifeUnits remain
};
#endif // LIFEFLD_HXX
```

In the methods for **LifeField**, the function **Randomize( )** uses the ANSI C library functions for random number generation to initialize the **LifeField** with a random pattern of **LifeUnit**s. The random number functions are **srand( )** to "seed" the random number generator, and **rand( )** to generate a random number.

This is a "pseudo-random" number generator. It takes the seed, and performs a calculation with it to generate a series of numbers that approximates randomness. However, if you give it the same seed every time, you will get the same series of numbers. True random number generators use some sort of random physical process to generate numbers. The only "physical process" you have access to in the ANSI C library is time. Although time itself isn't a particularly random process the time you start the program can be thought of as random. Thus, by seeding the random number generator with a number created from the current time, you get a different pattern every time. The ANSI C library function **time( )** fills its argument with a value representing the current time. (Chapter 10 has an example that converts this value to something readable.) This argument is used to seed **srand( )**.

The argument to **Randomize( )** is an integer that determines how sparsely the **LifeUnit**s will be distributed. **rand( )** returns a value from zero to **RAND_MAX** (**RAND_MAX** is defined in the **stdlib.h** header file). **RAND_MAX** is divided by the argument to **Randomize( )** to create a value called **cutoff**. The value returned by **rand( )** is divided by **cutoff** in an *integer* divide, so if the result of **rand( )** is less than **cutoff**, the divide produces zero (false) and if it greater than **cutoff** the divide produces a non-zero value (true). The result of the integer division is used in an **if** statement to determine whether to create a new **LifeUnit**.

To dynamically create a new **LifeUnit**, you simply say **new**, call the constructor with the appropriate arguments, and stash the address returned by **new** somewhere so you don't lose it.

```
// LIFEFLD.CXX : Methods for LifeField
#include "lifefld.hxx"
#include <time.h>  // to seed the random number generator

int LifeField::InRange(int r, int c) {
  if ( r <= rowmin || r >= rowmax )
    return 0;
  if ( c <= colmin || c >= colmax )
    return 0;
  return 1;
}

LifeField::LifeField( ) {
  // ANSI Clear Screen, Home Cursor:
  printf("\x1b[2J");  // <ESC>[2J
```

```
    // Initialize everything to zero:
    for (int fld = 0; fld < history; fld++) {
        for(int i = 0; i < rows; i++) {
            for(int j = 0; j < cols; j++)
                Field[fld][i][j] = NULL;
        }
    }
    CurrentField = 0;
}

void LifeField::Randomize(int factor) {
    // This is used to turn the random number into zero or 1.
    // Increase the divisor for a sparser randomization:
    const cutoff = RAND_MAX / factor;
    // Seed the random number generator using the current time:
    time_t tnow;
    time(&tnow);
    srand(tnow);

    for(int r = rowmin; r < rowmax; r++) {
        for(int c = colmin; c < colmax; c++)
            if ( !(rand( ) / cutoff) ) { // integer divide
                Field[CurrentField][r][c] = new LifeUnit(r,c, this);
                if (Field[CurrentField][r][c] == 0) {
                    fprintf(stderr,"new failed in randomize( )");
                    exit(1);
                }
            }
    }
}

int LifeField::NextGeneration( ) {
    int StillAlive = 0;
    int Change = 0;  // indicates change in the state
    // this calculation makes it count 0, 1, ... history-1
    int NextField = (CurrentField + 1) % history;
    for(int r = rowmin; r < rowmax; r++) {
        for(int c = colmin; c < colmax; c++) {
            // If one is there, and it's alive, copy it:
            if (Field[CurrentField][r][c]) {
                if (Field[CurrentField][r][c]- >Alive( )) {
                    Field[NextField][r][c] = Field[CurrentField][r][c];
                    StillAlive++;
```

```
        }
      else {
        delete Field[CurrentField][r][c];
        // (The destructor erases the character).
        Field[CurrentField][r][c] = NULL;
        Change++;
      }
    } else {  // one isn't currently there.
      // See if the space is ripe for new life:
      if (Fertile(r,c, *this)) {
        Field[NextField][r][c] = new LifeUnit(r,c, this);
        // A Birth!
        StillAlive++;
      }
    }
    }
  }
  }
  CurrentField = NextField;  // step forward in time
  if (!Change) return 0;
  return StillAlive;
}
```

The algorithm used here is pretty stupid, since it just marches through all the empty areas calculating the possibility of a birth in each one. A smarter algorithm would do its work in "live" areas and ignore ones that were all empty. You can improve the algorithm, but this usually requires the program to have a structure based on some special knowledge about the algorithm. This reduces the general-purpose nature of the design.

The function **NextGeneration( )** returns a zero when no changes are taking place. You can use this return value so you can quit when the number of changes drops below a certain value, or remains below a certain value for a set number of generations.

RUNNING THE SIMULATION   Here is the program that runs the simulation. It creates a **LifeField** and initializes it by calling **Randomize( )** with an integer argument from the command line. As long as the pattern continues to change, **NextGeneration( )** is called. Use CTRL-C to end the simulation. Note: There is a stack overflow problem with this project.

```
// LIFE.CXX : test the Life Simulation
#include "lifefld.hxx"
main(int argc, char * argv[ ]) {
   if( argc < 2 ) {

      fprintf(stderr, "usage: life integer\n"
         "The higher the integer, the sparser the life field");
      exit(0);
   }
   int factor = atoi(argv[1]);
   LifeField Simulation;
   Simulation.Randomize(factor);
   while(Simulation.NextGeneration( ))
      ;
}
```

LIFE EXTENSION   Here are some ideas for enhancements to the simulation system:

■ Expand it to use inheritance and **virtual** functions (Chapters 7 and 8) so you have many different kinds of **LifeUnit**s with different types of interactions. Many video arcade games are just elaborate simulations.

■ Give the **LifeUnit class** the ability to move around in a **LifeField**.

■ Add features to the **LifeField**, such as walls and rooms. A **LifeUnit** would interact with a **LifeField** feature differently than with another **LifeUnit**.

■ Often, you want to run a simulation to a certain point, then dump the data for analysis, and later restart the simulation from the same point. Create two member functions for **LifeUnit** called **read( )** and **write( )** that read the private data for a **LifeUnit** from an open file (the file or **istream** pointer is passed as an argument) and write the contents of a **LifeUnit** to an open file. Create functions for **LifeField** called **read( )** and **write( )** that open a file and read or write a field full of **LifeUnit** data points.

Arbitrarily Sized Objects

Let's review what you know so far about dynamic memory allocation.

■ Objects can be created dynamically when you don't know how many objects you will need until run time.

■ Objects can be created dynamically when you don't know what the lifetime of the object will be.

There is a third reason you may need to use dynamic memory allocation:

■ The constructor for an object can use dynamic memory allocation when you don't know how much memory the object will need until run time.

Examples of arbitrarily sized objects abound, once you start looking for them, for instance:

■ In the **matrix** class (see Appendix B) you generally don't know how many elements you need to store until the user creates the **matrix**, or tells the constructor what file the **matrix** data is in.

■ The whole idea of a linked list is that it can expand and contract to hold any number of objects.

■ The **window** class in Appendix C allocates memory to hold the patch of screen the window covers up (so it can be restored when the window is destroyed); the amount of memory allocated depends on the size of the window.

A Dynamically Sized Array

As an example of an arbitrarily sized object, this section presents a dynamically sized array object. A **DynArray** holds an array of pointers to objects; these are **void** pointers so they can point to any type of object (something outside of the **DynArray** is responsible for keeping track of what kind of objects are stored in the array, and casting them appropriately when they are dereferenced).

A **DynArray** can hold any number of pointers, and you don't have to keep track of the current size of the array. Simply call the **add( )** function with the pointer you want to add as an argument. The **DynArray** will make new space if it needs it, and you don't have to know when or how. In a sense, a **DynArray** is like an infinitely expandable bag. Because it can hold an arbitrary number of elements, it provides the same functionality as a linked list.

A **DynArray** gives you a few improvements over a linked list. While you can move to the top of a **DynArray** and hunt through it by moving to the **next( )** element as you would with a linked list, you can also select elements directly using the bracket operator and an index. The **add( )** function returns the index of the element you just added. You can also find out the index by calling **index( )**, which returns the index value of the current element.

DynArray keeps track of where it is in the array with a private integer **cursor**, and keeps track of the current size with **size**. The array where the data is stored is represented by a single pointer to a pointer—**void ** array**. Since a pointer can be used as if it were an array name, once memory is allocated for **array** you can think of it as **void * array[size]**. When memory is allocated, the **new** operator must be told what kind of objects it is creating (**void ***), and, in the case of an array, how big they are.

array = new void*[size];

Here is the header file for **DynArray**:

```
// DYNARRAY.HXX : Dynamically sized array of object pointers
#ifndef DYNARRAY_HXX
#define DYNARRAY_HXX

// how much to increase the array when it runs out of space:
const chunk = 10;

class DynArray {
    void ** array;  // starting address of array of void pointers
    int size;  // current size of the array
    int cursor;  // to index through the array
    void error(char * msg = " ");
public:
    DynArray( );
```

```
~DynArray( );
int add(void *); // stash an element in the array,
// increasing the size if necessary. Returns the index.
// Both remove( ) functions return 1 if successful:
int remove(void *); // remove an element by pointer
int remove(int); // remove an element using its index
// reset the cursor to the first nonzero element at the
// top of the array:
void reset( );
void * next( ); // return the pointer to the next element
                 // (empty elements are skipped). Returns NULL
                 // at end of array.
int index( ) { return cursor; } // index of current element
// return the pointer to the current element:
void * current( ) { return array[cursor]; }
void * operator[ ](int); // element selection
int count( ); // number of "live" items in the array
};

#endif // DYNARRAY_HXX
```

When an **array** element is initialized or cleared, you will see the value 0 cast to a **void** pointer—**(void *)0**. You could also use **NULL**, but this makes it explicit to the reader that you are dealing with a pointer, and not an integer.

The **add( )** function starts at the top of the list and looks for the first empty **array( )** space (this automatically recycles spaces when elements are removed). If it finds one, it places the user's **void** pointer in the space and returns the index number of that space. If, however, it reaches the end of **array** before it finds a space, it must extend the array.

The **array** is extended in increments of **chunk**, a constant that can be changed to optimize efficiency. To extend **array**, a temporary vector **temp** is allocated that is the current **size** plus an additional **chunk**. The old elements are copied into **temp**, the additional **chunk** is initialized to **(void *)** and the argument to **add( )** is inserted at the beginning of the additional **chunk**.

In this scheme, space is never removed from a **DynArray**. Generally, a **DynArray** will expand to whatever size you need and stay there (since it recycles its **array** elements). This is appropriate for most situations, but if you have an application where a **DynArray** needs to shrink, you can create a function that condenses all the empty spaces out of the array, copies it to a smaller piece of memory, and **delete**s the larger piece of memory. This function, unfortunately, will mix up all the index values.

The algorithm of searching down the array for the first empty space works fine for small arrays, but if you have a large array with very few empty spaces it becomes inefficient. In this situation you may want to add a second **private** array that contains the index numbers of empty spaces in the first.

The **next( )** function moves the **cursor** to the next non-empty element of **array** and returns the pointer there. If the end of the **DynArray** is reached, it returns **(void *)0**. You can get the address at the current **cursor** location with the **current( )** function, or the index of the location with the **index( )** function. Elements may be removed using the overloaded **remove( )** function and either the index or the pointer to be removed.

The **reset( )** function moves the **cursor** not just to the top of the array, but to the first non-zero element of the array. This way, you will always have a valid pointer available via **current( )** after **reset( )**.

Here are the methods for **DynArray**:

```
// DYNARRAY.CXX : The advantages of an array, with the
// dynamic flexibility of a linked list.
#include "dynarray.hxx"
#include <stream.hxx>
#include <stdlib.h>  // exit( )

void DynArray::error(char * msg) {
  cerr << "DynArray error: " << msg << "\n";
  exit(1);
}

DynArray::DynArray( ) {
  array = new void*[chunk];  // allocate a chunk of void *'s
  for(int i = 0; i < chunk; i++)
    array[i] = (void *)0;  // zero them
  size = chunk;
  cursor = 0;
}

// The destructor frees the dynamically allocated memory:
DynArray::~DynArray( ) {
  delete array;
}
```

```
int DynArray::add(void * new_element) {
  // Put it in the first empty space available:
  for(int i = 0; i < size; i++)
    if(array[i] == (void *)0) {

        array[i] = new_element;
        return i;
    }
  // at this point, no space was found.  Add new space:
  int tempsize = size + chunk;  // increase space by chunk
  void ** temp = new void*[tempsize];
  // copy the old array over:
  for(i = 0; i < size; i++)
    temp[i] = array[i];
  // initialize the rest of the new array elements:
  for( ; i < tempsize; i++)
    temp[i] = (void *)0;
  temp[i = size] = new_element;  // put at start of empty space
  delete array;  // free old memory
  array = temp;
  size = tempsize;
  return i;
}

int DynArray::remove(void * rp) {
  for(int i = 0; i < size; i++)
    if( array[i] == rp ) {
        array[i] = (void *)0;
        return 1;
    }
  return 0; // not found
}

int DynArray::remove(int ri) {
  if( ri < 0 || ri >= size)
    error("remove index out of range");
  // check to see if there's an element at that slot:
  if( array[ri] ) {
    array[ri] = (void *)0;
    return 1;
  }
  return 0; // not found
}
```

```
void DynArray::reset( ) {
   cursor = 0;
   while( (array[cursor] == (void *)0) && (cursor < size - 1)
      cursor++;  // find the first nonzero element
}

void * DynArray::next( ) {
   if( cursor == size -1 ) // last element, no next.
      return (void *)0;
   // Not at the end. Increment until you find a non-empty slot
   // or the end:
   while(array[++cursor] == (void *)0)
      if ( cursor == size -1 )  // no more elements in list
         return (void *)0;
   return array[cursor];
}

void * DynArray::operator[ ](int x) {
   if(x < 0 || x >= size)
      error("operator[ ] — index out of range");
   return array[x];  // even if it's empty...
}

int DynArray::count( ) {
   int cnt = 0;
   for(int x=0; x < size; x++)
      if(array[x])
         cnt++;
   return cnt;
}
```

To test **DynArray**, a simple class to hold a character string called **string** is created. It relies on getting a pointer to a statically initialized character string, for simplicity. The **string** class overloads the stream output **operator<<( )** for simple output.

In class **string**, you will see that **operator void*( )** has been defined. This reduces a great deal of typing, since all the calls to **DynArray::add( )** in **main( )** would otherwise have to look like this:

da.add((void *)string(" This is a "));

Since the compiler has a way to take a **string** object and produce a **void** pointer, you can say

da.add(string(" This is a "));

The test program creates a lot of strings (more than a single **chunk**, so the dynamic sizing can be tested) and puts them into the **DynArray da**. The entire array is printed, then a **string** containing the word "OOPS" is removed from **cp**, and the array is printed again.

To remove the **string** containing "OOPS," the ANSI C library function **strstr( )** is used to search for the pattern. **strstr( )** takes two arguments: a **char** pointer to the string to be searched and a **char** pointer to the pattern to search for. As mentioned in Chapter 4, the quoted string "OOPS" produces the starting address of the NULL-terminated ASCII character string that has been created statically and stashed in memory somewhere. To generate the address of the string to be searched, the **string class** has a member function **cp** that returns the address of the internal string.

Notice that whenever a pointer from **da** is produced, it must always be cast to a **string *** before it is used, otherwise you will get an error message for attempting to dereference a **void** pointer.

Here is the test program for **DynArray**:

```
// DYNATEST.CXX : test program for dynarray.
#include "dynarray.hxx"
#include <stream.hxx>
#include <string.h>
#include <stdlib.h>

// Very simple class to save a string and print
// it with streams:
class string {
    char * str;
public:
    string(char * msg = " ") { str = msg; }
    // create an automatic type conversion operator
    // so you don't have to cast string objects to
    // void pointer objects every time you want to
    // add them to a DynArray:
```

```
    operator void*( ) { return (void *)this; }
    char * cp( ) { return str; }
    friend ostream& operator<<(ostream &s, string * sp) {
        s << sp->str;
        return s;
    }
};

main( ) {
    DynArray da;
    da.add(string("This is a ")); da.add(string("test of the "));
    da.add(string("dynamic array ")); da.add(string("class "));
    da.add(string("to \n")); da.add(string("(OOPS! A Mistake) "));
    da.add(string("see ")); da.add(string("if "));
    da.add(string("it ")); da.add(string("will "));
    da.add(string("automatically make "));
    da.add(string("itself bigger "));
    da.add(string("when it \n")); da.add(string("runs out of "));
    da.add(string("room."));
    // First, print the whole list:
    da.reset( );
    do
        cout << (string *)da.current( );
    while( da.next( ) );
    cout << "\n\n";
    // Now, find the element with the "OOPS":
    da.reset( );
    while( strstr(((string *)da.current( ))- >cp( ), "OOPS") == 0 )
        if(da.next( ) == 0) {
            cerr << "OOPS not found\n";
            exit(1);
        }
    int rm = da.index( ); // number of element to remove
    cout << "removing " << (string *)da[rm] << "\n";
    if (da.remove(rm))
        cout << "removed successfully!\n";
    // Print the whole list again:
    da.reset( );
    do
        cout << (string *)da.current( );
    while( da.next( ) );
}
```

Duplicating Space for Strings

The **string class** in the DYNATEST program relies on being initialized with the address of a character string constant. Other programs in this book so far have also made that assumption. What if you want to handle the more general case of *any* type of **char** *? In particular, what if you want to make a string object from a local array? You don't want to point to an array that someone else can also change, or that can go out of scope and become invalid.

The solution to this problem is to allocate memory on the free store and copy the string into this private data area. Then you will have two separate copies of the data, and it is unimportant what happens to the data outside the class.

This is another situation when you don't know until run time how big an object will be. When you allocate memory on the free store, you must create enough for the whole string. Fortunately, the ANSI C library provides a package of string-handling functions to make this easy, including **strlen( )**, which returns the size of the string (not including the terminating NULL; you must add 1 to provide space for it), and **strcpy( )**, which copies the contents of its second argument into the contents of the first argument (both arguments are character pointers) *including* the NULL terminator.

The modified, general purpose **string class** looks like this:

```
// STRING.CXX : String class that handles any type of
// character pointer argument (static or automatic data)

#include <stream.hxx>
#include <string.h>

// Very simple class to save a string and print
// it with streams:
class string {
   char * str;
public:
   string(char * msg = " ") {
      // duplicate the message as private data:
      str = new char[strlen(msg) + 1];
      strcpy(str, msg);
   }
   operator void*( ) { return (void *)this; }
```

```
    char * cp( ) { return str; }
    friend ostream& operator<<(ostream &s, string & sp) {
        s << sp.str;
        return s;
    }
};


main( ) {
    char * msg1 = "This is msg1";
    string S(msg1);
    cout << "original msg1: " << msg1 << "\n";
    cout << "original S: " << S << "\n";
    msg1[0] = 'X';  // NOTE: modifying a string constant
    msg1[1] = 'X';  // is NOT portable.
    msg1[2] = 'X';
    cout << "msg1 after modification: " << msg1 << "\n";
    cout << "S after msg1 was modified: " << S << "\n";
}
```

The statement

str = new char[strlen(msg) + 1];

creates a character array on the free store. The size of the array is the length of the string **msg**, plus 1 for the terminating NULL. The pointer **str** holds the address of the character array. The contents of **msg** and the terminating NULL are copied into the newly allocated memory with the statement

strcpy(str, msg);

You can also allocate a single instance of a built-in type (as well as an array of built-in types, as shown previously). For instance, this creates a dynamically allocated **double**:

double * dp = new double;

ENCRYPTION EXAMPLE WITH DYNAMIC STRING ALLOCATION   Here is the encryption example from Chapter 4, modified to use (more appropriately) dynamic string allocation.

```
// ENCODE2.CXX : Re-implementation of class encode to use
// dynamic string allocation.
#define TEST
#include <stream.hxx>
#include <string.h>
// The following path is for this book's source-code disk.
// Your directory may be different:
#include "..\chap_4\encode.hxx"

unsigned char encode::make_key(char * keystring) {
  unsigned char ckey = 0;
  for(char * cp = keystring; *cp != 0; cp++)
    ckey += *cp;  // generate a number from the key
  return ckey;
}

encode::encode(char * msg, char * key) {
  unsigned char ckey = make_key(key);
  encrypted_string = new char[strlen(msg) + 1];
  strcpy(encrypted_string,msg);  // save the message
  for(char * cp = encrypted_string; *cp != 0; cp++)
    *cp += ckey;  // use the key to encrypt the msg
}

char * encode::decode(char * key) {
  unsigned char ckey = make_key(key);
  for(char * cp = encrypted_string; *cp != 0; cp++)
  *cp -= ckey;  // use the key to decrypt the string
  return encrypted_string;
}

#ifdef TEST

main( ) {
  encode hidden_message("This is a test string", "key string");
  cout << hidden_message.decode("key string") << "\n";
}

#endif // TEST
```

Notice the header is the same, so you can use the same programs as you used before with this class. The implementation changed, not the interface, so any program that used this class is unaffected. This is one of the advantages to programming in C++—changes are localized and don't tend to cause other changes throughout the program.

The Mechanics of Dynamic Object Creation

When you encounter some of the more subtle problems involved with the free store, it is helpful to know how C++ manages memory. Two subjects will be examined here: the functions called when you use **new** and **delete**, and what goes on inside the system.

The Order of Constructor And Destructor Calls

Because C++ has dynamic object creation and not just dynamic memory allocation, constructors must be called so **new** will return the address of a "live" object. Similarly, the destructor for an object must be called before the memory for that object is deallocated, in case cleanup is necessary.

When you use **new** to create an object, enough memory for the data items in the object structure (these items normally live on the stack or in the **static** memory area) is allocated on the free store, and then the constructor for the object is called. In case the object is a conglomeration of other objects, either through class inheritance or because the object contains member objects, the constructors are called in a particular order. First the constructor for the base class is called, then the constructor(s) for the member object(s), and finally the constructor for the derived class.

When you use **delete** to destroy an object that was previously created on the free store, the compiler performs any cleanup specified for the class by calling its destructor. If the object is a conglomeration of other objects, the destructors are called in a particular order that is the reverse of the order of constructor calls: first the derived class destructor is called, then the member object destructor(s), and finally the destructor for the base class.

Even though inheritance has not yet been explained in detail (see Chapter 7), for the sake of this discussion a small example will be used to show the order of constructor and destructor calls when the object contains a member object and is inherited from another class that also contains a member object. By running the program you can see what happens.

```
// ORDER.CXX : The order of constructor and destructor calls
// for inherited objects, and objects with member objects.
#include <stdio.h>

class member {  // to be used as a member object
    int x;  // to remember what object this is
public:
    member(int i) {
        printf("member constructor called with argument "
                "%d\n", i);
        x = i;
    }
    ~member( ) {
        printf("member destructor called, x = %d\n", x);
    }
};

class base {  // to be used as a base class
    int xx;  // to remember what object this is
    member M;  // a member object
public:
    // Here's how you initialize a member object:
    base(int a, int b) : M(b) {
        printf("base constructor called with arguments "
                "%d, %d\n", a, b);
        xx = a;
    }
    ~base( ) {
        printf("base destructor called, xx = %d\n", xx);
    }
};

// Here's where inheritance happens, as well as another member
// object.  Watch carefully!
class derived : public base {  // <--- inheritance!
    int xxx;  // to remember what object this is
    member MM;
public:
    // Here's how constructors for the base class AND the
```

```
    // member function are called, before the class body, to
    // remind you they are called before the constructor for
    // this class.  Notice the constructor call for the base
    // class is the one with no name:
    derived(int a, int b, int c) : (a,b), MM(c) {
        printf("derived constructor called with arguments "
            "%d, %d, %d\n", a, b, c);
        xxx = a;
    }
    ~derived( ) {
        printf("derived destructor called.  xxx = %d\n", xxx);
    }
};

main( ) {
    {
        puts("creating derived X(1,2,3);");
        derived X(1,2,3);
        puts("derived X(1,2,3) going out of scope");
    } // <- destructor called here
    puts("creating derived * dp = new derived(4,5,6);");
    derived * dp = new derived(4,5,6);
    puts("calling delete dp;");
    delete dp;
}
```

Each constructor and destructor in this example contains a **printf( )** call so you can see the order in which they are called. **class member** is used as a member object in both **class base** and **class derived**, to show the order in which member objects are constructed. **class base** is the "base class" for **class derived**; that is, **class derived** inherits **class base**. This hierarchy demonstrates the order of constructor and destructor calls for member objects, base classes, and the member objects contained in a base class.

A member object is used inside an enclosing class by simply defining an instance of the member object's class. The member object, however, must be initialized specially. When the body of the enclosing class's constructor is entered, the member object must have already been initialized. To show this initialization, the member object's constructor is called *after* the argument list for the enclosing class's constructor argument list but *before* the body.

base(int a, int b) : M(b) {

//... body of constructor

When a class inherits from another class, the base class must be initialized before the body of the derived class's constructor is entered. The constructor for the base class is also called before entering the derived class's constructor body. Since there is no instance of the base class (it is inherited), no identifier is given before the argument list.

derived(int a, int b, int c) : (a,b), MM(c) {

// ... body of constructor

The way you specify base-class and member-object constructor calls in a derived class serves as a reminder of the order in which they are called: before the body of the enclosing class and/or derived class constructor is called.

Here is the output from ORDER:

```
creating derived X(1,2,3);
member constructor called with argument 2
base constructor called with arguments 1, 2
member constructor called with argument 3
derived constructor called with arguments 1, 2, 3
derived X(1,2,3) going out of scope
derived destructor called.  xxx = 1
member destructor called, x = 3
base destructor called, xx = 1
member destructor called, x = 2
creating derived * dp = new derived(4,5,6);
member constructor called with argument 5
base constructor called with arguments 4, 5
member constructor called with argument 6
derived constructor called with arguments 4, 5, 6
calling delete dp;
derived destructor called.  xxx = 4
member destructor called, x = 6
base destructor called, xx = 4
member destructor called, x = 5
```

At first glance, the order of constructor calls doesn't seem quite right—a member constructor is called *before* the base-class constructor. But if you look closely, you'll see that the order is in fact correct. The **base** constructor is called, but before it has a chance to print its message, it must call the constructor for the member object that is *part* of **base**. Then **base** prints its message, and finally the message from the derived-class constructor is printed. The destructors are called in the same way, in reverse.

ARRAYS OF OBJECTS If you allocate an array of objects, the class the objects belong to must contain a constructor with no arguments. This constructor is called for each array element—since C++ implementations prior to release 2.0 don't perform aggregate initialization of automatics (that is, the compiler can't select arguments for the constructor of each array element from a list), the compiler must be able to call a constructor without arguments. For a class called **object**, the syntax for allocating an array of objects is

object * op = new object[10]; // array of 10 objects

When you **delete** an array of objects belonging to a class with a destructor, you must give the number of elements in the array, in brackets, preceding the starting address of the array.

delete [10]op;

This tells the compiler how many times it needs to call the destructor for that array. You can also use this notation for arrays of built-in types, but built-in types do not have destructors, so, like any object without destructors, the argument is ignored.

Constructors and destructors are called automatically for every element in an **auto** array, as well as if the array is created with **new** and destroyed with **delete**. The following example illustrates.

```
// NEWARRAY.CXX : Constructors and destructors are called
// for every object in an array.
#include <stdio.h>

class BobTheDog {
public: // no data elements!
```

```
// A constructor with no arguments is necessary
// to create arrays of objects.  A constructor where
// all the arguments have default values works too.
BobTheDog( ) { puts("constructor called"); }
~BobTheDog( ) { puts("destructor called"); }
};

void auto_objects( ) {
    BobTheDog spaniel[5];
}

void dynamic_objects( ) {
    BobTheDog * mutt = new BobTheDog[8];
    // note the number of elements in the array must be
    // given so the destructor is called for each element:
    delete [8]mutt;
}

main( ) {
    puts("calling auto_objects");
    auto_objects( );
    puts("calling dynamic_objects");
    dynamic_objects( );
}
```

The function **auto_objects( )** creates an array on the stack, and you will see a constructor call for each element when the scope is entered and a destructor call for each element at the end of the scope. The function **dynamic_objects( )** shows an array of the same object being created on the free store, and then deleted.

Internal Operations

When you use **new**, you must give the operator an argument so it knows how much memory to allocate. When you call **delete**, however, you only need to give it a starting address (for an array of objects, you must precede the address by the number of objects in the array). You may have surmised that **new** keeps tabs on how much memory is allocated, so the correct amount can be freed by **delete**.

The algorithm for **new** stores the amount of space allocated somewhere in memory. It might be stored next to the allocated block or in a table—the way **new** works varies between implementations. In addition, the location of the space allocated is stored somewhere, so subsequent calls to **new** do not allocate the same chunk of memory.

When you free a chunk of memory using **delete**, the system marks that block of memory as available, so the next time **new** is used that memory may be reallocated. Some implementations of C++ (such as Zortech) immediately write over portions of the deallocated memory. You should realize that it is never safe to use memory after it has been deallocated. After reading this explanation it may sound like a silly thing to do, but some people do it anyway. This goes into the same classification of taboos as "don't return addresses of local variables."

HEAP FRAGMENTATION If your program does a lot of memory allocation and deallocation, a phenomenon called *heap fragmentation* may result. Eventually, your heap may be so riddled with occupied space that, while enough free space exists to allocate a new chunk, there is no contiguous piece of memory large enough to allocate the size you request.

If you create a program that fragments the heap, you may need to add a routine to perform *heap compaction*. A compactor goes through the heap and moves all the chunks of allocated memory "down" (if you think of the heap as growing up from the bottom of memory, and the stack growing down) so that large chunks of free memory once again become available. Because a compactor changes all the addresses of the chunks of allocated memory, your program must have intimate knowledge of the compactor, and interact with it to keep all the addresses current. Because of this, you can't write a general purpose compactor and make it part of the language or part of a library function.

Some operating systems, such as the one for the Apple Macintosh, perform heap compaction for you. To accomplish this they use *double indirection*—whenever you request a chunk of memory from the operating system, you get back a pointer *to a pointer* to that chunk of memory. You must always use the address you get back, and dereference it twice. You cannot use the actual address of the chunk of memory because the operating system may change that address when it performs heap compaction.

Although many operating systems have methods to allocate chunks of memory, C++ and C do not generally go to the operating system when you use **new** and **delete**, although they may certainly be implemented that way. When a program starts, it takes a big chunk of data space. When you allocate free store, the memory is taken from that space, so C++ manages the free store, not the operating system.

NULL POINTERS   Generally, the value of NULL for a pointer has special meaning. It usually means the pointer isn't pointing anywhere. NULL is a convenient value because it is also a logical false, so you can use it in statements such as: **while(ptr)** or **if(ptr)**.

Although it's possible to dereference a pointer with a NULL value, you almost never want to. More sophisticated operating systems will trap an attempt to dereference a NULL pointer, but with simpler machines you may end up in some memory-mapped hardware, or in the operating system itself.

In C++, it is quite natural to use the value of NULL to indicate the pointer is empty. This is supported by a special feature—if you call **delete** with a NULL pointer it has no effect. You don't have to test to see if a pointer is empty before you delete the free store it points to.

ANSI C doesn't actually specify that the value of NULL must be zero. The implementation can use any value for NULL that it needs to. It must convert between that representation and zero under appropriate circumstances. Normally, you have no portable way of detecting how an implementation represents NULL.

MULTIPLE DELETIONS   Memory allocated on the free store should only be deleted once. If you call **new** once for a single allocation, and **delete** more than once for the same allocation, it can be disastrous.

Changing the Behavior
Of new and delete

C++ allows you to change the behavior of many of the aspects of the system. Dynamic memory allocation is no exception. You can redefine the function called when free store is exhausted, and you can redefine the operators **new** and **delete**.

Free Store Exhaustion

In some applications, exhausting the free store means you've made an error and your program has been wildly allocating free store. However, there are many situations when exhausting the free store is a normal and recoverable condition, for instance:

■ Your system may be designed to generate garbage, which can be collected to create more room.

■ You may be fragmenting the heap. If you design your system to allow it, the heap can be compacted.

■ You may have taken over free store allocation by redefining **new** and **delete** (demonstrated later in this section) and you may have some method of getting more memory when your local store is exhausted.

■ You may want to use as much memory as possible, to buffer disk I/O, for example. The only portable way to see if a certain amount of memory is available is to call **new** and see if it fails.

Normally, if there is no more free store, the **new** operator returns zero (instead of a pointer to memory). You can change this behavior by creating a new function and installing it with the function **set_new_handler( )**. When free store is exhausted, your new function will be called. For example, if you suspect you are running out of free store, you can make the program print a message and exit:

```
// FSHANDLR.CXX : Adding your own handler to be called when
// free store runs out.

#include <stdio.h>
#include <stdlib.h>

void no_more_free_store( ) {
   printf("You've exhausted the free store!");
   exit(1);
}

typedef void (*PF)( );  // PF is a pointer to function type
extern PF set_new_handler(PF);

main( ) {
   set_new_handler(no_more_free_store);
   while(1)
      new int;  // this loop will exhaust free store!
}
```

In this example, **set_new_handler( )** takes the address of **no_more_free_store( )** and installs it as the function to be called when free store is exhausted. The statement

while(1)

    new int;

eventually allocates all the free store, so you can see the handler called.

TRIVIAL GARBAGE COLLECTION   As a trivial example of a system with garbage collection, the following program defines a class called **garbage**. **garbage** objects are used for some mysterious purpose and then thrown away (perhaps the desired effect of a **garbage** object happens in the constructor). When the system runs out of free store, the **garbage** objects that are no longer in use are freed by the garbage collector. To find out if an object is still in use, the object itself is questioned. The **in_use** variable can be set according to criteria specific to your application.

To store the pointers efficiently, the **DynArray class** defined earlier in this chapter is used. Notice how convenient it is to use the **class** once it's defined—you just make a **DynArray**, throw pointers in, and fish them out later. Whenever an object is created, the **garbage** constructor passes its address to **DynArray::add( )**, so it is stored in the table.

```
// GARBAGE.CXX : A very simple example of how a garbage
// collector might work.
#include <stdio.h>
#include <stdlib.h>
#include "dynarray.hxx"

DynArray memtable;  // place for free store pointers
const garbage_chunk = 512;  // controls the size of an object

class garbage {
    int memory[garbage_chunk];
    int in_use;
public:
    garbage( ) {
        memtable.add(this);  // save the pointer
        in_use = 0;  // we're done, it's dead
    }
    int alive( ) { return in_use;}
```

```
    int dead( ) { return !in_use;}
};

void garbage_collector( ) {
    // print messages at the bottom of the screen using
    // ANSI terminal escape commands:
    printf("\x1b[25;1H\x1b[KGarbage Collecting...");
    printf("\x1b[24;40H\x1b[Kitems: %d", memtable.count( ));
    memtable.reset( );
    do
       if(((garbage *)memtable.current( ))- >dead( )) {
          printf("\x1b[25;40H\x1b[Kremoving %ld",
                 (long)memtable.current( ));
          delete (garbage *)memtable.current( );
          memtable.remove(memtable.index( ));
       }
    while( memtable.next( ) );
    printf("\x1b[25;22H\x1b[Kdone.");
}

typedef void (*PF)( );  // PF is a pointer to function type
extern PF set_new_handler(PF);

main( ) {
    set_new_handler(garbage_collector);
    while(1)
       new garbage;  // this loop will exhaust free store!
}
```

The program displays its garbage-collecting activities as they occur. If you are using a PC, you can try different memory models to get an idea of how much free store is allocated for each. Also, the program gives you an idea of how much stack space and heap space is allocated for a program, since you can see the number of chunks allocated before garbage collection occurs. The stack space is roughly the amount left over.

Redefining new *and* delete

There are situations where the actions of **new** and **delete** are not what you need. Conveniently, you can redefine **new** and **delete** to adapt to these problems. Here are some examples of when you might need to do this:

■ Suppose you are developing code in C++ for an *embedded system* (a program that is burned into ROM or EPROM and used for a specific application like a control system). Embedded systems generally have constraints on the placement and use of memory, so C++'s **new** and **delete** may be inappropriate. You can define a free store in your embedded system by redefining **new** and **delete**.

■ You may need to implement **new** and **delete** so they work more efficiently for your particular application.

■ A program that performs dynamic memory allocation can be difficult to debug. You may have access to a C package that provides debugging facilities through rewritten versions of **malloc( )** and **free( )**. These can be utilized in C++ by redefining **new** and **delete**. (Of course, you can also use **malloc( )** and **free( )** directly.)

The last case is worth making an example for; **new** and **delete** are redefined as operators, as shown here:

```
// RENEW.CXX : Redefining new and delete.  This code is useful
// if you have a malloc( ) and free( ) which perform memory bounds
// checking.
#include <stdlib.h>  // malloc( ), free( )
#include <stdio.h>
#include <stddef.h> // size_t

void* operator new(size_t sz) {
    void * mem = malloc(sz);
    printf("new: %ld bytes at %p\n", sz, mem);
    fflush(stdout);
    return mem;
}

void operator delete(void * dp) {
    printf("delete: %p\n", dp);
    fflush(stdout);
    free(dp);
}

class noisy {
    int dummy;
public:
```

```
    noisy( ) { printf("HI! I'm being created!\n"); }
    ~noisy( ) { printf("AAUUGH! Help, I'm being destroyed!\n"); }
};

main( ) {
    // notice that the constructors and destructors are still
    // called when you redefine new and delete:
    puts("noisy * na = new noisy[7];");
    noisy * na = new noisy[7];
    puts("delete [7]na;");
    delete [7]na;
    puts("noisy * x = new noisy;");
    noisy * x = new noisy;
    puts("delete x;");
    delete x;
}
```

The **printf( )** argument %**p** is a portable way to print a pointer.

There is a shortcoming with C++ compilers conforming to AT&T release 1.2. If you redefine **new** and **delete**, you cannot call the original versions of **new** and **delete**, so you always have to use some other method of allocating memory when redefining the two operators. If you want to perform your own memory management but still use the original **new** and **delete**, you must use assignment to **this**, described later in this chapter in "Inheritance and Assignment to **this**." (These problems are fixed in AT&T release 2.0).

IMPROVING DynArray   The ANSI C library function **realloc( )** takes a block of memory allocated by **malloc( )**, **calloc( )**, or **realloc( )** and expands it or contracts it. If you expand the block and **realloc( )** can't find enough space where the block is, it will copy the existing block into a new, larger memory space.

If you look back at the **add( )** method for **DynArray**, you can see the same activities taking place, only less efficiently—the block is *always* moved and copied, and the C++ code to perform the copy probably isn't as efficient as **realloc( )** (which is often written in assembly language).

If you are using a **DynArray** in a time-critical application, you may want to perform memory allocation in the constructor and in **add( )** using the ANSI C library functions instead of **new** and **delete**. Keep in mind, however, that some C++ packages may have problems if you use the ANSI C library functions for dynamic memory allocation *and* **new** and **delete** at the same time. (The ability to mix the two is the defined behavior; but not on the same object.)

Pitfalls in Dynamic Memory Allocation

When you decide to use dynamic memory allocation (for built-in types) or dynamic object creation (for user-defined types) there are certain potential traps you may encounter. As mentioned before, when you create a variable on the free store, it has an arbitrary lifetime. You are responsible for deleting the variable when you no longer need it. If you don't take care in cleaning up, you may run out of free store. You must also be sure that a class with a constructor that allocates free store has a complementary destructor that deallocates that free store or (again) you may run out of free store. For an example, look at the destructor for **class DynArray** in DYNARRAY.CXX.

You will encounter more subtle problems when you begin passing object arguments into functions and returning object arguments from functions. If the object contains pointers to memory on the free store, you will copy the structure that lives on the stack and contains the pointers. This is called a *shallow copy,* since the memory on the free store isn't copied. Assuming your destructor properly deallocates the free store, you will end up returning a structure that has pointers to deallocated free store. This problem is examined in detail in Chapter 9, "Arguments and Return Values."

Calculating Object Size

You must somehow know or calculate the size of the class when you call **new** or any other function that allocates dynamic memory. As with built-in types, you can usually just give the class name to **new**, and an object of the proper size will be created. The following example is a class that has a pointer to another class created on the free store:

```
// SIZES.CXX : Object sizes are automatically calculated for
// you when using "new."
```

```
class X {
   int i, j, k;
// ...
};

class Y {
   long u, v, w;
// ...
};

class Z {
   double a, b, c;
// ...
};

class conglomerate {
   X * xp;
   Y * yp;
   Z * zp;
public:
   conglomerate( ) {
      xp = new X; // just tell it the class, not the size
      yp = new Y;
      zp = new Z;
   }
};
```

Some classes contain hidden elements (for instance, classes with **virtual** functions, described in Chapter 8). Since **new** calculates the size of the class for you, you don't need to concern yourself with what's inside. Occasionally, you will need to calculate the size of your object while performing dynamic memory allocation. This can be accomplished using the **sizeof** operator. In the following example, a class contains a pointer to a **struct** that contains the size of a vector and the starting address of the vector itself:

```
// VVEC.CXX : Calculating sizes for dynamic memory allocation
// using sizeof.

class vec {
public: // so vvec has access to elements (struct works too)
    int size; // length of vector
    float v[1]; // trick -- this is only the start of the vector
};

class vvec {
    vec * vv;
public:
    vvec(int sz) {
        vv = (vec *)new char[sizeof(vec) + (sz-1) * sizeof(float)];
        vv->size = sz;
    }
    ~vvec( ); // appropriate destructor
};
```

Using References with Dynamic Memory Allocation

It is possible to bind the value returned by **new** to a reference variable instead of a pointer; for example:

```
// FREEREF.CXX : Using references for dynamic memory

class marilyn {
    double artist;
public:
    void paint( ) { }
    void draw( ) { }
    void tie_dye( ) { }
};
```

```
main( ) {
    // notice you must dereference the address, so the reference
    // sees an object (references must always bind to objects):
    marilyn & mc = *new marilyn;
    // now you can use it just like a scoped object:
    mc.paint( );
    mc.draw( );
    mc.tie_dye( );
    // but you are still responsible for cleaning up:
    delete &mc;
}
```

References can be attractive because they make a dynamically allocated object look like a local object, with the same syntax for calling member functions. They are deceiving because a destructor is called for a local object, while no destructor is called for a reference. Since a reference is less flexible than a pointer (you can't reassign a reference once it has been initialized) it generally isn't very useful in this facility. Again, references seem best left to their intended purpose—as function arguments and for returning addresses.

Assigning to this *In a Constructor*

Assignment to **this** allows you to take over dynamic memory allocation for an individual object (as opposed to redefining **new** and **delete**, which affects everything). You should only use assignment to **this** if

■ The built-in method for dynamic memory allocation is unsatisfactory *and*

■ You don't want to give up the predefined versions of **new** and **delete**

As noted earlier, when you redefine **operator new** and **operator delete**, you have no way to access the original **new** and **delete**. Assignment to **this** allows you to modify dynamic memory allocation without modifying **new** and **delete**. If you are using a C++ implementation that conforms to AT&T release 2.0, you should not use assignment to **this**. Release 2.0 allows overloading of **new** and **delete** on a class-by-class basis (see Chapter 11).

Reading and Writing this

While it is completely safe to *read* the value of **this** in any code you write, when you make an assignment to **this** in a constructor, the C++ compiler alters the way it generates code for that constructor. Specifically, it no longer generates code to perform dynamic memory allocation when that constructor is called with **new**. Ordinarily, code is secretly generated in a constructor to differentiate between objects created on the stack (the value of **this** when the constructor is called is non-zero) and objects created on the free store (the value of **this** when the constructor is called—but *before* the constructor body is entered—is zero). If **this** is equivalent to zero, the global **new** function (which you may have redefined) is called to allocate that memory.

When you perform an assignment to **this** anywhere within a constructor, the C++ compiler does not generate the code that checks to see if **this** is zero and calls the **new** function if it is. Normal dynamic memory allocation is not performed for that constructor. To override the normal dynamic memory allocation mechanism for an object, you simply figure out where you want the starting address of the object (either by calling some memory allocation routine or through other specific knowledge about the memory layout of your system), and assign that address to **this**, which is the starting address of the object.

Caveats

It is important to remember that assignment to **this** must only modify dynamic memory allocation. If you assign to **this** when an object is created on the stack, you will get no compiler errors or warnings, but erroneous results. A small example illustrates this.

```
// BADTHIS.CXX : Assignment to "this" for objects that haven't
// been created with "new" produces garbage!

#include <stdio.h>
class wrong{
   int i;
public:
   wrong(int x) {
      this = (wrong *) new int;
      i = x;
   }
   void print(char * msg = " ") {
      printf("%s : i = %d\n", msg, i);
   }
};

main( ) {
   wrong * heap_based = new wrong(100);  // This works
   heap_based->print("heap_based"); // correct answer printed
   wrong stack_based(100);  // this doesn't work
   stack_based.print("stack_based"); // garbage printed here!
}
```

Since **this** is a pointer to an object of the constructor's **class**, you must cast the address returned by **new** to the same type of pointer.

The problem in this example is that the constructor is attempting to assign to **this** for both stack-based objects and free store-based objects. You have two choices here: you can force the user of the class to only create objects with **new,** or you can check the value of **this** upon entry to the constructor, and perform an assignment to **this** *only* if **this** is equivalent to zero (indicating the object was created with **new**). The following example repairs the problems in BADTHIS.CXX using both methods:

```
// GOODTHIS.CXX : Fixing BADTHIS.CXX by only assigning to "this"
// if the constructor was called using "new."
#include <stdio.h>
#include <stdlib.h>

class right{
   int i;
```

```
public:
   right(int x) {
      if(this == 0) // means it was called with "new"
         this = (right *) new int;
      i = x;
   }
   void print(char * msg = " ") {
      printf("%s : i = %d\n", msg, i);
   }
};

class right2{
   int i;
public:
   right2(int x) {
      if(this != 0) { // means a stack-based object
         puts("error: cannot create a right2 on the stack!");
         exit(1);
      }
      this = (right2 *) new int;
      i = x;
   }
   void print(char * msg = " ") {
      printf("%s : i = %d\n", msg, i);
   }
};

main( ) {
   right * heap_based = new right(100);
   heap_based->print("heap_based");
   right stack_based(200);
   stack_based.print("stack_based");
   right2 * heap_based2 = new right2(300);
   heap_based2->print("heap_based2");
   right2 stack_based2(100); // generates an error at run time
}
```

Destructors

As you can imagine, you must change the way dynamic memory is
deallocated in the destructor when you change the way it is allocated in
the constructor. Ordinarily, the compiler generates some secret code in the

destructor to perform dynamic memory deallocation on objects that have been generated dynamically. The deallocation is performed by calling the **delete** function.

If you don't allocate memory using **new**, you probably have something different in mind when the object is destroyed, so you need to disable the normal dynamic deallocation method. To do this, you assign **this = 0** in the destructor. Similar to the situation with the constructor, assigning to **this** in the destructor only affects objects that are being destroyed with **delete**. It is important that you assign **this = 0** in the destructor whenever you perform your own memory allocation by assigning to **this** in constructors. Thus, the example GOODTHIS.CXX is still not complete. The following example works properly:

```cpp
// GOOD2.CXX : You must assign this = 0 in the destructor
// when you assign to "this" in the constructor.
#include <stdio.h>
#include <stdlib.h>

class do_right{
   int dudley;
   int dynamic; // whether it was dynamically allocated
public:
   do_right(int x) {
     if(this == 0) { // means it was called with "new"
       this = (do_right *) new int;
       dynamic = 1;  // set flag
     } else
       dynamic = 0;  // stack-based object
     dudley = x;
   }
   ~do_right( ) {
     if(dynamic)
       delete this;
     this = 0; // disable normal dynamic deallocation
   }
   void print(char * msg = " ") {
     printf("%s : dudley = %d\n", msg, dudley);
   }
};

class whiplash{
   int snidely;
```

```
public:
    whiplash(int x) {
        if(this != 0) { // means a stack-based object
            puts("error: cannot create a whiplash on the stack!");
            exit(1);
        }
        this = (whiplash *) new int;
        snidely = x;
    }
    ~whiplash( ) {
        delete this;  // all objects are stack-based
        this = 0;  // disable normal dynamic deallocation
    }
    void print(char * msg = " ") {
        printf("%s : snidely = %d\n", msg, snidely);
    }
};

main( ) {
    do_right * heap_based = new do_right(100);
    heap_based->print("heap_based");
    do_right stack_based(200);
    stack_based.print("stack_based");
    whiplash * heap_based2 = new whiplash(300);
    heap_based2->print("heap_based2");
}
```

There is no way for a destructor to tell if an object was created on the free store. In **do_right**, an extra flag is used so the destructor can decide what type of destruction to perform. In **whiplash**, since all objects are forced to be allocated on the free store, the destructor always knows that it must destroy a free store object. Notice the assignment to **this** happens *after* **this** is used to deallocate the memory.

As you can see, life is simpler if you force the user to create all objects on the free store. You can make life even more complicated (not recommended) if you assign to **this** in some constructors but not others. In this case, you can have three possibilities: stack-based objects, dynamically allocated objects created with **new**, and dynamically allocated objects created by your special constructor(s). To avoid havoc, you must either

■ Ensure that all constructors use the same dynamic memory allocation method—if one constructor assigns to **this**, all the other constructors should assign to **this** *or*

■ Store information about what method was used to dynamically allocate memory in the object, so the destructor can know how to deallocate the memory—it is unlikely that you will use more than one kind of dynamic memory allocation, since that would be a confusing way to program.

Recommendations for Assigning to this

If you must perform your own dynamic memory allocation for an object without redefining **new** and **delete**, life will be easiest if you

■ Force all objects to be created on the heap by ensuring that the value of **this** is zero upon entering all constructors.

■ Assign to **this** in *all* constructors. Examine your constructors to make sure there are no logical paths where no assignment to **this** occurs (the compiler will not help you if you make a mistake); for example:

example::example( ) { // example bad constructor

  if(condition)

   this = allocate_memory( );

} // what if condition == 0 ??

Here, there is a logical path that has no assignment to **this**. If this path is executed, you will end up with an object that has no memory allocated for its member data elements.

Inheritance and Assignment to this

When you assign to **this**, inheritance (covered in Chapter 7) can get fairly complicated. If a derived class assigns to **this**, the assignment to **this** in the derived class occurs before the base class constructor is called. If the base class assigns to **this**, the memory for the structure will be assigned to **this** in the base class and will then be initialized by the constructor in the derived class. If *both* the base and derived classes assign to **this**, you will have trouble—the derived class assignment to **this** will occur first, and then the base class assignment to **this** will write over it. You must write code in the derived class to protect against creating the object on the stack, and code in the base class to use a non-zero **this** if memory was already allocated by the derived class (since the derived class is often larger than the base class, it makes sense to give the responsibility for memory allocation to the derived class). Here's an example:

```
// INHERIT.CXX : Inheritance and assignment to "this"
#include <stdio.h>
#include <stdlib.h>

class base {
   int i;
public:
   base( );
   ~base( ) { delete this; this = 0; }
};

base::base( ) {
   if(this)
      this = this;  // assignment to "this" using memory allocated
                    // in the derived class
   else
      this = (base *)new int;
   i = 47;
}

class derived : public base {
   int x;
public:
   derived( );
   ~derived( ) { delete this; this = 0; }
};

derived::derived( ) : ( ) {
   if(this) {
```

```
        puts("derived must be created with new");
        exit(1);
    }
    this = (derived *)new int[2]; // for base & derived space
    x = 74;
}

main( ) {
    derived * D = new derived;
    delete D;
}
```

When you inherit and assign to **this** at the same time, you must carefully analyze your code to make sure there are no paths where memory for the object doesn't get allocated. It's complicated, and if you can instead use an implementation of C++ that conforms to AT&T release 2.0 (and avoid assignment to **this** altogether), you will be much better off.

Benefits of Assigning to this

Stroustrup and others show further examples of assignment to **this**. A common use is to increase the efficiency of dynamic memory allocation. For instance, if a large number of objects of a certain class are allocated (especially if the objects contain pointers to dynamically allocated data), the overhead of the built-in **new** function can cause significant performance degradation. If instead you allocate your own memory in big chunks with **new,** and then perform your own memory management inside the constructor that assigns to **this**, you can see significant performance improvements (without loss of portability). You can test the class using normal dynamic memory allocation, and then change to the improved method without modifying the interface. Of course, these same benefits can be realized in C++ release 2.0 *without* assigning to **this**.

Makefile for Chapter Examples

Here is the **makefile** for all the examples in this chapter:

```
# makefile for examples in chapter 6
# Zortech:
CPP = ztc
# Glockenspiel:
#CPP = ccxx

.cxx.exe:
            $(CPP) $*.cxx

.cxx.obj:
            $(CPP) -c $*.cxx

all:    dave.exe freestor.exe delete.exe life.exe garbage.exe \
        dynatest.exe string.exe encode2.exe order.exe \
        newarray.exe fshandlr.exe garbage.exe renew.exe \
        sizes.obj vvec.obj freeref.exe badthis.exe \
        goodthis.exe good2.exe inherit.exe

life.exe : life.obj lifefld.obj lifeunit.obj
            $(CPP) $**

dynatest.exe : dynatest.obj dynarray.obj
            $(CPP) $**

# On a PC, this is much more entertaining when compiled
# with the large memory model:
garbage.exe : garbage.obj dynarray.obj
            $(CPP) $**

freestor.exe : freestor.cxx tracker.hxx
delete.exe : delete.cxx tracker.hxx
life.obj : lifefld.hxx lifeunit.hxx life.cxx
lifefld.obj : lifefld.hxx lifeunit.hxx lifefld.cxx
lifeunit.obj : lifefld.hxx lifeunit.hxx lifeunit.cxx
dynarray.obj : dynarray.cxx dynarray.hxx
dynatest.obj : dynatest.cxx dynarray.hxx
garbage.obj : garbage.cxx dynarray.hxx
```

7 *Reusing Code In C++*

Programmers are very familiar with the concept of "reinventing the wheel." Often, it seems like every time you start a new project you end up rewriting a lot of code that you or someone else has written before. The existing code may be almost right for your application, but too complicated to be worth the effort of figuring out how to adapt it. If you've done this sort of thing before, you know you can burn up a lot of time trying to figure out how to modify old code—one project can mysteriously turn into several. Or in another scenario, the existing code may not need changes, but it may not be documented well enough for you to know how to use it.

The inability to easily reuse code is expensive. Not adding a feature to your program because learning to use someone else's code is too difficult is unfortunate; and it probably results in reducing the productivity of the end user. If you must write something from scratch, then you might just find a way to avoid writing it at all.

This chapter focuses on the support in C++ for the reuse of existing code (sometimes called *subclassing*). Classes can be reused in several ways. One way is by creating *member objects* of other classes inside your new class. This approach takes the view that an object can be a *collection* of other objects and is sometimes called *composition*. One object can also be a *kind* of another object. This is called *inheritance* or *derivation*. Just as a child inherits traits from its parents, a derived class (also called a *subclass*) inherits traits from a base class (also called a *superclass*). With composition, you are saying, "this **class** is some of these, and some of those, and one of these." For instance, a **building** has **doors** and **windows** and **rooms**. With derivation, you are saying "this new class is that old one with some changes." For instance, a **skyscraper** is a **building** with many floors.

This chapter looks at simply building new classes from old ones using member objects or inheritance. Inheritance, however, also creates another kind of relationship. When you inherit a new class from an old one, the new class doesn't just take on the characteristics of the old one. Instances of the new class are also instances of the old class. That is, any functions or operations that worked on objects of the old class work on objects of the new class as well. All classes inherited from the same base class have the same set of functions, or *interface,* as the base class. This concept of *class hierarchy* (also called *subtyping*) is very powerful, and will be explored in Chapter 8.

To use a class in C++, you must have the header file containing the class definition and, minimally, the object code file or a library containing the object code file. Coincidentally, this is exactly what you must have to derive a new class from an old one—you don't need the source code for the methods (although it can be useful). In the past, vendors of C libraries had the option of providing sources, often at a fee. With C++, any library that can be used can also be easily adapted to solve a new problem, whether or not you have the sources.

SINGLE VERSUS MULTIPLE INHERITANCE   C++ implementations that follow AT&T release 1.2 and earlier only allow a class to be a *kind* of one other class. For instance, you cannot say, "a **house** is a **building** and a **residence**; a **skyscraper** is a **building** and an **office_space**." Release 1.2 and earlier versions support *single inheritance;* you can only inherit from one base class. Release 2.0 supports *multiple inheritance,* which means you can inherit from more than one base class. This is further detailed in Chapter 11.

CLASS BROWSERS   Once C++ libraries start becoming commonly available, a new problem will arise: finding the code you want to reuse. The tool commonly used to keep track of code in object-oriented programming systems is called a *class browser.* A class browser shows you the hierarchy of classes and their member functions. But simply providing the names of classes and their member functions isn't enough; good C++ class browsers should provide support for textual information as well.

Reusing Code
With Member Objects

To reuse code using a member object, you simply declare an object of a class to be a member of a new class. Creating an object as a member of another class is very different than creating an ordinary (non-member) object, however. With an ordinary object, the constructor is called at the point where you define the object, and you may give an argument list after the identifier. If you do not give an argument list for an ordinary object, the constructor with no arguments, or all default arguments, is called. With a member object, you *never* give an argument list at the point the member object is declared in the class structure. The declaration of the member object tells the compiler to add space for the member object in any instances of the new class. However, the constructor cannot be called until the space is actually allocated, which does not occur until you create an instance of the new class and the new class's constructor is called. When the body of the new class's constructor is entered, you must be able to assume that all member objects have been initialized, thus the constructors for all member objects must be called *before* the constructor for the new class.

To remind you that constructors for member objects are called before the new class's constructor, C++ notation shows the calls being made *outside* the body of the new class's constructor, after the argument list (and a colon, to indicate the start of constructor calls) and before the opening brace. When calling the member object constructor, you must use the same form as if you were calling the constructor for an ordinary object—the identifier followed by an argument list. The syntax for using member objects is thus

class *classname* {

   // ...

   memberclass member_object_name;

   // ...

public:

   classname(arglist); // **constructor**

   // ...

};

classname::classname(arglist) : member_object_name(arglist2) **{**

   // **constructor body**

}

arglist2 is the argument list for the constructor of the member object; it may or may not contain arguments from *arglist*.

You can use as many member objects as you want in a class. For each member object you add, just add a constructor call to the *initializer list,* separating it from the other elements with commas. The constructors are called in the order they are shown in the class definition for C++ compilers conforming to releases 1.2 and before. You can also create arrays of member objects inside a class. (As with any array of objects, the constructor with no arguments is used for initialization, so no initializer needs to be specified in the new class constructor.)

A Class to Handle Errors

The need to handle errors when building classes is very common. When something goes wrong in an object, you often want to call a function that prints a sensible error message and either recovers to an earlier state or exits the program.

The following class, called **error_handler,** is meant to be used as a member object in other classes. The single argument to the constructor is a string that will be printed for all error messages the new class will issue; it is usually just the class name, followed by the word "error" and a colon. The two methods, called **message( )** and **terminate( ),** take a format string and arguments exactly like **printf( ),** so you can print virtually any kind of message with debugging information when an error occurs.

Here is the header file for **error_handler:**

```
// ERROR.HXX : A class to perform error management inside other
// classes.  This class demonstrates reuse via member objects.
// class_msg describes the class error_handler is being used
// in.  terminate( ) takes arguments just like printf( ) does.

#ifndef ERROR_HXX
#define ERROR_HXX

class error_handler {
   char * msg;
public:
   error_handler(char * class_msg) {
     msg = class_msg;
   }
   void message(char * format_string, ...);
   void terminate(char * format_string, ...);
};

#endif // ERROR_HXX
```

Notice the last line of the header file. While

#endif ERROR_HXX

will work with many compilers, it is not portable. Thus it is safer to comment out the rest of the line after an **#endif**.

The two methods for **error_handler** show you how to use a variable argument list with the macros contained in the ANSI C header file **stdargs.h**. Since you don't know how many arguments there will be in a list, you have to call the special macros to manage the argument list for you. Here is the implementation file for **error_handler**:

```
// ERROR.CXX : The variable argument list for terminate( ) is
// implemented using the ANSI C library functions for variable
// arguments (in stdarg.h) and the associated printf( )-like
// vfprintf( ) function.
```

```
#include <stdio.h>
#include <stdarg.h>
#include <stdlib.h>  // exit( )
#include "error.hxx"
// #define TEST  // un-comment this for a simple demonstration

void error_handler::message(char * format_string, ...) {
    va_list arg_pointer;
    va_start(arg_pointer, format_string);
    fprintf(stderr, "%s ", msg);  // print class message first
    vfprintf(stderr, format_string, arg_pointer);
    va_end(arg_pointer);
}

void error_handler::terminate(char * format_string, ...) {
    va_list arg_pointer;
    va_start(arg_pointer, format_string);
    fprintf(stderr, "%s ", msg);  // print class message first
    vfprintf(stderr, format_string, arg_pointer);
    va_end(arg_pointer);
    exit(1);
}

#ifdef TEST

class etest {
    error_handler error;
public:
    etest( ) : error("etest error:") { }
    void demonstration( ) {
        // Any time you perform a test and find something wrong,
        // you can terminate the program with an error message
        // that identifies the class, member function, and any
        // other useful information.  Use terminate( ) just like
        // you would use printf( ).
        error.terminate("in function %s, value %d\n", "test", 1);
    }
};
```

```
main( ) {
    etest E;
    E.demonstration( );
}
```

#endif // TEST

    arg_pointer is a special type of pointer that indexes through the argument list. To set this pointer up, the macro **va_start( )** is called. **arg_pointer** is handed to **vfprintf( )**, which knows how to select all the arguments in the list. When the function is finished, a call to **va_end( )** resets **arg_pointer**. For a more complete description of the use of variable argument lists, consult your local ANSI C guide.

    By removing the comment on the **#define TEST**, you will compile a very simple piece of test code. This code includes an example class called **etest** that includes an instance of **error_handler** (**error**) as a member object. In the constructor for **etest**, you can see the constructor call for **error** with an appropriate string. The member function **demonstration** shows an example call to **terminate( )**, using only two of the many possible types of arguments available for **vfprintf( )**.

    As you can see, adding sophisticated error messages to your classes is very easy. You will find that error messages are exceptionally useful when you start building large projects with many classes. The objects themselves will tell you where the problems are, which will greatly reduce your debugging time. You can also create a stand-alone instance of **error_handler** for use in **main( )**.

A Class to Handle Timing

Here's another class you might use to make a member object in another class. **class timer** allows you to **start( )** timing a process, **mark( )** the end of the process, and read the **elapsed_time( )** in seconds. It also has a function to allow you to **pause( )** for a number of seconds. The header file contains all the methods as **inline** functions.

```
// TIMER.HXX : A small class to handle delays and timing
#ifndef TIMER_HXX
#define TIMER_HXX
#include <time.h>

class timer {
   time_t start_time, mark_time;
public:
   void start( ) { // start the stopwatch
      time(&start_time);
   }
   void mark( ) {  // mark the time
      time(&mark_time);
   }
   double elapsed_time( ) { // how many seconds elapsed?
      return difftime(mark_time, start_time);
   }
   void pause(int seconds) {  // wait
      start( );
      do
         mark( );
      while ( elapsed_time( ) < seconds );
   }
};

#endif // TIMER_HXX
```

class timer uses the ANSI C library functions for keeping time, proto-typed in **time.h**. The ANSI committee could not force very stringent requirements on the time functions because some systems might not be able to meet them. As a result, the granularity of the time functions is one second. This means that if you ask for a pause of ten seconds, you will get a pause of no less than nine seconds and no more than ten seconds. For many applications, this is fine. If you need higher resolution, you can measure the number of clock ticks using the **clock( )** function. The number of clock ticks per second (**CLOCKS_PER_SEC** in **time.h**) is implementa-tion dependent and will often give you a better granularity than the methods used above. Here is **class timer** modified for (potentially) higher resolution:

```
// TIMER2.HXX : class timer modified to use the (implementation
// dependent) clock ticks instead of difftime.  This should
// provide higher resolution than TIMER.HXX.
#ifndef TIMER2_HXX
#define TIMER2_HXX
#include <time.h>

class timer {
   clock_t start_time, mark_time;
public:
   void start( ) { // start the stopwatch
      start_time = clock( );
   }
   void mark( ) {  // mark the time
      mark_time = clock( );
   }
   clock_t elapsed_time( ) { // how many seconds elapsed?
      return (mark_time - start_time)/ CLOCKS_PER_SEC;
   }
   void pause(int seconds) {  // wait
      start( );
      do
         mark( );
      while ( elapsed_time( ) < seconds );
   }
};

#endif // TIMER2_HXX
```

The implementation of **pause( )** is appropriate for a single-tasking environment. In a multi-tasking environment you may need to be careful not to hang up the machine during a **pause( )**.

The following program tests **class timer**. It takes an integer from the command line and counts that many seconds. It also checks the elapsed time and prints it at the end. To see the difference in the two implementations of **class timer**, try alternately including TIMER.HXX and TIMER2.HXX.

```
// TIMETEST.CXX : a test for class timer.  Takes the pause( )
// argument from the command line.
#include <stdio.h>
#include <stdlib.h>
//#include "timer.hxx"
#include "timer2.hxx"
#include "error.hxx"

main(int argc, char ** argv) {
  error_handler error("timetest error :\n\t");
  if(argc < 2)
    error.terminate("usage : timetest delay_in_seconds");
  timer T1, T2;
  T1.start( );
  T2.pause(atoi(argv[1]));
  T1.mark( );
  printf("elapsed time: %d seconds\n",
          (int)T1.elapsed_time( ));
}
```

Notice that an instance of **class error_handler** is used as an ordinary (non-member) object to print an error message if the user doesn't supply the right number of arguments.

Here's a more interesting use of **class timer**. It takes a command you would ordinarily type at the operating system command prompt and executes it using the ANSI C library **system( )** function. Then it tells you how long it took to execute.

```
// TIMECOM.CXX : Times the execution of a command.
#include <stdio.h>
#include <stdlib.h>
#include <string.h>
#include "timer2.hxx"
#include "error.hxx"

const comsize = 100;  // maximum size of command-line buffer

main(int argc, char ** argv) {
  error_handler error("timecom error :\n\t");
  if(argc < 2)
    error.terminate("usage : timecom command-line");
  timer T1;
  char combuf[comsize];
```

```
combuf[0] = '\0';
// copy the rest of the line into a single buffer:
for(int i = 1; i < argc; i++)
    sprintf(combuf + strlen(combuf), "%s ", argv[i]);
T1.start( );
printf("%s\n", combuf);
system(combuf);
T1.mark( );
printf("elapsed time: %d seconds\n",
        (int)T1.elapsed_time( ));
}
```

The **system( )** command can contain any number of arguments. The arguments are copied into the command buffer called **combuf** by using the **sprintf( )** library function. Each time **sprintf( )** is called, the address it will start writing the next argument to is calculated using the **strlen( )** library function. The result of **strlen( )** is added to the starting address of **combuf** to produce the new address.

Composition with Pointers to Objects

By creating an instance of an object as a member of another object, you decide at compile time how your new class will be composed. You can also delay the decision until run-time by using a pointer to an object instead of an object. This has been called *pluggable pointer composition* because you compose the object at run-time by "plugging in" a pointer to an object. It is a very powerful way to add run-time flexibility to your system.

As an example, suppose you have a base class:

class base { /* ... */ };

and two or more classes derived from that base class:

class derived1 : public base { /* ... */ };

class derived2 : public base { /* ... */ };

and finally, a class that has a pluggable pointer for **class base:**

```
class composed {
 base * pluggable:
 // ...
public:
 composed(base * plg) {
  pluggable = plg;
  // ...
 }
 // ...
};
```

Now you can decide at run-time, using the constructor call, what type of object will be used in **class composed**:

derived1 X;

derived2 Y;

composed c1(&X), c2(&Y);

c1 is created with a **derived1** object, and **c2** is created with a **derived2** object. This works because a derived-class object is also a member of the base class, so a derived-class pointer can be substituted any place a base class pointer is required. Because **base** provides a common interface (via **virtual** functions described in Chapter 8) and **derived1** and **derived2** can have different implementations, you can decide at run-time how an object with pluggable pointer composition will behave. You can also modify its behavior at run-time.

Reusing Code with Inheritance

So far, this chapter has been showing code reuse by including one object inside another object. This section examines code reuse through inheritance. Inheritance is used in two ways. The first, explored in this chapter, is when you have a class that you or someone else wrote and it isn't quite right. However, you don't want to throw away the code and rewrite it from scratch. That would require too much time and effort. Inheritance allows you to tweak the existing code by adding functionality here and there. You only change the features you need to and ignore the rest; you don't need to know how the whole thing works. By reusing code with inheritance, you can program faster.

The second way to use inheritance is to express a problem as a hierarchy of classes. The base class interface is common to all the derived classes. Subclasses can be manipulated using this common interface in some other part of the program. A well-designed program can be extended by simply deriving a new class from the base class—since the program already knows how to talk to any object in a class derived from the base class, the changes are minimal. Creating extensible programs by carefully designing the class hierarchy is investigated in the next chapter.

A Class to Manage the Screen

So far in this book, control of the screen has been implemented via ANSI terminal-control sequences. ANSI terminals are quite common; VT100 terminals or terminal emulators (available on many UNIX machines) use ANSI sequences, and the PC emulates an ANSI terminal when the device driver ANSI.SYS is loaded. However, using ANSI terminal-control sequences isn't particularly general or portable. The example in this section creates a general-purpose screen-control class and isolates the ANSI sequences in the methods. Later in the chapter, this class will be refined and expanded using inheritance.

The functionality of the base class will be limited. The cursor can be moved—you can erase to the end of the line, clear the whole screen, and move the cursor to the home position. You can also save and restore the cursor location. Notice that in the following header file there is no mention of ANSI terminals, or *any* kind of terminal. This means you can implement the functionality anyway you want.

```
// SCREEN1.HXX : Simple screen-handling class

#ifndef SCREEN1_HXX
#define SCREEN1_HXX
```

```
class cursor_controller {
public:
    // Simple cursor motion:
    void up(int rows = 1);
    void down(int rows = 1);
    void right(int cols = 1);
    void left(int cols = 1);
    void move(int row, int col); // absolute positioning
    void home( ) { move(1,1); }
    // Erasing portions of the screen:
    void clear_screen( );  // also send cursor "home"
    void clear_eol( );  // clear to end of line
    // Saving and restoring the cursor position:
    void save( );
    void restore( );
};

#endif // SCREEN1_HXX
```

The implementation of **cursor_controller** uses the ANSI control sequences, which always start with an escape (ASCII 27 or hexadecimal 1B) followed by a left bracket. This "attention sequence" is combined here into a preprocessor constant called **ATN** (for **AT**te**N**tion sequence). **ATN** is included in the print strings using the string concatenation feature of the ANSI preprocessor.

```
// SCREEN1.CXX : Methods for simple screen control

#include <stdio.h>
#include "screen1.hxx"
#define ATN "\x1b["

void cursor_controller::up(int rows) {
    printf(ATN "%dA", rows);
}

void cursor_controller::down(int rows) {
    printf(ATN "%dB", rows);
}

void cursor_controller::right(int cols) {
    printf(ATN "%dC", cols);
```

```
}

void cursor_controller::left(int cols) {
   printf(ATN "%dD", cols);
}

void cursor_controller::move(int row, int col) {
   printf(ATN "%d;%dH", row, col);
}

void cursor_controller::clear_screen( ) {
   printf(ATN "2J");
}

void cursor_controller::clear_eol( ) {
   printf(ATN "K");
}

void cursor_controller::save( ) {
   printf(ATN "s");
}

void cursor_controller::restore( ) {
   printf(ATN "u");
}
```

Here is a program to test **cursor_controller**:

```
// SCR1TEST.CXX : test for class cursor_controller
#include "screen1.hxx"
#include <stdio.h>
#include "timer2.hxx"
timer TT;

#define MESSAGE(function) \
   cursor.save( ); cursor.home( ); cursor.clear_eol( ); \
   printf("testing " function ); \
   cursor.restore( ); \
   TT.pause(2)

main( ) {
   cursor_controller cursor;
   MESSAGE("clear_screen");
```

```
   cursor.clear_screen( );
   MESSAGE("move");
   cursor.move(12,40);  // center of screen
   MESSAGE("right");
   cursor.right(20);
   MESSAGE("left");
   cursor.left(40);
   MESSAGE("up");
   cursor.up(4);
   MESSAGE("down");
   cursor.down(8);
   MESSAGE("clear_eol");
   for(int i = 0; i < 60; i++)
      printf("X");
   TT.pause(1);
   cursor.left(40);
   TT.pause(1);
   cursor.clear_eol( );
}
```

The test program contains a macro to print a message on the screen and delay for a few seconds (using an instance of **class timer**), so the effects of the screen control commands can be seen. Notice that there is no terminating semicolon in the macro definition. This forces all macro calls to be terminated with a semicolon.

Adding Functionality Through Inheritance

Now, suppose you want to control the screen, but the **cursor_controller** class doesn't do quite what you need. In particular, suppose you want to implement character attributes (blink or reverse video, for instance). With C++, you don't have to rewrite the class to add functionality; you simply inherit it into a new class.

When you inherit a new class from an old class, you indicate the name of the class you are inheriting from immediately after the name of the new class, separated by a semicolon. The syntax is

class *derivedclassname* **:** *baseclassname* {

    // body of class declaration

};

The members of a class default to **private** unless you explicitly declare them **public**. This is also true with inheritance: a base class is **private** unless you explicitly declare it **public**. In the above declaration, all the **public** members of *baseclassname* can only be used by member functions of *derivedclassname,* and are inaccessible to users of *derivedclassname*. If you want the **public** members of *baseclassname* to be available to users of *derivedclassname,* you must declare *baseclassname* **public** as it is being inherited. Thus, the more common syntax you will see for inheritance is

class *derivedclassname* **:** **public** *baseclassname* {

    // body of class declaration

};

When you inherit you get the base class data elements and base class member functions in the derived class. You can add your own data elements and member functions. Inside the derived class member functions, you can call **public** base class member functions and manipulate **public** base class data elements.

There are some member functions which are *not* automatically inherited into the derived class. Constructors, destructors, and the overloaded **operator=( )** all apply to the specific derived class structure. It would be a mistake to assume that what worked properly for constructing and destructing the base class would also work properly for the derived class. Therefore, the compiler forces you to treat constructors, destructors, and the **operator=( )** specially.

The **operator=( )** is usually a combination of destruction and construction (it is covered in Chapter 9). A new destructor must be created (if one is necessary) for each new derived class, and the destructors for the base classes and member objects are called automatically when an object goes out of scope. Constructors, however, are different because they are overloaded and they take arguments. There is a special syntax that allows you to call the constructor for the base class when you are creating the constructor for the derived class. This syntax echoes the syntax for inheritance: it starts with a colon, and ends with the left brace that opens the body. The syntax for a derived class constructor is

derivedclassname:: *derivedclassname(arglist1)* : *(arglist2)* {

   // derived class constructor body

};

where *arglist1* is the argument list for the derived class constructor, and *arglist2* is the argument list for the base class constructor. Notice there is no name associated with the call to the base class constructor, as there is when you have a member object. No instance of the derived class is being created; the derived class has simply been folded into the base class, so it has no name (other than **this**).

This works for C++ releases 1.2 and before or release 2.0 with exactly one base class (single inheritance). If you are deriving from more than one base class (multiple inheritance) you must specify the base class name for each argument list, just as you do with member objects.

If the constructor for the base class is overloaded, the particular constructor that is called depends on the argument list, just as in any overloaded function call. If no explicit call is made to the base class constructor in the derived class constructor, the base class constructor with no arguments is called.

If your derived class contains member objects, the member object constructor calls always occur after the base class constructor call, in the order in which the member objects are declared. The list of calls is separated by commas.

The following example demonstrates how constructors and destructors are called in derived classes. All the classes in the example simply print a message when their constructors and destructors are called, so you can see which ones are called and in what order. The file begins with a preprocessor macro that, given a name, creates a class with these message constructors and message destructors. There are two constructors so you can see the difference between an explicit constructor call (the constructor with an argument) and an automatic constructor call when no explicit call is made (the constructor with no arguments).

Three classes are created: **base**, **member1**, and **member2**. Three derived classes are then constructed, with **base** used as a base class and **member1** and **member2** used as member objects. In the first, **derived1**, the constructor explicitly calls the constructors for the base class and member objects, using arguments. In the second, **derived2**, no calls are made to the base class or member object constructors. In the third, **derived3**, the constructor calls are intentionally made out of their "proper" order to see what will happen. The output of the program is appended as comments at the end.

```
// INHTEST.CXX : demonstration of the order of constructor
// and destructor calls.
#include <stdio.h>

// A macro to create a class:
#define cldecl(CNAME) class CNAME { \
    int i; \
public: \
    CNAME( ) { puts(#CNAME "( ) constructor called"); } \
    CNAME(int) { puts(#CNAME "(int) constructor called"); } \
    ~CNAME( ) { puts(#CNAME " destructor called"); } \
}

cldecl(base);
cldecl(member1);
cldecl(member2);

// The "regular way":
class derived : public base {
    member1 m1;
    member2 m2;
public:
    derived( ) : (1), m1(1), m2(1) {
        puts("derived constructor called");
    }
    ~derived( ) { puts("derived destructor called"); }
};

// No explicit constructor calls
class derived2 : public base {
    member1 m1;
    member2 m2;
public:
    derived2( ) {
        puts("derived2 constructor called");
    }
```

```
    ~derived2( ) { puts("derived2 destructor called"); }
};

// Disordered constructor calls:
class derived3 : public base {
    member1 m1;
    member2 m2;
public:
    derived3( ) : m2(1), m1(1), (1) {
        puts("derived3 constructor called");
    }
    ~derived3( ) { puts("derived3 destructor called"); }
};

main( ) {
    {
        puts("\n\t derived X:");
        derived X;
    }
    {
        puts("\n\t derived2 X:");
        derived2 X;
    }
    {
        puts("\n\t derived3 X:");
        derived3 X;
    }
}

/* output from this program:

        derived X:
base(int) constructor called
member1(int) constructor called
member2(int) constructor called
derived constructor called
derived destructor called
member1 destructor called
member2 destructor called
base destructor called

        derived2 X:
base( ) constructor called
```

```
member1( ) constructor called
member2( ) constructor called
derived2 constructor called
derived2 destructor called
member1 destructor called
member2 destructor called
base destructor called

        derived3 X:
base(int) constructor called
member1(int) constructor called
member2(int) constructor called
derived3 constructor called
derived3 destructor called
member1 destructor called
member2 destructor called
base destructor called


*/
```

To test the classes, an instance of each class is put inside its own scope, so you can see all the constructor calls and then all the destructor calls for each object one at a time. As you can see from the output, the order you write the constructor calls for the inherited class and member objects is unimportant—the compiler always performs the calls the same way. The constructor with no arguments (or all default arguments) is called if no constructor call is explicitly written. And the destructor calls are out of your hands, since the compiler always calls the destructors in reverse order to the way the constructors were called, with the exception of member objects.

ADDING ATTRIBUTES TO CURSOR_CONTROLLER Now that you understand the mechanics of creating a derived class from a base class and/or member objects, the process of adding functionality to **cursor_controller** is straightforward. Here is the new class:

```
// SCREEN2.HXX : Adding new features to cursor_controller
// through inheritance.
#ifndef SCREEN2_HXX
#define SCREEN2_HXX
#include "screen1.hxx"  // must have the base class declaration
```

```
class cursor_controller2 : public cursor_controller {
public:
    void normal( );  // no attributes
    void high_intensity( );
    void blink( );
    void reverse( );
    void invisible( );
};

#endif // SCREEN2_HXX
```

And here are the methods for **cursor_controller2**:

```
// SCREEN2.CXX : Methods for screen control with attributes
#include <stdio.h>
#include "screen2.hxx"
// ANSI attributes:
#define ATTRIBUTE(A) printf("\x1b[" #A "m")

void cursor_controller2::normal( ) {
    ATTRIBUTE(0);
}
void cursor_controller2::high_intensity( ) {
    ATTRIBUTE(1);
}

void cursor_controller2::blink( ) {
    ATTRIBUTE(5);
}

void cursor_controller2::reverse( ) {
    ATTRIBUTE(7);
}

void cursor_controller2::invisible( ) {
    ATTRIBUTE(8);
}
```

When you inherit, you don't need access to the source code for the
methods of the base class. You *do* need the header file and the object code
for the methods. The derived class uses the declaration of the base class.

Thus, the header file for the base class must be included in the header for the derived class because the base class must be declared before the derived class. The object code for the base class must be searched by the linker to resolve all the calls to the methods of the base class. When SCREEN2 is linked, the object file from SCREEN1 must be searched by the linker (**class timer2** doesn't have an object code file since it consists solely of **inline** functions).

Here is a program to test **cursor_controller2**:

```
// SCR2TEST.CXX : test for class cursor_controller2
#include "screen2.hxx"
#include "timer2.hxx"
#incllude <stdio.h>

timer TT;

#define test(feature)   cursor.move(12,20); \
    cursor.clear_eol( ); \
    cursor.feature( ); \
    printf(#feature "text"); \
    TT.pause(1); \
    cursor.normal( )

main( ) {
    cursor_controller2 cursor;
    cursor.clear_screen( );
    test(normal);
    test(high_intensity);
    test(blink);
    test(reverse);
    test(invisible);
    // The finale:
    cursor.move(12,20);
    cursor.clear_eol( );
    cursor.reverse( ); cursor.blink( );
    printf("That's All, Folks!");
    TT.pause(2);
    cursor.normal( );
    // If you don't do a cursor.normal( ) as the very last
    // function, the program exits and leaves the attribute !
}
```

The **test( )** macro allows you to test all the new features of the class without writing a lot of code. Notice that both the "stringize" and string-concatenation features of the preprocessor are used in the statement

**printf(#feature " text"); **

MORE IMPROVEMENTS TO CURSOR_CONTROLLER2   **cursor_controller2** still lacks polish. For one thing, you may have noticed that when you use it, the program exits without resetting the screen attributes to "normal." If you forget to do this yourself, the terminal may be left with undesirable attributes. Also, what is to keep the user from declaring more than one instance of **cursor_controller2** ? This isn't a windowing system, which would allow multiple windows. There is only one screen.

It would also be helpful to print an error message if the user tries to move the cursor off the screen. Finally, it would be nice to add some support for display formatting: centering text, drawing vertical and horizontal lines of user-selected characters, and delays to allow end users time to read the screens.

To add these features, **cursor_controller2** will be inherited into a class called **screen_controller**. This new class will contain a member object of **class error_handler** to generate error messages, and a member object of **class timer** to allow pausing during output messages. **screen_controller** will also contain maximum row and column coordinates for the screen to use for bounds checking and display formatting. To prevent more than one instance of **screen_controller** in a program, **screen_controller** will contain a **static** data member the constructor can examine to ensure no other objects of the class already exist.

Here is the header file for **screen_controller**:

```
// SCREEN3.HXX : Inheriting cursor_controller2 and adding
// more improvements.
#ifndef SCREEN3_HXX
#define SCREEN3_HXX
#include "screen2.hxx"
#include "error.hxx"
#include "timer2.hxx"

class screen_controller : public cursor_controller2 {
    int rowmax, colmax; // screen boundaries
    error_handler error;
    timer interval;
```

```
        static object_count; // counts number of instances
public:
    // The defaults are for a "standard" terminal:
    screen_controller(int rows = 25, int cols = 80);
    // but you can change them:
    void setrows(int rows);
    void setcols(int cols);
    int maxrow( ) { return rowmax; }
    int maxcol( ) { return colmax; }
    // the destructor cleans up the screen:
    ~screen_controller( );
    // moving the cursor to the corners of the screen:
    void upper_left( );
    void lower_left( );
    void upper_right( );
    void lower_right( );
    // draw vertical line of lc;
    void draw_vertical(int row, int col, int length, char lc);
    // draw horizontal line of lc:
    void draw_horizontal(int row, int col, int length, char lc);
    // center text on a particular row
    void center(int row, char * text);
    // Replace inherited function with error-checking version:
    void move(int row, int col);
    // built-in time delay function:
    void pause(int seconds = 1);
    // draw a box around the edges of the screen.  The characters
    // used for the box are:
    //   hor = horizontal line character
    //   ver = vertical line character
    //   ul = upper-left corner character
    //   ur = upper-right corner character
    //   ll = lower-left corner character
    //   lr = lower-right corner character
    void drawbox(int hor, int ver,
                 int ul, int ur, int ll, int lr);
};

// Single global instance of this class:
extern screen_controller screen;

#endif // SCREEN3_HXX
```

Notice that one of the member functions in a base class, **move( )**, has been redeclared. Whenever you take a function that has been defined in a base class and redefine it in a derived class, you must redeclare it in the derived class. This makes it explicit to both the compiler and the user that the old definition of the function is being replaced. You can still *use* the old definition of the function; however, in the **screen_controller::move( )** code that follows, you will see a call to **cursor_controller::move( )**. The scope resolution operator (::) is necessary here because otherwise the compiler would take the nearest function and you would get an infinitely recursive call. (Well, not actually infinite. Only until the stack blows up.) The implementation of **screen_controller::move( )** is not very efficient because of the error checking and function call overhead. It is a demonstration of how to make particular function calls rather than how to write efficient code.

The preceding header file declares a single global instance of the **screen_controller** called **screen**, which is defined in the implementation file that follows:

```
// SCREEN3.CXX : methods for "polished" screen controller class
#include <stdio.h>
#include <string.h>
#include "screen3.hxx"

// Create a single global instance of screen_controller.  If
// the user tries to create another it generates a run-time
// error message.

screen_controller screen;  // use default parameters

screen_controller::screen_controller(int rows, int cols) :
   rowmax(rows), colmax(cols),
   error("screen_controller error :\n")
{
   if(object_count)
     error.terminate("only one instance of screen_controller "
     "is allowed.\nAn object called screen is automatically "
     "defined for you.");
   else
     object_count = 1;
   printf("\x1b[=7l"); // turn off line wrap
}
```

```
void screen_controller::setrows(int rows) {
   rowmax = rows;
}

void screen_controller::setcols(int cols) {
   colmax = cols;
}

screen_controller::~screen_controller( ) {
   normal( );  // return to normal text upon exit.
   printf("\x1b[=7h");  // turn on line wrap
}

void screen_controller::upper_left( ) {
   move(1,1);
}

void screen_controller::lower_left( ) {
   move(rowmax,1);
}

void screen_controller::upper_right( ) {
   move(1,colmax);
}

void screen_controller::lower_right( ) {
   move(rowmax,colmax);
}

void screen_controller::draw_vertical(
      int row, int col, int length, char l_char) {
   if(row > rowmax || (row + length) > rowmax)
      error.terminate("draw_vertical: row index out of bounds");
   if(col > colmax)
      error.terminate("draw_vertical: col index out of bounds");
   for(int rrow = row; rrow <= row + length; rrow++) {
      // call the more efficient version of move:
      cursor_controller::move(rrow,col);
      printf("%c", l_char);
   }
}

void screen_controller::draw_horizontal(
```

```
                 int row, int col, int length, char l_char) {
       if(col > colmax || (col + length) > colmax)
           error.terminate("draw_horizontal: row index out of bounds");
       if(row > rowmax)
           error.terminate("draw_horizontal: col index out of bounds");
       for(int ccol = col; ccol <= col + length; ccol++) {
           // call the more efficient version of move:
           cursor_controller::move(row,ccol);
           printf("%c", l_char);
       }
   }

   void screen_controller::center(int row, char * text) {
       move(row, (colmax - strlen(text))/2 );
       printf("%s", text);
   }

   void screen_controller::move(int row, int col) {
       if(row > rowmax)
           error.terminate("move: row index out of bounds");
       if(col > colmax)
           error.terminate("move: col index out of bounds");
       // call a base class function:
       cursor_controller::move(row,col);
   }

   void screen_controller::pause(int seconds) {
       interval.pause(seconds);
   }

   void screen_controller::drawbox(int hor, int ver,
                       int ul, int ur, int ll, int lr) {
       draw_vertical(0, 0, maxrow( ) - 1, ver);
       draw_vertical(0,maxcol( ), maxrow( ) - 1, ver);
       draw_horizontal(0, 0, maxcol( ) - 1, hor);
       draw_horizontal(maxrow( ), 0, maxcol( ) - 1, hor);
       upper_left( ); printf("%c",ul);
       lower_left( ); printf("%c",ll);
       upper_right( ); printf("%c",ur);
       lower_right( ); printf("%c",lr);
   }
```

Notice the calls to the member object constructors in the constructor for **screen_controller**. Even though the class is inherited, no call to the base class constructor is made because there is none. There is also no explicit call to the constructor for **interval** because that object has a constructor with no arguments that will be called automatically. The constructor first looks at the **static** variable **object_count**. A **static** variable, which is shared by all objects in a class, is initialized by the start-up code to zero. If **object_count** is non-zero, it means that an instance of this class has already been created, so the user is trying to create a second **screen_controller**. This is an error, so the program is terminated with a message to the user. If **object_count** is zero, this is the first object, so **object_count** is set to 1, and a command is given to turn off the line wrap (which causes the screen to shift up at inopportune times). The destructor returns the cursor type to normal and turns the line wrap back on.

The **draw_vertical( )** and **draw_horizontal( )** functions can be used to draw lines of arbitrary length starting at arbitrary positions on the screen. They first check the starting and ending positions of the line to make sure it doesn't exceed the boundaries. The **drawbox( )** command uses several of the other member functions to draw a border around the edge of the screen. You specify the characters used in the border in the argument list.

The following program uses some of the features of **screen_controller**. Un-comment the two statements at the beginning of **main( )** to see the effect of trying to define a second instance of **screen_controller** (other than the one defined in SCREEN3.CXX) and trying to move the cursor out of bounds.

```
// SCR3TEST.CXX : test for class screen_controller
#include "screen3.hxx"

// Charaters for making a box with double line characters
// on the PC.  Modify these for your own system.
const ulcorner = 201;
const urcorner = 187;
const llcorner = 200;
const lrcorner = 188;
const hbar = 205;
const vbar = 186;
```

```
main( ) {
    // generates error message:
//  screen_controller screen2;
    // generates error message when using default screen size:
//  screen.move(26,81);
    screen.clear_screen( );
    screen.drawbox(hbar, vbar, ulcorner, urcorner,
                   llcorner, lrcorner);
    screen.center(4, "Demonstration of class screen_controller");
    screen.reverse( ); screen.blink( );
    screen.center(8, "That's All, Folks!");
    screen.move(screen.maxrow( ) -1, 0);
    screen.pause(3);
}
```

The vertical bars, horizontal bars, and corners are specific to the PC. If you are using UNIX you will want to change them to something appropriate to your terminal.

Initializing static *Member Variables* SCREEN3.CXX shows the initialization of a **static** member variable, **object_count**, inside the constructor. In fact, **object_count** was already initialized to zero before the constructor was entered. In C++ release 2.0, you are not forced to use a constructor to initialize a static variable. Release 2.0 allows you to explicitly initialize a **static** member variable so it is something other than zero before any constructors are called. To do this, you use the scope resolution operator in an initialization statement specifying the type, full name (including class name), and initial value. The syntax is

type classname::staticmembername = initialvalue;

Initializing static *Objects* In plain C, if you want some initialization performed before **main( )** is called, the code you must write is very implementation dependent. In C++, you simply need to create an object with global lifetime; the object can be explicitly global or it can be **static**. Before **main( )** is called, the constructors for all static objects will be called, so you can put any code you need run before **main( )** inside the constructor. When the program exits, the destructor code for the objects will be called. The **screen** object in SCREEN3.CXX is an example—the destructor always calls the **normal( )** member function so the cursor is never left in an unknown state.

If the definition for one object with global lifetime appears before the definition of another in a single file, the first one's constructor is guaranteed to be called first. Other than that, the order of constructor calls for objects with global lifetime is not guaranteed in C++. If you have two objects with global lifetime defined in two separate files, you don't know which one will be called first. The only guarantee you get is that they will be called before **main( )** and the destructors will be called after **main( )** (unless you exit the program using the ANSI C library function **abort( )**. **exit( )** calls the destructors). If one object depends on another, this can cause problems. The simple solution, if you have enough control of the source code, is to put all objects with global lifetime that depend on one another into a single file, and control the order of constructor calls by the order of definition in the file. This doesn't solve the problem of a constructor for an object with global lifetime that depends on the existence of an initialized object defined in some other object file. For instance, if you want to use the **screen** object in a constructor for an object with global lifetime and you don't have control of the sources where **screen** is defined, you've got problems.

A partial solution to this problem has been presented by Schwarz.[1] He suggests adding a very simple class (referred to in this discussion as the *initializer class*) to the end of a header file for the object you want to create with global lifetime (which will be referred to here as the *static object*, even though it may also be a global object). You can always do this because you always have access to the header file even if you don't have access to the code for the methods. The initializer class has the sole task of initializing the static object. The static object is represented by a pointer, so the compiler doesn't call the constructor for the static object. The initializer class makes a single instance of the object using **new**. You must also add a **static** instance of the initializer class, referred to here as the *initializer object,* to the header, so the initializer object is created in every file where you include the header, but the initializer object is invisible outside the file (it has internal linkage). When the program starts up, *one* of the initializer object constructors will be called before any constructor that uses the global object (since the header must appear before the global object's use).

The initializer class contains a **static int** to count the number of times the global object is created. When the program starts, this **int** is initialized

---

1 Schwarz, Jerry. "Initializing Static Variables in C++ Libraries," *The C++ Report*, Volume 1, Number 1, February 1989

to zero. The first time the initializer class constructor is called, the global object is created and the **static int** is incremented. All the other times the initializer class constructor is called, the global object is not created. As an example, here's what you might add to the header file for **class screen_controller**:

```
class screen_controller { /* ... */ };
// New stuff here:
extern screen_controller * screen;
class screen_initializer {
    static int initialization_count;
public:
    screen_initializer( ) {
    if(initialization_count) return;
    initialization_count++;
    screen = new screen_controller;
}
~screen_controller( ) {
    delete screen;
    screen = 0;
}
};
static screen_initializer screen_init;
```

The destructor relies on the fact that a call to **delete** with an argument of zero has no effect, so the first call to the destructor will destroy the object while the other calls won't do anything.

Notice that **screen** is now a pointer to an object, and not an object, so the member function calls must be made with the arrow (**->**) and not the dot (**.**).

SUGGESTIONS FOR FURTHER IMPROVEMENTS The error checking is currently quite limited—the user is prevented from moving the cursor off the screen with the **move( )** command or the line drawing commands. You can still move the cursor to the right edge of the screen and then issue a **printf( )** statement. You can also move the cursor off the screen with the **up( )**, **down( )**, **left( )**, and **right( )** commands. Even if **class screen_controller** kept track of cursor coordinates whenever the cursor was explicitly moved with a member function, the implicit cursor motion from a **printf( )** statement would always make the system lose track of the cursor.

To solve these problems, you need to force all screen output to go through a member function in the class. You could call this member function **print( )**. To determine the new cursor position after a **print( )** statement, use the ANSI C library function **vsprintf( )** (a companion to **vfprintf( )** used in **class error_handler**) to print the output into a buffer. Use **strlen( )** to measure the length of the buffer and reposition the cursor (assuming it doesn't exceed the boundaries). Finally, send the buffer to the screen. You will also have to search the output string for tabs, carriage returns, and new-lines, and include those in your cursor calculations.

The approach of keeping track of the cursor has two further advantages: you could **center( )** a line without specifying the row number, and the class becomes much more portable. Since all screen I/O goes through the class, you could move code written using **class screen_controller** to a windowing system without too much effort.

Another improvement you might want to make is to replace the existing error function with one that can recover from problems, instead of exiting the program.

Speed is often a problem with screen output. You may want to use a local library of screen output functions to improve the performance. Since C++ classes separate the interface from the implementation, you can reimplement the methods for **class screen_controller** without modifying any programs that use the class. Simply modify and recompile SCREEN3.CXX and relink all the object files to create a new executable file. The efficiency could also be improved through the use of **inline** functions.

In the **makefile** at the end of this chapter, you will see that any program that uses **screen_controller** must link in **screen1.obj**, **screen2.obj** and **screen3.obj**. If you have a librarian, it makes sense to combine these three object files into a single library called **screen.lib**.

Storing Objects on Disk

Reusing code with member objects means defining a class as a collection of objects (composition). Reusing code with inheritance (derivation) means either you are adding successive refinements to the meaning of a class, as has been demonstrated up to now in this chapter, or you want to make the subclass a "kind" of the superclass and use the fact that a group of subclasses all belong to the same superclass, as will be shown in the next chapter, or you want to easily add a feature to other classes that has nothing to do with the hierarchy or successive refinement of a class. This last use will be illustrated in this section.

(The need to add features unrelated to hierarchy or successive refinement is one of the better arguments for multiple inheritance. It is completely reasonable to want to have a hierarchy in a group of classes *and* add a feature like the one in this section.)

It is very convenient to be able to store objects on disk, and to retrieve them later or with some other program. (These are sometimes called *persistent objects*.) The class developed in this section can be inherited into any class and will give the new class the ability to store itself to disk in a file with other instances of the same class. An instance of this class can also read itself from a file containing other instances of the class. This implementation should only be used for classes whose structures do not contain any pointers. If there are any pointers, the pointer is stored, but not the data it points to.

To store an object that has been inherited from class **storable**, the user opens a file with a call to the member function **open_output_file( )**. This function can be called with any object in the class, and the output file remains open and all objects are stored there until the user makes a call to **open_output_file( )**, **open_append_file( )**, or **open_input_file( )**. All files are automatically closed when the program exits. To store an object, the user calls the member function **write_record( )**. To retrieve an object (after **open_input_file( )**) the user creates an object and calls the member function **read_record( )**.

Design Considerations

To implement storability in your new class, you must do two things: create a **static struct** of type **storage_file** as a member of your class, and inherit your class from **class storable**. The **static storage_file** member allows you to successively store objects of your class in the same file, after opening the file only once. Because a different **static storage_file** member is defined for each different **storable** subclass, you can have a different file open for each class. You can only have one file open at a time for a class (this makes intermixed reading and writing tedious), but you can open and close several files sequentially in a session.

Your new class must be inherited from **class storable** instead of defining a **storable** member object because the member functions of **storable** must have access to **this**. **this**, the starting address of the object's structure, must be given to the functions that read a block of memory from disk and write a block of memory to disk. Of course, the base **class storable** has no way of knowing how big the derived class will be—you must specifically set the size of the object via a member function of **class storable**.

Many of the features of this system would have been much more elegant if **static** member objects had been implemented on the compilers available when the book was written. In the methods for the class derived from **storable**, you will see that each constructor must explicitly set the size of the object, when in fact it only needs to be done once for each class, when the program starts up and the single **static storage_file** object is created for the class. With release 2.0, this can be done with a global statement such as

storage_file mjm::disk(sizeof(mjm));

In addition, the destructor call for the static member **disk** (in program compiling under release 2.0) at the termination of the program would ensure that all files are cleaned up properly. This cannot be done in the destructor for **storable**, because every time an object belonging to a subclass of **storable** went out of scope, the file would be closed. To ensure the proper behavior in a program compiling under release 1.2, the ANSI C library function **atexit( )** must be used.

THE END RECORD   It is usually necessary to keep information in each file to describe the file's contents. With a **storable** subclass, you never know how many records the file will contain until you've written them all and are closing the file. Because of this, the information about the file is kept at the *end* of the file instead of the beginning. The information is stored in what will be called an *end record*. You could also reserve space at the beginning before you begin writing records, but the approach used here demonstrates the ability to read a record off the end of the file as well as the beginning.

In this example, the end record only contains the size of each object in the file and the number of objects in the file. This allows some rudimentary error checking, since you can compare the size of the objects in the file with the size of the object you are trying to read from the file. You can also keep track of how many objects are left in the file. You may want to add information to the end record to indicate the date the file was written, its full pathname, machine location, notes about the data, and so on. If you decide to do this, it is important that the size of the end record doesn't change just because you inherit it into a new class, and that any **class storable** can successfully read the end record in any file (so you can generate useful error messages). To do this, you will need to treat the end record as a header block with information leading to more sophisticated data in the file (for instance, the size and location of arbitrary-length text entries).

There are two **private** functions in **class storable** dealing with end records: **write_end_record( )** and **read_end_record( )**. **read_end_record( )** moves to the end of the file minus the size of an end record, reads the record into a temporary structure, and moves back to the beginning of the file. A temporary record is used so the size of the object in the file can be compared with the object opening the file.

In the header file for **class storable**, notice that the constructor must always be handed a pointer to a **storage_file**. This pointer is stored in each object of the derived class; it is the only space overhead in deriving from class **storable**. Here is the header file:

```
// DISKSTOR.HXX : A class designed to be inherited by
// a subclass that needs to store itself to disk and retrieve
// itself from disk.

#ifndef DISKSTOR_HXX
#define DISKSTOR_HXX
#include <stdio.h>

// a file can be unopened, opened for input or output:
```

```
enum ft { nil, input, output } ;

// Each storable class must contain a static object of struct
// storage_file so all storage for objects of that class goes
// to the same file.
// The implementations of C++ used for this book would not
// support static member objects, so the following had to be
// a struct.

struct storage_file {
    char * file_name; // name of file for storage/retrieval
    FILE * file_ptr; // pointer to actual file
    ft filetype;
    struct end_rec {
        int object_size;  // size of objects stored/read
        int object_count; // number of objects stored in file
    } end_record;
};

// A class to be stored on disk must be inherited from the
// following base class:

class storable {
    storage_file * sfile;
    void write_end_record( );
    void read_end_record(end_rec * er);
public:
    storable(storage_file * sf) {
        sfile = sf;
    }
    ~storable( );
    void close_file( );
    void open_output_file(char * filename);
    void open_append_file(char * filename);
    void open_input_file(char * filename);
    int record_count( ) { return sfile->end_record.object_count; }
    void write_record( );  // write the current object to the file
    void read_record( ); // read a record into the current object
    void set_size(int size) {
        sfile->end_record.object_size = size;
    }
};

#endif // DISKSTOR_HXX
```

So you can understand details of the implementation, the next section explains the ANSI C library functions that manipulate files.

ANSI C Library
Functions for File I/O

The ANSI C library functions used in this class read and write data in binary format. That is, if you have a floating-point number represented in 4 bytes in memory, those same 4 bytes will be transferred to disk; the floating-point number will not be converted to a sequence of ASCII digits. This method is generally more conservative with time and space, and you don't have to know anything about the data you are storing other than its size. A call to **write_record( )** will store an exact image of an object's structure on disk.

The primary library functions used for **storable** are **fopen( )**, which opens a file, **fread( )**, which reads a block of data from file into memory, and **fwrite( )**, which writes a block of data from memory into the file. The function **fseek( )** is also used to move around in the file.

You must pass arguments to all the file I/O functions. The most important argument, which is present in all the functions, is the *file pointer.* The file pointer contains all the information about the file and its current state; in particular, at what point in the file the next read or write will occur. When you call **fread( )**, **fwrite( )**, or **fseek( )**, you move the file pointer. **fread( )** and **fwrite( )** move the pointer forward according to the size of the block you read or write. **fseek( )** moves the file pointer to any point in the file relative to the beginning of the file, the current position of the file pointer, or the end of the file.

The file I/O library functions also take other arguments. **fopen( )** must know the filename (a character string) and the *access mode,* which tells it to open the file for reading, writing, or appending and specifies whether the file is text or binary. **fopen( )** returns a file pointer, denoted **FILE *.** Here is the syntax for **fopen( )**:

FILE * fopen(const char * filename, const char * access_mode);

fread( ) and **fwrite( )** need to know where to put the data in memory or where in memory the data is coming from, how big a record is, and how many records to read or write. **fread( )** and **fwrite( )** return the number of records actually read or written. Here is the syntax for **fread( )** (it is identical for **fwrite( )**):

size_t fread(void * buffer, size_t size, size_t count, FILE * stream);

where **size_t** is some integral type declared in **stdio.h**, **size** is the number of bytes in each record, and **count** is the number of records to read.

fseek( ) needs to know whether the new position is relative to the beginning of the file (**SEEK_SET**), the end of the file (**SEEK_END**) or the current position of the file pointer (**SEEK_CUR**). **fseek( )** must also know how far away the file pointer should be from the relative point; this number can be positive or negative. Here is the syntax for **fseek( )**:

int fseek(FILE * stream, long offset, int relative_to);

fseek( ) returns zero unless it fails.

```
// DISKSTOR.CXX : methods for storable base class
#include <stdlib.h>
#include "diskstor.hxx"
#include "error.hxx"
#include <string.h>

static error_handler error("storable error:");

// Private function to write the "end record", which
// holds a value indicating the size of the objects in
// the file and the number of objects.
void storable::write_end_record( ) {
    fwrite(&(sfile->end_record), sizeof(end_rec),
            1, sfile->file_ptr);
}

void storable::read_end_record(end_rec * er) {
    fseek(sfile->file_ptr, -(long)sizeof(end_rec), SEEK_END);
    fread(er, sizeof(end_rec), 1, sfile->file_ptr);
    // move back to beginning of file:
    fseek(sfile->file_ptr, 0L, SEEK_SET);
}

// Function to conditionally close file and
// free the space the filename was using.
void storable::close_file( ) {
```

```
    if(sfile->filetype != nil) {
        if(sfile->filetype == output)
            write_end_record( );
        fclose(sfile->file_ptr);
    }
    if(sfile->file_name)
        delete sfile->file_name;  // free old space
}

storable::~storable( ) {
    // All files are automatically closed by exit( );
    // but you must call close_file( ) yourself or
    // the end record won't get written.  This is solved
    // in release 2.0, which supports static member objects.
}

void storable::open_output_file(char * filename) {
    close_file( );
    sfile->file_name = new char[strlen(filename) + 1];
    strcpy(sfile->file_name, filename);
    sfile->filetype = output;
    // open file:
    if((sfile->file_ptr = fopen(filename, "wb")) == NULL)
        error.terminate("can't open %s for writing\n", filename);
}

void storable::open_append_file(char * filename) {
    close_file( );
    sfile->file_name = new char[strlen(filename) + 1];
    strcpy(sfile->file_name, filename);
    sfile->filetype = output;
    // open file:
    if((sfile->file_ptr = fopen(filename, "rb+")) == NULL)
        error.terminate("can't open %s for appending\n", filename);
    end_rec er;
    read_end_record(&er);  // find out size and number of records
    if(er.object_size != sfile->end_record.object_size) {
        error.message("%s objects wrong size\n", filename);
        error.message("object size = %x\n",
                    sfile- >end_record.object_size);
        error.terminate("file object size = %x\n", er.object_size);
    }
```

```
      if(er.object_count <= 0)
         error.terminate("%s contains 0 objects\n", filename);
      // set file pointer so next write overwrites the end record:
      fseek(sfile->file_ptr, -(long)sizeof(end_rec), SEEK_END);
}

void storable::open_input_file(char * filename) {
   close_file( );
   sfile->file_name = new char[strlen(filename) + 1];
   strcpy(sfile->file_name, filename);
   sfile->filetype = input;
   // open file:
   if((sfile->file_ptr = fopen(filename, "r")) == NULL)
      error.terminate("can't open %s for reading\n", filename);
   end_rec er;
   read_end_record(&er);  // find out size and number of records
   if(er.object_size != sfile->end_record.object_size) {
      error.message("%s objects wrong size\n", filename);
      error.message("object size = 0x%x\n",
                  sfile- >end_record.object_size);
      error.terminate("file object size = 0x%x\n",
                  er.object_size);
   }
   if(er.object_count <= 0)
      error.terminate("%s contains 0 objects\n", filename);
   sfile->end_record = er;  // copy the record
}

void storable::write_record( ) {
   if(sfile->filetype == nil)
      error.terminate("tried to write a file that wasn't open");
   if(sfile->filetype == input)
      error.terminate("tried to write to an input file");
   if ( fwrite(this, sfile->end_record.object_size,
         1, sfile->file_ptr) != 1)
      error.terminate("error writing to %s\n", sfile- >file_name);
   sfile->end_record.object_count++;
}

void storable::read_record( ) {
   if(sfile->filetype == nil)
      error.terminate("tried to read a file that wasn't open");
```

```
    if(sfile->filetype == output)
        error.terminate("tried to read from an output file");
    storage_file * temp = sfile;  // save correct pointer
    if(sfile->end_record.object_count) {
        sfile->end_record.object_count--;
        if ( fread(this, sfile->end_record.object_size,
                1, sfile->file_ptr) != 1)
            error.terminate("tried to read past end of %s\n",
                        sfile->file_name);
    } else
        error.message("can't read past last record in %s\n",
                sfile->file_name);
    sfile = temp;  // recopy correct pointer
}
```

In **open_output_file( )**, **open_input_file( )**, and **open_append_file( )**, a call to **close_file( )** is always made at the beginning of each function. **close_file( )** checks to see if a file is open. If so, it writes the end record, closes the file, and frees the space used by the filename. Thus, the user only has to open files. Unfortunately, the user is required to call **close_file( )** explicitly before the program ends (a condition that can be eliminated by a compiler that supports **static** member objects).

Carefully examine the member functions **read_record( )** and **write_record( )**. After the error checking, the functions make calls to **fread( )** and **fwrite( )**, respectively. Notice that the first argument to **fread( )** and **fwrite( )** is **this**. The representation of the object on disk is being read directly into the current object in **read_record( )**, and the representation is being copied from the current object to disk in **write_record( )**. This is the reason it is so important to inherit **storable** into a new class rather than making it a member object—a member object would use the member's **this**, which wouldn't be right. Notice also that in **read_record( )**, the pointer to **disk** is saved before the read and restored after it. This is because the pointer that was saved to disk was only valid at the time the object was saved.

As objects are read from a file, the **object_count** is decremented so the program knows when there are no more objects. As objects are written to a file, the **object_count** is incremented, so when the end record is written it contains an accurate count of the objects in the file.

Creating a Storable Class

To show you how to make a class with objects that can store themselves to and retrieve themselves from disk, here's an example class that contains some integer and floating-point data:

```
// STORTEST.HXX : test for disk storage classes

#ifndef STORTEST_HXX
#define STORTEST_HXX
#include "diskstor.hxx"

class mjm : public storable {
    int i, j, k;
    double monica, matt, mike, moira, mark;
    static storage_file disk;
public:
    mjm( );
    mjm(int ii, int jj, int kk, double d1, double d2,
        double d3, double d4, double d5);
    void print(char * msg = " ");
};

#endif // STORTEST_HXX
```

The only thing that distinguishes this class from any other is that it contains a **static** instance of **storage_file** and it is inherited from **class storable**. Here is the implementation of **class mjm**:

```
// STORTEST.CXX : test for disk storage classes

#include "stortest.hxx"
#include <stdio.h>

mjm::mjm( ) : (&disk) {
    // there's a more elegant way to do things in 2.0:
    set_size(sizeof(mjm));
}
```

```
mjm::mjm(int ii, int jj, int kk, double d1, double d2,
         double d3, double d4, double d5) : (&disk) {
  // there's a more elegant way to do things in 2.0:
  set_size(sizeof(mjm));
  i = ii;
  j = jj;
  k = kk;
  monica = d1;
  matt = d2;
  mike = d3;
  moira = d4;
  mark = d5;
}

#define PRI(arg) printf(#arg " = %d\n", arg)
#define PRD(arg) printf(#arg " = %f\n", arg)

void mjm::print(char * msg) {
  printf("%s\n", msg);
  PRI(i); PRI(j); PRI(k);
  PRD(monica); PRD(matt); PRD(mike); PRD(moira); PRD(mark);
}
```

The base class constructor takes the address of the **static** instance of **storage_file** as an argument. Because release 1.2 of C++ doesn't handle **static** member objects, the **set_size( )** function must be called upon the entry to each constructor. The size really only needs to be set once, before the program is begun (as would be handled by a **static** constructor), but since you never know which constructor will be called first, you have to do it everywhere.

The **PRI( )** preprocessor macro to print an integer and the **PRD( )** macro to print a floating-point number are simply used to reduce typing and mistakes.

To test **class mjm**, here are two programs. The first creates four instances of **mjm** and writes them to disk.

```
// MJMTEST1.CXX : driver for disk storage test class.  This
// program writes a file of objects.
#include <stdio.h>
#include "stortest.hxx"
```

```
main( ) {
    mjm A(1,2,3, 1.1, 2.2, 3.3, 4.4, 47.0),
        B(4,5,6, 5.5, 6.6, 7.7, 8.8, 47.0),
        C(7,8,9, 9.9, 10.10, 11.11, 12.12, 47.0),
        D(10,11,12, 13.13, 14.14, 15.15, 16.16, 47.0);
    A.print("A");
    B.print("B");
    C.print("C");
    D.print("D");
    A.open_output_file("mjm.dat");  // could use B, C, or D also
    A.write_record( );
    B.write_record( );
    C.write_record( );
    D.write_record( );
    D.close_file( );  // could use A, B, or C also
}
```

The second test program creates four instances of **mjm** and reads them from the same disk file.

```
// MJMTEST2.CXX : driver for disk storage test class.  This
// program reads a file of objects.
#include <stdio.h>
#include "stortest.hxx"

main( ) {
    mjm A, B, C, D;
    A.open_input_file("mjm.dat");
    A.read_record( );
    B.read_record( );
    C.read_record( );
    D.read_record( );
    A.print("A");
    B.print("B");
    C.print("C");
    D.print("D");
}
```

Both programs print out the contents so you can see that the second program does indeed reconstruct the objects that the first program wrote to the disk.

Suggestions for Improvements

Not all file systems keep track of file systems in units of bytes. This means that when you open a file, the "end" may be farther out than where the last record was written. Thus, the implementation shown here may not be portable to all platforms. You can avoid this problem by storing the location of the last record in the beginning of the file.

Several of the features of **class storable** could have been implemented much more elegantly if the compilers used had supported **static** member objects in classes; the constructors and destructors for the static member could have been used for initialization and cleanup. Instead the creator of the new class must pay more attention to this since a **struct** with no member functions had to be used instead.

The approach taken to errors is to **exit( )** the program, which is somewhat hostile. C++ doesn't currently support exception handling, and will not, except experimentally, in AT&T version 2.0, so it takes clever programming to unwind back to a known good state if you hit an exception.

You may want to modify the end record to include more information. Notice you only need to change the declaration of **end_rec**, since all the reading and writing uses **sizeof( )** to determine the size of the record.

Consider what is necessary to allow the system to store and retrieve objects that occupy a piece of memory the size of which is unknown at compile time. Objects like this would consist of a structure containing pointers to data on the free store; this data would have to be stored on disk after the object's structure. The structure, which is always a fixed size, would be read from disk first. From the structure, the size of the arbitrary-sized portion would be determined, so the proper **fread( )** could be performed to reconstruct the rest of the object.

A List That Can Save And Retrieve Itself

The solutions to certain types of problems can be expressed very cleanly using lists of objects. It can be useful to store entire lists to disk, and retrieve those lists from disk. The example presented in this section combines **class storable** with **class DynArray** to create a list that can save and retrieve itself. The objects in the list will be small database records for holding names and addresses; they will belong to **class db_re-**

cord, which is inherited from **class storable**. **class db_list** will be inherited from **class DynArray** to further specify the type of items **DynArray** can hold from **void *** to **db_record ***, and to add methods to store and retrieve the entire list. You may find this example useful not only because you can make a general-purpose list that can store and retrieve itself, but also because you can see various methods of building up a complex class out of simpler classes.

A Class to Hold
A Database Record

A database record is a group of string buffers that are encapsulated into an object. Each string buffer is a field in the record. You can read or write the strings in the fields.

To hold each database record, a class called **db_record** is created. The structure in the class is a fixed size, and you must recompile the program when you add or remove fields—this harks back to the early days of inflexible database managers. To simplify the task of adding a field, two macros are defined. The first, **SIZE( )**, specifies the size of the field. You will notice it adds one to the field size; this is so you don't have to remember to put in space for the **\0** string terminator. The second macro, **FIELD( )**, takes a field name and creates space for it in the structure. **FIELD( )** also defines a function to put data into the field and one to access the data in the field. Notice that the **private** and **public** keywords are used repeatedly in the class declaration. An example of the use of the macros is shown here:

```
// DBRECORD.HXX : database records.  You could take this one
// step further by creating a program that generates all the
// macro calls from a script file.
#ifndef DBRECORD_HXX
#define DBRECORD_HXX
#include <stdio.h>
#include <stdlib.h>
#include <string.h>
#include "diskstor.hxx"

const maxwidth = 100;  // maximum size of a field

// Macros for adding new fields:
```

```
// establish field size.  1 is added for terminating null
#define SIZE(fieldname, fieldsize) \
    const fieldname##_size = fieldsize + 1

// declare a field and create methods for putting information
// into a field and accessing information in a field:
#define FIELD(fieldname) \
private: \
    char fieldname[fieldname##_size]; \
public: \
    void get_##fieldname( ) { \
    get_field(fieldname, fieldname##_size); } \
    const char * read_##fieldname( ) { \
    return fieldname; }

// To add a new field, add SIZE( ) and FIELD( ) macro calls.

SIZE(last, 20);
SIZE(first, 20);
SIZE(business, 40);
SIZE(street, 40);
SIZE(city, 15);
SIZE(state, 10);
SIZE(zip, 15);
SIZE(area, 3);
SIZE(phone1, 8);
SIZE(phone2, 8);


class db_record : public storable {
    static storage_file disk;  // for disk storage
    // simple input from standard input.  You can modify the
    // implementation to make it more sophisticated:
    void get_field(char * field, int maxsize) {
        char buf[maxwidth];
        gets(buf); // gets( ) replaces newline with '\0'
        buf[maxsize - 1] = '\0'; // truncate string
        strncpy(field, buf, maxsize);
    }
public:
    char bstart;  // marks the start of the block
```

```
    FIELD(last);
    FIELD(first);
    FIELD(business);
    FIELD(street);
    FIELD(city);
    FIELD(state);
    FIELD(zip);
    FIELD(area);
    FIELD(phone1);
    FIELD(phone2);
    char bend;    // marks the end of the block
public:
    db_record( ); // constructor
};

// This
// constructor is inline so it doesn't generate multiple
// definition errors at link time.
inline db_record::db_record( ) : (&disk) {
    set_size(sizeof(db_record));
    // zero the block:
    memset(&bstart,'\0', &bend - &bstart);
}
#endif // DBRECORD_HXX
```

The constructor sets the contents of all the data fields to **\0** using the ANSI C library function **memset( )**. **memset( )** must be given a starting address, the value to set the block to, and the size of the block. To calculate the size of the block without knowing the names of the data fields in the block (which could easily change), two dummy pieces of data are placed in the structure: **bstart**, to give the address of the beginning of the block, and **bend**, to get the address of the end of the block. The size of the block is then calculated as **&bend - &bstart**.

The **private** member function **get_field( )** gets an input string from the user and truncates it to the proper size before copying it into the appropriate field in the **db_record** object's structure. You can modify **get_field( )** to do fancier input handling.

In the TAWK example in Chapter 10, a different kind of database file is manipulated. In that example, the fields are also objects. You could use that approach here as well, but the design used is simpler to understand.

A Class to Make
A List of db_records

A **db_record** knows how to store and retrieve itself because it is inherited from **class storable**. To make this system flexible, you must be able to create an arbitrary number of **db_records**—as many as are contained in the database file. **class DynArray** is used because it can handle any number of objects and the mechanism is hidden. **DynArray** handles **void** pointers. The new list should not accept anything but **db_records**. In the following header file, you can see that **class db_list** is inherited from **class DynArray**, and that the methods in **DynArray** that take **void** pointers as arguments, or return **void** pointers, are redefined to pass or return **db_list** objects as pointers.

```
// DBLIST.HXX : a storable list of database records.
#ifndef DBLIST_HXX
#define DBLIST_HXX
// This file organization corresponds to the source-code
// disk for this book.  Yours may be different:
#include "..\chap_6\dynarray.hxx"
#include "dbrecord.hxx"

class db_list : public DynArray {
public:
    // Force all member functions of DynArray that handle void *
    // to only use db_record *
    int add(db_record * dbr) { return DynArray::add(dbr); }
    int remove(db_record * dbr) { return DynArray::remove(dbr); }
    db_record * next( )  { return (db_record *)DynArray::next( ); }
    db_record * current( ) {
        return (db_record *)DynArray::current( );
    }
    db_record * operator[ ](int index) {
        return (db_record *)DynArray::operator[ ](index);
    }
    // New methods for this class:
    void save_list(char * filename) {  // save list to a file
        db_record temp;
        temp.open_output_file(filename);
        reset( );
        do {
            current( )->write_record( );
```

```
      } while(next( ));
      temp.close_file( );
   }
   void retrieve_list(char * filename) { // get from a file
      db_record temp;
      temp.open_input_file(filename);
      // while there are records left, read them from the file:
      while(temp.record_count( )) {
         db_record * dbrp = new db_record;
         dbrp->read_record( );
         add(dbrp);
      }
      temp.close_file( );
   }
};
#endif // DBLIST_HXX
```

The two new member functions, **save_list( )** and **retrieve_list( )**, use local instances of **db_record** called **temp** to open and close the database file, and to see if there are any records left. Since all instances of **db_record** have access to the **static** member **struct disk**, it doesn't matter what object you use to manipulate the file—the modifications to the file affect all of the objects in **db_record**. Thus, **temp** is only used to manipulate the file and never contains any valid data. The need to create a dummy object to call a function like this is removed in C++ release 2.0 by using *static functions*.

Adding Records
To the Database File

Using **db_record** and **db_list**, you can create a set of utilities to work with your database files. The two utilities shown here will add new data to a file, and look up data according to a last name. You may also want to write utilities to sort a file (using the ANSI C library function **qsort( )**), remove records from a file, import and export records in the comma-separated ASCII format used by TAWK in Chapter 10 (the easiest way to do this is to use **class csascii** from that chapter), edit records, print an envelope, and so forth.

The first utility program adds a single record to a file. The file has a fixed name. Both of these decisions were made with the consideration that you will probably have a single database file with all your important names and addresses, and you will probably only add one record at a time. These decisions speed startup and use.

If the program is started and it cannot find the database file (called **namelist.dbf**), it creates one with a single, empty record (so it doesn't contain zero records, which would cause an error), and exits.

Most of the space taken up by the following program is for reading and displaying the information. Because most of the work is hidden in the classes, the key statements are very simple.

db_list database;

database.retrieve_list(dbfile);

opens the database file and reads it in, and

database.add(&new_record);

database.save_list(dbfile);

adds the new record and updates the file with the new list.

```
// DBADD.CXX : Add a single new record to a database file.
// Tests db_record & db_list.  The name of the database file is
// hard-wired into this end-user application to reduce typing
// when adding an entry, but you may want to pick it off the
// command line.
#include "dblist.hxx"
#include "screen3.hxx"

char * dbfile = "namelist.dbf";

main( ) {
    // Check to see if file exists.  If not, create it.
    // Might want to make this into a member function.
    FILE * tmp;
    if ((tmp = fopen(dbfile, "r")) == NULL) {
        db_record temp;
        fprintf(stderr, "initializing %s\n", dbfile);
        temp.open_output_file(dbfile);
        temp.write_record( ); // write an empty record
        temp.close_file( );
```

```
        exit(1);
    } else
        fclose(tmp);
    // Read file into array:
    db_list database;
    database.retrieve_list(dbfile);
    // add new records:
    db_record new_record;

// macro to get the different fields:
#define FGET(fieldname) \
    printf("enter " #fieldname ": "); \
    new_record.get_##fieldname( )

    screen.clear_screen( );
    FGET(last);
    FGET(first);
    FGET(business);
    FGET(street);
    FGET(city);
    FGET(state);
    FGET(zip);
    FGET(area);
    FGET(phone1);
    FGET(phone2);

// macro to display the different fields:
#define FD(fieldname) \
    printf( #fieldname ": %s\n", new_record.read_##fieldname( ))
    screen.clear_screen( );
    FD(last);
    FD(first);
    FD(business);
    FD(street);
    FD(city);
    FD(state);
    FD(zip);
    FD(area);
    FD(phone1);
    FD(phone2);

    database.add(&new_record);
    database.save_list(dbfile);
}
```

Once again, two macros are used to save typing and mistakes in repetitive coding.

Looking Up Records In the Database File

The program presented here uses **db_list** to read a database file (the same one that was created in the above example). It searches for a key phrase—in this case, the last name. The first time it encounters the name it stops looking and displays the name. (Notice the **screen_controller class** is used to clear the screen.) This is somewhat crude, since you may have several entries with the same last name, but this is a simple example. (See LOOKUP.CXX in Chapter 10 for a more elegant way to handle the multiple-name problem.) The code looks like a condensed version of DBADD.CXX.

```
// DBFIND.CXX : Find a record in the database file created by
// DBADD.CXX.  Uses a linear search and requires an exact match
// with no duplications, which is somewhat hostile but gives
// the reader room to improve the project.
#include "dblist.hxx"
#include "screen3.hxx"
#include "error.hxx"

char * dbfile = "namelist.dbf";

error_handler error("dbfind error:");

main(int argc, char ** argv) {
   if(argc < 2)
      error.terminate("usage: dbfind lastname");
   // Read file into array:
   db_list database;
   database.retrieve_list(dbfile);
   // hunt through the database:
   database.reset( );
   int found = 0;
   do {
      if(strcmp(database.current( )->read_last( ), argv[1]) == 0) {
         found++;
         break;
```

```
    }
  } while(database.next( ));
  if(!found) error.terminate("name not found");

// macro to display the different fields:
#define FD(fieldname) \
  printf( #fieldname ": %s\n", \
          database.current( )- >read_##fieldname( ))

  screen.clear_screen( );
  FD(last);
  FD(first);
  FD(business);
  FD(street);
  FD(city);
  FD(state);
  FD(zip);
  FD(area);
  FD(phone1);
  FD(phone2);
}
```

You can see that an instance of **class error_handler** is used for simple error messages. Display code is simplified through macros.

For large, sorted files you can improve the speed of the search by utilizing the ANSI C library function **bsearch( )** instead of a simple sequential search, as shown here.

Accessing Elements of the Base Class

If you are designing a class you intend to be inherited, you may want to give the programmer access to **private** elements in your class, and at the same time prevent the user of your class from manipulating those elements directly. This is a problem, because **private** elements in the base class cannot be accessed by any functions except members or friends of the base class. This means you can't get access to private elements of a class by simply inheriting it.

If you think about it, this makes sense—you don't want the **private** mechanism broken just because a class is inherited. If that were true, then you would no longer have control over what functions could change the **private** data, or even know what those functions were.

The use of the keyword **public** while inheriting a class doesn't affect the **private** elements of the base class, either. It only says whether the **public** members of the base class will be **public** in the derived class. If you leave off the **public** keyword when inheriting a class, the **public** elements of that class will only be accessible to members of the derived class, and not to users of the derived class.

How, then, do you make elements of the base class **private** to users of the base class but available to members of the derived class? The **protected** keyword has the desired effect. Here is an example of the use of the **protected** keyword:

```
// PROTECT.CXX : Use of the "protected" keyword
#include <stdio.h>

class base1 {
    int i;  // i is private
public:
    base1(int ii = 0) { i = ii; }
    void print( ) { printf("base1 i = %d\n", i); }
};

class base2 {
protected:
    int i;  // i is private to users, public to inheritors
public:
    base2(int ii = 0) { i = ii; }
    void print( ) { printf("base2 i = %d\n", i); }
};

class derived1 : public base1 {
public:
    // this won't work:
// print( ) { printf("derived1 i = %d\n", i); }
};

class derived2 : public base2 {
public:
// This will work:
    void print( ) { printf("derived2 i = %d\n", i); }
};
```

In **derived1**, the **print( )** member function won't work because it cannot access the **private** element **i** in **base1**. In **derived2**, however, the **print( )** function has access to the **protected** element **i** in **base2**.

Disabling Member Functions In an Inherited Class

Sometimes you want to inherit a class, but you don't want the user to be able to use certain functions in the base class. There are two methods for solving this problem. The first is to simply to redefine the function in the derived class and make it something innocuous, or have it generate an error message. For example:

```
// HIDE1.CXX : Redefining a base class function in order
// to hide it.
#include "error.hxx"

class base {
    int i, j, k;
public:
    base(int ii = 0, int jj = 0, int kk = 0) {
        i = ii; j = jj; k = kk;
    }
    void setall(int val) {
        i = j = k = val;
    }
    void nullify( ) {
        i = j = k = 0;
    }
};

class derived : public base {
    error_handler error;
public:
    derived(int x, int y, int z)
        : (x,y,z), error("derived error: ") { }
    // setall( ) is automatically available in derived.
    // To prevent the user from calling nullify( ), you can
    // redefine it to generate an error message:
    void nullify( ) {
```

```
        error.message("nullify( ) not available");
      }
};

main( ) {
   base A;
   A.setall(1);
   A.nullify( );
   derived B(1,2,3);
   B.setall(2);
   B.nullify( );  // this generates a run time error
}
```

This method works, but you don't know you've done something wrong until run time. If you want the error messages to be generated at compile time, you can make all the **public** members of the base class **private** in the derived class. Then you can selectively "export" base class functions by stating their names in the **public** section of the derived class. In the following example, the **private** keyword is used explicitly during inheritance. You don't have to do this, but it reminds the user of the class that those members are not available.

```
// HIDE2.CXX : Hiding members by letting the base class be
// private and explicitly "exporting" the acceptable functions.
// This causes compile time errors if you try to use the
// unacceptable functions.

class base {
   int i, j, k;
public:
   base(int ii = 0, int jj = 0, int kk = 0) {
      i = ii; j = jj; k = kk;
   }
   void setall(int val) {
      i = j = k = val;
   }
   void nullify( ) {
      i = j = k = 0;
   }
};
```

```
class derived : private base {
public:
   derived(int x, int y, int z) : (x,y,z) { }
   // all the members of base are private, unless you
   // explicitly "export" them:
   base::setall;
};

main( ) {
   base A;
   A.setall(1);
   A.nullify( );
   derived B(1,2,3);
   B.setall(2);
// B.nullify( );  // this generates a compile time error
}
```

Notice that when you are exporting a function name, you simply state the name—no argument list is given for functions. This method has the advantage of generating errors sooner in the development cycle (during compilation rather than during execution).

Makefile for Chapter Examples

Here is the **makefile** for all the examples in this Chapter:

```
# makefile for examples in chapter 7
# Zortech:
CPP = ztc
# Glockenspiel:
#CPP = ccxx

.cxx.exe:
        $(CPP) $*.cxx

.cxx.obj:
        $(CPP) -c $*.cxx
```

```
all :      timetest.exe timecom.exe inhtest.exe \
           scr1test.exe scr2test.exe scr3test.exe \
           mjmtest1.exe mjmtest2.exe dbadd.exe dbfind.exe \
           protect.obj hide1.exe hide2.exe

timetest.exe : timetest.obj error.obj
           $(CPP) $**

timecom.exe : timecom.obj error.obj
           $(CPP) $**

scr1test.exe : scr1test.obj screen1.obj
           $(CPP) $**

scr2test.exe :  scr2test.obj screen2.obj screen1.obj
           $(CPP) $**

scr3test.exe : scr3test.obj screen3.obj screen2.obj \
               screen1.obj error.obj
           $(CPP) $**

mjmtest1.exe : mjmtest1.obj stortest.obj diskstor.obj error.obj
           $(CPP) $**

mjmtest2.exe : mjmtest2.obj stortest.obj diskstor.obj error.obj
           $(CPP) $**
dbadd.exe : dbadd.obj ..\chap_6\dynarray.obj diskstor.obj \
               error.obj screen3.obj screen2.obj screen1.obj
           $(CPP) $**

dbfind.exe : dbfind.obj ..\chap_6\dynarray.obj diskstor.obj \
               error.obj screen3.obj screen2.obj screen1.obj
           $(CPP) $**

hide1.exe : hide1.obj error.obj
           $(CPP) $**

depend:
           +awk depend makefile > makefile.new
           +makedep -s *.cxx | tformat +downcase >> makefile.new

## dependencies generated by make depend after this line:
##!!
error.obj : error.hxx error.cxx
```

```
timetest.obj : timer2.hxx error.hxx timetest.cxx
timecom.obj : timer2.hxx error.hxx timecom.cxx
screen1.obj : screen1.hxx screen1.cxx
screen2.obj : screen2.hxx screen1.hxx screen2.cxx
screen3.obj : screen3.hxx screen2.hxx screen1.hxx \
              error.hxx timer2.hxx screen3.cxx
diskstor.obj : diskstor.hxx error.hxx diskstor.cxx
scr1test.obj : screen1.hxx timer2.hxx scr1test.cxx
scr2test.obj : screen2.hxx screen1.hxx timer2.hxx scr2test.cxx
scr3test.obj : screen3.hxx screen2.hxx screen1.hxx error.hxx \
              timer2.hxx scr3test.cxx
stortest.obj : stortest.hxx diskstor.hxx stortest.cxx
mjmtest2.obj : stortest.hxx diskstor.hxx mjmtest2.cxx
mjmtest1.obj : stortest.hxx diskstor.hxx mjmtest1.cxx
dbadd.obj : dblist.hxx ..\chap_6\dynarray.hxx dbrecord.hxx \
              diskstor.hxx screen3.hxx screen2.hxx \
              screen1.hxx error.hxx timer2.hxx dbadd.cxx
dbfind.obj : dblist.hxx ..\chap_6\dynarray.hxx dbrecord.hxx \
              diskstor.hxx screen3.hxx screen2.hxx \
              screen1.hxx error.hxx timer2.hxx dbfind.cxx
hide1.obj : hide1.cxx error.hxx
```

As you can see, the dependency list is rather large. Maintaining a correct dependency list can be a real problem as you add more and more classes to your program. Many people have created programs called *dependency list generators,* which go through all your files and determine the dependencies for you. A dependency list generator does not need to be created by the same company that created your compiler—like **make**, it is a separate program.

The dependencies in this **makefile** were generated by a dependency list generator called **makedep** written by Walter Bright, who wrote Zortech C++. You can see how it is used in the rule called **depend**. When you say **make depend**, the **makedep** program looks through all the .cxx files and finds the header-file names. If those header files include other header files, those names are also included on the dependency list. The **-s** flag for **makedep** prevents the inclusion of system files (files in angle brackets).

The dependencies generated by **make depend** are shown below the line with pound signs (#). Before you do another **make depend**, you must remove all the data past the pound signs. In UNIX, you can use AWK or SED to do this automatically; there are also public-domain versions of AWK available for MS-DOS.

8 Writing Extensible Programs in C++

In the previous chapter, inheritance was used to modify a class when it didn't fit the needs of the problem at hand. **public**, **private**, and **protected** data and functions can be added through inheritance to increase the functionality of a class, and **public** members of a base class can be redefined or removed in a derived class. Using inheritance to modify existing classes is a very powerful way to develop code incrementally, especially since you can inherit a class even if you don't have the source code for the methods of that class. Incremental code development with inheritance also isolates bugs. If you have a working base class that you inherit into a derived class that has bugs, there is a reasonable certainty the bugs were introduced in the methods of the derived class.

Using inheritance to change the functionality of an existing class is an excellent programming aid. One of the great benefits of object-oriented programming, however, is not just in writing code but in designing programs. Inheritance is a way of classifying concepts. Many problems can be cast into a hierarchy, or tree, of these concepts; the tree shows which concepts share common features.

As an example, Figure 8-1 shows a hierarchy illustrating various different kinds of transportation. At the base of the tree, all transportation has certain things in common: a certain number of passengers can be carried, a certain speed may be attained, there is a certain fuel efficiency, and so on. In Figure 8-1, transportation is subdivided into types depending on the medium: water, land, air, space, and other dimensions. All of these types of transportation inherit the characteristics of the base class. These types are further subdivided according to their specific idiosyncrasies.

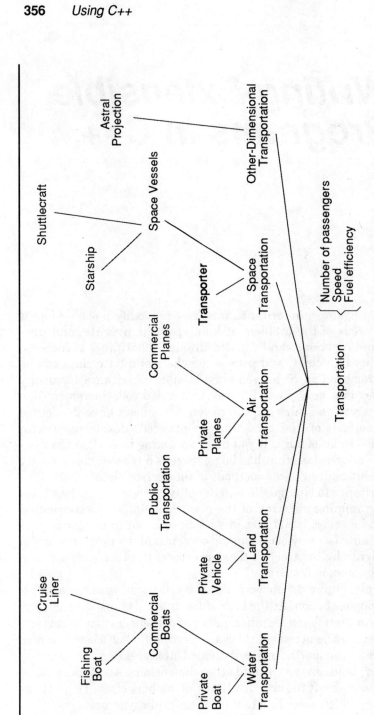

***Figure 8-1.** A transportation tree*

Regardless of the specific subclass of transportation you are dealing with, you know it will have the methods available in the base class (unless those methods have been hidden by privately inheriting the base class). This means that all modes of transportation have a certain common interface, which is the same as saying that all forms of transportation have certain things in common. By creating this tree of subclasses, you can, for instance, always find out how many passengers can be carried by a mode of transportation (assuming there is a method in the base class to tell you this information). A program that manipulates objects of **class transportation** is extensible—all you need to do is derive a new subclass of **transportation**. The program already knows how to handle it.

Coding the transportation Hierarchy *in C++*

To illustrate this point, a portion of the tree in Figure 8-1 will be turned into C++ code, and a small program will be written to manipulate objects of **class transportation**. The program will be extended by adding a new subclass. Here is the code that implements a portion of the tree in Figure 8-1:

```
// TRANSPRT.HXX : Implementing the transportation tree

class transportation {
    char * name;
    int passengers;
    int speed;
    int fuel_use;   // scale of 0 to 100
    int safety;   // scale of 0 to 100
    int range;
    char * difficulty;
    int expense;   // scale of 0 to 100
    char * comfort;
    char * notes;
public:
    transportation(char * nm, int pass, int spd, int fuel,
        int safe, int rng, char * difficult, int exp, char * comf,
```

```
        char * nte) :
            name(nm),
            passengers(pass),
            speed(spd),
            fuel_use(fuel),
            safety(safe),
            range(rng),
            difficulty(difficult),
            expense(exp),
            comfort(comf),
            notes(nte)
            { }
    const char * trans_name( ) { return name; }
    int num_of_pass( ) { return passengers; }
    int max_speed( ) { return speed; }
    int fuel_usage( ) { return fuel_use; }
    int degree_of_safety( ) { return safety; }
    int distance_possible( ) { return range; }
    const char * degree_of_difficulty( ) { return difficulty; }
    int cost( ) { return expense; }
    const char * level_of_comfort( ) { return comfort; }
    const char * other_observations( ) { return notes; }
};

class water_transport : public transportation {
    int crew;
    int hulls;
    char * navigation;
public:
    water_transport(char * nm, int pass, int spd, int fuel,
        int safe, int rng, char * difficult, int exp, char * comf,
        char * nte, int crw, int hls, char * nav) :
            (nm, pass, spd, fuel, safe, rng, difficult, exp,
            comf, nte), crew(crw), hulls(hls), navigation(nav) { }
    int crew_complement( ) { return crew; }
    int number_of_hulls( ) { return hulls; }
    const char * navigational_system( ) { return navigation; }
};

class private_boat : public water_transport {
    int owners;
public:
```

```
        private_boat(char * nm, int pass, int spd, int fuel, int safe,
            int rng, char * difficult, int exp, char * comf,
            char * nte, int crw, int hls, char * nav, int ownrs) :
                (nm, pass, spd, fuel, safe, rng, difficult, exp, comf,
                    nte, crw, hls, nav), owners(ownrs) { }
        int number_of_owners( ) { return owners; }
};

class commercial_boat : public water_transport {
    int fare;
public:
    commercial_boat(char * nm, int pass, int spd, int fuel,
        int safe, int rng, char * difficult, int exp, char * comf,
        char * nte, int crw, int hls, char * nav, int fre) :
            (nm, pass, spd, fuel, safe, rng, difficult, exp, comf,
                nte, crw, hls, nav), fare(fre) { }
    int fare_per_passenger( ) { return fare; }
};

class cruise_liner : public commercial_boat {
    int feed_rate;
public:
    cruise_liner(char * nm, int pass, int spd, int fuel,
        int safe, int rng, char * difficult, int exp, char * comf,
        char * nte, int crw, int hls, char * nav, int fre,
        int feeding) :
            (nm, pass, spd, fuel, safe, rng, difficult, exp, comf,
                nte, crw, hls, nav, fre), feed_rate(feeding) { }
    int meals_per_day( ) { return feed_rate; }
};

class fishing_boat : public commercial_boat {
    int refrigerator_capacity;
public:
    fishing_boat(char * nm, int pass, int spd, int fuel,
        int safe, int rng, char * difficult, int exp, char * comf,
        char * nte, int crw, int hls, char * nav, int fre,
        int refer_cap) :
            (nm, pass, spd, fuel, safe, rng, difficult, exp, comf,
                nte, crw, hls, nav, fre),
                refrigerator_capacity(refer_cap) { }
    int fish_storage_capacity( ) { return refrigerator_capacity; }
};
```

// End of that branch of the tree. Now develop a new branch.

```
class land_transportation : public transportation {
    int wheels;
public:
    land_transportation(char * nm, int pass, int spd, int fuel,
        int safe, int rng, char * difficult, int exp, char * comf,
        char * nte, int whls) :
            (nm, pass, spd, fuel, safe, rng, difficult, exp,
                comf, nte), wheels(whls) { }
    int number_of_wheels( ) { return wheels; }
};

class private_vehicle : public land_transportation {
    int stereo;
    int sunroof;
public:
    private_vehicle(char * nm, int pass, int spd, int fuel,
        int safe, int rng, char * difficult, int exp, char * comf,
        char * nte, int whls, int ster, int sunrf) :
            (nm, pass, spd, fuel, safe, rng, difficult, exp, comf,
                nte, whls), stereo(ster), sunroof(sunrf) { }
    int has_stereo( ) { return stereo; }
    int has_sunroof( ) { return sunroof; }
};

class public_transportation : public land_transportation {
    int schedule;  // how often it comes by
public:
    public_transportation(char * nm, int pass, int spd,
        int fuel, int safe, int rng, char * difficult, int exp,
        char * comf, char * nte, int whls, int sched) :
            (nm, pass, spd, fuel, safe, rng, difficult, exp, comf,
                nte, whls), schedule(sched) { }
    int regularity( ) { return schedule; }
};
```

// And so on, for the other branches of the tree ...

You will notice that the initializations for the member data look like
constructor calls. If your initialization for a variable of a built-in type
consists only of assignment, you can use this "pseudo-constructor call"

format, but only in the constructor initializer list for the enclosing class. That is, you can say

class X {

   int a;

public:

   X( ) : a(1) {}

};

but you cannot say

class Y {

   int b;

public:

   Y( ) { int b(1); }

};

Built-in types have no constructors, so the pseudo-constructor call format for built-in types can only be used in a limited context.

The following file contains a function called **print_info( )**, which asks a **transportation** object some questions. Every object belonging to a class derived from **transportation** also belongs to **class transportation**. You can pass any object derived from **transportation** to **print_info( )** and the function will work properly.

```
// TRANSPRT.CXX : a function that investigates various modes of
// transportation.
#include <stdio.h>
#include "transprt.hxx"

void print_info(transportation & transport) {
    printf("name = %s\n", transport.trans_name( ));
    printf("number of passengers = %d\n",
             transport.num_of_pass( ));
    printf("maximum speed = %d\n", transport.max_speed( ));
    printf("fuel consumption = %d\n", transport.fuel_usage( ));
}
```

Notice that **print_info( )** takes an address (as a reference; a pointer may also be used). You cannot pass an object of a derived class by value to a function that is expecting an object of a base class. The function will not know how big the object is (because you often add elements when you derive a new class) and will be unable to manipulate it. Thus, the compiler generates an error unless you use an address, which is the same size for all objects. This is an important point. When you are treating objects of a derived class as objects of a base class, you must use addresses.

Here's a small program that tests **print_info( )** and some of the transportation classes:

```
// TRANTST1.CXX : Test for print_info( ) and some of the
// transportation classes
#include "transprt.hxx"
void print_info(transportation & transport);

main( ) {
    cruise_liner princess("Love Boat", 800, 14, 1, 99,
        5000, "easy", 100, "very comfortable", " ", 80, 1,
        "electronic", 4000, 8);
    private_vehicle volkswagen("bug", 4, 55, 25, 5, 400,
        "moderate", 10, "somewhat uncomfortable", " ", 4, 1, 1);
    public_transportation bus("greydog", 56, 60, 12, 80, 600,
        "fairly easy",  4, "more uncomfortable", " ", 6, 4);
    print_info(princess);
    print_info(volkswagen);
    print_info(bus);
}
```

Now suppose you want to derive a new class from **transportation** and use **print_info( )** on that class. The **print_info( )** function doesn't need to be changed a bit, as shown here:

```
// TRANTST2.CXX : Deriving a new class and using print_info( )
// on it.  Demonstrates extensibility.
#include "transprt.hxx"
void print_info(transportation & transport);

class other_dimensional : public transportation {
    int dimension;
public:
```

```
    other_dimensional(char * nm, int pass, int spd, int fuel,
        int safe, int rng, char * difficult, int exp, char * comf,
        char * nte, int dim) :
            (nm, pass, spd, fuel, safe, rng, difficult, exp,
            comf, nte), dimension(dim) { }
    int dimension_number( ) { return dimension; }
};

main( ) {
    other_dimensional time_travel("Tardis", 47, 0, 0, 10, 0, "?",
        100, "quite comfortable", " ", 7);
    other_dimensional Buckaroo("Overthruster", 1, 0, 0, 1, 0, "?",
        100, "very jarring", "Can cause insanity", 8);
    print_info(time_travel);
    print_info(Buckaroo);
}
```

Any function or program you write that manipulates objects of a base class (via addresses) is extensible. You can add to its capabilities by deriving a new class from the base.

Virtual Functions

Suppose you want to create functions and programs that manipulate base class objects so those functions and programs are extensible through inheritance. Sooner or later you will run into a problem, which can best be illustrated by an example. **description** is a simple class that carries a description of itself and has a method to print the description.

```
// DESCRIP1.HXX : A class that contains a self-description.
#include <stdio.h>
#ifndef DESCRIP1_HXX
#define DESCRIP1_HXX

class description {
protected: // so derived classes have access
    char * information;
public:
```

```
      description(char * info) : information(info) { }
      void print( ) { printf("%s\n", information); }
};


#endif // DESCRIP1_HXX
```

Now suppose you want to extend the abilities of the class and any function or program that uses **class description** by inheriting the class into a more specific form of **description** containing more information. To print the additional information, the **print( )** function must be redefined for each new class. Here are some examples:

```
// DESCRIP2.HXX : subclasses of class description
#include "descrip1.hxx"
#ifndef DESCRIP2_HXX
#define DESCRIP2_HXX

class sphere : public description {
   float radius;
public:
   sphere(char * info, float rad) : (info), radius(rad) { }
   // redefine the base-class member function:
   void print( ) {
      printf("%s\n", information);
      printf("radius = %g\n", radius);
   }
};

class cube : public description {
   float edge_length;
public:
   cube(char * info, float edge) : (info), edge_length(edge) { }
   // redefine the base-class member function:
   void print( ) {
      printf("%s\n", information);
      printf("edge length = %g\n", edge_length);
   }
};

#endif // DESCRIP2_HXX
```

So far, things look fine. However, there is a discrepancy between treating an object as a member of the base class and treating it as a member of a derived class. This test program illustrates the problem:

```
// DESCRIP.CXX : test of derived description classes
#include "descrip2.hxx"

sphere small_ball("mini", 1.0),
       beach_ball("plastic", 24.0),
       planetoid("moon", 1e24);
cube crystal("carbon", 1e-24),
     ice("party", 1.0),
     box("cardboard", 16.0);

description * shapes[ ] = {
   &small_ball,
   &beach_ball,
   &planetoid,
   &crystal,
   &ice,
   &box
};

main( ) {
   // print the descriptions individually:
   small_ball.print( );
   beach_ball.print( );
   planetoid.print( );
   crystal.print( );
   ice.print( );
   box.print( );

   // print all the descriptions in the list:
   for(int i = 0; i < sizeof(shapes)/sizeof(shapes[0]); i++)
      shapes[i]->print( );
}
```

When the member function **print( )** is called for the specific object, the desired method is used and all the information about the object is printed. However, when the object is treated as an instance of the base class by calling **print( )** for all the pointers in the array **shapes**, the base class method for **print( )** is used! This is clearly not the desired effect. What you want in a case like this is the best of both worlds: the common interface provided by the base class, but the different implementations of the methods created in the derived classes.

The problem occurs because the function call to **print( )** must be resolved before the program executes. When the compiler generates the call to **print( )** for each element of an array of **description** pointers, it generates a call to **description::print( )**, because that's the only function it knows about in that context. Resolving the function call at compile time is called *early binding* or *static binding*.

To implement a common interface with different implementations for the member functions, the resolution of function calls must be delayed until run time. The goal is to be able to say, "you, you're an object of **class description**; **print( )** yourself!" This should not call **description::print( )**, but instead **sphere::print( )** or **cube::print( )**, depending on whether the object is a **sphere** or a **cube**. Resolving a function call at run time is called *late binding* or *dynamic binding*.

To perform dynamic binding of a function in a C++ class, you declare the function **virtual**. You can declare any or all of your class member functions **virtual**. When you declare any functions in a class to be **virtual**, the compiler secretly adds a data member to the class. This data member is referred to here as VPTR and is a pointer to a table of function pointers, referred to here as VTBL. VTBL contains pointers to all the functions that have been declared **virtual** in the class, or in any of the classes that were inherited. Here is a brief example that shows evidence of the secret existence of VPTR:

```
// VPTRSIZE.CXX : Using sizeof( ) to detect the existence of VPTR
#include <stdio.h>

class novirtual {
    int x;
public:
    void foo( ) { }
};

class withvirtual {
    int x;
public:
    virtual void foo( ) { }
};
```

```
main( ) {
    printf("sizeof(novirtual) = %d\n", sizeof(novirtual) );
    printf("sizeof(withvirtual) = %d\n", sizeof(withvirtual) );
}

/* Output of this program on a PC with Zortech C++,
    compact model:

sizeof(novirtual) = 2
sizeof(withvirtual) = 4

*/
```

Whenever a call to a virtual function is made in a C++ program, the compiler generates code to treat VPTR as the starting address of an array of pointers to functions. The function call code simply indexes into this array and calls the function located at the indexed address. The binding of the function call always requires this dynamic indexing activity—it always happens at run time. This means that if you call a virtual member function while treating the object in question as a member of its base class, the correct derived class function will always be called.

To illustrate this, look at the effect of virtual functions on **class description**. The code here is repeated in a single file for the files DESCRIP1.HXX, DESCRIP2.HXX, and DESCRIP.CXX shown previously. Notice that the only change that has been made to the code is the addition of the keyword **virtual** to the **print( )** function in the base class. Everything else is untouched.

```
// DESCRFIX.CXX : Fixing class description w/ virtual functions
#include <stdio.h>

class description {
protected: // so derived classes have access
    char * information;
public:
    description(char * info) : information(info) { }
    // ONLY CHANGE IS RIGHT HERE: ADDITION OF "virtual" :
    virtual void print( ) { printf("%s\n", information); }
};

class sphere : public description {
    float radius;
```

```
public:
    sphere(char * info, float rad) : (info), radius(rad) { }
    // redefine the base-class member function:
    void print( ) {
        printf("%s\n", information);
        printf("radius = %g\n", radius);
    }
};

class cube : public description {
    float edge_length;
public:
    cube(char * info, float edge) : (info), edge_length(edge) { }
    // redefine the base-class member function:
    void print( ) {
        printf("%s\n", information);
        printf("edge length = %g\n", edge_length);
    }
};

sphere small_ball("mini", 1.0),
       beach_ball("plastic", 24.0),
       planetoid("moon", 1e24);
cube crystal("carbon", 1e-24),
     ice("party", 1.0),
     box("cardboard", 16.0);

description * shapes[ ] = {
    &small_ball,
    &beach_ball,
    &planetoid,
    &crystal,
    &ice,
    &box
};

main( ) {
    // print the descriptions individually:
    small_ball.print( );
    beach_ball.print( );
    planetoid.print( );
    crystal.print( );
    ice.print( );
```

```
    box.print( );

    // print all the descriptions in the list:
    for(int i = 0; i < sizeof(shapes)/sizeof(shapes[0]); i++)
        shapes[i]->print( );
}
```

```
/* Output of this program:

mini
radius = 1
plastic
radius = 24
moon
radius = 1e+024
carbon
edge length = 1e-024
party
edge length = 1
cardboard
edge length = 16
mini
radius = 1
plastic
radius = 24
moon
radius = 1e+024
carbon
edge length = 1e-024
party
edge length = 1
cardboard
edge length = 16


*/
```

```
/* Output of this program WITHOUT the "virtual" keyword in
    the base class:

mini
radius = 1
plastic
radius = 24
```

```
moon
radius = 1e+024
carbon
edge length = 1e-024
party
edge length = 1
cardboard
edge length = 16
mini
plastic
moon
carbon
party
cardboard


*/
```

You can see from the output that the virtual function is essential for creating objects with the same interface but different implementations. You may wonder why the programmer is given the option of making a function virtual—why not just let the compiler create *all* functions as virtual? This was another design decision made in favor of run time efficiency. A virtual function requires an extra dereference to make a function call. The language defaults in favor of maximized efficiency, which is accomplished through static binding. This means the programmer is forced to be aware of the difference between early and late binding, and to know when to apply late binding. Several other object-oriented languages, Smalltalk in particular, always use late binding, so the programmer never has to think about it.

Rules for Virtual Functions

When you create a virtual function in a base class, you must have a definition in the base class even if you will never actually call the base class version of the function. (Release 2.0 allows you to define *pure virtual functions* by assigning the definition to zero. See Chapter 11.) You can make the base class definition empty or an error message (if you want to ensure that the user never uses the base class version of the function). If you redefine a virtual function in a derived class, you must redeclare the function in the derived class definition.

The prototypes for the base class version of a virtual function and all the derived class versions must be identical for the virtual function to work properly. This makes sense, since otherwise it wouldn't be a "common interface." In compilers conforming to C++ releases 1.2 and earlier, the compiler generated an error message if you tried to change the prototype of a virtual function in a derived class. In release 2.0, the compiler doesn't complain, but the function definition for that derived class becomes non-virtual. Note that you *can* change the prototype for a non-virtual derived class member function that has been defined in the base class. This is essentially the same as declaring a new function. If you change the prototype of a non-virtual function, the original function in the base class is not hidden (unless the base class is **private**).

You cannot have virtual constructors, but you *can* have virtual destructors. In fact, virtual destructors are essential to the solution of some problems. It is also possible to have virtual operator overloading.

An Extensible Menu System

As a useful example of extensible programming, consider the problem of building menus. Adding functionality to menus is a typical task, and you want it to be as painless as possible. In addition, while the process of selecting one menu item is identical to the process of selecting any other menu item (that is, the interface is the same), what happens when a menu item is selected can vary widely. This sounds like virtual functions could be used to advantage.

The menu system will be broken into two parts. The fundamental unit will be the **class menu_item**, which represents a single item on the menu and its associated functionality. These fundamental units will be contained by a second class called **menu_driver**, which manages a group of **menu_items**. A class that has the sole task of managing objects of another class is often called a *container class*.

Different types of **menu_items** will be derived from the base class. **menu_item** will contain functions to display the item and to test to see if a keystroke matches the item's **activation_letter**. If a match is made, the **virtual execute( )** function is called.

ISOLATING NON-PORTABLE CODE   Before launching into the menu system, a separate problem must be solved. ANSI C doesn't provide any library support for "raw" I/O. The lack of raw I/O means you cannot, for instance, just grab a keyboard character—you must wait until an entire line is entered, followed by a carriage return. Many compiler vendors and/or operating systems *do* provide functions that grab keyboard keys, but they are, of course, non-portable. A good way to handle a problem like this is to isolate the non-portable code. The following header file isolates the non-portable function to get a character from the keyboard. It is designed for Zortech C++; check your compiler manuals for an appropriate function for your local environment.

```
// GETKEY.HXX : isolation of non-portable console I/O.
// Zortech C++ (and many other packages for the PC) use
// getch( ) to do "raw" I/O from the keyboard.  You may need
// to investigate your system to find out how to grab a
// keyboard character without waiting for a carriage return.
#ifndef GETKEY_HXX
#define GETKEY_HXX

#ifdef __ZTC__
#include <conio.h>
#define get_console_key( ) getch( )
#else
// if all else fails, force the user to enter a CR after
// the character:
#define get_console_key( ) getchar( )
#endif

#endif //  GETKEY_HXX
```

The macro **get_console_key( )** is simply redefined for the local environment. You will see this header file used several places in the menu system.

A Class to Represent a Single Menu Entry

Here is the header file for **menu_item**. In the constructor, notice the "constructor syntax" for member variables is again used, even though they are built-in types.

```
// MENUITEM.HXX : class to represent a single item on the menu
#ifndef MENUITEM_HXX
#define MENUITEM_HXX

class menu_item {
    char activation_letter;
    char * item_name;
    char * item_description;
public:
    menu_item(char activ_let, char * name, char * descrip) :
        activation_letter(activ_let), item_name(name),
        item_description(descrip) { }
    // menu action is empty for the base class:
    virtual const char * execute( ) { return " "; }
    void display(int line_number);
    int execute_if_match(char test_char);
};

#endif // MENUITEM_HXX
```

Notice that the function **execute( )** is declared as **virtual**. The function **execute_if_match( )** compares its argument to **activation_letter**. If there is a match, it calls **execute( )**, which has usually been redefined in a derived class (examples will be shown in a test program). The **execute( )** can be anything.

Here are the methods for **menu_item**:

```
// MENUITEM.CXX : methods for single menu item.
// This header file organization is for the book's
// source-code disk.  Yours may be different.
// Use the screen controller from Chapter 7:
#include "getkey.hxx"
#include "menuitem.hxx"
#include "..\chap_7\screen3.hxx"
#include <stdio.h>
// Use the error handler from Chapter 7:
#include "..\chap_7\error.hxx"
static error_handler error("menu_item error: ");
```

```
const key_col = 1;  // column for activation letter
const name_col = 4; // column for item name
const descr_col = 20;  // column for item description

void menu_item::display(int line_number) {
    screen.move(line_number, key_col);
    screen.clear_eol( );
    screen.reverse( );
    printf("%c", activation_letter);
    screen.normal( );
    screen.move(line_number, name_col);
    screen.high_intensity( );
    printf("%s", item_name);
    screen.normal( );
    screen.move(line_number, descr_col);
    printf("%s", item_description);
}

int menu_item::execute_if_match(char test_char) {
    const char * return_message;
    if(test_char == activation_letter) {
        if(*(return_message = execute( )) != '\0') {
            error.newline( );
            error.message(return_message);
            error.newline( );
            error.message("any key to continue");
            get_console_key( );
        }
        return test_char;
    }
    return 0;  // not a match
}
```

Two of the classes from Chapter 7 are being reused here: **class screen_controller,** which automatically defines a single object called **screen** and prevents you from creating any other instances, and **class error_handler,** to report errors. **error,** the instance of **error_handler,** is declared **static,** so it has file scope (internal linkage) and will not interfere with any other file with the same **error_handler** name.

display( ) simply prints the line of information on the screen via the **screen** object. **execute_if_match( )** calls **execute( )** if the key pressed matches **activation_letter. execute( )** returns a pointer to a **const**

character string. If this string is empty, it means that the function has executed successfully. If the string is not empty, there was a problem and the string contains an error message, which can be printed. **execute_if_match( )** returns the key pressed if the key matched with **activation_letter,** or 0 if there was no match (and no call to **execute( )**).

A Class to Manage A Collection of Menu Entries

Now that the base class for a menu entry has been defined, a container class can be created to manipulate an array of pointers to **menu_item.** Since you usually do not create a menu at run time (although this can be desirable, as you will see later), the array of **menu_item** pointers will be created globally, and the starting address of the array will be handed to the constructor, along with the size of the array and a headline to print at the top of the menu. Here is the header file for **class menu_driver:**

```
// MENUDRIV.HXX : container class for menu_item.  Displays a
// menu on the screen and gets a response.
#ifndef MENUDRIV_HXX
#define MENUDRIV_HXX
#include "menuitem.hxx"

// problem with Zortech C++ version 1.07 & earlier forced
// the use of #define instead of const here:
#define quit_character  'q'
#define forward_screen  '+'
#define backward_screen  '-'

// spacing for menu items:
#define linespacing 2

class menu_driver {
    menu_item ** menu; // array of pointers to menu items
    char * headline;  // to print at the top of the screen
    int total_items; // total number in menu
    int items_per_page; // how many you can fit in a screen
    int current_page; // current screen of commands
    int max_pages;   // maximum number of screens
public:
```

```
    menu_driver(char * head, menu_item ** menu_array, int size);
    void display_current_page( );
    int get_and_execute( ); // get a command and do it, return key
    void run( ) {
        do
            display_current_page( );
        while(get_and_execute( ) != quit_character);
    }
    void dump( ); // for testing
};

#endif // MENUDRIV_HXX
```

The value of **linespacing** is used by the constructor to calculate the number of menu items per page. The argument **size** is the size of the menu array and is used to calculate the total number of menu items, which is used to calculate the number of pages. These calculations and the value of **current_page** are used to move back and forth through the menu pages. **display_current_page( )** clears the screen, writes the headline and all the menu items that will fit on the page, and a line at the bottom that tells the user how to quit or move forward or backward through the menu pages (if there is more than one page). The user moves through the menu pages or quits by selecting one of the character constants: **forward_screen**, **backward_screen**, or **quit_character**.

get_and_execute( ) waits for a keystroke and, after checking that it doesn't match with **forward_screen**, **backward_screen**, or **quit_character**, tests each **menu_item** on the current screen of the array until it finds a match. It will return the value of the keystroke if it is **forward_screen**, **backward_screen**, or **quit_character**, or a successfully completed function; otherwise it returns 0.

Here are the methods for **class menu_driver**:

```
// MENUDRIV.CXX : methods for menu_driver class
// This header file organization is for the book's
// source-code disk.  Yours may be different.
#include <stdio.h>
#include "..\chap_7\screen3.hxx"
#include "menudriv.hxx"
#include "getkey.hxx"
const lines_per_page = 25;
```

```
menu_driver::menu_driver(char * head, menu_item ** menu_array,
                          int msize)
    : menu(menu_array), headline(head), current_page(0) {
//   items_per_page = (screen.maxrow( ) - 4) / linespacing;
// the above line doesn't always work with static objects
// because the screen object may not get initialized before
// this object.
        items_per_page = (lines_per_page - 4) / linespacing;
        // two lines for the top and two for the bottom.  Notice the
        // integer divide truncates any remainder.
        // The total number of items is the size of the list
        // divided by the size of a single item (the first one):
        total_items = msize / sizeof(*menu);
        max_pages = total_items / items_per_page;
        if(total_items % items_per_page) // if there's a remainder
            max_pages++;
}

void menu_driver::display_current_page( ) {
    screen.clear_screen( );
    screen.home( );
    screen.reverse( );
    screen.center(1, headline);
    int line = 3;  // current line to write on
    screen.normal( );
    for(int i = current_page * items_per_page;
        (i < (current_page + 1) * items_per_page)
        && (i < total_items) ;
        i++ ) {
      menu[i]->display(line);
      line += linespacing;
    }
    screen.move(screen.maxrow( ), 1);
    screen.reverse( );
    printf("%c", quit_character);
    screen.normal( );
    printf(" to quit   ");
    if(current_page < max_pages - 1) {
      screen.reverse( );
      printf("%c", forward_screen);
      screen.normal( );
      printf(" for next screen   ");
    }
```

```
    if(current_page > 0 ) {
        screen.reverse( );
        printf("%c", backward_screen);
        screen.normal( );
        printf(" for previous screen   ");
    }
}

int menu_driver::get_and_execute( ) {
    int key = get_console_key( );
    switch(key) {
        case quit_character: return quit_character;
        case forward_screen:
            if(current_page < max_pages - 1)
                current_page++;
            return forward_screen;
        case backward_screen:
            if(current_page > 0)
                current_page--;
            return backward_screen;
    }
    // only look at the items on this page:
    for(int i = current_page * items_per_page;
        (i < (current_page + 1) * items_per_page)
        && (i < total_items) ;
        i++ )
        if(menu[i]->execute_if_match(key))
            return key;
    return 0;  // nothing found to execute
}

void menu_driver::dump( ) {
    printf("menu = %p\n", menu);
    printf("headline = %s\n", headline);
#define PR(x) printf(#x " = %d\n", x)
    PR(total_items);
    PR(items_per_page);
    PR(current_page);
    PR(max_pages);
    get_console_key( );
}
```

In the constructor, you may wonder why the size of the **menu_item** pointer array must be passed into the function. The reason is that an array identifier is different than a pointer to an array. If you take the **sizeof( )** an array identifier, you get the size of the entire array. If you take the **sizeof( )** a pointer to an array, you get the size of the pointer. When you pass an array identifier to the constructor as the argument **menu_array**, the starting address of the array is produced and assigned to the **menu_array**. At that point, inside the function, you have no way to figure out how big the array is, since all you have is a pointer. Thus the size of the array must be taken and passed to the constructor. The constructor uses this information to determine the number of menu items per page and the number of pages.

The constructor contains a "wart" in the commented-out line

// items_per_page = (screen.maxrow( ) - 4) / linespacing;

which has been replaced with this calculation:

items_per_page = (lines_per_page - 4) / linespacing;

The first calculation depends on a global object; the second doesn't. The reason the change was made will be discussed in "Initialization of Static Variables" later in this chapter.

display_current_page( ) is primarily a series of calls to **screen**, the **screen_controller** object. After the screen is cleared and the headline is written, the **display( )** function is called for each **menu_item** on the page. At the bottom of the page, the **quit_character** is printed with a message. If there are more pages, the user is told how to move forward, and if it isn't the first page the user is told how to move backward.

In **get_and_execute( )**, the **quit_character**, **forward_screen**, and **backward_screen** selections are handled in a **switch** statement; each of the cases returns from the function, so no **break** statement is needed. If the function makes it through the **switch** statement, then the selected key is tested against all the menu items on the current page with the **menu_item::execute_if_match( )** function. Because only the items on the current page are checked, you can reuse activation letters from page to page. The **dump( )** function has been included for debugging.

Testing the Menu System

To test the menu system, subclasses with different definitions of **execute( )** must be derived from the base **class menu_item**. A global array of pointers to instances of these subclasses must be created, and the starting address of the array must be handed to the constructor for **menu_driver**, along with the size of that array and a headline.

The subclasses derived from **menu_item** in the following example show only a small sample of the possible ways you can redefine **menu_item**. Essentially, anytime you want a new type of menu functionality, you should derive a new subclass. Notice in particular the derived **class submenu**, which allows you to create a menu that is activated by selecting an item from another menu.

```
// MENUTEST.CXX : test for the menu_driver class.
// Note screen size can be changed by commands to the
// screen object before initializing the menu.
#include "getkey.hxx"
#include "menudriv.hxx"
#include "..\chap_7\screen3.hxx"
#include <time.h>
#include <stdio.h>
#include <stdlib.h>

// First, derive some subclasses of menu_item to perform
// different kinds of actions:

class display_time : public menu_item {
public:
    display_time( ) :
        ('t', "display time", "shows you the time and date") { }
    const char * execute( ) {
        time_t now;
        time(&now);
        screen.clear_screen( );
        screen.move(10, 10);
        printf("current time is %s", ctime(&now));
        screen.move(12, 10);
        printf("any key to continue");
        get_console_key( );
        return " ";  // execution finished OK
    }
```

```
} disp_time;  // instance of display_time

// a class to view environment variables:
class environment : public menu_item {
   char * envname;
public:
   environment(char kn, char * en) :
      (kn, en, "displays the value of this environment variable"),
      envname(en)
      { };
   const char * execute( );
};

const char * environment::execute( ) {
   screen.clear_screen( );
   screen.move(10, 10);
   char * envstr = getenv(envname);
   if(envstr == NULL)
      return "Environment variable not found";
   printf("environment variable %s is %s", envname, envstr);
   screen.move(12, 10);
   printf("any key to continue");
   get_console_key( );
   return " ";  // execution finished OK
}

environment path('p', "PATH"),  // instances of this class
             library('L', "LIB"),
             includes('i', "INCLUDE"),
             foo('f', "FOO"); // for testing the error system

class system_command : public menu_item {
protected:
   char * command_name;
public:
   system_command(char ck, char * cname) :
      (ck, cname, "the operating system executes this command"),
      command_name(cname) { }
   const char * execute( );
};
const char * system_command::execute( ) {
   screen.clear_screen( );
   if(system(command_name)) // non-NULL means error
```

```
            return "error executing system command";
        screen.move(screen.maxrow( ), 1);
        screen.reverse( );
        printf("any key to continue");
        screen.normal( );
        get_console_key( );
        return " ";  // execution finished OK
}
system_command directory('l', "ls"),
                    fulldirect('a', "ls -l"),
                    subtree('s', "ls - R"),
                    sysdate('d', "DATE");

// Here's a second tier of inheritance.
// A system command with a single command-line argument:
class syscom_1arg : public system_command {
    char * argprompt;
public:
    syscom_1arg(char ck, char * cname, char * argp) :
        (ck, cname), argprompt(argp) { }
    const char * execute( );
};

const char * syscom_1arg::execute( ) {
    char buf[50], cbuf[100];
    screen.clear_screen( );
    screen.move(10,10);
    printf("%s : ", argprompt);
    gets(buf);
    sprintf(cbuf,"%s %s", command_name, buf);
    if(system(cbuf)) // non-NULL means error
        return "error executing system command";
    screen.move(screen.maxrow( ), 1);
    screen.reverse( );
    printf("any key to continue");
    screen.normal( );
    get_console_key( );
    return " ";  // execution finished OK
}

syscom_1arg emacs('e', "emacs", "name of file to edit"),
                changedir('c', "cd", "directory to change to"),
                more('m', "more", "name of file to view");
```

```cpp
// Here's a class which is a gateway to another menu:
class submenu : public menu_item {
   menu_driver newmenu;
public:
   submenu(char smk, char * smd, char * head,
           menu_item ** sma, int size) :
      (smk, "sub-menu", smd), newmenu(head, sma, size)
      { }
   const char * execute( );
};

const char * submenu::execute( ) {
   newmenu.run( );
   return " ";  // execution finished OK
}

// Here are three classes to display data in
// different number formats.  They will be placed
// in the submenu.  First, a base class to build the others
// with:

class display_number : public menu_item {
   char buf[100];
   char * description;
protected:
   int decimal;
public:
   display_number(char nc, char * nn, char * nd,
      char * descrip) :
      (nc, nn, nd), description(descrip) { }
   void get_decimal( ) {
      screen.clear_screen( );
      screen.move(10, 10);
      printf("decimal value: ");
      gets(buf);
      decimal = atoi(buf);
      screen.move(11, 10);
      printf("%s : ", description);
   }
   void finish( ){
      screen.move(12, 10);
      printf("any key to continue");
      get_console_key( );
```

```
       }
  };

  class display_binary : public display_number {
  public:
     display_binary( ) :
        ('b', "display binary", "converts decimal to binary",
          "binary value") { }
     const char * execute( );
  };

  const char * display_binary::execute( ) {
     get_decimal( );
     // Assume 8-bit bytes here:
     for(int i = 8 * sizeof(int) - 1; i >= 0; i--)
        printf("%c", (decimal & (1 << i)) ? '1' : '0');
     finish( );
     return " ";  // execution finished OK
  }
  display_binary disp_binary;

  class display_hex : public display_number {
  public:
     display_hex( ) :
        ('h', "display hex", "converts decimal to hex",
          "hex value") { }
     const char * execute( ) {
        get_decimal( );
        printf("0x%x", decimal);
        finish( );
        return " ";  // execution finished OK
     }
  };
  display_hex disp_hex;

  class display_octal : public display_number {
  public:
     display_octal( ) :
        ('o', "display octal", "converts decimal to octal",
          "octal value") { }
     const char * execute( ) {
        get_decimal( );
```

```
            printf("0%o", decimal);
            finish( );
            return " ";  // execution finished OK
        }
    };
    display_octal disp_octal;

    // the array holding the submenu menu_item pointers:
    menu_item * submenu_array[ ] = {
        &disp_binary,
        &disp_octal,
        &disp_hex
    };

    // create an object to perform the submenu function:
    submenu number_conversion('n',
        "convert from decimal to other number formats",
        ">>> Number Conversion <<<",
        submenu_array, sizeof(submenu_array));

    // The array holding all the menu_item pointers:
    menu_item * tstmenu1[ ] = {
        &disp_time,
        &number_conversion,
        &path,
        &library,
        &includes,
        &foo,
        &directory,
        &fulldirect,
        &subtree,
        &changedir,
        &sysdate,
        &emacs,
        &more
    };

    main( ) {
        menu_driver menu(">>>> A test menu <<<<",
                            tstmenu1, sizeof(tstmenu1));
        menu.run( );
    }
```

The first class, **display_time**, has such a limited and focused functionality that you would never make more than one instance of it. Since it is so focused, it doesn't need any arguments either. Of course, not using any arguments puts some limitations on the flexibility of choosing activation keys for the other menu items. **display_time** uses the ANSI C library functions for time located in **time.h**.

class environment will display a selected environment string using the ANSI C library function **getenv( )**. The name of the environment variable is displayed as part of the menu display line. This class also demonstrates the use of the error function—if the environment variable is not found (as will probably be the case with **foo**), an error message is returned. You can test it by selecting **foo** from the menu.

class system_command uses the ANSI C library function **system( )** to send a command to the operating system. The name of the command is stored in a **protected** data area (so it can be accessed by derived classes), and is used on the menu display line. When you select a **system_command** object from the menu, the screen is cleared and the command is run. If **system( )** returns a non-zero value, there was a problem executing the command, so an error message is returned; otherwise, the output is held on the screen until the user presses a key. Four instances of **system_command** are defined: three with the **ls** listing program (available on all UNIX machines or on MS-DOS as an add-on or from the public domain), and one with the DATE command. You may have to change the commands used here to suit those available on your local system.

class syscom_1arg is derived from **system_command**. A **syscom_1arg** object executes a system command that takes a single command-line argument. The constructor takes an extra argument that is a string, to prompt the user for the extra command-line argument. **execute( )** prompts the user for the argument and builds the command from the program name and the user-supplied argument by using the ANSI C library function **sprintf( )** to print the formatted string into a buffer called **cbuf. cbuf** is handed to **system( )** to execute the command. Three instances of this class are created, one each to run **emacs** (an editor), **cd** (change directory), and **more** (to view a document a page at a time). All three of these programs are available in one form or another on both UNIX and MS-DOS.

The next class, **submenu**, is particularly interesting because it is a **menu_item** that has as a member object an instance of **menu_driver**, which means that it is a menu item that selects another menu. As you can see, **execute( )** simply runs the menu. To demonstrate the **submenu** function, three subclasses of **menu_item** are created to perform data conversion from decimal to binary, hexadecimal, and octal. (As an exercise, create subclasses to convert numbers in the other direction and add them to the submenu.)

First, **class display_number** is derived from **menu_item**, so the common activities of the classes won't have to be repeated. All the number conversion classes are derived from **display_number** and use the **get_decimal( )** and **finish( )** functions from **display_number**. The number conversion classes are **display_binary**, **display_hex**, and **display_octal**, and the instances of those classes are **disp_binary**, **disp_hex**, and **disp_octal**. An array of **menu_item** pointers called **submenu_array[ ]** is created from the addresses of those instances; and an instance of **submenu** called **number_conversion** is initialized with this array. **number_conversion** is now a **menu_entry** that is a gateway to another menu.

Finally, the array of **menu_item** pointers called **tstmenu1[ ]** is created from the addresses of all the instances of **menu_item** that have been previously defined (including, you will notice, **number_conversion**). In **main( )**, an instance of **menu_driver** called **menu** is initialized with this array, and the **run( )** function is called for the menu. As you can see, all the work is in setting up the menu—running it is a snap!

You will notice, as you derive your own subclasses of **menu_item** and add instances of them to the menu system, that it is very difficult to break the system by adding new subclasses. Any problems you have will be isolated to the new code you write, not to the way your code interacts with the rest of the system. The system interaction is defined by the inheritance hierarchy.

INITIALIZATION OF STATIC VARIABLES The "wart" mentioned about listing MENUDRIV.CXX occurs because the line that was commented out

// items_per_page = (screen.maxrow( ) - 4) / linespacing;

depends on the object **screen** being initialized before the calculation is performed. **screen** is a global object, and its lifetime lasts throughout the whole program. The ANSI C specification describes variables like these as having *static storage duration* (note that **static** variables that are local to a function or class also have static storage duration). C++ programmers often refer to these variables as "static variables" (yet another confusion to the use of the word "static"). What they mean is "static storage duration."

The only guarantees about initialization of static variables are that variables that occur earlier in a file will be initialized first, and that all static variables will be initialized before **main( )** is entered. There are no rules about the order of initialization across different files. In MENU-TEST.CXX, as long as all the **menu_driver** objects were created inside **main( )**, the **screen** object was certain to be initialized, so any calculation in the constructor that depended on **screen** works fine. However, to add a **submenu** object to the main menu, the **submenu** object must be created as a global object so its address can be taken and added to **tstmenu1**. This means that the constructor for **menu_driver**, which is used to create a member object in **submenu**, must be called for a static object. When this was attempted, the preceding commented-out calculation did not work, because the **screen_controller** constructor had not yet been called for the **screen** object, so **screen** was not initialized and the calculation produced the wrong answer.

The solution used in MENUDRIV.CXX robs the system of its flexibility. You can no longer call **screen.setrows( )** and **screen.setcols( )** at the beginning of **main( )** and change the size of the screen. There is no solution in sight in terms of changes to the language. The only way to recapture the flexibility of this system is to rewrite **menu_driver** to dynamically build its own array of **menu_items** at run time (using **DynArray** from Chapter 6, or something like it). This would allow all **menu_driver** objects to be created inside **main( )** or inside the scopes of other functions, so it would be guaranteed that **screen** was properly initialized whenever the **menu_driver** constructor was called. A **menu_driver** that can be created at run time also has a greater flexibility than the one shown in this system, since you could also construct new menus "on the fly," based on user input or other dynamic considerations.

Unfortunately, the inability to control the order of initialization of static objects is not addressed in AT&T release 2.0, so you'll have to learn to live with it (or use the solution presented in the previous chapter).

IMPROVEMENTS YOU MIGHT WANT TO ADD TO THE MENU SYSTEM
Simple improvements include adding page numbers or other messages at the top of the menu, which change depending on what page you are on. You might want to allow a string representation of a key that has no printable representation (ESC for example, or the function keys on a PC). You might also want to add a way to force a page break in menu pages, to group menu items logically on separate pages.

Abstract Classes

In the previous example, **class menu_item** is an *abstract class.* An abstract class is one that has no instances, and is not designed to be used to create objects. An abstract class is only designed to be inherited. It specifies an interface at a certain level of inheritance, and provides a form upon which other classes can be created. In the previous example, all the derived menu items are treated by **class menu_driver** as members of the abstract base **class menu_item**. The abstract class is the most important class in the example, because it is the pathway to extending the system. To create a new type of menu item that can be used by the existing system, you must derive it from the abstract **class menu_item**.

Abstract classes have other benefits. Because an abstract class provides a framework upon which you can build other classes, you don't have to use the C programmer's trick of creating skeleton code and then copying and modifying the skeleton to create new functionality. One problem with skeleton code is if you want to change the skeleton, the changes must be propagated by hand throughout the system—an error-prone process at best. In addition, you don't know if bugs are in the original skeleton or in the modified versions. By using an abstract class, you can change the interface and immediately propagate the changes throughout the system with no errors. All changes made by the programmer who derived the new class are shown explicitly in the code for the derived class, and any bugs that show up are almost always isolated in the new code.

An Abstract
Class to Aid Debugging

Suppose you want to build a project consisting of a large number of classes, possibly using a large number of programmers. If you want to make sure that every class in your project has a common debugging interface, a good approach is to create an abstract class from which all the other classes in your project will be inherited. Since any new classes for your project must inherit from your base class, programmers are not free to create a different interface, so you are guaranteed that all objects in the project will respond to the same debugging commands. DEBUG1.HXX is an example of an abstract base class for debugging.

```
// DEBUG1.HXX : Abstract class for debugging

#ifndef DEBUG1_HXX
#define DEBUG1_HXX
#include <stdio.h>

class debuggable {
public:
   virtual void dump( ) {  // dump contents of an object
      puts("debuggable error: no dump( ) defined for this class");
   }
};

#endif // DEBUG1_HXX
```

If someone derives a new class from **debuggable** and doesn't redefine **dump( )**, you will get a reminder when you try to dump any objects of that new class because the base-class version of **dump( )** will be used.

Here are some examples of classes derived from **debuggable**:

```
// DBGTEST.CXX : testing class debuggable
#include "debug1.hxx"

class X : public debuggable {
   int i, j, k;
public:
   X(int ii = 0, int jj = 0, int kk = 0) {
      i = ii; j = jj; k = kk;
   }
   // Other member functions ...
   void dump( ) {
      printf("i = %d, j = %d, k = %d\n", i, j, k);
   }
};

class Y : public debuggable {
   float f, g, h;
public:
   Y(float ff = 0.0, float gg = 0.0, float hh = 0.0) {
```

```
        f = ff; g = gg; h = hh;
    }
    // Other member functions ...
    void dump( ) {
        printf("f = %f, g = %f, h = %f\n", f, g, h);
    }
};

main( ) {
    X x(1,2,3);
    Y y(4.1, 5.2, 6.3);
    x.dump( );
    y.dump( );

    // you can also treat x & y as members of debuggable:
    debuggable * dba[2];
    dba[0] = &x;
    dba[1] = &y;
    dba[0]->dump( );
    dba[1]->dump( );
}
```

Any objects in your system can be dumped, and you can add the object addresses to a list of **debuggable** pointers and call **dump( )** for members of the list.

The abstract class becomes very powerful when it is integrated into your system and you want to change the interface. Imagine how difficult this would be with a conventional language—first, you would have to make sure the debugging interface was properly implemented in all parts of your system. If you ever wanted to change the interface, you would have to check each separate part to make sure the new interface was properly added. A headache like this will probably keep you from doing it in the first place. With abstract classes in C++, you simply change the abstract class and recompile the system. The new interface automatically propagates through the system; when the virtual function(s) added in the new interface are redefined in the derived classes, the compiler ensures strict conformance to the interface. For example, suppose you wanted to add a function called **trace( )** to **class debuggable**.

```
// DEBUG2.HXX : Changing the interface of an abstract class.
#ifndef DEBUG2_HXX
#define DEBUG2_HXX
#include <stdio.h>

class debuggable {
public:
    virtual void dump( ) {  // dump contents of an object
        puts("debuggable error: no dump( ) defined for this class");
    }
    virtual void trace( ) { }
};

#endif // DEBUG2_HXX
```

When this is used in DBGTEST.CXX, the virtual function **trace( )** may or may not be redefined in **class X** and **class Y**. It is optional until you need it. This means you can design the debugging framework into your classes, and even change the framework midway through your project without any problems. When you do redefine **trace( )**, you must use the identical function prototype as in **debuggable** or release 2.0 compilers will make the function non-virtual, and pre-2.0 compilers will generate an error.

An Abstract Class For Garbage Collection

Suppose you want to create a more general version of the garbage-collection system suggested in Chapter 6. That example showed only one type of garbage object. In practice, you might want to collect the garbage generated by many different classes. This is another situation where an abstract class is appropriate.

The following header file contains the redesigned abstract class for classes that create objects to be collected by a garbage collector. There are only three member functions in the abstract class: the constructor, which adds the pointer to the object to a list used by the garbage collector; a virtual function, which determines whether the object is "dead" (ready to be collected); and a virtual destructor.

```
// GARBAGE2.HXX : Abstract class for objects designed to be
// destroyed by a garbage collector.
#ifndef GARBAGE2_HXX
#define GARBAGE2_HXX

class garbage {
public:
    // this will always be called when the class
    // is inherited, even if the programmer forgets to make
    // the explicit call to the base-class constructor:
    garbage( );
    // It is very important that the destructor be virtual,
    // so the derived class is destroyed properly by the
    // garbage collector:
    virtual ~garbage( ) { }
    // You must redefine this in your derived class so it
    // determines (by some algorithm) whether your object is
    // alive or dead:
    virtual int dead( ) { return 1; }
};

#endif // GARBAGE2_HXX
```

Because the destructor is virtual, the actual destructor for the derived class will be called by the garbage collector. This is very important because the abstract class knows nothing about the intricacies of destroying the derived class object. Virtual destructors make things work properly.

The trickiest function in any garbage-collection scheme is the one that tells the garbage collector whether this object can be safely destroyed. It is the subject of much debate and many papers and algorithms and will not be discussed here. If you can figure out whether your object is not being used, then the function **dead( )** should return a non-zero value. If the object is still in use, **dead( )** should return zero (false).

Here are the methods for the abstract **garbage class** and an example that you can use by defining the preprocessor macro **example**:

```
// GARBAGE2.CXX : methods for improved garbage-collection scheme
#include "garbage2.hxx"
#include <stdio.h>
#include <stdlib.h>
#include "..\chap_6\dynarray.hxx"
```

```
#include "..\chap_7\error.hxx"

// The following #define should be removed after testing:
#define DISPLAY
#ifdef DISPLAY
#include "..\chap_7\screen3.hxx"
#endif

// The following #define creates an example:
#define EXAMPLE

static DynArray memtable;  // place for free store pointers
static error_handler error("garbage error : ");

// the constructor simply adds its address to the array:
garbage::garbage( ) {
    memtable.add(this);  // save the pointer
}

void garbage_collector( ) {
#ifdef DISPLAY
    screen.move(screen.maxrow( ), 1);
    screen.clear_eol( );
    screen.reverse( );
    printf("Garbage collecting...");
    screen.normal( );
#endif
    memtable.reset( );
    do
        if(((garbage *)memtable.current( ))- >dead( )) {
#ifdef DISPLAY
            screen.move(screen.maxrow( ) -1, 1);
            printf("removing %p", memtable.current( ));
#endif // DISPLAY
            delete (garbage *)memtable.current( );
            memtable.remove(memtable.index( ));
        }
    while( memtable.next( ) );
#ifdef DISPLAY
    screen.move(screen.maxrow( ), 22);
    screen.reverse( );
    printf("...done");
```

```
    screen.normal( );
#endif
}


// This is the prototype for the function that sets the
// "new handler" to the function of your choice:
typedef void (*PF)( );  // PF is a pointer to function type
extern PF set_new_handler(PF);

// Here's a class who's only job is to initialize the
// "new handler" to the garbage_collector( ) before main( )
// is entered:
class init_garbage_collector {
public:
   init_garbage_collector( ) {
      set_new_handler(garbage_collector);
   }
} handler_initializer;  // single global instance

#ifdef EXAMPLE

#define chunk 512

class garbage_obj : public garbage {
   int memory[chunk];
public:
   // redefinition of the dead( ) virtual function:
   int dead( ) { return 1; }
};

main( ) {
   // This continues until you interrupt the program.
   // Control-C often does the trick.
   screen.clear_screen( );
   while(1)
      new garbage_obj;  // this loop will exhaust free store!
}

#endif // EXAMPLE
```

If you don't want to see the activities of the garbage collector, you should remove the line

#define DISPLAY

memtable is an instance of **class DynArray** (from Chapter 6) that is used by **class garbage** to store pointers to **garbage** objects when they are created. The garbage collector hunts through **memtable** to find objects that can safely be destroyed. The garbage collector asks each object in the table if it is **dead( )**; if it is, the object is destroyed by calling its (virtual) destructor via **delete**. Notice that you can only create **garbage** objects on the free store.

The C++ function **set_new_handler( )** must be called to install the garbage collector before the program starts. This way, the garbage collector will be called when the free store is exhausted. So that the user doesn't have to worry about this task, a special class is created called **init_garbage_collector**. This class has a single global instance that is called **handler_initializer**. The sole task of **handler_initializer** is to call **set_new_handler( )** and install the garbage collector. This technique of creating a special class and a single global instance is very useful for pre- and post-**main( )** initialization and cleanup. Of course, whenever you do something like this, you run the risk of getting snagged by the order of initialization of static objects.

To test the garbage collector and to show you how to use it, a simple class called **garbage_obj** is created. Its sole purpose is to take up space and exhaust the free store so the garbage collector will be called. **main( )** consists of an infinite loop that calls **new** to create new **garbage_obj**s.

Simulation Using Abstract Classes

As a final example for this chapter, consider the simulation problem introduced in Chapter 6 as the Life program. The Life simulation was somewhat limited in flexibility because inheritance and virtual functions had not yet been introduced. Now that you know about these very important features of C++, you can see a more flexible implementation of a simulation problem.

The abstract class that will be the fundamental unit in this example is called **simulation_unit**. A **simulation_unit** knows where it is on a grid, and how to **display( )** and **erase( )** itself from the screen. A **simulation_unit** can also move itself about on the grid (unlike **LifeUnit**s that were stationary), and it has a member function called **cycle( )** that causes it to move through a step of its existence. Here is the header file for **class simulation_unit**. Notice that most of the functions are virtual.

```
// SIMULATE.HXX : An abstract class for simulation.
#ifndef SIMULATE_HXX
#define SIMULATE_HXX
// Should use const here, if compiler allows it:
#define xsize 25
#define ysize 80

class simulation_unit {
protected:
    int x,y; // location on grid
public:
    virtual void display( ) { }
    virtual void erase( ) { }
    simulation_unit(int x_loc, int y_loc) : x(x_loc), y(y_loc) { }
    virtual ~simulation_unit( ) { erase( ); }
    virtual void cycle( ) { } // execute one cycle of activity
    void move(int x_steps, int y_steps); // to a new location
};

extern simulation_unit * s_grid[xsize][ysize];

#endif // SIMULATE_HXX
```

If **simulation_unit** were derived into a class (to simulate the Life game, for instance), **cycle( )** would be redefined to look at the nearest neighbors and decide whether the current object will live to the next generation. The simulation presented here, however, is quite different than Life because it exists on a passive grid (called **s_grid**, for simulation grid) and the **simulation_unit**s initiate all activities, while Life was created with an active grid—the grid controlled the creation and destruction of **LifeUnit**s. This was not necessarily the best solution, but it solved the problem of figuring out who was to decide when to create and destroy **LifeUnit**s. If you were to create Life using the simulation in this section, the classes derived from **simulation_unit** would have to work it out among themselves how objects are to be created and destroyed. This might seem more realistic for many types of problems, but it is a more difficult problem to solve since it requires that each object essentially be an independent task. In this example, the problem of objects negotiating with each other to determine the outcome of a particular transaction will be completely avoided. With classes derived from **simulation_unit**, objects can perform imperious actions (they can even destroy one another!) but there is no facility for negotiated behavior. As in real life, it seems much easier to act first and ask questions later (albeit far less civilized).

In **simulate.hxx** you can see definitions for the size of the display. Because **s_grid** is an array, it must be declared with constant indices. This can be eliminated with more programming if it becomes a problem, but it would not have added to your understanding of the current example.

There is really only one method for **simulation_unit** that isn't defined in-line, but an additional class is included in the file to initialize the **s_grid**. **class init_grid** has a single global instance called **grid_initializer**. The entire effect of **grid_initializer** takes place in the constructor, where all the elements of **s_grid** are set to zero. **s_grid** could have been encapsulated in a class of its own, but since all the grid elements are **public** anyway, and it would have required an extra level of indirection, nothing would be gained by doing so.

Here is the file containing the definition of **s_grid**, **init_grid**, and the **move( )** method for **simulation_unit**:

```
// SIMULATE.CXX : simulation_unit methods
#include "simulate.hxx"
#include <stdio.h>

// For simplicity, a global array is used:
simulation_unit * s_grid[xsize][ysize];

// A class whose sole task is to initialize grid[ ][ ]
// before main is entered:
class init_grid {
public:
 init_grid( );
};
init_grid grid_initializer; // single global instance

// constructor does the initialization:
init_grid::init_grid( ) {
    for(int i = 0; i < xsize; i++) {
```

```
            for(int j = 0; j < ysize; j++)
                s_grid[i][j] = NULL;
        }
}

void simulation_unit::move(int x_steps, int y_steps) {
    int x_new = x + x_steps;
    int y_new = y + y_steps;
    if (x_new < 0 || x_new >= xsize)
        fprintf(stderr, "move: x coordinate out of bounds");
    if (y_new < 0 || y_new >= ysize)
        fprintf(stderr, "move: y coordinate out of bounds");
    if(s_grid[x_new][y_new] == NULL) { // place is currently empty
        s_grid[x][y] = NULL; // leave old place
        erase( );  // erase old place on screen
        s_grid[x = x_new][y = y_new] = this; // land in new place
        display( ); // display new place on screen
    }
}
```

The responsibility for making sure that the arguments to **move( )** do not attempt to go out of bounds is left to the caller—**move( )** will inform you that you're trying to go out of bounds, but it won't do anything about it. **move( )**, however, will only place the object at the destination if there isn't an object currently at the destination. If the current object is a chess piece, for example, and it is taking another piece from the board, it is responsible for destroying that piece and clearing the position before moving. When a **move( )** is successful, it is quite simple: the old position is cleared (set to NULL), the old place on the screen is erased, the new grid position is set to **this**, the internal object coordinates are set to the new position, and the object's symbol is displayed at the new position on the screen.

To test the simulation system, two classes are derived from **simulation_unit** in the following file. The first class, **pop_around**, simply jumps around the screen in random leaps. The **virtual cycle( )** function calculates a landing point that is within the bounds of the screen and tries to jump there using **move( )**. **move( )**, of course, only moves the object to the destination if no one is already there. The second class, **crawl_around**, can only move one step at a time diagonally from its present position.

Both **pop_around** and **crawl_around** use the ANSI C library function **rand( )**, the pseudo-random number generator, to calculate their next position. The pseudo-random number generator is seeded by calling

srand( ) with some integral argument. As with the Life example in Chapter 6, this seed is obtained from a number generated by the ANSI C library **time( )** function (that is, it is based on the current time). The seeding is accomplished before **main( )** is entered by creating a class called **init_random** with a single global instance called **random_number_initializer**. The seeding takes place in the constructor for **init_random**.

Here is the file containing the class definitions for **pop_around**, **crawl_around**, **init_random**, and the **main( )** file to test the system:

```
// SIMTEST.CXX : simple test of simulation class.  First,
// classes must be derived from the abstract simulation_unit
#include "simulate.hxx"
#include "..\chap_7\screen3.hxx"
#include "..\chap_7\error.hxx"
#include <stdio.h>
#include <stdlib.h>  // srand( ) and rand( )
#include <time.h>  // to seed the random number generator

// This class generates objects that jump around on the
// screen:
class pop_around : public simulation_unit {
public:
    void display( ) {
        screen.move(x,y);
        printf("@");
    }
    void erase( ) {
        screen.move(x,y);
        printf(" ");
    }
    pop_around(int xi, int yi) : (xi, yi) {
        display( );
    }
    void cycle( ) {
        // Generate two random numbers, one to control x-motion
        // and one to control y-motion.  The possible motion in
        // any direction is factored in.
        // First, choose a direction to move -- 0 means positive,
        // 1 means negative.  Note that a zero value for x or y
        // must move in a positive direction and a size-1 value
        // for x or y must move in a negative direction (otherwise
        // divide-by-zero happens in a later calculation).
```

```
      int x_direction;
      int y_direction;
      if ( x == 0 )
         x_direction = 0;  // must move positively
      else if ( x == xsize - 1 )
         x_direction = 1;  // must move negatively
      else
         x_direction = rand( ) / (RAND_MAX / 2);
      if ( y == 0 )
         y_direction = 0;  // must move positively
      else if ( y == ysize - 1 )
         y_direction = 1;  // must move negatively
      else
         y_direction = rand( ) / (RAND_MAX / 2);
      // Now generate a random amount to move in that direction.
      // The amount of space left in that direction is used
      // in the calculation.  Note the use of the ternary
      // if-else operator.
      int x_jump = x_direction ?
         ( -rand( ) / (RAND_MAX / x) ) /* - calculation */
         : (rand( )/(RAND_MAX/(xsize - x -1))); /* + calculation */
      int y_jump = y_direction ?
         ( -rand( ) / (RAND_MAX / y) ) /* - calculation */
         : (rand( )/(RAND_MAX/(ysize - y - 1))); /* + calculation */
      move(x_jump, y_jump); // won't move anyplace if
      // there's already something at the destination.
   }
};

// Objects of this class move one step at a time:
class crawl_around : public simulation_unit {
public:
   void display( ) {
      screen.move(x,y);
      printf("*");
   }
   void erase( ) {
      screen.move(x,y);
      printf(" ");
   }
   crawl_around(int xi, int yi) : (xi, yi) {
      display( );
   }
```

```
    void cycle( ) {
        // random number decides which direction the step is in
        int x_step = (rand( ) / (RAND_MAX / 2)) ? -1 : 1;
        if ( x + x_step < 0 ) x_step = -x_step;
        if ( x + x_step >= xsize ) x_step = -x_step;
        int y_step = (rand( ) / (RAND_MAX / 2)) ? -1 : 1;
        if ( y + y_step < 0 ) y_step = -y_step;
        if ( y + y_step >= ysize ) y_step = -y_step;
        move(x_step, y_step);
    }
};

// This class is just to initialize the random number generator
// before main( ) is entered:
class init_random {
public:
    init_random( ) {
        // Seed the random number generator using the current time:
        time_t tnow;
        time(&tnow);
        srand(tnow);
    }
};
// single global instance:
init_random random_number_initializer;

static error_handler error("simtest error : ");

// initialize grid with pop_around and crawl_around objects,
// and make it run.
main(int argc, char * argv[ ]) {
    if(argc < 3)
        error.terminate("usage : \n\t"
            "simtest pop_factor crawl_factor\n"
            "Where pop_factor determines the density of pop_around\n"
            "objects, and crawl_factor determines the density of\n"
            "crawl_around objects on the display.");
    screen.clear_screen( );
    // Convert the command-line arguments into factors that will
    // turn the random number into a zero or 1, to decide whether
    // to place an object at that point in the grid:
    int pop_factor = RAND_MAX / atoi(argv[1]);
    int crawl_factor = RAND_MAX / atoi(argv[2]);
```

```
// randomly lay down objects in the grid:
for(int x = 0; x < xsize; x++) {
    for(int y = 0; y < ysize; y++) {
        if( !(rand( ) / pop_factor) ) // integer divide
            if(!s_grid[x][y])  // make sure place is empty
                s_grid[x][y] = new pop_around(x,y);
        if( !(rand( ) / crawl_factor) )
            if(!s_grid[x][y])  // make sure place is empty
                s_grid[x][y] = new crawl_around(x,y);
    }
}
// To run the simulation, random x,y locations are chosen and
// if there's a simulation_unit there, it's virtual cycle( )
// is called.  The values xrand and yrand take the value
// returned by rand( ) and turn it into a number that is
// between 0 and xsize for x, or 0 and ysize for y.  The value
// is only calculated once for efficiency (although many
// compilers will fold the constants in so this wouldn't
// be a problem):
int xrand = RAND_MAX / (xsize - 1);
int yrand = RAND_MAX / (ysize - 1);
while(1) {
    int x_location = rand( ) / xrand;
    int y_location = rand( ) / yrand;
    if(s_grid[x_location][y_location])
        s_grid[x_location][y_location]->cycle( );
}
}
```

In **main( )**, **pop_factor** and **crawl_factor** are created from the value of **RAND_MAX** (the largest number the random number generator will create, contained in **stdlib.h**) and the command-line arguments. The number of **pop_around** and **crawl_around** objects that are placed on the grid is controlled by **pop_factor** and **crawl_factor**. The command-line arguments give the user control over the numbers.

In this implementation of the simulation, the location to be "cycled" is chosen randomly; you can perform your cycling in many other different fashions if you wish.

SUGGESTIONS FOR FURTHER DEVELOPMENTS You might want to add a piece of **private** data to the derived classes **pop_around** and **crawl_around** so they can hold unique symbols that will be printed on the screen by **display( )**. This way you can visually track the motion of the objects. Keep in mind that there's nothing here that says an object must only be one character position. You can use up any number of positions, but you might want to make sure that objects can't overlap each other on the screen. There's also nothing that says you are limited to text for your **display( )** function. If you have access to a graphics package, you can easily use that.

You might also want to try creating an arcade-type simulation where the objects run around eating each other, shooting each other, or performing some other hostile activity. Without the ability to negotiate, that's about the level at which you find yourself.

Makefile for Chapter Examples

Here is the **makefile** for all the examples in this chapter. The target **depend** shows one way to set up automatic dependency-list generation. The old dependencies are first removed by running an **awk** script on the **makefile** to generate a file called **makefile.new**. The **awk** script file is shown after the **makefile**. The **awk** script removes everything after the ##!! (you could use any unique token for this). The dependencies were generated by a program called **makedep**, formatted by a program called **tformat** (shown in Chapter 10) and then appended to **makefile.new**. **makefile.new** can then be copied back to **makefile**. This way anytime you add new files, you can just run **make depend** to generate a complete dependency list.

```
# makefile for examples in chapter 8
# Zortech:
CPP = ztc
# Glockenspiel:
#CPP = ccxx

.cxx.exe:
        $(CPP) $*.cxx

.cxx.obj:
        $(CPP) -c $*.cxx
```

```
all :      trantst1.exe trantst2.exe descrip.exe \
           descrfix.exe vptrsize.exe menutest.exe \
           garbage2.exe dbgtest.exe simtest.exe

trantst1.exe : trantst1.obj transprt.obj
           $(CPP) $**

trantst2.exe : trantst2.obj transprt.obj
           $(CPP) $**

menutest.exe : menutest.obj menudriv.obj menuitem.obj \
                   ..\chap_7\screen3.obj ..\chap_7\screen2.obj \
                   ..\chap_7\screen1.obj ..\chap_7\error.obj
           $(CPP) $**

garbage2.exe : garbage2.obj ..\chap_6\dynarray.obj \
                   ..\chap_7\screen3.obj ..\chap_7\screen2.obj \
                   ..\chap_7\screen1.obj ..\chap_7\error.obj
           $(CPP) $**

simtest.exe : simtest.obj simulate.obj ..\chap_7\screen3.obj \
                   ..\chap_7\screen2.obj ..\chap_7\screen1.obj \
                   ..\chap_7\error.obj
           $(CPP) $**

depend:
           +awk ..\depend makefile > makefile.new
           +makedep -s *.cxx | tformat +downcase >> makefile.new

## dependencies generated by make depend after this line:
##!!
transprt.obj : transprt.hxx transprt.cxx
trantst1.obj : transprt.hxx trantst1.cxx
trantst2.obj : transprt.hxx trantst2.cxx
descrip.obj : descrip2.hxx descrip1.hxx descrip.cxx
menuitem.obj : ..\chap_7\screen3.hxx ..\chap_7\screen2.hxx \
                   ..\chap_7\screen1.hxx ..\chap_7\timer2.hxx \
                   ..\chap_7\error.hxx menuitem.cxx menuitem.hxx
menudriv.obj : ..\chap_7\screen3.hxx ..\chap_7\screen2.hxx \
                   ..\chap_7\screen1.hxx ..\chap_7\error.hxx \
                   ..\chap_7\timer2.hxx \
```

```
                        menudriv.hxx menuitem.hxx menudriv.cxx
menutest.obj : menudriv.hxx menuitem.hxx menutest.cxx
dbgtest.obj : debug1.hxx dbgtest.cxx
garbage2.obj : ..\chap_6\dynarray.hxx ..\chap_7\error.hxx \
                    ..\chap_7\screen3.hxx ..\chap_7\screen2.hxx \
                    ..\chap_7\screen1.hxx ..\chap_7\timer2.hxx \
                    garbage2.cxx
simulate.obj : simulate.hxx simulate.cxx
simtest.obj : simulate.hxx ..\chap_7\screen3.hxx \
                    ..\chap_7\screen2.hxx ..\chap_7\screen1.hxx \
                    ..\chap_7\error.hxx ..\chap_7\timer2.hxx \
                    simtest.cxx
```

If you want the dependency list to be generated properly when you are using header files from other directories, you must examine those other header files. If they include any other header files, those other header files must be described in such a way that the dependency generator can find the other files. This usually means using double dots in the path (to mean, "the directory above this one") enough times to get to a common directory between where you are and where the other files exist, and then specifying the path from there. In the source-code listing disk for this book, all the code for each chapter is placed in a subdirectory by itself, and all these subdirectories are off of a single main directory. Thus, the header files in Chapter 7 include entries such as

#include "..\chap_7\screen1.hxx"

so they can be included in files in other directories, and everything will work fine.

Here is the **awk** script used in **make depend. awk** exists on most UNIX machines and is available for MS-DOS commercially or free from a number of sources.

```
# DEPEND.AWK :
# Awk file to strip off all lines after ##!!
# Used in "make depend" to get rid of old
# dependency list.
```

```
# This line says: "print every line"
    {print}

# This line says: "exit when the line consists of ##!!"
# $0 means the whole line, $1 means the first word on
# the line, $2 means the second, etc.
$0 == "##!!" {exit}
```

Most **awk** packages come with documentation; it is very similar to programming in a C-like language that understands strings and automatically breaks up input text lines into words.

9 *Arguments and Return Values*

The primary activity in object-oriented programming is creating new classes of objects. Program complexity is generally hidden in these objects. Writing the **main( )** function consists of managing objects.

In C++ creating a new **class** of object is an extension to the compiler. This is different from "extensible languages" in that the new **class** of objects must be truly integrated into the compiling environment rather than just casually added to the language. In C++, new types of objects are made as "first class" as possible. *First class* means objects of a user-defined type are treated the same as objects of a built-in type. Although classes in C++ are not completely first class, it usually appears that they are: static type checking is performed, objects are initialized and cleaned up, operators may be used with the objects (if operators have been defined for the class), and so on.

This chapter focuses on a more complex issue of creating a first-class user-defined type: passing objects to and returning objects from functions. For simple classes, passing and returning objects is transparent, but when a class becomes more complex a number of issues arise that can be quite confusing to the new C++ programmer. This chapter will teach you to build complex classes that can be passed and returned correctly.

Passing by Name, Value, or Reference

A *function frame* is the place where all the function variables are manipulated. It is bounded by the opening and closing braces of the function. The function communicates with the "outside world" in two ways: by changing values that are global to the function, or through passing and returning. Passing and returning moves values across the boundaries of the function frame.

Information can be moved across the frame boundary in two ways:

- A copy of the entire variable is made.

- Only the address of the variable is transferred across the boundary.

The first method is called *pass-by-value*. Since a copy of the variable is made, the variable can be changed inside the function frame without affecting the variable it was copied from. The second method is called *pass-by-name* when a pointer is passed, and *pass-by-reference* when references are used. In both cases an address is manipulated. (**inline** functions may be treated differently. Some implementations treat references to built-in types as aliases.)

Addresses are passed for two reasons. The first is simply for efficiency; if you know the variable will only be read (and this can be enforced by using the **const** keyword in the argument list), then it is generally faster to pass the address when using objects larger than a pointer. There is an additional benefit to passing an address. The address you pass is for an *initialized* object, and the size of the address is always the same, so there are none of the problems (described later in this chapter) involved with copying and initialization. If the programmer can avoid passing objects by value or returning objects, these problems can be ignored.

The second reason for passing an address is to physically manipulate the object the address points to, that is, to change an object that is external to the function. Normally, the results of a function call should be expressed through the function's return value, but there are situations where this is unsatisfactory. For example, the function may need to have an effect on more than one object. If object addresses are passed, the function may directly affect any number of objects on the other side of the function frame boundary.

Pass-by-Reference

It is said that all argument passing in C is pass-by-value since you explicitly declare pointers and pass addresses. C++ adds a new type of argument passing: pass-by-reference. Passing by reference is the same as declaring an argument to be a pointer and then passing an address. With references, however, the compiler does all the work for you—it forces the address to be passed into the function, even though the user doesn't explicitly take the address. Inside the function you can manipulate the item as if it were an object. This is a big improvement since a lot of errors when using C libraries can be attributed to confusion over whether to pass an address.

Because the C++ compiler handles the details for you when you pass by reference, fewer mistakes are made. Thus, pass-by-reference is the preferred scheme whenever you won't be modifying the argument. It is also often more efficient to pass an address than to copy an entire object into the called function's frame.

When to Pass by Value

There are cases where you genuinely need a copy of an object to be created inside the frame of a function. You may need to modify the object, and you don't want the original touched. In these cases, you must pass the object by value. If the compiler passes an **int**, **float**, or other built-in type by value, it knows what to do: a copy of the data is pushed on the stack before the function is called. When passing a user-defined type, however, the compiler has no idea how to handle it—you may need all kinds of complicated initialization.

If you have a "simple" class (none of the member data are pointers) and you haven't defined a copy-constructor, the compiler resorts to a bitcopy. A bitcopy copies all the bytes of the **struct** in the old object into the **struct** of the new object. A bitcopy is "usually the right thing to do" in the absence of any other instructions by the programmer, but other types of initialization that may take place in the "regular" constructor are then ignored. The bitcopy scheme is often referred to as a *shallow copy,* since it ignores anything but what is in the class structure.

If some of the class members are pointers, a *deep copy* is usually required to allocate free memory and copy the items that are pointed to. Some C++

implementations issue a warning when pointers are copied and no copy-constructor has been defined.

Hidden Activities

Arguments and return values are transparently controlled by the compiler in C. Since the user can define new types in C++, it is important to understand the way arguments are passed and values are returned.

How Arguments Are Passed

When a function is called, the caller pushes arguments on the stack and an assembly-language call is executed. In plain C the last argument in the list is pushed first, but some C++ implementations do not follow this scheme.

Inside the function call, the stack pointer is moved down to make space for local variables, and the arguments are used right on the stack. After the call is completed, the caller cleans the arguments off the stack. This reduces the risk, in old C, of crashing the system by calling a function with the wrong number of arguments, because the caller always pushes and cleans the same number of arguments. In ANSI C, and C++, function prototyping allows the compiler to generate error messages if the function call is made with an incorrect number or type of arguments.

The C compiler knows the sizes of all built-in types and how to pass them by pushing them on the stack. There are a finite number of built-in types, and they are all known when the compiler is written, so dealing with pass-by-value is a straightforward problem. Structures are simply pushed on the stack piece by piece. Passing by name means a pointer is pushed on the stack.

How Values Are Returned

In plain C, values are normally returned in registers. The compiler writer decides which registers will be used to return an **int**, which for a **short**, **double**, etc. It is important that values be returned in registers because C is designed to be *reentrant:* it can be interrupted at any point without destroying data. Well-behaved interrupts always save the register contents, so returning values in registers is safe. If, however, a compiler was created that returned values on the stack, the process would occur as follows: the return value would be pushed on the stack, then the stack pointer would be restored to the point above the return value where the return address is located so an assembly-language **return** can be performed. (The return address is popped off the stack into the instruction pointer.)

Since the stack space where the return value lived would be below the stack pointer in this hypothetical compiler, that stack space might be overwritten by an interrupt routine *after* the return from the function but *before* the caller has a chance to retrieve the result. This would not allow programming with interrupts. Since C and C++ are both intended to be used as systems programming languages, interrupts must be supported so values are returned in registers.

The Problem with Structures

You might wonder what happens when the return value is too large to fit into the register set—particularly when the return value is a **struct**, as is the case when an instance of a **class** is returned. (Physically, a **class** looks like a structure.) The original solution in plain C—and the one most C compilers follow—was to copy the return value to a global **static** data area, return from the function, and then copy the global **static** data area into the destination **struct**. This, of course, is a non-reentrant solution. If an interrupt happens during a return it is possible for the global **static** data area contents to be overwritten. Since most system-level programmers don't return **structs** from functions this non-feature of C has gone largely unheralded.

Because of the way **structs** are returned, the statement

A = B = C;

is not allowed if **A**, **B**, and **C** are structures; **structs** are not completely first class. It is allowed for other types in C.

Some C compilers and all implementations of C++ use a different scheme to return **structs** (and objects, which are just glorified **structs**). The address of the destination **struct** is secretly passed into the function, possibly in registers. The function copies the return value directly into the destination before exiting. Not only is this more efficient since it eliminates a copy, it is reentrant.

You should be aware that the "new, improved" solution to structure copying doesn't necessarily happen automatically in all C++ implementations. The only time you are guaranteed to avoid the global **static** data area when returning an object is if a copy-constructor and an **operator=( )** are defined for the object's class. Both are described in this chapter.

Hidden Activities Specific to C++

C++ also performs hidden activities when handling arguments and return values. Built-in objects, such as **int**, **float**, **long**, and **char**, are treated just as they are in C. The compiler writer knows about these types and can build passing and returning rules into the compiler. The compiler writer doesn't, however, know anything about the new types *you* define.

Since an object looks like a **struct** when it is just sitting in memory, the easy way out is to handle arguments and return values as if an object *is a* **struct**. When the user doesn't intervene this is exactly what the C++ compiler does. A **class**, however, isn't just a structure—it is a true data type and generally has some associated initialization and cleanup. The **class** may also contain pointers to other items. A simple structure copy will not satisfy the general case.

When copying is inappropriate or initialization and cleanup must occur for variables being passed into or out of a function frame, C++ allows the user to implicitly take over the hidden activities that occur by defining a function that is automatically called by the compiler to perform argument passing and value returns. This function is called the *copy-constructor*.

Dangers of Returning Addresses

The novice programmer may wish to avoid all this trouble by only passing and returning addresses of objects. Passing the address of objects *into* a function frame is a very good idea and should be practiced whenever possible (preferably using references), but passing the address of a variable that is local to the function frame *out* of the function frame is usually a bad idea. (See the function **mmtrace::oname( )** in "Tracing the Creation and Destruction of Objects" at the end of this chapter for an example of when it is acceptable.) Once a variable goes out of scope it is never reliable to use that variable, even if the variable is immediately copied. This means that any object requiring initialization or cleanup that is passed by value or returned from a function must have a copy-constructor.

The Copy-Constructor X(X&)

The copy-constructor handles three cases: two for copying, and one for initialization. It is a constructor that takes as its argument a reference to an object of the same class as itself.

Let's look at the simplest case first: initialization. The copy-constructor is called when you want to declare and initialize an object from another object of the same type. Here is an example:

```
// CI.CXX: An example of the copy-constructor
// being used for initialization.
#include <stdio.h> // puts() declaration

class ci {
    int i;
public:
    ci(int j) { i = j; }
    // copy-constructor:
    ci(ci & rv) {
        puts("copy-constructor called");
        i = rv.i; // copy in the rvalue
    }
};

main() {
    ci original(1);
    ci copy1(original); // copy-constructor called.
    ci copy2 = original; // here, too
}
```

Notice that the more common type of constructor call, **copy1**, or the more confusing equals sign, **=**, can be used. It's confusing because most people are familiar with the **operator=( )** being called whenever the compiler encounters an equals sign used with that class. The single case when **operator=( )** is *not* called is *classname object = object;*

Fortunately, it is the only exception so it isn't too hard to remember.

If the class will not be passed or returned, and no objects of the class will be created from other objects in the class, it is not necessary to define a copy-constructor. In the above example, if the declaration and initialization proceed as follows:

classname object1;

classname object2;

object1 = object2;

then the copy-constructor is not called. (**operator=( )** is called instead, if it has been defined. More about that later.)

Copying into and out of Functions

The second, and more complicated use, of the copy-constructor is passing by value and returning a value from a function. If a copy-constructor is available, it is automatically called by the compiler whenever an object is passed or returned by value.

The copy-constructor must perform all the necessary initialization when creating one object from another. When passing objects into a function frame boundary, the object on the inside (the local, or *automatic,* variable) must be initialized from the object on the outside. When returning objects out from a function frame boundary, the object on the outside must be initialized from the object on the inside. Initialization often means simply copying, but it can mean much more, as the example later in this chapter will show.

As an example of a class that requires a copy-constructor, let's look at an integer vector.

```
// VEC.CXX: An integer vector to illustrate the
// need for the copy-constructor
#include <stdio.h>
#include <stdlib.h>

class vec { // an integer vector
    int size;
    int * vp;
```

```
public:
    vec(int i = 0, int j = 0);
    vec(vec & rv);
    ~vec() { delete vp; }
    vec operator=(vec & rv);
    void print(char * msg = "");
    int & operator[](int x);
    int length() { return size; }
};

vec::vec(int i, int j) {
    vp = new int[size = i];
    for (int x = 0; x  size; x++)
        vp[x] = j;
}

vec::vec(vec & rv) {
    vp = new int[size = rv.size];
    for (int x = 0; x  size; x++)
        vp[x] = rv.vp[x];
}

vec vec::operator=(vec & rv) {
    delete vp; // release old memory
    vp = new int[size = rv.size];
    for (int x = 0; x  size; x++)
        vp[x] = rv.vp[x];
    return *this;  // return a copy of this object
}

void vec::print(char * msg) {
    printf("%s",msg);
    for(int x = 0; x  size; x++)
        printf("%d ",vp[x]);
    printf("\n");
}

int & vec::operator[](int x) {
    if (x  size)
        return vp[x];
    else {
        puts("vec index out of range");
        exit(1);
    }
```

```
}
// pass in by value, return by value:
vec func1(vec value) {
    if (value.length() = 1)
        value[0] = 0;
    return value;
}

main() {
    vec A(4,3);
    vec B;
    A.print("A: ");
    B.print("B: ");
    B = func1(A);
    A.print("A after func1: ");
    B.print("B after func1: ");
}
```

The copy-constructor is used to pass a **vec** by value to **func1( )**, and to return a **vec** from **func1( )**. The copy-constructor is essential here since the compiler would default to simply copying the source object structure into the destination object structure, and the dynamically allocated memory, which is destroyed when **value** goes out of scope in **func1( )**, isn't reproduced for the returned value. The pointer to the memory would be copied, but when the free store was released it would either be written over immediately (depending on the implementation of **new** and **delete**) or overwritten when **new** is called at some unknown later time.

When you define a copy-constructor, you take all responsibility for the process—the default structure copy isn't performed. As you can see in the copy-constructor for **class vec**, the value of **size** is copied just as it would be in the default case, but new memory is allocated, initialized, and assigned to **vp**.

Both uses of the copy-constructor—copying and initialization—are invoked secretly by the compiler under certain conditions: in copying when you pass arguments by value into and out of a function, and with initialization when you declare a new value as created from an old one.

Object Assignment

The **operator=( )** function is another situation where the compiler defaults to a simple structure copy if assignment (*not* initialization, as discussed before) is used and no **operator=( )** has been defined. This is often an equally satisfactory solution for simple objects. When pointers and more elaborate initialization occur, an **operator=( )** must be defined.

Unique Characteristics of operator=( )

Assignment falls into an category by itself, and the programmer must be aware that **operator=( )** is unlike any other operator or member function.

operator=( ) CANNOT BE INHERITED   Although **operator=( )** is not a constructor in the usual sense, it does not inherit—just as constructors do not inherit. Assignment must perform the same duties as both the destructor and the copy-constructor. To perform these duties, **operator=( )** must have specific knowledge of the derived class; that is, the derived class often contains new elements. Thus an inherited **operator=( )** is incorrect and the compiler should generate an error message.

operator=( ) IS DESTRUCTION PLUS COPY-CONSTRUCTION   As you can see in **class vec**, assignment is nearly identical to copy-construction. The difference is that the copy-constructor is a constructor, so you must assume the object has never been initialized. Assignment, however, is simply another function called for an initialized object, so the object is "live" and the initialized parts must be properly dealt with. In **class vec**, memory is allocated when **operator=( )** is called, and that memory must be freed before assigning **vp** to a new vector.

Here is a general guideline: when defining an **operator=( )** you must perform the duties of the destructor on the current object before performing the duties of the copy-constructor with the argument to the right of the equal sign. Thus the **operator=( )** for a complicated object often looks like the code for the destructor followed by the code for the copy-constructor.

operator=( ) HAS A RETURN VALUE   The **operator=( )** has another difference from the copy-constructor in that it has a return value. (Constructors have a return value but the programmer has no control over it. All constructors return **this** automatically.) The return value can be anything, but the most common practice is to return a copy of the newly assigned-to object by saying **"return *this"**. This allows sequential assignment to be performed, as in **"A = B = C;"**. As noted before, this kind of structure assignment is not allowed in C. The result of the assignment may also have a member function called, as in **"if ((A=B).is_ok( )) ... "**.

Hidden Intermediate Variables

The statement

B = func1(A);

from the preceding program is rather elaborate and can cause confusion, especially if you print a message whenever destructors are called. This statement causes hidden objects to be created.

In C, a function can be called for its return value or for its side effects—modifications to its arguments or to data external to the function. Thus the user must always have the option of ignoring the return value. The compiler knows how to ignore return values in C, but C++ objects are generally more complicated, so a *hidden intermediate variable* must be created to catch the return value as the function passes it out. A reference to this return value is then passed to **vec::operator=( )**. As discussed earlier, **operator=( )** usually has a return value; this value is assigned to a *second* hidden intermediate variable. In fact, for any function that returns an object by value the compiler generates a hidden intermediate variable when the function is called, if the object's **class** has a copy-constructor.

If **func1( )** is being called for its side effects, as in

func1(A);

the hidden intermediate variable is simply ignored after the return value is copied into it. Note that, as it is written, **func1( )** has no side effects. The address of the hidden intermediate variable is secretly passed into **func1()** so the result can be copied into it at the end. Thus the code generated for a call to **func1( )** will show an extra argument being passed.

Walking Through an Assignment

Here is a review of the statement

B = func1(A);

At the beginning of the function, stack space is allocated for the **struct** of the local object **value**. The copy-constructor is called for **value** with **A** as an argument so **A** can be reproduced in the local frame. The address of the hidden intermediate variable is also passed into the function. At the end of the function, the copy-constructor is called for the hidden intermediate variable with **value** as an argument. The copy-constructor copies the return value out of the function frame. Since the return value of **func1( )** is being used here, its address (the address of the hidden intermediate variable) is passed to the next function in line, **vec::operator=( )**.

   operator=( ) is called as a member function for **B**. Since **B** will be bound again to new data, the old representation of **B** must be cleaned up first. In this case, "cleaned up" simply means deleting the free memory allocated for the vector. New memory is then allocated to hold the new vector and the data is copied in, just as with the copy-constructor. Finally, **operator=()** returns a copy of itself by secretly calling the copy-constructor for a second hidden intermediate variable with its own address, **this**, as an argument. This last hidden intermediate variable is unused so it is ignored (except by the destructor, which cleans it up at the end of the scope). For further clarification, see "Tracing the Creation and Destruction of Objects" later in this chapter for an example that generates output to show the creation and use of hidden intermediate variables.

An Example of Deep Copy: class matrix

A matrix class is a good example of the proper use of the copy-constructor. Since you never know until run time the size or dimensions of a matrix, the data space for the matrix must always be dynamically allocated. In addition, matrices are often too unwieldy to copy around when passing and returning, so the **class matrix** will simply move a pointer around.

Reference Counting

Since a pointer is moved, the bulk of the matrix data lives in the free store so the program must be very careful not to delete "live" data from the free store. The destructor must ensure that no objects are pointing to the data before it is released. To accomplish this, a device called a *reference counter* is used. The reference counter tells how many objects are currently using the data. Since the reference count must be associated with data rather than with any particular object, it is allocated on the free store as part of a **struct** that also contains information about the size of the matrix and a pointer to the actual matrix data. This structure is called a **matrep** in the program, for "matrix representation." Matrix objects only contain a pointer to a **matrep**; the rest of the information is in the **matrep** itself, on the free store.

When a new object is tied to a particular **matrep**, the reference count is increased. When an object is removed the reference count is decreased. Whenever the reference count is decremented it is tested—if it goes to zero the **matrep** and the matrix data are deleted. Note that the destructor simply decrements the reference count, and only deletes the data if the subsequent reference count is zero. The copy-constructor simply increments the reference count of the argument and copies the pointer.

How operator=( ) Works

The **operator=( )** follows these general guidelines. First, cleanup is performed, just as in the destructor. Then the object's pointer is copied from the argument and the new reference count is increased to indicate another object is using the data, as is done in the copy-constructor. Finally, a copy of the object is returned.

Element Selection

The function **val( )** allows element selection. It returns a reference to an element in the matrix. Since the reference is not declared as a **const** the element may be read or written. Notice that **val( )** also performs bounds checking to make sure the user isn't trying to index outside the matrix. This error checking is quite valuable but it slows the process down a fraction. The member functions all directly access the elements, ensuring that the indexes don't go out of bounds. The speed of element selection can be increased by making the function **val( )** an **inline**.

Matrix Multiplication and Addition

The **operator*( )** and **operator+( )** define multiplication and addition for the matrices. These functions show how the proper definition of the copy-constructor is critical for complicated classes. Both functions create their results in a local **matrix** and then return that local variable. The functions also follow the basic "pass *in* by reference, pass *out* by value" rule that, except in unusual cases, you should use.

When either **operator*( )** or **operator+( )** is called, the compiler creates a hidden intermediate variable and secretly passes its address as an argument. When the local **matrix** variable is created, there is only one object using the dynamically allocated portion, so the reference count is 1 (see the constructor definition). At the **return** statement, the compiler calls the copy-constructor for the hidden intermediate variable, with the local variable as an argument. The copy-constructor copies the pointer from the local variable to the hidden intermediate variable and increments the reference count. At that point, the reference count is 2. After the return statement, the destructor is called by the compiler. The destructor decrements the reference count to 1 but doesn't destroy the dynamically allocated portion of the matrix since the hidden intermediate variable is still using it. This way, the matrix is returned very quickly without destroying and reallocating memory and copying the entire matrix.

Messages to Hidden Intermediate Variables

In **main( )**, the matrix functions are exercised. The last statement in **main( )** shows how you can call a member function for a hidden intermediate variable: the function **print( )** is called for the result of **B∗identity**. Understanding the concept of the hidden intermediate variable makes it much easier to determine what is happening here. In particular, if you call a member function that changes the result, it will have no effect since the action will be on the hidden intermediate variable. For example,

(B∗identity).val(1,1) = 0;

will set element 1,1 of the hidden intermediate variable to 0, and promptly forget about that matrix until cleanup time. It is a perfectly valid statement, but it makes no sense.

A Matrix Class Framework

The following code only shows a framework for a matrix class, but it shows the portion that is most relevant to C++ programming. The remainder of the class is primarily mathematical and not appropriate to the subject of this chapter. The complete matrix class is given in Appendix B.

While studying this code, remember that what is going on here isn't trivial. It may take a while before you understand it all. Here is the header file.

```
// MMATRIX.HXX: simple matrix class to show complexities
// of a "deep copy."  See text for description of
// reference counting.

// A structure to hold matrix information.  This structure
// is always created on the free store.
struct matrep {
    double **m; // pointer to the matrix
    int r,c;    // number of rows and columns
    int n;      // reference count
};
```

```
class matrix {
   matrep *p;
   void error(char * msg1, char * msg2 = ""); // private function
public:
   matrix(int rows = 1, int columns = 1, double initval = 0);
   matrix(matrix& x); // copy-initializer
   ~matrix();
   matrix operator=(const matrix& rval); // matrix assignment
   matrix operator+(const matrix& rval); // matrix addition
   matrix operator*(const matrix& rval); // matrix multiplication
   double & val(int row, int col); // element selection;
   // can be used to read or write an element.
   void print(char * msg = "");
};
```

This is the implementation file.

```
// MMATRIX.CXX: implementation of simple matrix
#include <stdlib.h>

#include <stdio.h>
#include "mmatrix.hxx"

void matrix::error(char * msg1, char * msg2) {
   fprintf(stderr,"matrix error: %s %s\n", msg1, msg2);
   exit(1);
}

matrix::matrix(int rows, int columns, double initval) {
   // create the structure:
   p = new matrep;
   // allocate memory for the actual matrix:
   p->m = new double *[rows];
   for (int x = 0; x  rows; x++)
      p->m[x] = new double[columns];
   p->n = 1;  // so far, there's one reference to this data
   p->r = rows;
   p->c = columns;
   for (int i=0; i  rows; i++) {
      for (int j = 0; j  columns; j++)
         p->m[i][j] = initval;
   }
```

```
    }

  matrix::matrix(matrix& x) {
    x.p->n++; // we're adding another reference.
    p = x.p;  // point to the new matrep.
  }

  matrix matrix::operator=(const matrix& rval) {
    // clean up current value:
    if(—p->n == 0) {  // If nobody else is referencing us...
      for (int x = 0; x  p->r; x++)
        delete p->m[x];
      delete p->m; // ...nobody else can clean us up...
      delete p;
    }
    // connect to new value:
    rval.p->n++;  // tell the rval it has another reference
    p = rval.p;  // point at the rval matrep
    return *this;
  }

  matrix::~matrix() {
    if (—p->n == 0) { // if reference count goes to 0
      for (int x = 0; x < p->r; x++)
        delete p->m[x];
      delete p->m; // delete data
      delete p;
    }
  }

  double & matrix::val(int row, int col) {
    if (row < p->r && col < p->c)
      return (p->m[row][col]);
    else
      error("index out of range");
  }

  matrix matrix::operator*(const matrix& rval) {
    if( p->r != rval.p->c)
      error("# cols of second mat must equal ",
            "# rows of first for multiply!");
```

```
    matrix result(p->r,rval.p->c);
    for(int row = 0; row < p->r; row++) {
       for(int col = 0; col < rval.p->c; col++){
          double sum = 0;
          for(int i = 0; i < p->c; i++)
             sum += p->m[row][i] * rval.p->m[i][col];
          result.p->m[row][col] = sum;
       }
    }
    return result; // Returning a local variable?
    // copy-initializer happens before the destructor,
    // so reference count is 2 when destructor is called,
    // thus destructor doesn't free the memory.
}


matrix matrix::operator+(const matrix& rval) {
    if(( p->r != rval.p->r) || ( p->c != rval.p->c))
        error("must have equal dimensions for addition!");
    matrix sum(p->r,p->c);
    for (int i=0; i< p->r; i++) {
       for (int j = 0; j < p->c; j++)
          sum.p->m[i][j] = p->m[i][j] + rval.p->m[i][j];
    }
    return sum; // see note for operator*()
}

void matrix::print(char *msg) {
    if (*msg) printf("%s\n",msg);
    for (int row=0; row< p->r; row++){
       for (int col = 0; col < p->c; col++)
          printf("%6.6g  ", p->m[row][col]);
       printf("\n");
    }
}

main() {
    matrix A(4,4,3);
    matrix B(4,4);
    int w = 0;
    for (int u = 0; u < 4; u++) {
```

```
    for (int v = 0; v < 4; v++)
        B.val(u,v) = w++;
}
matrix identity(4,4);
for(int i = 0; i < 4; i++)
    identity.val(i,i) = 1;
matrix C = B + A;
A.print("A:");
B.print("B:");
C.print("C = A+B:");
(B*identity).print("B*identity:");
}
```

Caveat

It is not a good idea to have two objects pointing to the same data (unless one of those objects is a hidden intermediate variable, in which case it is the compiler's responsibility). If this happens, any change one object makes in the data is reflected in the other object, with unpredictable results. There are two ways to prevent this. One is to disallow **matrix** assignments such as

A = B;

There is no elegant way to prevent the user from doing this; it should simply be advised against. The second way is to create a scheme that allocates new memory and duplicates the object whenever the user attempts to write to a memory space that has two objects using it. This is even less elegant.

It has been suggested that reference counting is not always the best solution to the problem **class matrix** has of passing and returning large amounts of data.

Using printf( ) Versus Streams

You will notice that **printf( )** was used in this example instead of a stream function. Streams are often the best choice for I/O because they tend to be more efficient—each function is specified for the task at hand, instead of the **printf( )** approach of "one function conquers all." However, using streams slows the compiler down noticeably, which can be tedious during development.

Tracing the Creation And Destruction of Objects

It can be confusing to try to imagine how a complex program works. Since each object has a unique identifier—its address, available via the keyword **this**—it is possible to display all the calls of the constructors and destructor. The following modified **matrix** class shows both user-created variables and compiler-created hidden intermediate variables. The logic of **class mmtrace** is the same as **class matrix** except for the addition of the tracing information.

User-created variables are identified by their variable names; a string with the name is an argument to the constructor. When the normal constructor is called the string is always present. When the copy-constructor is called, however, the name string for the current object may be empty, indicating a hidden intermediate variable. If this is the case, the **hidden** flag is set.

The private member function, **oname( )**, returns a pointer to a string that describes the object. This pointer can be handed to **printf( )** for output. Notice this is one of the unusual cases when it is acceptable to return an address. The address is either **name**, which is valid outside the scope of **oname( )**, or the address of **static char buf[20]**. Since **buf** is static, it is also valid outside the scope of **oname( )**. Notice the return value is declared **const** so the string may not be modified.

The **oname( )** function checks to see if the object is associated with a variable name; if so, the address of **name** is returned. If the **hidden** flag is set, the variable is described as hidden and the object address (**(int)this**) is used to give it a unique identifier. This information is placed in the **static** buffer using the C library function **sprintf( )** (like **printf( )**, except it writes to a buffer) and the buffer address is returned.

The function **object_data( )** is called to display information about an object. To help clarify the trace, a tiny class called **tformat** with a single instance called **TAB** is used to perform indentation.

The program output is the trace of a single expression

$$E = A + B + C + D;$$

where all the elements are matrices.
Here is the header file.

```
// MMTRACE.HXX : matrix class with tracing to show
// initialization & destruction
class mmtrace {
    char * name; // to keep track of which object this is
    int hidden; // indicates a hidden variable
    struct matrep {
        double **m; // pointer to the matrix
        int r,c;    // number of rows and columns
        int n;      // reference count
    } *p;
    void error(char * msg1, char * msg2 = ""); // private function
    const char * oname(); // an identifier string for the object
public:
    mmtrace(char * object_name,
        int rows = 1, int columns = 1, double initval = 0);
    mmtrace(mmtrace& x); // copy-constructor
    ~mmtrace();
    mmtrace operator=(mmtrace& rval); // matrix assignment
    mmtrace operator+(mmtrace& rval); // matrix addition
    void object_data(char * msg); // trace information
};
```

Notice that the definition of **struct matrep** was moved inside the class definition. This is only to enhance readability; the structure definition is not scoped inside the class definition as it seems to imply. The **matrep** name is still global.

This is the implementation file.

```
// MMTRACE.CXX: Implementation of matrix class with
// tracing to show initialization & destruction

#include <stdlib.h>
#include <stdio.h>
#include <string.h>
#include "mmtrace.hxx"
```

```
// a tiny class to perform indentation
class tformat {
    int depth;
public:
    tformat() : depth(0) {}
    void operator++() { depth += 2; }
    void operator--() { depth -= 2; }
    void indent() {
        for (int i = 0; i  depth; i++ )
            printf(" ");
    }
} TAB;

void mmtrace::error(char * msg1, char * msg2) {
    fprintf(stderr,"matrix error: %s  %s\n", msg1, msg2);
    exit(1);
}

// returns a character pointer to a printable
// description of the object
const char * mmtrace::oname() {
    static char buf[20];
    if (hidden) {
        sprintf(buf,"hidden:this = %d",(int)this);
        return buf;
    }
    else
        return name;
}

void mmtrace::object_data(char * msg) {
    TAB.indent();
    printf("%s: [%s], p = %d\n", msg, oname(), (int)p);
}

mmtrace::mmtrace(char * object_name,
        int rows, int columns, double initval) {
    hidden = 0;
    p = new matrep;
    name = new char[strlen(object_name) + 1];
    strcpy(name,object_name);
    p->m = new double *[rows];
```

```
    for (int x = 0; x < rows; x++)
       p->m[x] = new double[columns];
    p->n = 1;  // so far, there's one reference to this data
    p->r = rows;
    p->c = columns;
    for (int i=0; i< rows; i++) {
       for (int j = 0; j < columns; j++)
          p->m[i][j] = initval;
    }
    object_data("constructor called");
    TAB++;
}

mmtrace::mmtrace(mmtrace& x) {
    // if there is no string this is a hidden variable
    if (name == (char *)0) hidden++;
    object_data("before copy-constructor");
    x.object_data("copying from");
    x.p->n++;    // we're adding another reference,
    p = x.p;    // so increase the count.
    object_data("after copy-constructor");
}

mmtrace mmtrace::operator=(mmtrace& rval) {
    object_data("op= before assignment");
    rval.object_data("op= argument");
    rval.p->n++;
    TAB.indent();
    printf("before decrement, reference count = %d\n",p->n);
    if(—p->n == 0) {
       TAB.indent();
       printf("op= releasing old contents of [%s]\n",oname());
       for (int x = 0; x < p->r; x++)
          delete p->m[x];
       delete p->m;
       delete p;
    } else {
       TAB.indent();
       printf("[%s] contents not released\n",oname());
    }
    p = rval.p;
    object_data("op= returning *this");
    return *this;
```

```
}
mmtrace::~mmtrace(){
   object_data("destructor called");
   TAB.indent();
   printf("before decr, reference count = %d\n",p->n);
   if(—p->n == 0) {
      TAB.indent();
      printf("destructor releasing contents of [%s]\n",oname());
      for (int x = 0; x < p->r; x++)
         delete p->m[x];
      delete p->m;
      delete p;
   } else {
      TAB.indent();
      printf("contents of [%s] not released\n",oname());
   }
   TAB—;
}

mmtrace mmtrace::operator+(mmtrace& rval) {
   if(( p->r != rval.p->r) || ( p->c != rval.p->c))
         error("must have equal dimensions for addition!");
   object_data("in op+ called for");
   rval.object_data("op+ argument");
   mmtrace sum("op+ local: sum",p->r,p->c);
   for (int i=0; i< p->r; i++) {
      for (int j = 0; j < p->c; j++)
         sum.p->m[i][j] = p->m[i][j] + rval.p->m[i][j];
   }
   TAB.indent(); printf("in op+; returning sum\n");
   return sum;
}

main() {
   TAB.indent(); printf("declaring A\n");
   mmtrace A("A",4,4,3);
   TAB.indent(); printf("declaring B\n");
   mmtrace B("B",4,4);
   TAB.indent(); printf("declaring C\n");
   mmtrace C("C",4,4,5);
   TAB.indent(); printf("declaring D\n");
   mmtrace D("D",4,4,6);
   TAB.indent(); printf("declaring E\n");
```

```
    mmtrace E("E");
    TAB.indent(); printf("Entering E = A + B + C + D\n");
    E = A + B + C + D;
    TAB.indent(); printf("After E = A + B + C + D\n");
    E.object_data("E");
    TAB.indent(); printf("Program finished, time for cleanup\n");
}
```

The way hidden intermediate variables are handled is implementation dependent. For example, the Zortech compiler copies the return value into a temporary object, then makes an image of the result into the hidden intermediate variable. This gives the impression of more hidden intermediate variables than actually exist. But if you carefully examine the output you will see the destructor is only called for the hidden intermediate variables (with the high **this** numbers) and never for the temporaries (with the low **this** numbers).

C code generators do not use the "temporary" scheme; they simply call the copy-initializer for the actual hidden intermediate variables. This is easier to read. The output used here comes from Glockenspiel C++ for the small model.

```
declaring A
constructor called: [A], p = 6382
  declaring B
  constructor called: [B], p = 6542
    declaring C
    constructor called: [C], p = 6702
      declaring D
      constructor called: [D], p = 6862
        declaring E
        constructor called: [E], p = 7022
          Entering E = A + B + C + D
          in op+ called for: [A], p = 6382
          op+ argument: [B], p = 6542
          constructor called: [op+ local: sum], p = 7050
            in op+; returning sum
            before copy-constructor: [hidden:this = 6112], p = 116
            copying from: [op+ local: sum], p = 7050
            after copy-constructor: [hidden:this = 6112], p = 7050
            destructor called: [op+ local: sum], p = 7050
            before decr, reference count = 2
            contents of [op+ local: sum] not released
          in op+ called for: [hidden:this = 6112], p = 7050
```

op+ argument: [C], p = 6702
constructor called: [op+ local: sum], p = 7224
  in op+; returning sum
  before copy-constructor: [hidden:this = 6106], p = 1
  copying from: [op+ local: sum], p = 7224
  after copy-constructor: [hidden:this = 6106], p = 7224
  destructor called: [op+ local: sum], p = 7224
  before decr, reference count = 2
  contents of [op+ local: sum] not released
in op+ called for: [hidden:this = 6106], p = 7224
op+ argument: [D], p = 6862
constructor called: [op+ local: sum], p = 7398
  in op+; returning sum
  before copy-constructor: [hidden:this = 6100], p = 5273
  copying from: [op+ local: sum], p = 7398
  after copy-constructor: [hidden:this = 6100], p = 7398
  destructor called: [op+ local: sum], p = 7398
  before decr, reference count = 2
  contents of [op+ local: sum] not released
op= before assignment: [E], p = 7022
op= argument: [hidden:this = 6100], p = 7398
before decrement, reference count = 1
op= releasing old contents of [E]
op= returning *this: [E], p = 7398
before copy-constructor: [hidden:this = 6094], p = 7398
copying from: [E], p = 7398
after copy-constructor: [hidden:this = 6094], p = 7398
After E = A + B + C + D
E: [E], p = 7398
Program finished, time for cleanup
destructor called: [hidden:this = 6094], p = 7398
before decr, reference count = 3
contents of [hidden:this = 6094] not released
destructor called: [hidden:this = 6100], p = 7398
before decr, reference count = 2
contents of [hidden:this = 6100] not released
destructor called: [hidden:this = 6106], p = 7224
before decr, reference count = 1
destructor releasing contents of [hidden:this = 6106]
destructor called: [hidden:this = 6112], p = 7050
before decr, reference count = 1
destructor releasing contents of [hidden:this = 6112]
destructor called: [E], p = 7398

```
    before decr, reference count = 1
    destructor releasing contents of [E]
destructor called: [D], p = 6862
before decr, reference count = 1
destructor releasing contents of [D]
destructor called: [C], p = 6702
before decr, reference count = 1
destructor releasing contents of [C]
destructor called: [B], p = 6542
before decr, reference count = 1
destructor releasing contents of [B]
destructor called: [A], p = 6382
before decr, reference count = 1
destructor releasing contents of [A]
```

After all the constructors are called, the evaluation of **A + B + C + D** proceeds from left to right. First, **operator+( )** is called for **A** with an argument of **B**. Inside the function **operator+( )**, the constructor is called for the local variable **sum**. **sum** is returned by calling the copy-constructor for a hidden intermediate variable with **sum** as the argument. The destructor is called for **sum** when it goes out of scope, but the reference count is 2 since the hidden intermediate variable is also using it. Next, **operator+( )** is called for the hidden intermediate variable with **C** as the argument.

Each local **sum** is bound by the copy-constructor to a new hidden intermediate variable until the expression has been evaluated. The hidden intermediate variable representing the sum is passed to **operator=( )**, which is called for **E**. Notice the result of **operator=( )** is also bound to a hidden intermediate variable; this is the effect of the statement **return *this;** in the definition for **operator=( )**. This final hidden variable is not used in this code.

You can see that destructors are called for the hidden intermediate variables as well as the visible ones, and that the reference count works out correctly.

*Returning Objects with *new*

The **new** keyword creates and initializes (by calling the appropriate constructor) an object on the free store. This section shows why you should never return an object created on the free store by value, that is, with **return *new ....**

More About References

In addition to their use in argument passing, references can be created as independent variables. A variable created this way looks and acts exactly like a regular object, but it is actually an address (or an alias, for inline functions in some implementations of C++). The compiler secretly performs all the proper dereferencing. It isn't usually very useful to declare reference variables other than as function arguments or return values. Reference variables initialized with ***new** are an exception.

All references must be initialized, and the address contained in a reference must always point to an initialized object. The following is an error (except in a **class** definition; see Chapter 4):

int & intref; // ERROR: must be initialized to something

There are two correct ways to initialize references. The first is to bind the reference to a named object.

```
// REF1.CXX : Binding a reference to an initialized object

#include <stdio.h> // printf() declaration

class RC {
   int i;
   char * name;
public:
   // The compiler allocates space for the name string, so
   // assigning "name" (instead of allocating space and
   // copying) is a safe thing to do:
   RC(char * nm,int j = 0) { name = nm; i = j; }
   void set(int k) { i = k; }
   void print(char * msg = "") {
      printf("%s: %s : i = %d\n",msg,name,i);
   }
};
```

```
main() {
    RC A("A",5);  // create an object
    RC & B = A;   // create a reference
    A.print("A after initialization");
    B.print("B, a reference to A");
    B.set(20);    // changing B ...
    A.print("A after B.set(20)");  // ... also changes A!
}
```

The output generated by this program is

```
A after initialization: A : i = 5
B, a reference to A: A : i = 5
A after B.set(20): A : i = 20
```

The object **A** is created, then a reference **B** is made from **A**. Notice that a reference is treated by the compiler as an object, not an address; thus the value of **A** and not the address of **A** must be used in the expression.

This situation is subject to the same caution as given for the **matrix** class when reference counting was used. Since **A** and **B** point to the same object, changing A or B will modify that object. This is generally more confusing than it is useful.

Proper Use of *new

The second and more practical way to use an independent reference is to initialize it with a variable created on the free store. Since destructors are never called for references unless the user explicitly calls **delete**, the object created this way is not subject to the normal scoping rules, so it "lives" until the user explicitly destroys it. Scoping may also be disabled by using pointers in a similar fashion.

When initializing a reference from an object created on the free store, keep in mind that the keyword **new** returns an *address,* and a reference must be initialized with an *object*. Thus the address returned by **new** must be dereferenced with an *, as shown here.

```
// REF2.CXX: Initializing a reference from
// an object created on the free store

#include <stdio.h> // printf() declaration

class RCF {
    int i;
public:
    RCF(int j = 0) { i = j; }
    ~RCF() { printf("destructor called!"); }
};

main() {
    RCF & C = *new RCF(47);
    // destructor is never called for a reference
}
```

In this program, the destructor will never be called.

When initializing a reference, the compiler secretly takes the address of the source object, so the address of the object which is actually on the free store is bound to **C**.

Improper Use of *new

It may be tempting for the new C++ programmer to return an object created on the free store instead of worrying about reference counting or creating a copy-initializer that performs proper deep copying. It seems to be a very neat solution: since the destructor is never called (destructors are not automatically called for objects created on the free store) there is no need to worry about the copy-constructor. The statement

return *new *classname(arguments);*

appears to work just fine.

The problem with the preceding statement can be seen by executing the following program:

```
// STARNEW.CXX: why the statement:
// return *new classname;
// is disastrous
#include <stdio.h>

class starnew {
   int * intarray;
   char * chararray;
public:
   void data(char * msg = "") {
      printf("%s:\n\tthis = %d intarray = %d chararray = %d\n",
             msg,(int)this,(int)intarray, (int)chararray);
   }
   starnew(int intsize, int charsize) {
      intarray = new int[intsize];
      chararray = new char[charsize];
      data("constructor called");
   }
   starnew(starnew &rval) {
      rval.data("argument of copy-constuctor");
      intarray = rval.intarray;
      chararray = rval.chararray;
      data("after copy-constuctor");
   }
   ~starnew() {
      delete intarray;
      delete chararray;
      data("destructor called");
   }
};

starnew return_starnew() {
   printf("return_starnew, before return *new starnew(5,5);\n");
   return *new starnew(5,5);
}

main() {
   starnew A = return_starnew();
   A.data("A");
   starnew & B = *new starnew(6,6);
```

```
    B.data("B");
    delete &B; // explicit destructor call for reference
}
```

The problem can be seen in the trace generated by program execution.
Glockenspiel C++ was used here.

```
return_starnew, before return *new starnew(5,5);
constructor called:
        this = 4696 intarray = 4702 chararray = 4714
argument of copy-constuctor:
        this = 4696 intarray = 4702 chararray = 4714
after copy-constuctor:
        this = 4444 intarray = 4702 chararray = 4714
A:
        this = 4444 intarray = 4702 chararray = 4714
constructor called:
        this = 4722 intarray = 4728 chararray = 4742
B:
        this = 4722 intarray = 4728 chararray = 4742
destructor called:
        this = 4722 intarray = 4728 chararray = 4742
destructor called:
        this = 4444 intarray = 4702 chararray = 4714
```

Inside the function **return_starnew( )**, an object is created on the free
store and a pointer to that object is produced by **new**. When the pointer is
dereferenced and returned via **return *new**, a (shallow) copy of the
structure is returned and copied into **A**'s structure. The copy includes
pointers to the two arrays, so when a destructor is called for **A**, the two
arrays are destroyed. However, the original structure created on the free
store is *never destroyed!* In fact, you couldn't destroy it if you tried, since
the address of that structure is immediately lost when the **return *new**
statement is executed. Thus, no destructor is ever called to free the memory
that is allocated for the structure inside the function **return_starnew( )**.

   A program written using **return *new** will work fine until some number
of free store allocations and deallocations have occurred; then it will run
out of memory. This occurs because all the structures left lying around in
the free store eventually fill it up or fragment it so much that no block of

memory can be found in the size desired. The example also shows the creation and destruction of a reference **B**. This is the proper way to call a destructor for a reference.

Makefile for Chapter Examples

Here is the **makefile** for all the examples in this chapter.

```
# makefile for examples in chapter 9

CPP = ztc

all: mmtrace.exe mmatrix.exe ci.exe vec.exe ref1.exe \
        ref2.exe starnew.exe

mmtrace.exe : mmtrace.hxx mmtrace.cxx
        $(CPP) mmtrace.cxx

mmatrix.exe : mmatrix.hxx mmatrix.cxx
        $(CPP) mmatrix.cxx

ci.exe : ci.cxx
        $(CPP) ci.cxx

vec.exe : vec.cxx
        $(CPP) vec.cxx

ref1.exe: ref1.cxx
        $(CPP) ref1.cxx

ref2.exe: ref2.cxx
        $(CPP) ref2.cxx

starnew.exe: starnew.cxx
        $(CPP) starnew.cxx
```

10   *Complete Examples*

This chapter contains examples to help create polished programs and to demonstrate object-oriented design. The first example shows you how to handle command-line arguments, flags, and opening files as stream objects. The second is a file-listing program that numbers the lines of each file and prints a header including the filename and the date and time the file was printed.

The third example reads and manipulates a comma-separated ASCII database file according to a scriptfile; it demonstrates techniques of parsing and recursive analysis. The fourth example is a clock-based control system. It parses a user script and creates a linked list of generic **event** objects. These objects are continuously tested; when an object is ready, it is run and removed from the list. This example demonstrates **virtual** functions, parsing, and linked lists. Additional examples can be found in the appendixes.

Command-Line Arguments, Flags, and Files

C and C++ contain convenient facilities for processing arguments on the command line. Arguments are usually filenames, but often some form of flags are also needed to allow the user options in the way the program operates.

The programs in this section comprise a template for processing command-line arguments and include a class to make the handling of flags easy. This class can be modified to manage flags for any other program by simply changing the contents of the **flags.h** file. The class makes the main program much clearer and the template reduces errors.

Command-Line Arguments

When a C or C++ program starts, the command line is passed to the **main( )** routine in the form of two arguments. As with any argument list in a function, you may call the arguments anything you want as long as they are of the correct type. Traditionally, however, the arguments are called **argc** (for "argument count") and **argv** (for "argument values"). **argc** is an integer that tells the number of arguments in the command line including the program name (**cat filename** has an **argc** of 2). **argv** is an array of character pointers that point to strings of the names on the command line, including the program name. You may see **main( )** declared in two equivalent forms: **main(int argc, char ∗∗ argv)** or, more typically, **main(int argc, char ∗ argv[ ])**. In either case, **argv[0]** produces a character pointer to the program name string, **argv[1]** points to the first argument, and so on. Command-line processing consists of determining the number of arguments (via **argc**) and processing each one (via their character strings in **argv**).

As an example, here's a program that simply lists its arguments:

```
// ARGLIST.CXX : list command-line arguments

#include <stream.hxx>

main(int argc, char * argv[ ] ) {
   for(int i = 0; i < argc; i++)
      cout << "arg[" << i << "] is : " << argv[i] << "\n";
}
```

Command-Line Flags

A program often has a number of options. These options may be set by a configuration file, by interaction with the user, or via arguments on the command line. Command-line flags are usually differentiated by a leading character; for this example, '+' will turn the flag on (enable the desired option) and '-' will turn the flag off (disable the option).

The programs in this section demonstrate a system to easily add flag options to the command line. To change the flag options, edit a special file containing only the flag names, string representations for the command line, and the number of flags. For the first program, the file looks like this:

```
// TSTFLAG.H: flag definitions for CLTEST.CXX
// This file must be changed to reflect the flags
// needed for each program; this is the only place
// changes need to be made.

#define FLAG_NAMES var1, var2, var3, var4, var5
#define FLAG_STRINGS "var1", "var2", "var3", "var4", "var5",
#define FLAG_COUNT 5
```

These definitions are used by the header file, as follows:

```
// CLFLAGS.HXX: class to manage command-line flags
// NOTE: the file FLAGFILE (a #define on the compiler
// command line) is different for each program.  This
// is controlled in the makefile

#ifndef FLAGFILE
// The "error" preprocessor directive emits error
// messages during compilation
#error FLAGFILE must be defined on the
#error command line with -DFLAGFILE="filename"
#endif
```

```
#include FLAGFILE

enum FLAG_NUMBER {
   FLAG_NAMES
};

class CL_flags {
   int flag_value[FLAG_COUNT];
 public:
   CL_flags( );
   int is_flag(char * cl_arg); // true if a flag
   void set(FLAG_NUMBER n) { flag_value[n]++; }
   void clear(FLAG_NUMBER n) { flag_value[n] = 0; }
   int is_on(FLAG_NUMBER n) { return flag_value[n]; }
   int is_off(FLAG_NUMBER n) { return !flag_value[n]; }
};
```

The macros are inserted into the flag definitions. Notice that if the header file defining the flags hasn't been included, an error message is emitted using the **#error** directive. You can use this any time you want to send a message to the person compiling the program.

The **class CL_flags** keeps track of the number and value of all the flags. You should only make one **CL_flags** object per program. Once the object is initialized, you can set or clear flags, and you can test to see if a flag is on or off. Because of the **enum**, you can refer to flags by name; this makes the program much easier to read and write.

Here are the definitions for **CL_flags**:

```
// CLFLAGS.CXX: manages command-line flags

#include <string.h>
#include <stream.hxx>
#include "clflags.hxx"
#include <stdlib.h>

const char * FL_STRING[ ] = {
   FLAG_STRINGS
};
```

```
CL_flags::CL_flags( ) {
    for (int i = 0; i < FLAG_COUNT; i++)
        flag_value[i] = 0; // clear all flags
}

int CL_flags::is_flag(char * cl_arg) { // true if a flag
    if ( cl_arg[0] != '-' && cl_arg[0] != '+')
        return 0; // not a flag
    for (int i = 0; i < FLAG_COUNT; i++) {
        // note we must start the comparison at the character
        // after the '+' or '-' by adding 1 to the pointer:
        if ( strcmp( FL_STRING[i], cl_arg + 1 ) == 0) {
            switch (cl_arg[0]) {
                case '+' : set((FLAG_NUMBER)i); break;
                case '-' : clear((FLAG_NUMBER)i);
            }
            break; // quit "for" loop (efficiency)
        }
    }
    if ( i == FLAG_COUNT ) {
        cerr << "command-line error: flag not found: "
            << cl_arg << "\n"
            << "available flags are:\n";
        for (int j = 0; j < FLAG_COUNT; j++)
            cerr << "\t" << FL_STRING[j] << "\n";
        cerr << "+ to turn on, - to turn off\n";
        exit(1);
    }
    return 1; // return true since it was a flag
}
```

An alternative approach is to hand **argc** and **argv** to the constructor, and let it hunt through the command line for flags. When it finds a flag, it can remove it from the command line and adjust **argc** and **argv** accordingly. Although this is more automatic, it doesn't have the same level of flexibility. With the design shown here, the *order* of the flags on the command line can be important. You can turn on a feature for one file and turn it off for the next one. This can be very useful.

The constructor turns off all the flags. **is_flag( )** checks to see if an argument is a flag; if so, the flag value is noted and a Boolean true (non-zero value) is returned, so the user can ignore the argument. If an unknown flag is encountered, an error message is printed along with a list of the acceptable flags.

Here's an example using **CL_flags**:

```
// CLTEST.CXX: test clflags
#include "clflags.hxx"
#include <stream.hxx>

CL_flags FLAG;  // only make one CL_flags object per program
extern const char * FL_STRING[ ];

main(int argc, char * argv[ ]) {
   for (int i = 1; i < argc; i++)
      if ( ! FLAG.is_flag(argv[i]))
         cout << "argument " << i << " isn't a flag\n";
   for (i = 0; i < FLAG_COUNT; i++)
      cout << "flag " << FL_STRING[i] << " is "
      << (FLAG.is_on((FLAG_NUMBER)i) ? "ON" : "OFF") << "\n";
}
```

It prints out the state of the arguments that are flags and the arguments that aren't flags. With this program, you can turn a flag on and off, and, since it processes the flags all at once, it will only notice the final value.

To compile any program using **CL_flags**, you must specify on the compiler command line the name of the file containing the flag names. This is done by setting a preprocessor macro on the command line.

-DFLAGFILE="tstflag.h"

This has the same effect as the preprocessor directive.

#define FLAGFILE "tstflag.h"

The **makefile** at the end of this section shows how the command-line macro is used to compile these programs.

A SIMPLE UTILITY This example also uses the **CL_flags** system. It takes standard input, processes it according to the flag settings, and sends the result to standard output. The flags default to "option disabled." This table shows the effect of each flag.

Flag	Effect
+zero	Zero the high bit of each character (high bits are set by some word processors)
+number	Put line numbers on the output
+upcase	Make all characters uppercase
+downcase	Make all characters lowercase
+xtab	Expand tabs to spaces

If you want to number the lines of a file called INFILE and send the result to a file called OUTFILE, type

format +number < infile > outfile

Notice that the program uses a set of plain C functions declared in the file **ctype.h** to perform the upper- and lowercasing. Using plain C library functions simply entails including the header file and calling the function, just as you would in plain C. This assumes that your plain C header files either come from an ANSI C implementation (and use prototypes) or have been rewritten using prototypes or ellipses (...) in the argument lists to disable type checking.

Here is the flag name header file for the format program:

```
// FORMFLAG.H: flag definitions for the format program

#define FLAG_NAMES zero, number, upcase, downcase, xtab
#define FLAG_STRINGS "zero","number","upcase","downcase","xtab"
#define FLAG_COUNT 5
```

The format program just interrogates the flags to see what is to be done with each input character.

```
// TFORMAT.CXX: format standard input according to command-
// line flags; send result to standard output
#include "clflags.hxx"
#include <stream.hxx>
#include <ctype.h> // toupper( ) & tolower( )
```

```
CL_flags FLAG;

main(int argc, char * argv[ ]) {
  for (int i = 1; i < argc; i++)
    FLAG.is_flag(argv[i]); // process flags
  char c;
  int linecount = 1;
  if (FLAG.is_on(number))
    cout << linecount << ": ";
  while( cin.get(c) ) {
    if (FLAG.is_on(zero))
      c &= 0x7f; // zero the high bit
    if (FLAG.is_on(upcase))
      c = toupper(c); // all but a-z are unchanged
    if (FLAG.is_on(downcase))
      c = tolower(c); // all but A-Z are unchanged
    if (c != '\t' || FLAG.is_off(xtab))
      cout.put(c); // ordinary output
    else {
      for (int x = 0; x < 8; x++)
        cout.put(' '); // expand tabs to spaces
    }
    if ( c == '\n' ) {
      linecount++;
      if (FLAG.is_on(number))
        cout << linecount << ": ";
    }
  }
}
```

IMPROVEMENTS You can make two modifications to the **CL_flags** system. First, you can add a default message that is printed whenever an incorrect flag is used. The message should be constructed at compile time from a text file, and the user should be able to call it via a member function.

The second modification is to allow arguments to flags; for example:

programname size=20

This means you must differentiate between on-off flags and variable flags, and look for an '=' in the flag.

Not all programs use all the features of an object-oriented programming language. Many, such as this one, benefit from encapsulation but don't use inheritance or virtual functions.

Opening Files with streams

The **streams class** is designed to manipulate files as well as **cin, cout,** and **cerr.** Creating file objects with streams is not as simple as it could be, so here are a pair of macros to abbreviate the process:

```
// FILE.HXX : file creation macros
/* creates an istream called name from the string
    called ifile, checking for errors */
#define OPEN_INPUT(name, ifile) \
filebuf f ## name; \
if ((f##name).open(ifile, input) == 0) { \
    fprintf(stderr, "cannot open %s\n", ifile); \
    exit(1); \
} \
istream name(& f ## name)

/* creates an ostream called name from the string
    called ofile, checking for errors */
#define OPEN_OUTPUT(name, ofile) \
filebuf f ## name; \
if ((f##name).open(ofile, output) == 0) { \
    fprintf(stderr, "cannot open %s\n", ofile); \
    exit(1); \
} \
ostream name(& f ## name)
```

Macros are used instead of functions here because a **filebuf** and an **istream** must be given variable names. The macros allow you to open a file without writing the variable definitions. The macros use the ANSI C "token-pasting" preprocessor operator **##**. This takes the left side and pastes it to the right side; if either side is an argument, the argument is substituted. For instance, if **name** is **bob,** the line

filebuf f ## name;

produces the line

filebuf fbob;

When you call **OPEN_INPUT( )** or **OPEN_OUTPUT( )**, the macro will attempt to open a file (and quit with an error message if it fails) and create a stream object. Manipulating this file is as simple as manipulating any other stream object; all the stream functions are available.

ifile and **ofile** can be strings or pointers. Here's an example that copies a file from the first argument on the command line into the second, and simultaneously into a file called TEMP:

```
// SCOPY.CXX : copies a file from arg1 to arg2
// and makes an extra copy in TMP.$$$

#include <stdlib.h>
#include <stream.hxx>
#include "file.hxx"

main(int argc, char * argv[ ]) {
    if(argc < 2) {
        cerr << "usage: scopy from to\n";
        exit(1);
    }
    OPEN_INPUT(infile, argv[1]);
    OPEN_OUTPUT(outfile, argv[2]);
    OPEN_OUTPUT(tmpfile, "TMP.$$$");
    char c;
    while(infile.get(c)) {
        outfile.put(c);
        tmpfile.put(c);
    }
}
```

You don't need to worry about closing files that are stream objects. When the object goes out of scope, the compiler calls the destructor that closes the file.

makefile *for Preceding Examples*

Here is the **makefile** for the examples in this chapter so far. Notice that the **clflags.cxx** file is recompiled for the three programs that use

CL_flags, and a different object filename is given in both cases (using the compiler command-line flag **-o**).

```
# makefile for cltest.exe, clformat.exe, arglist.exe
# and scopy.exe.  Notice the FLAGFILE must be defined
# on the command line for the system to work properly.
# STRMLIB can be set with:
# make STRMLIB=oldstrms.lib
# if your C++ doesn't explicitly use the "old" streams library
# For Zortech:
CPP = ztc


all: cltest.exe tformat.exe arglist.exe scopy.exe

cltest.exe : cltest.obj clftst.obj
        $(CPP) cltest.obj clftst.obj $(STRMLIB)

cltest.obj : cltest.cxx clflags.cxx clflags.hxx tstflag.h
        $(CPP) -c -DFLAGFILE="tstflag.h" cltest.cxx

clftst.obj : clflags.cxx clflags.hxx tstflag.h
        $(CPP) -c -DFLAGFILE="tstflag.h" -oclftst.obj clflags.cxx

tformat.exe : tformat.obj clformat.obj
        $(CPP) tformat.obj clformat.obj  $(STRMLIB)

tformat.obj : tformat.cxx clflags.cxx clflags.hxx formflag.h
        $(CPP) -c -DFLAGFILE="formflag.h" tformat.cxx

clformat.obj : clflags.cxx clflags.hxx formflag.h
        $(CPP) -c -DFLAGFILE="formflag.h" -oclformat.obj clflags.cxx

arglist.exe : arglist.cxx
        $(CPP) arglist.cxx $(STRMLIB)

scopy.exe : scopy.cxx ..\..\include\file.hxx
        $(CPP) scopy.cxx $(STRMLIB)
```

A Program to List Files

This program sends any number of files to standard output after adding headlines and line numbers. It is intended that the output be redirected to your printer, as in

list file1 file2 file3 > PRN:

(or piped to a print spooler in UNIX). There are several lines in the program that are specific to a particular printer (in this case, the Hewlett-Packard LaserJet). The line

const int PAGELENGTH = 95;

gives the number of lines in a page; since compressed print is used there are more lines than on a typical page.
    The lines

cout << chr(27) << "&15C";

cout << chr(27) << "(s16.66H";

send escape codes to initialize the LaserJet, and the line

cout << chr(27) << "E";

ejects the last page and resets the printer.
    To manage paging, a **class** called **pager** is created, and a single instance **line** is made. When **line** is incremented (using **operator++( )**), it checks to see if the number of lines (**linecount**) is greater than **PAGELENGTH**. If so, it ejects the page, increments the number of pages (**pagecount**), and generates a new headline. Every time the file is changed, the member function **name( )** changes the name so the headline can reflect the new filename.
    class pager also maintains a time when the listing started, to print in the headline. ANSI C time function declarations are contained in the header file **time.h**. Consult your manual for a full description of the time functions.

```
// LIST.CXX: produce program listings on an HP LaserJet
// (change the escape sequences for your favorite printer)
// Demonstrates:
// Use of streams for file reading
// command-line argument manipulation
// data encapsulation

#include <stdlib.h>
#include <stream.hxx>
#include "file.hxx"
#include <string.h>
#include <time.h>
const int PAGELENGTH = 95; // number of lines per page
const int TABSIZE = 8; // number of spaces in a tab


// In the date and time function, the structure element
// tm_wday is a number representing the day of the week.
// This array converts a number in tm_wday to a weekday name.
// Since this array is is defined outside of all functions
// (i.e., it is not an auto), it can be initialized by
// the compiler.
char * weekday[ ] = {
    "Sunday",
    "Monday",
    "Tuesday",
    "Wednesday",
    "Thursday",
    "Friday",
    "Saturday",
};


// Class to hide the details of paging the output.  Inline
// functions should not generally be used this much, but
// they make the code easier to read.
class pager {
    int linecount;  // count lines per page
    int pagecount; // pages for whole job
    char * filename;
    time_t ltime;  // holds encoded time
    tm t; // the time and day
    int namecount; // counts the number of times the name( )
                    // function has been called.
public:
```

```
pager( ) {
    linecount = pagecount = 1;
    filename = (char *)0;
    namecount =0;
    time(&ltime); // get time
    // convert time & make a local copy:
    t = *localtime(&ltime);
}
void tab(int i = 1) {
    for(int j = 0; j < i * TABSIZE; j++)

        cout.put(' ');
}
void header( ) {
    cout << "FILE: " << filename;
    tab(2);
    int hr = t.tm_hour, pm = 0;
    int hour = hr > 12 ? (pm++, hr -12) : hr;
    cout << weekday[t.tm_wday] << ", " <<
        t.tm_mon << "/" << t.tm_mday << "/" << t.tm_year <<
        "   " << hour << ":" <<
        (t.tm_min < 10 ? "0" : " ") << t.tm_min << " " <<
        (pm ? "pm" : "am");
    tab(2);
    cout << "page " << pagecount << "\n\n";
}
void eject( ) {
    cout << chr('\f'); // Form Feed
    pagecount++;
    linecount = 2;
    header( );
}
// add one to the linecount and conditionally eject:
void bumpline( ) {
    if ( ++linecount % PAGELENGTH == 0)
        eject( );  // and print new header
}
void operator++( ) { bumpline( ); }
void name(char * fn) { // change name
    // The first 2 times, don't print the name.  This would
    // generate duplicates for the first file in the list:
    if (namecount++ >= 2) {
        cout << "\nFILE: " << fn;
```

```
            bumpline( );
            cout <<"\n"; bumpline( );
            cout <<"\n"; bumpline( );
        }
        delete filename; // free old name (delete 0 has no effect)
        filename = new char[strlen(fn) + 1];
        strcpy(filename,fn); // attach new name
    }
} line;  // declare a global

main(int argc, char * argv[ ]) {
    const int BSIZE = 100;  // better than #define
    if (argc < 2) { // argc: # of arguments including program name
        cerr << "usage: list filelist\n";
        exit(1);
    }
    // these two lines are HP LaserJet-specific:
    cout << chr(27) << "&l5C";  // 5/48" (approx 10 lines/inch)
    cout << chr(27) << "(s16.66H"; // small typeface
    line.name(argv[1]); line.header( ); // first page header
    // do for all files:
    for (int filenum = 1; filenum < argc; filenum++) {
        OPEN_INPUT(infile,argv[filenum]);
        line.name(argv[filenum]); // change & print the name
        int count = 1;  // count of lines in file
        char buf[BSIZE], c;
        while(infile.get(buf,BSIZE, '\n')) { // reads each line
            // until '\n' or line size == BSIZE, but DOESN'T read
            // the terminating character (left on the input stream)
            cout << count++ << ": " << buf << "\n";
            infile.get(c);  // throw away the terminating character
            line++;  // count lines & automatically page
        }
    }
    // this line is HP LaserJet-specific:
    cout << chr(27) << "E";  // eject page and reset printer
}
```

Notice that the member function **name( )** changes the name in the **pager** object and prints the new filename. The first time you call **name( )**, it sets the name for use by the headline. The second call to **name( )** is also for the first file, but after the **while** loop. You don't want the name printed in either case because the name is printed at the top of the first page. A counter, **namecount**, keeps track of the number of times the function has been called. After two times, the filename is printed.

Although there are no inheritance or **virtual** functions in this program, it is a good example of the value of abstract data typing and data encapsulation.

TAWK: A Simple Database Interpreter

Most microcomputer database management systems will read and write records in a "comma-separated ASCII" format. This is probably an artifact from the days when BASIC (which uses that format) was the only common language on microcomputers. Comma- separated ASCII files are useful not only because they allow the records from one DBMS to be moved to another, but because they can be manipulated using programming languages.

Here's an example of a comma-separated ASCII file:

```
"cfront","AT&T","Source Code"
"Gnu C++","Free Software Foundation","Unix"
"Glockenspiel C++","Glockenspiel","Unix, MSDOS, OS/2, VMS"
"Guidelines C++","Guidelines","MSDOS"
"Oregon C++","Oregon Software","Sun Workstation"
"Zortech C++","Zortech","MSDOS"
```

Each field in a record is delimited by double quotes. The fields are separated from each other by commas, and each record is terminated by a new-line. Commas are allowed inside fields, but double quotes are not.

While BASIC automatically reads and writes these records, other languages must be programmed to do so. In C++, this tedious task can be encapsulated into several classes; the user of the class doesn't need to worry about the details. In the first part of this project, two classes are created: the constructor for **class field** reads a single quoted and comma-separated field and makes an object from it. The constructor for **class csascii** opens a comma-separated ASCII file and reads records (as arrays of field objects) one at a time until the file ends. A simple application is shown that uses the classes to search through a database file for a last name.

Database files must often be manipulated or output in an organized way as a "report." It becomes tedious to write and compile code for each different report, and non-programmers must often design reports. A common solution to a problem like this is the creation of a "scripting language" tailored to the task at hand. The second part of this project is the creation of a very simple language that outputs the comma-separated ASCII records to standard output according to a script in a separate file.

The program is called TAWK for "tiny AWK," since the problem it solves is vaguely reminiscent of the AWK pattern-matching language found on UNIX (versions of AWK have also been created for DOS). It demonstrates one of the thornier problems in computer science—parsing and executing a programming language. The data-encapsulation features of C++ prove very useful here, and a recursive technique is used to read arbitrarily long fields and records.

Recursive Descent

A *recursive descent* algorithm is very useful if you don't know how long or complicated a statement will be when you start looking at it. In programming languages, for instance, recursive descent parsers are often used in expression evaluation, since expressions can contain other expressions. In this project, the expressions aren't particularly complicated, but you don't know how long a string of text is going to be.

When scanning an expression using recursive descent, a central function is used. This function munches along, absorbing input until it runs into a delimiter that indicates a change in the type of input (white space, for example, or a number). At this point it might call another function, to eat the white space or to get the string of digits and turn it into a number. Then, if the expression is finished, it will just return. If the expression *isn't* finished (and here's the tricky part) it *calls itself;* that is, it *recurses.* Every time it encounters a new sub-expression within the one it is evaluating, it just calls itself to evaluate the expression. When solving more complex problems (such as a programming language), a set of functions is used. Each function may call any of the others during expression evaluation.

At some point the evaluation must bottom out. When this happens, the function performs some termination activities and then returns. As the stack unwinds from all the recursive calls, the tail end of each function call performs some operation to store the information it was able to glean, and then it returns. When the function finally completes, the expression has been evaluated.

Recursive scanning is used in three places in this project. The **field** class, which creates an object containing a single quote-delimited field, has a recursive function **field::getfield( )** (shown in file FIELD.CXX) to read one character at a time, keeping track of the number of characters encountered, until the end of the field. When the closing quote is encountered, memory is allocated for exactly the right number of characters, and the function returns. As it unwinds, characters are placed in the object's **data** buffer. Using recursive descent means there are no restrictions on the field size, assuming you have an infinite stack. For very large records, you may need to change **field::getfield( )** so it doesn't blow up the stack.

The **token class** (in file PARSE.HXX) uses recursive descent in a more sophisticated way. When a **token** object is created by handing it an input stream (via the constructor function **token::token(istream & input)**) it reads the input stream until it has scanned a complete token. When the constructor completes, a new token has been created.

A token is a group of symbols that represent a single concept. A C++ compiler uses a large number of tokens: { means "begin a scope," **for** means "start a **for** loop," **foo** means "an identifier." TAWK has a much smaller number of tokens. All tokens in TAWK are delimited by @, which starts a new command. When @ is encountered it is pushed back onto the input stream (for use in the next **token** object) and the current token is completed. The central recursive function for **token** is **token::get_token( )**, shown later in file PARSE.CXX.

The class **parse_array** builds an array of tokens by recursively calling **parse_array::build_array( )**. This function makes a new token, then looks at the token to decide what to do next.

The two programs (LOOKUP and TAWK) are built from several classes. Each of these classes will be examined.

A Class to Manage a Single Field

Here is the declaration for **class field**:

```
// FIELD.HXX: Used by csascii class to build a single field.
// Fields are collected by csascii to create a record.
#include <stream.hxx>

class field { // one field in a comma-separated ASCII record
    istream * input; // where to get the data
    char * data;
    int length, fsize;
    int end_of_file; // flag to indicate the end of file happened
    void getfield( );  // recursive function to read in a field;
                // treats data, length & input as globals
    int infield; // flag used by getfield( ) to determine whether
            // it's inside a quoted field
```

```
  public:
    field(istream & instream);
    ~field( );
    friend ostream& operator<<(ostream &s, field & f) {
      s << f.data;
      return s;
    }
    int eof( ) { return end_of_file; }  // to check for end
    int size( ) { return fsize;}
    int last_length( ) {return length; }
    char * string( ) { return data; }
};
```

Here are the definitions for **class field**:

```
// FIELD.CXX: Definitions for class field.
// A recursive scanning scheme is used because field
// length is always unknown.
#include "field.hxx"

field::field(istream & instream) {
    input = &instream;
    length = 0;
    end_of_file = 0; // set flag to say "we're not at the end"
    infield = 0; // set flag to say "we're not inside a field"
    data = (char *)0; // to show no memory has been allocated
    getfield( );  // recursively get characters until end of field
}

field::~field( ) {
    delete data;  // if no memory has been allocated,
    // data = (char *)0 so this will have no effect.
}

// A comma-separated ASCII field is contained in quotes to allow
// commas within the field; these quotes must be stripped out
void field::getfield( ) {
    char c;
    // This happens when descending:
    if((input->get(c)).eof( ) ) {
       end_of_file++;  // just say we reached the end...
       return;
```

```
    }
  else  // watch out for the Unix vs. DOS LF/CR problem here:
    if (((c != ',') || infield) && (c != '\n')) {
      if ( (c != '"') && (c != '\r')) // watch for quotes or CR
        length++;  // no quotes -- count this character
      else {
        if ( c == '"')
          infield = !infield;  // If we weren't inside a field
          // and a quote was encountered, we are now inside
          // a field.  If we were inside a field and a quote
          // was found, we're out of the field.
        c = 0; // a quote or CR; mark it so it isn't included
      }
      getfield( );  // recursively get characters in field
      // after returning from function call, we jump past
      // the following "else" part to finish the recursion
    }
    else {  // This happens once, when the terminator is found:
      fsize = length;  // remember how long the string is
      data = new char[length + 1]; // space for null terminator
      data[length] = '\0';  // highest index is "length"
        // when you allocate an array of length + 1
      length--;  // notice we don't insert the delimiter
      // Now the first "if" statement evaluates to TRUE and
      // the function rises back up.
      return;
    }
  // This happens when ascending:
  if ( c ) // if it wasn't a quote or CR,
    data[length--] = c;  // put chars in as we rise back up...
}
```

The field object doesn't control opening or closing files; it is simply handed an **istream** from which it takes its input. If it finds the end of input, it just makes an internal note (by setting its **end_of_file** flag) and returns. It's up to the caller to check for end of file with the function **field::eof( )**. The **operator<<( )** is overloaded so that a field object may be put to a stream output object. When this occurs, the **data** field is copied to the output.

The field constructor **field::field(istream & instream)** initializes all the variables to zero and sets the member **istream * input** equal to **instream**. This allows **field::getfield( )** to treat **input** as a global variable, and to simply get the next character. The last thing the constructor does is call the recursive function **field::getfield( )**, which recurses until it reaches the end of the field. When the constructor finishes, the field is complete.

The function **field::getfield( )** reads a character from the input stream. A special flag called **infield** determines if the character is inside a quoted phrase. If the character is a comma inside a quoted phrase, it is included as a part of the field. If a character is a comma outside a quoted phrase, it terminates the field. If the character is a carriage return, it terminates the record. If no terminator is found, the function counts the current character and calls itself to get the next character. If a terminator is found, memory is allocated to hold the string (using the C++ dynamic memory allocation keyword **new**) and the string terminator **'\0'** is inserted. As the function returns from calling itself, each character is inserted, from right to left, into the buffer.

Memory is not always allocated for a field. The constructor for a field object sets the **data** pointer to zero. If memory is never allocated, the destructor will delete a NULL pointer, which is defined to have no effect.

class csascii

Here is the **csascii** (for comma-separated-ASCII) **class** declaration:

```
// CSASCII.HXX: Class to manipulate comma-separated ASCII
// database files.
#include <stream.hxx>
#include "field.hxx"

class csascii { // Manipulates comma-separated ascii files,
// generated by most database management systems (generated and
// used by the BASIC programming language).  Each field
// is separated by a comma; records are separated by new-lines.
   int fieldcount;
   field ** data; // an array to hold the entire record
   istream * datafile; // file with comma separated ASCII input
   int readrecord( ); // private function to read a record
public:
   csascii( char * filename );  // Open file, get first record
   ~csascii( ); // destructor
   int next( ); // get next record, return 0 when EOF
   field & operator[ ](int index); // select a field
```

```
      int number_of_fields( ) { return fieldcount; }
};
```

And here is the definition file for **csascii**:

```
// CSASCII.CXX: Function definitions for comma-separated
// ascii database manipulation class.
#include <stdlib.h>
#include "csascii.hxx"
#include <file.hxx> // for opening stream files
int csascii::readrecord( ) {
    for (int fieldnum = 0; fieldnum < fieldcount; fieldnum++ ) {
        data[fieldnum] = new field(*datafile);
        if (data[fieldnum]->eof( )) return 0;
    }
    return 1;
}

csascii::csascii( char * filename ) {
    char c;
    fieldcount = 0;
    int quote = 0;
    // first, determine the number of fields in a record:
    {
        // See text for dangers of opening files this way:
//      istream infile(new filebuf->open(filename, input));
        OPEN_INPUT(infile,filename);
        while(infile.get(c), c != '\n') {
            // keep track of being inside a quoted string:
            if (c == '"') quote = !quote;  // invert the flag
            // fields are delimited by unquoted commas:
            if ( c == ',' && !quote)
                fieldcount++;
        }
    } // infile goes out of scope; file closed
    fieldcount++; // last field terminated by new-line, not comma
    // an array of field pointers:
    data = new field * [ fieldcount ];
    // re-open at start; dynamically allocate so it isn't scoped:
    datafile = new istream(new filebuf->open(filename, input));
    readrecord( );
}
```

```
csascii::~csascii( ) {
    delete data;
    delete datafile; // calls istream destructor to close file
}

int csascii::next( ) {
    for (int i = 0; i < fieldcount; i++ )
        delete data[i];  // free all the data storage
    return readrecord( ); // 0 when end of file
}

field & csascii::operator[ ](int index) {
    if (index >= fieldcount) {
        cerr << "index too large for number of fields in record\n";
        exit(1);
    }
    return *(data[index]);
}
```

Notice the use of the FILE.HXX macros for opening files as streams. The **#include** uses angle brackets instead of quotes. For this to work, you must copy FILE.HXX into the directory where your include files are located; otherwise you must put it in the local directory and change the angle brackets to quotes.

The constructor opens the input file, counts the number of fields in a record, and closes the file. It then creates an array of pointers to field objects, reopens the file, and reads the first record in. Every time **csascii::next( )** is called, a new record is read until the end of the file.

The **operator[ ]( )** is overloaded so the individual fields may be selected from each record. This function checks to ensure that the index is within bounds.

ONE-LINE FILE OPENING   The method of opening files should be examined here. The line

istream infile(new filebuf->open(filename, input));

is a very succinct way to create a buffer and open a file. The **new filebuf** creates a **filebuf** object (necessary to open a file as an **istream**) on the free store and returns a pointer to this object. The pointer is used to call a member function, **filebuf::open( )**. The pointer is also handed to the constructor of **istream** to create an object called **infile.**

This is a clever piece of code, and nice for quick programming. Unfortunately, it isn't robust unless you *know* that the file exists. If the file doesn't exist on DOS machines, the system locks up. For this reason, the line is commented out and the FILE.HXX macro is used instead.

Notice that in **csascii::csascii( )**, the file is closed implicitly by putting braces around the first clause in the constructor where the fields are counted. When the **istream** object goes out of scope, the file is closed. This is the only purpose for putting the braces there. Anytime you want to control the destruction of a local object, simply put it in braces.

Testing field *and* csascii

Here is a short program to show the use of **class csascii**:

```
// LOOKUP.CXX: simple use of csascii to find name in a database
#include "csascii.hxx"
#include <string.h>
#include <stdlib.h>
#include <conio.h>

main(int argc, char ** argv) {
    if (argc < 2) {
        cerr << "usage: lookup lastname\n";
        exit(1);
    }
    // create object & open file:
    csascii file("\\nut\\PPQUICK.ASC");
    int found = 0;  // indicates one record was found
    do {
        if (strcmp(file[0].string( ),argv[1]) == 0) {
            found++;  // found one.  File is sorted, so if we stop
            // finding them, quit instead of wasting time.
            cout << chr(27) << "[2J"; // ANSI clear screen
            for (int i = 0; i < file.number_of_fields( ); i++)
                cout << file[i] << "\n";
            cout << chr(27) << "[7m" << "press any key" <<
                chr(27) << "[0m"; // ANSI display reverse video
            if( getch( ) == 27) break;
        } else if (found) exit(0);  // quit if that was the last
    } while (file.next( ));
}
```

TAWK — Tiny database processor, vaguely like "AWK"

usage: tawk tawkfile csafile [-s]
where:

Optional '-s' pages output to the screen

csafile contains comma-separated ASCII records. Each field in a record is contained in quotes, and each record is delimited by a new-line. These are standard records that can be generated by the BASIC language and most database management systems.

tawkfile is a file that contains formatting commands. Each record in the csafile is read, and fields in the record are printed out according to the formatting commands in the tawkfile. Everything in the tawkfile (characters, spaces, new-lines) is printed literally except for the following:

@(n) Print field number n; @(3) prints field 3 of the current record. The first field in a record is field 0.

@<n> Print an ascii character number n;

@<27> prints the escape character

@!   This line is a comment until the end of the line

@?nn@: ("then" statements) @~ ("else" statements) @.
      An "if-then-else" conditional. If field nn is not empty, the "then" statements are executed, otherwise the "else" statements are executed. A conditional must have all three parts, but the statements may be empty. Conditionals can be nested.

@Preamble or @P or @p
      When a tawkfile is begun, all statements until @main are considered to be part of the preamble. The preamble is only executed once, at the beginning of the program. The preamble must be strictly text, it cannot contain field numbers or conditionals. The @preamble statement is optional; @preamble is assumed until @main.

@Main or @M or @m
      The main section is executed once for each record in the file. All statements between @Main and @Conclusion are part of the main section. @Main may contain field numbers and conditionals. The @main statement is required.

@Conclusion or @C or @c
      The conclusion is executed after the last record in the database file is read and the file is closed. The conclusion, like the preamble, may only contain text. All other characters on the same line as @preamble, @main or @conclusion are ignored. The @conclusion statement is required.

@end This must be at the end of the tawkfile

@@   Print an '@'

Figure 10-1.   *The manual page for the TAWK program*

Example tawkfile:
@! A comment, which isn't printed
@! The @preamble is optional, but promotes understanding
@main
      This is field 1: @(1)
      This is field 10: @(10)
      @?4@: @(4) @~Field 4 is empty @.
      print an escape: @<27>
      Regenerate comma-separated ASCII record:
"@(0)","@(1)","@(2)","@(3)"
@conclusion This is a comment
That's All, folks!!
@end

Figure 10-1.   *The manual page for the TAWK program (continued)*

The **csascii** object file is created by giving it the name of the comma-separated ASCII file PPQUICK.ASC. Then the records are read one at a time, and field 0 is compared to the first argument on the command line (presumably the last name of the person in the database). When a record is found, it is displayed on the screen (notice the use of the ANSI screen control codes). A flag called **found** is set to indicate that at least one record is found, so when no more matches occur, the program knows to exit. (It is assumed the file has been sorted by the database manager.)

The ANSI C library function **strcmp( )** has been used here for compatibility. To ignore upper- or lowercase in the comparisons, Microsoft C and Turbo C++ provide **strcmpi( )** and Zortech provides **strcmpl( )**.

The TAWK Program

Figure 10-1 gives the complete syntax for the TAWK language. You can see that each TAWK command consists of an @ and a single character. In the case of @( ) and @<>, the commands are @(and @<; the) and > are used by the function that reads the number, to find the end.

The execution of a **tawk** script parallels the compilation or interpretation of other programming languages. The **tawk** script is parsed into arrays of tokens when the program starts up. An execution routine steps through the arrays and performs actions based on the tokens to "run" the **tawk** script.

Here are the declarations for **class token** and **class parse_array**:

```
// PARSE.HXX: Class to parse a tawk script file.  Creates
// a structure that can be used at run time to "execute"
// the tawk script.
#include <stream.hxx>

// types of tokens the scanner can find:
enum tokentype {
    fieldnumber, string, if_, else_, endif_, phase_change
};

// preamble and conclusion of the tawk script are only executed
// once, while main is executed once for every data record
enum phase { preamble, tmain, conclusion};

class token {
    tokentype ttype;
    union {  // an "anonymous union"
        int fieldnum;  // if type is a fieldnumber
        unsigned char * literal; // if type is a string
    };
    int if_level;  // if this is an if_, then_, or else_
    // private functions:
    void get_token( );  // recursive descent scanner
    // Functions to help in scanning:
    void getnext(char & c); // used by get_token( );
    unsigned char get_value(char delimiter, char * msg);
    void dumpline( ); // for @! comments
    void error(char * msg = " ", char * msg2 = " ");
public:
    token(istream & input);
    ~token( );
    friend ostream & operator<<(ostream &s, token &t);
    int field_number( ) { return fieldnum; }
    int token_type( ) { return ttype; }
    int nesting_level( ) { return if_level;}
};

// The following is called a "container class," since its sole
// purpose is to hold a list of objects (tokens, in this case):
class parse_array {
```

```
        token ** tokenarray; // an array of token pointers
        istream * parse_stream;
        int token_count;
        int end; // the size of the array
        phase p_section; // of the program (preamble, etc.)
        void build_array( ); // another recursive function
    public:
        parse_array(istream & input);
        ~parse_array( );
        int size( ) { return end; } // how big is it?
        token & operator[ ](int index); // select a token
        phase section( ) { return p_section; }
};
```

Here are the definitions for **token** and **parse_array**:

```
// PARSE.CXX: class parse function definitions
#include "csascii.hxx"
#include "parse.hxx"
#include <ctype.h>
#include <stdlib.h>

// The following have file scope, which means no one outside
// this file can know about them.  This is the meaning when a
// variable outside all functions is declared "static."
static istream * tokenstream;
static int length; // to remember size of string
static int line_number = 1;  // line counting for errors
static int if_counter = 0; // monitors "if" statement nesting
static phase program_section = preamble;  // ... until @main
static int end_of_file = 0; // zero means not end of file

token::token(istream & input) {
    // initialize values and start the descent
    tokenstream = &input;
    length = 0;
    get_token( );  // recursively get characters to end of token
}

token::~token( ) { // delete heap if any has been allocated:
    if (ttype == string)
        delete literal;
}
```

```
void token::error(char * msg, char * msg2) {
    cerr << "token error on line " << line_number << ": " <<
        msg << " " << msg2 << "\n";
    exit(1);
}

ostream & operator<<(ostream &s, token &t) {
    switch (t.ttype) {
        case string:
            s << (char *)t.literal;
            break;
        case fieldnumber: // only for testing
            s << " fieldnumber: " << t.fieldnum << "\n";
    }
    return s;
}

// Get a character from the tokenstream, checking for
// end-of-file and new-lines
void token::getnext(char & c) {
    if(end_of_file)
        error("attempt to read after @end statement\n",
            "missing @conclusion ?");
    if((tokenstream->get(c)).eof( ) )
        error("@end statement missing");
    if (c == '\n')
        line_number++; // keep track of the line count
}

// See text for description of tokens
void token::get_token( ) {
    char c;
    // This happens when DEscending:
    getnext(c);
    if ( c == '@') {
        if (length == 0) { // length 0 means start of token
            getnext(c);
            switch(c) {
                case '!': // comment
                    dumpline( ); // dump the comment
                    get_token( ); // get a real token
                    break;
                case 'p' : case 'P' : // preamble statement
```

```
        if ( program_section != preamble )
            error("only one preamble allowed");
        dumpline( ); // just for looks, ignore it
        get_token( ); // get a real token
        break;
    case 'm' : case 'M' : // start of main loop
        dumpline( ); // toss rest of line
        program_section = tmain;
        ttype = phase_change;
        return; // very simple token
    case 'c' : case 'C' : // start conclusion
        dumpline( );
        program_section = conclusion;
        ttype = phase_change;
        return; // very simple token
    case 'e' : case 'E': // end statement
        end_of_file++; // set flag
        ttype = fieldnumber; // so destructor doesn't
                            // delete free store for this token.
        if (if_counter)
            error("unclosed 'if' statement(s)");
        return;
    case '(' :
        if ( program_section == preamble ||
            program_section == conclusion )
            error("@( ) not allowed in preamble or conclusion");
        fieldnum = get_value(')',"@( )");
        ttype = fieldnumber;
        // This is a complete token, so quit
        return;
    case '<' :
        c = get_value('>',"@<>");
        length++;
        get_token( ); // get more...
        break;
    case '?' : // beginning of an "if" statement
        if ( program_section == preamble ||
            program_section == conclusion )
            error("@? not allowed in preamble or conclusion");
        fieldnum = get_value('@',"@?@");
        ttype = if_;
        getnext(c); // just eat the colon
        if(c != ':')
```

```
                error("@? must be followed by @: (then)");
            if_level = ++if_counter;  // for nesting
            return;
        case '~' : // the "else" part of an "if" statement
            ttype = else_;
            if_level = if_counter;
            return;
        case '.' : // "endif" terminator of an "if" statement
            ttype = endif_;
            if_level = if_counter--;
            if(if_counter < 0)
            error("incorrect nesting of if- then-else clauses");
            return;
        case '@' : // two '@' in a row mean print an '@'
            length++;  // just leave '@' as the value of c
            get_token( );
            break;
        default:
            error("'@' must be followed by:",
                "'(', '<', '?',':','~','.','p','m','c' or '@'");
        }
    } else { // an '@' in the middle of a string; terminate
        // the string.  Putback( ) is part of the stream class.
        // It is only safe to put one character back on the input
        tokenstream->putback(c); // to be used by the next token
        // allocate space, put the null in and return up the stack
        literal = new unsigned char[length + 1]; // space for '\0'
        literal[length--] = '\0'; // string delimiter
        ttype = string; // what kind of token this is
        return; // back up the stack
    }
    } else { // not an '@', must be plain text
        length++;
        get_token( );
    }
    // This occurs on the "tail" of the recursion:
    literal[length--] = c;  // put chars in as we rise back up...
}

// This function is used by get_token when it encounters a @(
// or a @< to get a number until it finds "delimiter."
// If an error occurs, msg is used to notify the user what
// kind of statement it is.
```

```
unsigned char token::get_value(char delimiter, char * msg) {
    char c;
    char buf[5];
    int i = 0;
    while(getnext(c), c != delimiter) {
        if (!isdigit(c))
            error("must use only digits inside", msg);
        buf[i++] = c;
    }
    buf[i] = 0;
    return atoi(buf);
}


void token::dumpline( ) { // called when '@!' encountered
    char c;
    while(getnext(c), c != '\n')
        ; // just eat characters until new-line
}

// Since there's no way to know how big a parse_array is
// going to be until the entire tawkfile has been tokenized,
// the recursive approach is again used:

parse_array::parse_array(istream & input) {
    parse_stream = &input;
    token_count = 0;
    p_section = program_section; // so we know at run time
    build_array( );
}

void parse_array::build_array( ) {
    token * tk = new token(*parse_stream);
    if( ! end_of_file && tk->token_type( ) != phase_change) {
        // normal token, not end of file or phase change:
        token_count++;
        // recursively get tokens until eof or phase change:
        build_array( );
    } else { // end of file or phase change
        // only done once per object:
        // allocate memory and return up the stack
        tokenarray = new token * [end = token_count];
        if(token_count) token_count--; // only if non-zero
        return;
```

```
   }
   tokenarray[token_count—] = tk;  // performed on the "tail"
}


parse_array::~parse_array( ) {
   for (int i = 0; i < end; i++)
      delete tokenarray[i];
   delete tokenarray;
}

token & parse_array::operator[ ](int index) {
   if ( index >= end ) {
      cerr << "parse_array error: index " << index
         << " out of bounds\n";
      exit(1);
   }
   return *tokenarray[index];
}
```

Here is the **main( )** function for TAWK:

```
// TAWK.CXX: Parses a tawk script and reads an ascii file;
// generates results according to the tawk script.
#include "csascii.hxx"
#include "parse.hxx"
#include "..\\..\\include \\file.hxx"
#include <stdlib.h>
#include <conio.h> //DOS only

main (int argc, char * argv[ ]) {
   int screen = 0;  // flag set true if screen output desired
   if (argc < 3) {
      cerr << "usage: tawk tawkfile datafile\n" <<
         "trailing -s pages output to screen";
      exit(1);
   }
   if (argc == 4) {
      if (argv[3][0] != '-') {
         cerr << "must use '-' before trailing flag\n";
         exit(1);
      } else
```

```
    if (argv[3][1] != 's') {
        cerr << "'s' is only trailing flag allowed";
        exit(1);
    } else
        screen++; // set screen output flag true
}
OPEN_INPUT(tawkfile,argv[1]);
parse_array Apreamble(tawkfile); // the @preamble
parse_array Amain(tawkfile);  // the @main section
parse_array Aconclusion(tawkfile); // the @conclusion
csascii datafile(argv[2]); // make a comma-separated ASCII
                                // object from the second arg
// ———— @preamble ————
for (int i = 0; i < Apreamble.size( ); i++)
    cout << Apreamble[i]; // preamble can only contain strings
if(screen) {
    // ANSI reverse video sequence:
    cout << chr(27) << "[7m" << "press any key" <<
        chr(27) << "[0m";
    getch( );
}
// ———— The Central Loop (@main) ————
do { // for each record in the data file
    if(screen) cout << chr(27) << "[2J"; // ANSI clear screen
    for(int i = 0; i < Amain.size( ); i++) {
        switch(Amain[i].token_type( )) {
            case fieldnumber:
                cout << datafile[Amain[i].field_number( )];
                break;
            case string:
                cout << Amain[i];
                break;
            case if_:
                int fn = Amain[i].field_number( );
                if (datafile[fn].size( ) == 0) { // conditional false
                    int level = Amain[i].nesting_level( );
                    // find the "else" statement on the same level:
                    while ( !(Amain[i].token_type( ) == else_
                        && Amain[i].nesting_level( ) == level))
                            i++;
                } // conditional true — just continue
                break;
            case else_: // an "if" conditional was true so skip
```

```
            // all the statements in the "else" clause
            int level = Amain[i].nesting_level( );
            // find the "endif" statement on the same level:
            while ( !(Amain[i].token_type( ) == endif_
                && Amain[i].nesting_level( ) == level))
                    i++;
            break;
        case endif_: // After performing the "else" clause
            break; // ignore it; only used to find the end
            // of the conditional when "if" is true.
        default: // should never happen (caught in parsing)
            cerr << "unknown statement encountered at run-time\n";
            exit(1);
        }
    }
    if(screen) {
        cout << chr(27) << "[7m" <<
            "press a key (ESC quits)" << chr(27) << "[0m";
        if( getch( ) == 27) break;
    }
} while (datafile.next( )); // matches do { ...
// ———— @conclusion ————
for ( i = 0; i < Aconclusion.size( ); i++)
    cout << Aconclusion[i]; // conclusion contains only strings
}
```

The **tawk** script is parsed into three different **parse_array**s, one each for **@preamble**, **@main**, and **@conclusion**. These arrays are executed using the database file as input.

class token

Each token must be of a particular type. The kind of information a token contains depends on what type it is. In TAWK, the possible token types are as follows: a field number, for printing out a field or testing if a field is empty in an **if** statement; a string, simple text including non-printable characters; parts of a conditional statement, **if, else**, and **endif**; or a phase change, which indicates a transition from **@preamble** to **@main** or **@main** to **@conclusion**. Since a phase change is never executed but is simply used to terminate the creation of a **parse_array**, it isn't a token in the same sense as the others, but some form of communication was necessary.

The different types of tokens and phases are enumerated in the **token-type** and **phase** declarations. The **phase** information is kept by the main program, but each **token** contains a **tokentype** identifier. Since a **token** can never be a field number and a string at the same time, the data container in a **token** is combined into an *anonymous union,* which is like a regular union except that it has no name. The union is used to save space.

A **token** also contains information about the level of **if** statement. Because **if** statements can be nested, each token that is an **if**, **else**, or **endif** must have information about the nesting level. If the conditional evaluates to false (the field is empty), the interpreter must hunt through tokens in the **parse_array** until it finds the **else** statement *at the same level,* and continue executing statements from there.

While **token::get_token( )** is performing its recursive scanning, it calls several other functions, which are made private since they aren't needed by the user. **token::get_next( )** gets a character and tests for end of file (which is an error condition, since an **@end** statement should always terminate the **tawk** script). **token::get_value( )** is used for the **@( )** and **@<>** statements. **token::dumpline( )** is called for comments.

The PARSE.CXX file starts with a number of **static** variables that have file scope. This means they cannot be accessed outside the file. When the constructor is called, it establishes the source of input characters (**tokenstream**), sets the length of the string that has been read so far to zero, and begins the recursion by calling **token::get_token( )**.

There are three possibilities in **token::get_token( )**.

■ The next character in the input stream is an **@** and the length is zero. This means you are at the beginning of a command; the next character will determine what the command is. In this case, a large **switch** statement is executed.

■ The next character is an **@** and the length is not zero. This means you are in the middle of a string and a command is starting. In this case, the **@** is pushed back on the input stream (for use by the next token), space is allocated for the string, and the "unwinding" of the stack is started with a **return**.

■ The next character is not an **@**. This means it must be plain text. In this case, **token::get_token( )** calls itself to get more characters.

class parse_array

The class **parse_array** is a *container class,* since it is only used to contain objects of another class (**token**). There is no way to know how many tokens a **parse_array** will contain, so the recursive approach is used again. The constructor initializes some variables and calls the recursive function **parse_array::build_array( )**, which keeps getting tokens and calling itself until a phase change or the end of the input (an **@end** statement). At this point, it allocates space to hold all the tokens (which it has been counting during the descent) and ascends, storing a token on each function return.

The individual tokens in a **parse_array** can be selected by using brackets ([ ]). This is because the bracket operator has been overloaded in **parse_array::operator[ ]( )**. Since **token** has a stream function defined, tokens can be put directly to **cout**.

Executing a tawk *Script*

TAWK.CXX contains the **main( )** function. After the command-line arguments are checked, the **tawk** script is opened and three **parse_arrays** are created, one for the **@preamble**, one for **@main**, and one for the **@conclusion**. The second command-line argument is used to create a **csascii** object.

At the beginning and end of the script execution, the preamble and conclusion **parse_arrays** are simply sent to standard output (**cout**). Since they can only contain text, no other action is necessary.

The central loop executes the statements in the **@main** phase for each record the **csascii** object reads from the database file. After a record is read, the type of each token in **parse_array Amain** is used in a **switch** statement to choose the proper action. Strings are sent to **cout**, field numbers send the selected field to **cout**.

In an **if** statement, if the selected field is empty in the current record, the **parse_array** index is incremented until the **else** token at the same level is found. If the field is not empty, no action is taken (the subsequent statements are executed). When an **else** is encountered, it means the **if** evaluated to true, so the **else** clause is skipped over until the **endif** of the same level is found.

makefile *for TAWK*

Here is the **makefile** for all the examples in this project:

```
# makefile for tawk.exe & lookup.exe
# Zortech C++:
CPP = ztc
# Glockenspiel C++
#CPP = ccxx

all: tawk.exe lookup.exe

tawk.exe : tawk.obj parse.obj csascii.obj field.obj
        $(CPP)  tawk.obj parse.obj csascii.obj field.obj

lookup.exe : lookup.cxx csascii.obj field.obj
        $(CPP) lookup.cxx csascii.obj field.obj

tawk.obj : tawk.cxx parse.hxx csascii.hxx field.hxx
        $(CPP)  -c tawk.cxx

parse.obj : parse.cxx parse.hxx
        $(CPP)  -c parse.cxx

csascii.obj : csascii.cxx csascii.hxx field.hxx
        $(CPP)  -c csascii.cxx

field.obj : field.cxx field.hxx
        $(CPP)  -c field.cxx
```

Example tawk *Scripts*

Here are two example **tawk** scripts. The first reformats a file with six fields into one with five fields, combining the last two fields. If both of the last two fields are not empty, a space is inserted between them.

```
@! REFORM.TWK
@! A tawk script to reformat a comma-separated ASCII file
@! with 6 fields.  This creates a new CS-ASCII file with
@! fields 4 and 5 combined.
@main
"@(0)","@(1)","@(2)","@(3)","@(4)@?4@:@~@.@(5)"
@conclusion
@end
```

The next script shows the usefulness of the preamble and conclusion. It creates a tiny phone list on an HP LaserJet printer. The preamble and conclusion are used to send special control codes to the printer. The use of nested if-then-else statements is shown here: if field 3 exists, it is printed followed by a carriage return and a test to see if field 4 exists, which is printed with a linefeed if it does (nothing happens if it isn't). If field 3 doesn't exist, field 4 is tested and printed with a linefeed, or else only a linefeed is printed. When everything is completed, a "reset" is sent to the LaserJet.

```
@! WALLET.TWK
@! Tawkfile to create a tiny phone listing for a wallet
@! on a Hewlett-Packard Laserjet-compatible printer
@! from a comma-separated ASCII file generated by a DBMS
@preamble
@<27>&l5C@! approximately 10 lines per inch
@<27>(s16.66H@! small typeface, built into Laserjet
@main
@! last, first, (area code) phone1
@(0),@(1)(@(2))@?3@:@(3)
@ phone2, if it exists
@?4@:@(4)
@~@.@~@?4@:@(4)
@~
@.@.@conclusion
@<27>E @! Reset the Laserjet
@end
```

If you want a further challenge, try adding a "goto" system to TAWK. You will need to create a label command and a goto command. Gotos can be executed from if-then-else statements.

Hiding Complexity in TAWK

The **main( )** program for TAWK is actually quite small for what it does. Because the details are hidden in the **csascii** and **parse_array** objects, you can imagine creating a much more sophisticated program without losing control of the complexity. This is typical of C++; indeed, the language was designed to allow one programmer to handle the same amount of code that previously required several. The compiler supports the creation of large projects by hiding initialization and cleanup and enforcing the correct use of user-defined types.

A Clock-Based Control System

The final project in this chapter parses an ASCII script file to create a list of events that it constantly checks. When an event is ready, the program runs it and removes it from the list. The program is designed to be easy to modify, even for the novice C++ programmer. The modification process is straightforward, and several examples are given. In addition, there are a number of interesting techniques demonstrated, both in C++ and plain C.

This project is quite complete—with a very small amount of customization, you can turn it into a deliverable package that allows customers to configure their own control systems to run selected events at certain times. An inexpensive computer, along with whatever control hardware you need, becomes a stand-alone, time-based controller! The program design can be changed to add hardware events (in addition to clock events). Some degree of interrupt support is even conceivable.

This isn't the ultimate real-time control system. The adequacy of the system depends on the speed and of the computer and the speed/accuracy requirements of your problem. Many problems simply don't require a complicated, preemptive control system.

Using the CONTROLR Program

Figure 10-2 is the "manual page" for CONTROLR. TSTSCRPT is a sample script file for the program.

Usage: controlr <scriptfile> [r|n]

The second argument is optional. 'r' reprints the scriptfile in a form readable by controlr and quits. 'n' turns off the event display to speed things up. Warning: reboot is required to get out of program when the 'n' flag is used!

<scriptfile> is an ASCII file containing commands and comments. Each line in the file can be empty, or contain a single command (including a comment) or contain a comment alone. A comment is started with a single quote (') and continues to the end of the line. There are two types of commands: system commands (which control the execution of the program) and controller commands (which control the target devices). Available system commands are

cycle(CC:CC:CC)
force(FF:FF:FF)
align(AA:AA:AA)

CC:CC:CC is the cycle time. The cycle command restarts the system after each cycle period.

FF:FF:FF is the force time. The force command restarts the system at the force time.

AA:AA:AA is the align time. If the align hours are non-zero, the system restarts on the hour (even if the align hours are greater than zero). If the align hours are zero but the align minutes are nonzero, the system restarts every even multiple of the align minutes. If align hours and minutes are zero, the system restarts every even multiple of the align seconds.

If there are no system commands, the events in a script will only run once.

It doesn't make any sense to have more than one "cycle" command (only the shortest cycle will ever get used) but you can use as many "force" commands as you want. If any of the force commands are in the future, they are added to the list.

Controller commands consist of the command word (specified by the programmer), optional modifiers, and optional comment. The command word and modifiers may appear in any order on the line. If a command word appears alone, as in

LIGHT_ON

that command is executed immediately, upon startup. Thus it is an initializer.

A controller command may have three types of modifiers. All consist of a single character and a time argument. If the character is a

'+': the event occurs at the startup time plus the modifier time.

'@':the event occurs at the modifier time.

'R':the event time (relative or absolute) is randomized by adding a time between zero and the modifier time

---

Figure 10-2.   *The manual page for the CONTROLR program*

An example script:

'This is a comment
@align(00:00:15) ' repeat every 15 seconds, on the 15-second mark
LIGHT_ON 'start with light on
LIGHT_OFF +00:00:02 'light off 2 seconds after start
LIGHT_ON +00:00:02 R00:00:08 'on between 2 and 10 seconds
+00:00:12 LIGHT_OFF ' order doesn't matter
LIGHT_OFF @12:00:00 'light off at noon
LIGHT_ON @12:45:00 R00:30:00 'light on at 12:45 + up to 30 minutes

Figure 10-2. *The manual page for the CONTROLR program (continued)*

```
'TSTSCRPT : A sample script for CONTROLR.EXE
cycle(00:03:00) ' restart every 3 minutes
force( 16:15:00 ) 'restart at an absolute time
force( 21:20:00 ) 'notice spaces are ignored
force( 21:25:00 )
align(00:05:00)  ' restart on the five-minute mark
""""""  start up conditions  """"""""
LIGHT_ON
THERMOSTAT_NIGHT
BELL
"""""""""""""""""""""""""""""""""""""""""""
LIGHT_OFF  +00:00:10 ' light off ten seconds after startup
THERMOSTAT_DAY +00:00:15 ' heater high 15 seconds after startup
THERMOSTAT_DAY @13:50:00 ' heater high at 1:00 pm
LIGHT_ON    +00:00:30 R00:00:10 'light on 30 secs after start
LIGHT_OFF @14:00:00 R01:00:00 '2 pm plus up to 1 hour
R00:00:10 +00:01:00 GREENHOUSE_WATER_ON ' order is unimportant
R00:00:10 +00:01:30 GREENHOUSE_WATER_OFF
```

To modify the program for your own use, edit the file CONTROLR.CXX (shown later in the chapter in "Parsing the Script"). Two preprocessor macros are used in the file, **EVENT_TYPE** and **MAKE_EVENT**. You can see how a new kind of event is added to the system by looking at the example definitions at the beginning of CONTROLR.CXX (**light_on,**

light_off, **bell**, and so on). Each definition consists of a call to the **EVENT_TYPE** macro, which is followed by member definitions for **name::action( )** and **name::description( )**, where **name** is what you've called the new kind of event. The **action( )** function is run when the event is "ready" (in this case, when the clock time is greater than or equal to the event time), and the **description( )** is used to describe the event on the display.

Remove all the event definitions except for **system_restart**. Now create your own definitions. For each **EVENT_TYPE** macro call and associated definitions, you also need to add a **MAKE_EVENT** call farther down in the program. If you search for the label **CREATE:**, you will see a **while(1)** loop containing a number of **MAKE_EVENT** definitions corresponding to the **EVENT_TYPE** definitions at the beginning of the file. The arguments to the macro are the class name and a string that is the command name used in the script file. Remove these macro calls and replace them with your own. Then recompile the program with C++ by typing "make." That's all there is to it.

The remainder of this chapter describes the internal workings of the program.

Object-Oriented Event Control

This program is "truly" object-oriented. It manipulates generic objects. Each object belongs to the abstract base class, **event** (see the file EVENT.HXX), and to a specific derived class that has special properties in two **virtual** functions, **description( )** and **action( )**. A **virtual** function is declared in the base class and defined in the derived class, so two objects can have the same interface but different implementations.

Objects of the base class are kept in a list and constantly checked to see if they are ready to run. ("Ready" in this case is only tied to the clock. To modify the system to respond to hardware events, make **ready( )** a virtual function and define it to test hardware in the derived class.) When an event is ready, its **action( )** is performed and it is removed from the list.

A class *to Manage Time*

Here is the header file **event.hxx**, which contains two **class** definitions: **class time_point**, to represent a single point in time; and **class event**, to represent a single event.

```
// EVENT.HXX: Each event object has a scheduled time,
// and a virtual function to be executed at that time.
// The event class should be derived into a class with
// the desired "action" function; a list of events is
// managed in main( ).

#include <stdio.h>

// A point in time:
class time_point {
    int hours;
    int minutes;
    int seconds;
public:
    time_point( ); // get current time
    void normalize ( );
    // set a specific time:
    time_point ( int hr, int min = 0, int sec = 0 ) {
        hours = hr; minutes = min; seconds = sec;
        normalize( );
    }
    // the copy-initializer: (create one point from another)
    time_point (time_point & rv);
    time_point (char *); // from string, i.e.: "09:45:23"
    void randomize(time_point & random_f);
    time_point operator=(time_point & rv); // assignment
    // compare one time point to another:
    int operator>=(time_point & rv);
    time_point operator+(time_point & rv);
    void display( ){
        printf("%2.2d:%2.2d:%2.2d",hours,minutes,seconds);
    }
    int & hr( ) { return hours; }
    int & min( ) { return minutes; }
    int & sec( ) { return seconds; }
};

// an event object is scheduled to occur at some point in time:
class event {
    time_point event_time; // when the event should happen
public:
    // note the initialization of the member object:
    event( ) : event_time( ) { }; // no arguments -- do it now
```

```
    event(time_point & tp)  : event_time(tp) { } ; // absolute
    event(time_point & tp, time_point & rst_time) // from restart
        : event_time(tp + rst_time) { }
    event(time_point & tp, time_point & rst_time,
            time_point & random_f)
        : event_time(tp + rst_time) {
            event_time.randomize(random_f);
        }
    // "ready" is true if event is ready to run:
    int ready(time_point & now) {
        return now >= event_time;
    }
    void display( ) { event_time.display( ); }
    // The following function is redefined for each specific
    // subclass:
    virtual void action( ) { // what happens at event_time
        fprintf(stderr, "error — base class used; %s\n"
            "no action specified for this event");
    }
    // This is optionally redefined so you can see what
    // events are waiting to be run:
    virtual void description( ) { puts("no description"); }
};


// This macro derives a new class from class event.  It saves
// typing and errors when you want to make a new type of event.
// To use it: EVENT_TYPE(event_class_name);  you must also
// define a function for the new action which is to happen
// when the event is ready to run:
// void event_class_name::action( ) { /* defintion here */ }
// See the examples in CONTROLR.CXX

#define EVENT_TYPE(ENAME) class ENAME : public event { \
    public: \
    ENAME( ) : ( ) { } \
    ENAME(time_point & p) : (p) { } \
    ENAME(time_point & p, time_point & s) : (p,s) { } \
    ENAME(time_point & p, time_point & s, time_point & r) \
            : (p,s,r) { } \
    void action( ); \
    void description( ); \
};
```

class event contains a member object called **event_time** that belongs to **class time_point**. **time_point**s can be assigned, added, compared to see if one is greater than or equal to another, and "randomized" (increased by a random amount of time, bounded by a random factor). Once **class time_point** is defined, details of time calculations can be ignored.

Each object in **class event** is associated with a single **time_point**. When the clock time is greater than or equal to the **event_time**, the member function **ready( )** returns true. This way you can ask an event if it is ready to run.

To create a new type of event, a new class must be inherited from **class event** so the virtual functions **description( )** and **action( )** may be redefined. This inheritance is always the same except for the name, so the code to inherit a new subtype is packaged into the macro **EVENT_TYPE**, defined in event.hxx and used in CONTROLR.CXX. Notice that a macro can be continued as long as you keep putting backslashes at the end of each line.

Here are the definitions:

```
// EVENT.CXX: definitions for event.hxx
// (class event functions are all in-line)
#include "event.hxx"
#include <time.h>
#include <stdlib.h> // for rand( ), srand( ), atoi( )

#define db(var) printf(#var " = %d\n", var)

// Correct the time so hours < 24, minutes & seconds < 60
void time_point::normalize ( ) {
   if ( seconds >= 60 ) {
      minutes += seconds / 60; // integer division
      seconds = seconds % 60; // integer remainder
   }
   if ( minutes >= 60 ) {
      hours += minutes / 60;
      minutes %= 60; // short form of " = minutes % 60 "
   }
   if ( hours >= 24 ) {
      hours %= 24;
   }
}
```

```
time_point::time_point( ) { // get current time
    time_t ltime;  // holds encoded time
    struct tm *t; // the time and day
    time(&ltime); // get time
    t = localtime(&ltime); // convert time
    hours = t->tm_hour;
    minutes = t->tm_min;
    seconds = t->tm_sec;
}

time_point::time_point (time_point & rv) {
    hours = rv.hours;
    minutes = rv.minutes;
    seconds = rv.seconds;
}

time_point time_point::operator=(time_point & rv) {
    hours = rv.hours;
    minutes = rv.minutes;
    seconds = rv.seconds;
}

time_point::time_point (char * ts) {
    hours = atoi(ts);
    ts += 3; // move pointer past first ':'
    minutes = atoi(ts);
    ts += 3; // move pointer past second ':'
    seconds = atoi(ts);
    normalize( );
}

void time_point::randomize(time_point & random_f) {
    time_point now;
    // seed the random number generator:
    srand(now.hours + now.minutes + now.seconds);
    // create a random number between 0 and 1:
    float r = (float)rand( )/(float)32767;
    seconds += (int)(r * random_f.seconds);
    minutes += (int)(r * random_f.minutes);
    hours += (int)(r * random_f.hours);
    normalize( );
}
```

```
int time_point::operator>=(time_point & rv) {
   if ( hours > rv.hours )
      return 1;
   if (hours < rv.hours)
      return 0;
   // here, hours == rv.hours
   if ( minutes > rv.minutes )
      return 1;
   if ( minutes < rv.minutes )
      return 0;
   // here, minutes == rv.minutes
   if ( seconds >= rv.seconds  )
      return 1;
   return 0; // seconds < rv.seconds
}

time_point time_point::operator+(time_point & rv) {
   time_point sum(0);
   sum.seconds = seconds + rv.seconds;
   sum.minutes = minutes + rv.minutes;
   sum.hours = hours + rv.hours;
   sum.normalize( );
   return sum;
}
```

You may want to improve the **randomize( )** function. Notice you can
change the implementation without modifying the interface, so the rest of
the program does not need to be modified.

A C++-Oriented Linked List

"Completely" object-oriented programs often manage an arbitrary number
of generic objects (from classes that use polymorphism, or **virtual** functions). A linked list is often the best way to handle these objects. Here is
the linked list definition for this project. Notice all the function definitions
are **inline**. This makes it easier to create different lists.

```
// EVLIST.HXX: a self-contained linked list
// The first object must be created as a named variable
// with no arguments.  This is the name of the list.
// All the rest are created with "new" and arguments,
```

```
// but the return value of "new" is never used (normally
// a no-no). Because "head" is static, only one list name
// can be used for each different list class.
#include "event.hxx"
#include <stdio.h>
#include <stdlib.h>

class event_el {
    // the start of all members of this class:
    static event_el * head;
    // used to step through the list:
    static event_el * cursor;
    event_el * next_el; // link to the next element
    event * ddata; // holds the information in this node
    void error(char * msg = " ") {
        printf("list error: %s\n", msg);
        exit(1);
    }
public:
    event_el( ) { // create a named list (don't use "new" on this!)
        next_el = 0;
        ddata = 0; // to mark end of list
        // point to yourself as the only element:
        cursor = head = this;
    }
    event_el(event * info) { // only use "new" on this!
        ddata = info;
        // insert this element at the head of the list:
        next_el = head;
        head = this;
    }
    ~event_el( ) {
        event_el * current = head, * old = head;
        while ( current != this ) {
            // find our place in the list, and the element before
            if (current == 0) error("can't delete nonexistent link");
            old = current;
            current = current->next_el;
        }
        if ( this == head )
            head = next_el; // move head to next link
        old->next_el = next_el; // unlink this from list
        delete ddata; // does nothing if ddata == 0
```

```
    }
    event * data( ) { return ddata; }
    void reset( ) { cursor = head; }
    event_el * next( ) { // step through the list
      // return the current element and step forward one,
      // if we can.
      event_el * llp = cursor;
      if (cursor->next_el != 0)
        cursor = cursor->next_el;
      if (llp->ddata != 0)
        return llp;
      else // tail element has empty ddata pointer (don't use it)
        return 0;
    }
};
```

This linked list uses the unique features of C++ to advantage, in particular constructors, destructors, and **static** class variables.

Many linked lists define a link element and then a "container" to manage the links. The **class event_el** in **evlist.hxx** contains *itself*. It does this by using a *static member variable* for the **head** pointer (the pointer to the beginning of the list).

static class *VARIABLES* A **static** member variable is a way for all objects in a class to share common information. It is available to all objects of the class, but space for only one variable of that name is defined, and all objects share the same data space for the variable. Like a static variable in a C function body, a **static** member variable is not automatic (so it has the same lifetime as a variable defined outside all functions), but it has a "hidden" name that is only known to members of the class (assuming the element is private).

Unlike **static** variables in C functions, **static** class variables should not be initialized when they are declared. Initialization tells the C++ compiler to make space for the variable, so if you include the header containing the class declaration in more than one place, you will get a conflict when you try to link the program. The **static** member variable should only be initialized by a special constructor.

This special constructor in **class event_el** is the constructor without arguments. Because of the **static** variable, you can only create one linked list for each unique class name, so this constructor can only be called once (at the beginning of CONTROLR.CXX). If you want to make another list, copy the class definition to a new file and give the class a new name.

The **event_el** class contains itself via the **static** member variable

static event * head;

A new list called **event_list** is created in CONTROLR.CXX with the line

event_el event_list;

This points **head** to an empty element (used to indicate the end of the list). The constructor with an argument, **event_el::event_el(event * info)**, should only be called with the **new** keyword, which creates an object on the free store. **new** normally returns the address of the object it created, and in most cases if you lose this address you can never release that heap space. Here, however, the constructor ties the element into the linked list by inserting it at the head, so the address isn't lost. What normally invites disaster,

new event_el(new event);

is the proper way to add an element to the list.

Notice the **cursor** pointer is also static. This means there is only one cursor for the entire list.

***REMOVING ELEMENTS WITH* delete**   Most linked lists have a function to unlink elements. This linked list is unique because it uses C++'s destructor to neatly remove objects from the linked list. The compiler automatically calls the destructor when an object created on the stack goes out of scope. The user can explicitly call the destructor for an object created on the free store using the keyword **delete**. If you call **delete** with a pointer to an **event_el,** the destructor removes that **event_el** from the linked list and deletes the data. This produces very tidy code when using the linked list. (See the last part of CONTROLR.CXX, which follows.)

Parsing the Script

Here is the file CONTROLR.CXX, which contains the subclass definitions of the **event**s, the parser, and the list manager. Notice that at the beginning of **main( )**, the program tests for a single trailing flag, '**-s**'. You can improve the program by using the **CL_flags** system shown at the beginning of this chapter.

```
// CONTROLR.CXX: The main controller.  Parses a file of
// commands and creates a list of events  When it is time to
// run an event, the event's action is executed and the event
// is removed from the list.

#include <stdlib.h>
#include <stream.hxx>
#include <string.h>
#include <setjmp.h> // setjmp( ) & longjmp( )
#include "evlist.hxx"

jmp_buf system_restart_buf; // for setjmp & longjmp

event_el event_list; // make only one named event_el list!

// To add a new type of event, mimic the following definitions
// (call the macro EVENT_TYPE and create an action for your new
// event) and add a new macro call of MAKE_EVENT in the
// "while(1)" loop with the comment "CREATE." That's all there
// is to extending the system. (The description( ) definition is
// optional).

EVENT_TYPE(light_on);
void light_on::action( ) {
    // put hardware control code here to physically
    // turn on the light.
}
void light_on::description( ) {
    puts("light is on");
}
// End of a user-defined event definition.
// More user-defined event definitions:
EVENT_TYPE(light_off);
void light_off::action( ) {
```

```
    // put hardware control code here to physically
    // turn off the light.
}
void light_off::description( ) {
    puts("light is off");
}

// an example of an action( ) which inserts a new
// one of itself into the event list:
EVENT_TYPE(bell);
void bell::action( ) {
    // ring bell every 10 seconds:
    cout << chr(7); cout.flush( );
    time_point now;
    new event_el(new bell(now + time_point(0,0,10)));
}
void bell::description( ) {
    puts("ring bell");
}

EVENT_TYPE(greenhouse_water_on);
void greenhouse_water_on::action( ) {
    // put hardware control code here
}
void greenhouse_water_on::description( ) {
    puts("greenhouse water is on");
}

EVENT_TYPE(greenhouse_water_off);
void greenhouse_water_off::action( ) {
    // put hardware control code here
}
void greenhouse_water_off::description( ) {
    puts("greenhouse water is off");
}

EVENT_TYPE(thermostat_night);
void thermostat_night::action( ) {
    // put hardware control code here
}
void thermostat_night::description( ) {
    puts("thermostat on night setting");
}
```

```
EVENT_TYPE(thermostat_day);
void thermostat_day::action( ) {
   // put hardware control code here
}
void thermostat_day::description( ) {
   puts("thermostat on day setting");
}


// The above EVENT_TYPEs are just examples, but the following
// is used by the system:
EVENT_TYPE(system_restart);
void system_restart::action( ) {
   event_list.reset( );
   // remove all entries from the list:
   event_el * ep;
   while ( (ep = event_list.next( )) != 0)
      delete ep;
   // "nonlocal goto" back to beginning of main( ):
   longjmp(system_restart_buf,1);
}
void system_restart::description( ) {
   puts("system restart");
}


// This specifies when an event is to happen.
// relative: from system startup time
// absolute: 24-hour clock time
enum whenis { now, relative, absolute, unassigned };


// A "token" structure to hold the information in
// the line from the event description file:
struct tk {
   whenis when;
   int randomize;
   char * descriptor;
   time_point etime;
   time_point randomization;
   tk( ) : when(unassigned),
           randomize(0), descriptor(" ") ,
           etime(0), randomization(0)
           { }
   ~tk( ) { if ( when != unassigned )
                delete descriptor;
```

```
    }
    void display( );
};

// output the event description in such a way
// that it can be re-parsed by this program:
void tk::display( ) {
    if ( when != unassigned ) {
        cout << descriptor;
        int dl = 25 - strlen(descriptor);
        for (int i = 0; i++ < dl; cout.put(' ') )
            ;
        if(when == relative) cout << "+";
        if(when == absolute) cout << "@";
        if ( when != now) {
            etime.display( ); cout << "\t";
        }
        if(randomize) {
            cout << "R";
            randomization.display( );
        }
        cout << "\n";
    }
}

main (int argc, char * argv[ ]) {
    if ( argc != 2 && argc != 3 ) {
        cerr << "Usage: controlr <scriptfile> [r|n]\n"
            "Second argument is optional. 'r' reprints the\n"
            "scriptfile in a form readable by this program.\n"
            "'n' turns off the event display to speed things up.\n"
            "Warning: reboot is required to get out of program\n"
            "when the 'n' flag is used!\n"
            " <scriptfile> is an ASCII file containing controller"
            " commands\n";
        exit(1);
    }
    int evdisplay = 1; // flag means "display events"
    int reprint = 0; // flag means reprint scriptfile & quit
    if ( argc == 3 ) {
        if ( *argv[2] == 'n' )
            evdisplay = 0;
        if ( *argv[2] == 'r' )
```

```
        reprint++;
}
// set the restart buffer so longjmp comes back here:
setjmp(system_restart_buf);
time_point startup_time;  // time at startup or restart
{ // forces istream eventscript out of scope at closing
    // brace, which closes file so it is re-opened when
    // this scope is entered again.
filebuf f1;
if (f1.open(argv[1], input) == 0) {
    cerr << "cannot open %s\n" << argv[1] << "\n";
    exit(1);
}
istream eventscript(&f1);
// for use by strtok( ), the token grabber.  Tokens are
// whitespace or paren delimited:
const char * delimit = " \t\n\r( )";
const int BSIZE = 100;
char buf[BSIZE], c;
while( eventscript.get(buf,BSIZE) ) {
    eventscript.get(c); // throw away new-line delimiter
    { // to force tk token out of scope after each loop
    tk token; // to save information about event
    char * tokptr = strtok(buf, delimit); // get first token
    while ( tokptr != NULL ) { // do for all tokens in line
        if ( * tokptr == '\' ) { // start of comment
            break; // throw away to end of line
        }
        if ( strcmp(tokptr,"cycle") == 0 ) {
            // make cycle time from next token:
            time_point cycle_time(tokptr = strtok(NULL, delimit));
            if (reprint) {
                cout << "cycle(";
                cycle_time.display( );
                cout << ")\n";
            }
            cycle_time = cycle_time + startup_time;
            // enter it into the event list:
            new event_el(new system_restart(cycle_time));
        } else
        if ( strcmp(tokptr,"force") == 0 ) {
            // make force time from next token:
            time_point force_time(tokptr = strtok(NULL, delimit));
```

```
    if (reprint) {
        cout << "force(";
        force_time.display( );
        cout << ")\n";
    }
    // if we aren't already past the force_time,
    // enter it into the event list:
    if ( ! (startup_time >= force_time))
        new event_el(new system_restart(force_time));
} else
if ( strcmp(tokptr,"align") == 0 ) {
    // make align time from next token:
    time_point align_time(tokptr = strtok(NULL, delimit));
    if (reprint) {
        cout << "align(";
        align_time.display( );
        cout << ")\n";
    }
    if ( align_time.hr( ) != 0 ) { // XX:00:00 align to hours
        align_time.hr( ) = startup_time.hr( ) + 1;
        align_time.min( ) = align_time.sec( ) = 0;
    } else {
        align_time.hr( ) = startup_time.hr( );
        if ( align_time.min( ) != 0 ) { //00:XX:00 align minute
            int next_min =
                ( (startup_time.min( )/align_time.min( )) + 1 )
                    * align_time.min( );
            if (next_min > 60 )
                align_time.hr( )++;
            else
                align_time.min( ) = next_min;
            align_time.sec( ) = 0;
        } else { // 00:00:XX align seconds
            align_time.min( ) = startup_time.min( );
            if (align_time.sec( ) != 0) {
                int next_sec =
                    ( (startup_time.sec( )/align_time.sec( )) + 1 )
                        * align_time.sec( );
                if (next_sec > 60 )
                    align_time.min( )++;
                else
                    align_time.sec( ) = next_sec;
            }
```

```
          }
        }
        align_time.normalize( );
        new event_el(new system_restart(align_time));
      } else
      if ( *tokptr == '+' ) {
        token.when = relative;
        token.etime = time_point(++tokptr);
      } else
      if ( *tokptr == '@' ) {
        token.when = absolute;
        token.etime = time_point(++tokptr);
      } else
      if ( *tokptr == 'R' || *tokptr == 'r' ) {
        token.randomize++;
        token.randomization = time_point(++tokptr);
      } else {
        // it wasn't anything else -- assume a name
        token.descriptor = new char[strlen(tokptr) + 1];
        strcpy(token.descriptor,tokptr);
      }
      tokptr = strtok(NULL, delimit); // get next token
    }
    // line parsed.  Now perform actions based on token.
    if(!*token.descriptor)
        // A line with an empty descriptor means a comment line
        // or a system command (which was executed in the parser).
        // Go back to beginning of while loop and get next line:
        continue;
    // If the token isn't empty but it isn't relative or
    // absolute, it means the event should happen now:
    if(token.when != relative && token.when != absolute)
            token.when = now;
    if(reprint)
      token.display( );

    // Add an event to the list.  First, a macro that creates
    // the right event based on the token information.  This
    // saves a great deal of typing and mistakes.  The final
    // "break" gets out of the "while(1)" loop that follows.
    // The macro is placed here instead of at the beginning of
    // the file (as is conventional) because it makes the code
    // easier to understand.
```

```
//    STRING is the string the parser finds in the
// script file.  ENAME is the name of the class.
#define MAKE_EVENT(STRING,ENAME) \
if (strcmp(token.descriptor,STRING) == 0) { \
    switch(token.when) { \
        case relative: \
            if (token.randomize) \
                new event_el(new ENAME( startup_time, \
                                        token.etime, \
                                        token.randomization)); \
            else \
                new event_el(new ENAME(startup_time, token.etime)); \
            break; \
        case absolute: \
            if (token.randomize) \
                new event_el(new ENAME(token.etime, \
                                 time_point(0), \
                                 token.randomization)); \
            else \
                new event_el(new ENAME(token.etime)); \
            break; \
        case now: \
            new event_el(new ENAME); \
    } \
    break; \
}
// End of macro definition

    // Create the event and add it to the list, using the
    // information parsed from the script file.
    // CREATE:
    while(1) {
        // When a match is found, a "break" statement in the
        // macro jumps out of the "while(1)" loop.
        MAKE_EVENT("LIGHT_ON", light_on);
        MAKE_EVENT("LIGHT_OFF", light_off);
        MAKE_EVENT("BELL", bell);
        MAKE_EVENT("GREENHOUSE_WATER_ON", greenhouse_water_on);
        MAKE_EVENT("GREENHOUSE_WATER_OFF", greenhouse_water_off);
        MAKE_EVENT("THERMOSTAT_DAY", thermostat_day);
        MAKE_EVENT("THERMOSTAT_NIGHT", thermostat_night);
        // if there wasn't a match, it's an error:
        cerr << "unrecognized line in " << argv[1] << "\n";
```

```
        token.display( );
        exit(1);
      } // end of "while(1)"
    } // end of tk token scope (token destroyed)
  } // all lines in file are parsed
} // end of scope enclosing istream eventscript
if (reprint) exit(0);  // just reprint script
cout << chr(27) << "[2J"; // ANSI clear screen
// The list of events has been completely built.
// Now loop through the list and look for events to be run.
while(1) {
  { // this '{' forces "current_time" to go out of scope so it
    // is destroyed and created for each pass through the loop
    time_point current_time;
    if (evdisplay) {
      cout << chr(27) << "[s"; // ANSI save cursor position
      cout << chr(27) << "[1;40H"; // ANSI move cursor to 1,40
      cout << chr(27) << "[7m"; // ANSI reverse video
      current_time.display( );
      cout << " started: "; startup_time.display( );
      cout << chr(27) << "[m"; // ANSI no attributes
      cout << chr(27) << "[u"; // ANSI restore cursor position
    }
    event_list.reset( );
    event_el * ep;
    while ( (ep = event_list.next( )) != 0) {
      if ((ep->data( ))- >ready(current_time)) {
        if(evdisplay) {
          cout << "\nRUNNING an event:\n";
          (ep->data( ))- >description( );
        }
        (ep->data( ))->action( ); // run the event
        delete ep; // remove event from list
        // print out remaining list times and descriptions:
        if(evdisplay) {
          cout << "\n\n Event list:\n";
          event_list.reset( );
          while ( (ep = event_list.next( )) != 0) {
            (ep->data( ))- >display( );
            cout << " ::: ";
            (ep->data( ))- >description( );
          }
```

```
            }
        }
    }
    } // close of "current_time" scope
  } // end of while(1) looping through event list
}
```

After the subclasses are derived, you will see a definition for a **struct** called **tk** (for "token"). A **tk** is a place to store all the information about a particular event while parsing a line. When the parser is finished with the line, a new **event** can be created based on the information in the **tk**.

This approach has several advantages. It generally separates the analysis from the action (except for system commands, which can easily be added to **tk**) to keep the code easy to understand and maintain. By creating an internal representation instead of executing events as soon as you figure out what they are, you allow the possibility of saving the internal representation of the entire file (instead of handling it a line at a time, as is done here) so the design can easily be changed to allow faster system restarts.

The C++ **stream class** is used for console and file I/O. In **main( )**, the script file is opened as an **istream,** and one line is read at a time from the **istream** using the member function **get( )** until the file ends. Since **get( )** only reads to a terminating character (and pushes the terminator back on the input stream), an extra **get( )** of a single character is necessary before the next line **get( )**. (**get( )** is an overloaded function. The same function name can take several different types of arguments.) This terminator defaults to '**\n**'.

The ANSI C function **strtok( )** breaks each line into pieces. **strtok( )** is a very useful function when you want to parse input. The function name means "break a string into tokens." (The word "token" as used here means "a piece of text.") **strtok( )** looks for a single character terminator from among the characters you give it in the third argument. The possible terminators (given by the constant string **delimit**) are white space (space, tab, linefeed, carriage return) or an open or closing parenthesis.

The first time you call **strtok( )** for a line, you give it the starting address of the buffer as the first argument. For subsequent calls using the same line, give it NULL as the first argument. **strtok( )** will return a pointer to a null-terminated string token until it can't find any more (in which case it returns **NULL**).

Each token is analyzed in a large **if-else** statement until the entire line has been parsed.

SYSTEM COMMANDS You can see that the *system commands* (**force, cycle, align**; commands that modify the control system) are handled differently in the parser than the *control commands* (which modify the system being controlled). System commands are executed by the parser ("Execute" in this case means "an event is added to the event list.") Control commands require string matching and argument checking before an event can be added to the event list.

PARSER IMPROVEMENTS You can improve the design of the parser by adding **cycle, force**, and **align** to the enumeration **whenis**. During parsing simply assign **token.when** to the type of system command and **token.etime** to the time, and delay the event creation until after the parsing is completed. This improvement is also the first step necessary to allow you to turn the entire file into a representation in memory.

One system command you may want to add is **commandfile** to change the name of the controller script file used when the system restarts.

Adding an Event to the List

After each line is parsed, an event is added to the list based on the information in the line. The macro **MAKE_EVENT** compares the **token.descriptor** to a string; if there is a match it makes a new **event**. This occurs inside what appears to be an infinite **while** loop. You can think of it as a **case** statement that matches strings (instead of simple integers, as an ordinary **case** does); it was implemented this way to simplify the addition of new event types. An **if-else** construct would not have fit neatly into a macro, since **else** would occur at the end of the macro. By using a **break** at the end of the macro to jump out of the **while(1)** loop the code fits together nicely.

Managing the List

After the script file is parsed and the list is constructed, the program loops through the list looking for events to run. At the beginning of each loop, a new **current_time** object is created and all the **event** objects in the list are tested with their **ready( )** functions, using **current_time** as the argument.

Notice the extra set of braces in the final **while(1)** loop. The only purpose of these braces is to force **current_time** out of scope at the end of the loop.

When it goes out of scope, the destructor is called, and when the loop is started again, the constructor is called. This updates **current_time.** The trick of forcing an object to go out of scope (and thus calling a constructor or destructor) is used several places in the program.

If you ignore the display code in the list manager, the remaining code is surprisingly compact, as you can see from this code fragment:

```
while(1) {

  {

  time_point current_time;

  event_list.reset( );

  event_el * ep;

  while((ep = event_list.next( )) != 0)

    if((ep->data( ))->ready(current_time)) {

    (ep->data( ))->action( );

    delete ep;

    }

  }

}
```

The list is reset, and each element is tested against the current time until there are no more elements in the list. If one is found, it is run and removed from the list. This abbreviated code is executed when the **n** command-line option is used. Notice that object pointers are used, so arrows dereference the member functions.

Design Guidelines

When designing an object-oriented system, it is important that your concept of an object encompass all the possible uses for that object. In this system, for example, an **action( )** can be anything, including restarting the system. (See **EVENT_TYPE(system_restart)** in CONTROLR.CXX.) Notice also the flexibility of the system—the action of one event can add other events to the list, as shown in **EVENT_TYPE(bell)**.

The system restart commands are necessary for two reasons: you may want to create a process that repeats itself, and you may want the controller to resynchronize itself in the event of a power failure.

Restarting the System

To make a system command just another type of **event, system_restart::action( )** must be able to jump to the beginning of the **main( )** function. This isn't as easy as using **goto**, since any labels in **main( )** are outside the scope of **system_restart::action( )**.

C solves this kind of problem with a concept called *non-local goto*, implemented with the ANSI C library functions **setjmp( )** and **longjmp( )**. The **setjmp( )** function stores the contents of the stack and the program counter in a type of structure called a **jmp_buf**. When **longjmp( )** is called with that same structure as an argument, it goes back to the spot where **setjmp( )** was called and restores the same stack. Except for the return value of **setjmp( )**, it looks exactly like the first time **setjmp( )** was called. Notice that **longjmp( )** is called inside the **system_restart::action( )** function, which has no idea where the jump will end up. Because **setjmp( )** is called at run time, and can be called in several different spots, you can not only jump *anywhere,* you can decide at run time where you will jump.

Increasing Restart Speed

The controller script file is reopened and reparsed every time the system is restarted. If this isn't as quick as you'd like (if you are restarting at very short intervals) then you can rewrite the parsing section to store the information in a linked list of **tk** pointers (copy the file **evlist.hxx** and modify the linked list). When the system restarts, you won't have to open and reparse the file. Just build the new list of events from the list of **tk** pointers. If you're a very good programmer, you can create an image of the list and duplicate it using **memcpy( )** when the system is restarted. This is more complicated than it sounds, and not for the faint of heart. A second, much quicker alternative is to create a small disk cache, just large enough to hold the script file.

If you are concerned about the execution speed of the **events**, use the **n** command-line flag to eliminate display. Screen display can be notoriously slow. This option, unfortunately, requires you to reboot the system to get out of the program (or kill the process, in UNIX). You can fix this in MS-DOS by adding the non-ANSI C statement **if(kbhit( )) exit(0);** inside the last **while(1)** loop.

Advantages of Object-Oriented Design

Pay special attention here to the ease with which you can extend the system. Extending the system consists essentially of deriving a new data type from the base **class event**. (You must also add a line at the **CREATE:** label, but no thinking is involved.) Since the system already knows how to handle **event**s, you only need to focus your efforts on what is new; the rest of the program doesn't break because you've added a new data type.

The idea of "designing a program for extensibility" is often new to users of traditional procedural languages. Those languages make the implicit assumption that a program will be designed once, and never changed. Experience has shown that modifying programs is a rule, rather than an exception. When you design a program, look for items that can be thought of as objects, and see what those objects have in common. Create an abstract base class containing all those common features as **virtual** functions, and create code to manage objects of that base class. You will find yourself building programs that are much easier to read, maintain, and extend.

Remember, however, that the real point of object-oriented programming is not **virtual** functions, operator overloading, or other frills. Those are just features in a language to *support* object-oriented programming. The point is to capture the parts of the program that are least likely to change—the objects being manipulated.

Makefile for CONTROLR

Here is the **makefile** for the event controller project:

```
# Makefile for event manager.
# The -C prevents inline expansion; this is a very nice
# feature in Zortech C++ because when you run out of memory
# from too many inline functions, you don't have to do a lot
# of editing; just use this flag.
```

```
CPP = ztc -C
controlr.exe : controlr.obj event.obj
        $(CPP) controlr.obj event.obj

controlr.obj : controlr.cxx evlist.hxx event.hxx
        $(CPP) -c controlr.cxx

event.obj : event.cxx event.hxx
        $(CPP) -c event.cxx

# NOTE: this code may not compile with the version of
# Glockenspiel C++ available at the time the book was written.
# The 31-character limit imposed on identifiers by
# Microsoft C is exceeded by the names generated in this
# program.  When the names are truncated by MSC they are no
# longer unique.  ANSI C says that 31 characters is the
# minimum number a compiler must use internally for
# identifiers.  C++ release 2.0 will add even more
# characters to identifier names and compound the problem
# for C-code generators.
```

On MS-DOS, the excessive use of **inline** functions in the **class** definitions caused both Zortech C++ and Glockenspiel C++ to run out of memory. The -**C** flag in Zortech C++ forces **inline**s to be compiled as non-**inline** functions, so the problem can easily be repaired if you are using Zortech C++. If you are using Glockenspiel C++, you will have to edit the **inline** functions into non-**inline** functions in a separate definition file. Turbo C++ automatically changes inlines to non-inlines when they become too complicated or otherwise inappropriate.

11 *C++*
Release 2.0

A living language changes and grows according to the needs of its community. Since the birth of C++, programmers have discovered new and creative ways to use the language and also found deficiencies in the features that C++ provides. Some of these deficiencies were removed in later releases of C++ by adding new features to the language. As you will appreciate the longer you work with C++, each feature is carefully integrated into the entire language, so a new feature must work sensibly across the spectrum of possibilities.

The changes in the C++ language have been indicated by the AT&T release numbers. Release 1.0 was the language as specified in Stroustrup's *The C++ Programming Language*. Release 1.1 added pointers to class members (although not all implementations claiming conformance to release 1.1 contained this feature), and the **protected** keyword. Release 1.2 added the ability to use **unsigned int**s and **unsigned long**s to distinguish one overloaded function from another.

Most of the early popularity of the language occurred with release 1.2. As its popularity grew, certain problems were discovered with release 1.2, and some inadequacies as well. In the summer of 1989, AT&T publicized the specification for AT&T C++ release 2.0. The new version contains important changes to fix problems in earlier releases. It also contains some new features, most notably multiple inheritance. Release 2.0 gives C++ even greater object-oriented power and ensures its place as "the successor to C."

Continuing Incompatibilities
With ANSI C

Several incompatibilities between ANSI C and the "C features" of C++ release 1.2 have been noted throughout this book. You might expect that these incompatibilities would be fixed in release 2.0, since that release and the final vote on the ANSI C specification were almost simultaneous. However, certain fundamental philosophical differences remain between the two. These differences exist because of the way C *has* been used and the way C++ is *intended* to be used. The differences are often small, but you can run into trouble if you aren't aware of them. In particular, you must take special care if you want to create header files that are to be included in both C++ and ANSI C programs. This section details the differences between the two languages and points out ways to get around problems in combined C and C++ header files.

Many times in combined C and C++ header files, the preprocessor can isolate the C++ incompatibilities or extensions using **#ifdef** statements and the special preprocessor name **__cplusplus**, which is defined for all implementations of C++. Since C++ now modifies *all* function names to achieve *type-safe linkage* (described in this chapter), you must explicitly disable this modification when a C header file is included in a C++ file. Here is the typical way to accomplish this in a C header file that is intended to be included in a C++ file:

```
#ifdef __cplusplus

extern "C" { // Allows linkage to non-C++ objects

#endif /* __cplusplus */

/* C declarations here: */

/* .... */

#ifdef __cplusplus

}

#endif /* __cplusplus */
```

Keywords Specific to C++

Because C++ is essentially an extension to C, there are keywords that implement the language extensions and cannot be used in C header files to be included in C++ files. For release 2.0, these keywords are

asm	**operator**	**throw**
class	**private**	**try**
delete	**protected**	
friend	**public**	
catch	**template**	
inline	**this**	
new	**virtual**	

The only keywords that are new in release 2.0 are **template, catch, throw**, and **try** which will be described later. **asm** is actually part of the original C++ and many C implementations, but it has no defined meaning (that is, it is implementation dependent). Usually **asm** is used to pass information to the assembler. The keyword **overload** is obsolescent in release 2.0 (but still accepted for backward compatibility); it has been obviated by type-safe linkage.

const *Defaults to Internal Linkage*

As noted in Chapter 3, **const** means different things in C++ and ANSI C. In ANSI C, the keyword **const** adds the information "this cannot be changed" to an ordinary variable. Everything else is the same; in particular a **const** defaults to external linkage (meaning that it is globally visible). In C++, however, **const** is intended to replace the use of **#define** values in header files. This means that C++ can do type checking on constants to provide an additional level of safety that isn't there with **#define** values. In C++ you can also use a **const** in a constant expression, such as

```
const bufsize = 20;
```

```
char buf[bufsize];
```

which is illegal in C.

To allow easy use of **const** in header files, **const** in C++ defaults to internal linkage. This means it is local to every file in which the header file is included. Effectively, wherever you say **const** in C++, the compiler treats it as if you had said **static const**. This avoids the normally disastrous effect of defining a variable in a header file and then including that header in several other files across the system (which may generate multiple definition errors at link time, depending on how the linker works). It also allows the compiler to do more powerful optimization.

Notice that this is precisely the opposite of **const** in ANSI C, which defaults to external linkage (global). You *may* get multiple-definition errors at link time if you put a **const** in a header file in ANSI C, unless you explicitly modify the linkage with **static**, as in

static const x = 10; // necessary in ANSI C for header files

This still doesn't allow you to use an ANSI C **const** in a constant expression, however.

Because **const** defaults to internal linkage in C++, an **extern const** declaration will not automatically reference a **const** defined in some other file. That is, for the two files

// PC1.CXX :

const PC = 47;

// PC2.CXX :

extern const PC;

the linker will be unable to resolve the reference in **pc2.cxx**, since **PC** in **pc1.cxx** has file scope (internal linkage) in C++. To achieve the desired effect, you must explicitly change the linkage of **PC** when it is defined in **pc1.cxx**, as follows:

// PC1.CXX :

extern const PC = 47; // extern forces external linkage (global)

If **const** is to be used in a header file that is to be included in both C and C++ programs, it must be given explicit linkage with **static** or **extern** when the **const** is defined. Usually, a header file included in a C program must have all its constants declared **static**, so there will be no multiple definition errors at link time. For example:

static const both = 74;

Note that in C++, a **const** definition must always have an initializer, while in ANSI C a **const** will default to zero if there is no initializer with the definition. Thus a **const** definition in a header file intended to be used with both C and C++ should always have an initializer, even if it is zero.

An Empty Argument List Means "No Arguments"

Unlike ANSI C, C++ requires that a function name be declared before the function can be called (for backward compatibility with old C, ANSI C assumes that an undeclared function call has any number or type of arguments and returns an **int**). In ANSI C, a declaration with an empty argument list such as

int foo( );

means "an unspecified number of arguments." In C++ it means "exactly zero arguments." Although ANSI C lists this type of function declaration as "obsolescent," it is still allowed (which, essentially, eliminates argument type checking for that function). For C++ to support strong type checking, the empty argument list can only mean "no arguments," so if **foo( )** is called with arguments in C++ you will get an error message.

Function declarations with no arguments in header files for use in both C and C++ programs should use the explicit form

int foo(void);

A void * Cannot Be Assigned
To Another Pointer Type

In both C++ and ANSI C, you can assign any pointer type to a **void** pointer without using a cast. In ANSI C, you can also assign a **void** pointer to a non-**void** pointer without using a cast to the non-**void** pointer type. This is an invitation to errors, and is not allowed in C++.

Character Constants Are
Of Type char

In ANSI C, character constants are of type **int**. Since functions are not overloaded in plain C, this doesn't cause problems. In C++, however, the compiler needs to be able to distinguish between two overloaded functions based on their argument lists. For example:

void print(int);

void print(char);

When you call the function

print('z');

the compiler should call **print(char)** and not **print(int)**. For this to work, C++ treats character constants as being of type **char**.

enum Definitions Can Be Local
To a class, struct, or union

ANSI C allows an **enum** to be defined within a structure, but the **enum** is globally visible. In C++, an **enum** defined within a structure is only visible inside the structure. For instance:

class numtype {

enum ntp { integer, real, matrix };

```
// ...
};
```

// In C, "integer," "real," and "matrix" would be visible here.

// In C++, they are only visible within members of "numtype."

Note that you can use local enumerations with assigned values to simulate local **const** definitions. Note also that an **enum** definition in C++ creates a new type (which is not an **int**). This means, for instance, that you cannot increment an enum variable.

Multiple Definitions Are Illegal

ANSI C allows the following:

int x;

int x;

The first statement is treated by the compiler as a declaration and the second as a definition. This is not acceptable in C++ since it would have to extend to user-defined types. For a **class foo** used in the code

foo f;

foo f;

the compiler would have to decide which is a declaration and which is a definition, and only call the constructor for one of them. This was deemed to add unnecessary complexity to the C++ compiler, so code that can be interpreted as containing multiple definitions will generate an error message. This means that all but one declaration of an object must use the **extern** specifier. That is, the difference between an object declaration and an object definition must be made explicit by the programmer.

Character Array Initialization

When initializing character arrays in ANSI C, the compiler will allow you to declare an array of one character less than a normal string constant requires, (that is without leaving enough space for the terminating \0). This means a statement like

char x[2] = "AA";

is legal in ANSI C. It assumes the programmer intends to leave out the **\0** in the definition. C++ generates an error message for this code.

A goto *Cannot Skip Variable Initialization*

ANSI C allows a **goto** to jump past variable initialization; for instance:

```
void show( ) {
   goto after_init;
   {
      int x = 1;
      after_init:
      x++;
      /* ... */
   }
}
```

If this was allowed in C++, constructor calls for objects could be skipped. If those objects also had complementary destructor calls at the end of the block, a destructor could be called for an object that never had a constructor call. This is an invitation to disaster; C++ doesn't allow **goto**s to skip initialization.

C++ *Allows Nonconstant Initializers For Static Objects*

ANSI C requires that all initializers for objects with global storage lifetime be constant expressions. Release 2.0 allows nonconstant expressions. In files that are used in both C and C++, you must restrict yourself to constant expressions for initializers.

Multiple Inheritance

One of the most important and fundamental changes to C++ in release 2.0 is the ability to create a new derived class from more than one base class. This is called *multiple inheritance*. Multiple inheritance is especially useful when you want to add features that are unrelated to a hierarchy to a class that is part of that hierarchy. For instance, you may want to make a class that is part of the transportation hierarchy shown at the beginning of Chapter 8, but also has the ability to store itself by inheriting from **class storable** in Chapter 7. The only way to accomplish this is through multiple inheritance.

The syntax for multiple inheritance is fairly straightforward. With single inheritance, you say

class bc {

   //...

};

class dc : public bc {

   // ...

};

With multiple inheritance, you say

class bc1 {

   // ...

};

class bc2 {

   // ...

```
};
class bc3 {
  // ...
};
class midc : public bc1, public bc2, public bc3 {
  // ...
};
```

As with single inheritance, if you don't specify the access to the elements of the base class with the keyword **public**, it defaults to **private**. You cannot use **protected** to specify access to a base class.

You may not specify a class in the list of base classes more than once. The order of classes in the list determines the order of initialization if you don't specify it in the constructor (that is, if you let the compiler call the constructors for you). The order of destruction for the base classes is always in the reverse order of their declaration.

Constructors for Multiple Inheritance

When using single inheritance, it was redundant to give the name of the base class in the constructor initializer list, so it was left out. For example:

```
class bc {
    int i;
public:
    bc(int x = 0) { i = x; }
};
class dc : public bc {
public:
    dc(int y = 0) : (y) {} // base class constructor call
};
```

With release 2.0, this syntax is still accepted for single inheritance, although it is not recommended. When using multiple inheritance, however, this syntax is ambiguous—the compiler doesn't know which base class you are talking about. To solve this problem, you must specify the name of the base class in the constructor initializer list.

```
class bc1 {
public:
    bc1(int x);
};
class bc2 {
public:
    bc2(int x);
};
class mdc : public bc1, public bc2 {
public:
    // Names of base classes are given in the initializer list:
    mdc(int a, int b) : bc1(a), bc2(b) { }
};
```

In release 2.0 you can also give the name of the base class in the constructor initializer list for single inheritance.

Virtual Base Classes

While multiple inheritance adds a great deal of power to C++ programming, it also introduces some potential ambiguities. In particular, what happens if two classes share the same base class and are both inherited into a single derived class? To understand the problem, some new terminology is necessary.

A *direct base class* is one that is in the list of base classes for a particular derived class. For instance, in the following

class dc : public bc1, public bc2, public bc3 { /* ... */ };

the classes **bc1**, **bc2**, and **bc3** are direct base classes. An *indirect base class* is a class that doesn't appear in the preceding list of base classes, but is inherited into one or more classes in the list. For example:

class ibc {

public:

  void print( );

};

class dbc1 : public ibc { };

class dbc2 : public ibc { };

class derived : public dbc1, public dbc2 {

public:

  void print_derived( ) { print( ); } // ambiguous

};

Here, **dbc1** and **dbc2** are direct base classes, and **ibc** is an indirect base class. Notice that because **ibc** is used in both **dbc1** and **dbc2**, the call to the function **ibc::print( )** is ambiguous in **derived::print_derived( )**. The problem occurs because when an object of **class derived** is created, it contains two *sub-objects* (areas of memory to hold base classes) of **class ibc**. The compiler has no idea which one to use, and an error message is generated. In addition, having two sub-objects is often a waste of space.

You can solve the problem in two ways. The first way is to specify the base class sub-object to call by using the scope resolution operator. For instance:

void derived::print_derived( ) { dbc1::print( ); } // no ambiguity

However, the user of a derived class may not have enough knowledge of the base classes to do this, and it is an extra confusion. Release 2.0 has a more elegant way to solve the problem, by ensuring that only one sub-object of the indirect base class is used (and thus eliminating the ambiguity). To do this, the class designer must declare the common base class **virtual** when it is being derived into the direct base classes. For the preceding example

class dbc1 : virtual public ibc { };

class dbc2 : virtual public ibc { };

class derived : public dbc1, public dbc2 {

public:

    void print_derived( ) { print( ); } // not ambiguous

};

Here, there is only one sub-object of **class ibc**, so calling **print( )** is not ambiguous. The sub-object of **class ibc** is shared by **dbc1** and **dbc2**.

You can have virtual and non-virtual sub-objects in the same class. If another direct base class is created *without* using the **virtual** keyword when inheriting from **class ibc**,

class dbc3 : public ibc { }

and this base class is also used in **class derived**,

class derived : public dbc1, public dbc2, public dbc3 {

public:

    void print_derived( ) { print( ); } // ambiguous again!

};

you get another ambiguity because there are two sub-objects of **class ibc**: the one in **dbc3** and the one shared by **dbc1** and **dbc2**.

The compiler checks for ambiguities before checking to see if the access is legal (that is if a derived class is trying to access a **private** member of a base class) and before types are checked. If an ambiguity is discovered, an error message is generated. You must remove all ambiguities by either qualifying a member with its class name or by using **virtual** base classes.

INITIALIZING VIRTUAL BASE CLASSES Virtual base classes are always initialized by the most derived class. A virtual base class can be initialized explicitly, but it should also have a constructor that can be called without arguments (a constructor with no arguments, a constructor where all arguments have default values, or no constructor at all). All virtual sub-objects are initialized before any non-virtual sub-objects.

Type-Safe Linkage

Chapter 5 pointed out a very sticky problem that occurs when overloading functions. To allow plain C header files to be included in C++ programs, C++ implementations before release 2.0 overload function names in the following manner: the first use of the overloaded name was not *mangled* into a new name by the compiler (mangling means adding information about the arguments and return values to the function name so there are no ambiguities when the function is called; this forces the linker to perform type checking). All subsequent uses of the overloaded name were mangled. The assumption here is that the plain C function names will always be declared first, thus the plain C header files must always be included first. As was demonstrated in Chapter 5, this is not a good assumption to make. The declarations can easily get out of their "proper" order and generate hard-to-track bugs.

To solve this problem, type-safe linkage has been introduced in C++ release 2.0. With type-safe linkage, *all* function names are mangled with information about their arguments and return values. Any problems or ambiguities will be flagged by the compiler and will not show up at link time.

Because name mangling happens automatically for all function names whether you specifically direct the compiler to overload them or not, the **overload** keyword is obsolete in release 2.0. It is still accepted for backward compatibility with older code.

Specifying Alternate Linkage

When including plain C header files, you must be able to turn the mangling of function names off, because the linker would otherwise be unable to find the function name in the plain C library. Release 2.0 allows you to specify alternate linkage by the use of a string after the **extern** keyword. For example:

extern "C" printf(...);

This establishes a reference to an external function of the C variety called **printf( )**. You can also include whole groups of alternate-linkage function names inside braces, such as

extern "C" {

    printf(...);

    puts(char ∗);

}

or

extern "C" {

#include <stdio.h>

}

Generally, header files that are intended to be included in both C and C++ files are already modified to provide C linkage, but in many cases you will have to do it yourself.

The declaration of objects in other files can also be modified, but the effect is implementation- and language-dependent. For instance,

extern "C" {

    special_buf foo[10];

}

gives **foo** C linkage.

Each C++ implementation must support the linkage-specifier strings **"C"** and **"C++"**, but the effect of these strings is implementation-dependent. A C++ implementation may support other linkage-specifier strings (for instance, **"Pascal"**).

Function Matching

When the compiler encounters a function call, it goes through three steps while attempting to determine which function to call. All three steps try to find a match for the arguments and return value given in the function call.

First, an exact match is sought. This means that all the given argument types match the types in the function prototype, and the required return value matches the return value given in the prototype.

If no perfect match is found, **float** values may be converted to **double** values and/or integral promotions may be performed in an attempt to find a match.

Finally, user-defined conversions (user-defined casting operators or constructors taking arguments of the other type; see Chapter 5) may be used to modify the arguments and return value in order to find a match.

Taking the Address
Of an Overloaded Function

Attempting to take the address of an overloaded function introduces an ambiguity, because there is more than one function for the compiler to choose from. This ambiguity must be resolved by specifying the argument types of the function pointer that will receive the address of the overloaded function. For example:

void foo(int);

void foo(float);

void (*foo_ptr_int)(int) = foo;

void (*foo_ptr_float)(float) = foo;

The 31-Character-Limit Problem

ANSI C specifies that a compiler must support a minimum of 31 characters for internal identifier names. (In addition, the language only requires the linker to handle six characters, single-case.) This means that any implementation of C++ that is a C-code generator is technically restricted from generating names of more than 31 characters that must be disambiguated, or requires a C compiler that uses more than 31 characters to represent identifiers internally.

Prior to release 2.0, C-code generators derived from **cfront** did not pay any attention to this problem. As a result, it isn't too hard to break a pre-2.0 C-code generator when it is used with a C compiler that has a 31-character limit. For an example, try compiling the CONTROLR example in Chapter 10 with Glockenspiel **cfront** (before 2.0) and Microsoft C 5.1.

Type-safe linkage could conceivably generate longer names than ever. Release 2.0 has addressed this problem in **cfront** by encoding the last two characters (using a hashing algorithm) in the identifier; that is, characters 30 and 31. This way, **cfront** can be ported to any system that has an ANSI-conforming C compiler and a linker that supports at least 31 characters in identifiers, upper- and lowercase.

The only limitation occurs if the hashing algorithm generates a collision between two similar identifiers; in that case you're out of luck and must change one of the identifier's names. This may cause problems when porting code developed on any implementation that doesn't use the encoding scheme (and instead uses the entire name internally) to a **cfront**-based C++.

Explicit Support for Abstract Classes

Abstract classes were introduced in Chapter 8. An abstract class serves only as a framework upon which to derive other classes. It provides the "common interface" (via **virtual** functions) upon which the derived classes may build differing implementations (by re-defining those **virtual** functions). An abstract class is never intended to have instances (although before release 2.0 you could make objects of abstract classes).

Release 2.0 has provided explicit support for abstract classes by allowing you to differentiate between "ordinary" classes and abstract classes. The mechanism for doing this is the *pure virtual function*. You can specify that a **virtual** function is "pure" by using a *pure-specifier,* which simply means assigning the definition of that **virtual** function to zero. You cannot make objects of any class containing pure virtual functions; the compiler will treat any attempt to do so as an error.

Here is an example of the use of the pure-specifier to create an abstract class:

```
class abstract {
    // ...
public:
    abstract( );
    virtual void expressionism( ) = 0; // pure virtual function
    // ...
};
```

An abstract class is not restricted to **virtual** functions nor to having pure-specifiers for every **virtual** function. The existence of one or more pure **virtual** functions is all that is necessary to make a class abstract.

An abstract class may not be passed by value to a function or be returned from a function (this would require the creation of a temporary variable, which would be an instance of the abstract class). You may pass pointers and references, however (this is the idea, since a pointer or reference to an object of a class derived from the abstract class can then be substituted).

The Copy-Constructor and operator=( ) *Can Be Created by the Compiler*

Chapter 9 demonstrated some of the difficulties, especially with new C++ programmers, when dealing with the copy-constructor and **operator=( )**. The copy-constructor (termed "copy-constructor" in the C++ Reference Manual), also referred to as **X(X&)**, is a constructor that takes as its argument a reference to an object of the same class. It is a function that is used secretly by the compiler to initialize a new object from an old one in the following expression:

X a;

X b = a; // X(X&) called here

The copy-constructor is also used to copy objects by value into a function when the objects are used as arguments, and out of a function when an object is returned by value. For instance:

void thizbin(X c) { // c is passed by value; X(X&) called

   return c; // c is returned by value; X(X&) called

}

Prior to 2.0, if the programmer did not define a copy-constructor (which often happened because new programmers don't see the need for it since it is never called explicitly) the compiler resorted to a *bitwise copy,* which means that the structure of one object is directly copied into the structure of another object. This works fine for very simple objects (ones that don't contain pointers or instances of other classes), but definitely does not have the desired effect when the object contains pointers or members that are other objects. Prior to 2.0, the programmer was forced to write the copy-constructor to handle these cases.

Similarly, **operator=( )** is called when one already initialized object is assigned to another already initialized object. For example:

X d;

X e = d; // X(X&) called

X f;

f = d; // X::operator=(X&) called

In this example, if **f** contains pointers or member objects, **operator=( )** is responsible for cleaning those up. As with the copy-constructor, if **operator=( )** is not defined by the programmer in C++ implementations earlier than release 2.0, the compiler resorts to a bitwise copy of the right-hand side onto the left-hand side, ignoring the need to clean up the left-hand side first. This can result in real problems, since if the left- hand side object contains pointers to free store, the old pointers are copied over and the address of the block of free store is lost, which may eventually cause the program to run out of memory. The programmer who writes the **operator=( )** must be sure to properly clean up the left-hand side before performing the assignment activities.

In release 2.0 the programmer may still take over the duties of copy-constructor and assignment by writing **X(X&)** and **operator=( )**. As before, those who do so are completely responsible for the activities during copy-construction and assignment, since the default activity (bitwise copy, before 2.0) is disabled when these functions are defined. However, release 2.0 has introduced an improvement when the programmer doesn't define either **X(X&)** or **operator=( )**. Instead of the previous bitwise copy, release 2.0 automatically generates a copy-constructor and an **operator=( )** (if either or both weren't defined) that use *member-wise initialization* and *member-wise assignment,* respectively. Member-wise initialization calls the copy-constructors for each member object in a class. If a member object contains member objects, the copy-constructors for those objects are called, and so on. Member-wise assignment calls the **operator=( )** functions for each member object in a class. If a member object contains member objects, their **operator=( )** functions are called, and so on. These activities more closely match "the right thing to do" when the programmer doesn't define a copy-constructor or **operator=( )**, and removes a lot of confusion for new C++ programmers.

Note that if any version of the copy-constructor has been defined, the compiler will not generate a default copy-constructor. If any version of the **operator=( )** has been defined, the compiler will not generate a default **operator=( )**. This is true even if the version doesn't solve your particular problem.

Operator new *and* delete
Can Be Overloaded

Chapter 6 showed how to take over the dynamic allocation of memory when creating objects on the free store. You have two choices: you can overload **operator new** and **operator delete**, or you can perform assignment to **this**. If you overload the global **operator new** and **operator delete**, you lose access to the previous versions of **new** and **delete** and you also change the way **new** and **delete** behave for the entire program. If you want to take over free-store allocation on a class-by-class basis, you must resort to using assignment to **this** (in pre-2.0 versions of C++), which is a tricky and arcane process.

Release 2.0 allows you to overload **operator new** and **operator delete** on a class-by-class basis. That is, **operator new** and **operator delete** are now member functions. This means that you can still use the global **new** and **delete** when you create member functions of **new** and **delete**. It also means that you don't change the entire system when you create member functions of **new** and **delete**, and that you can completely ignore the "assignment to **this**" confusion. Assignment to **this** is still accepted for backward compatibility with old code, but it is obsolete and shouldn't be used for new code.

An **operator new** must take a **long** argument and return a **void** ∗. An **operator delete** must take a **void** ∗ argument and return **void** (nothing). Here's a very simple example, where the member **operator new** keeps track of how many times **new** has been called (via a static member) and then calls the global **new**. The member **operator delete** decrements the count and then calls the global **delete**.

```
// KEEPTRAK.CPP : class-by-class overloading of operators
// new and delete.
#include <stddef.h>  // definition of size_t
#include <stdio.h>

  class keep_track {
  static int newcalls;
  public:

  void * operator new(size_t sz) {
    newcalls++;
    puts("keep_track::operator new () called");
    return ::new unsigned char[sz];
  }
  void operator delete(void * dp) {
    newcalls—;
```

```
        puts("keep_track::operator delete() called");
        ::delete(dp);
    }
};
```

```
    main() {
      keep_track * kt = new keep_track;
      delete kt;
      int * i = new int; // to make sure global new & delete
      delete i;      //remain the same...
    }
```

You can also define an **operator delete** with a second argument indicating the size of the object to be deleted.

class xx {

//...

public:

   void operator delete(void ∗ dp, long dsz);

};

This form is used if you need to know the size of the object being deleted inside the user-defined **operator delete**. The compiler will automatically pass the size into the function, but the size will only be correct under the following two conditions:

1. The pointer **dp** is the exact type of the object being deleted. If you derive a new **class uu** from **class xx** and you delete a **uu** through a pointer to the base **class xx**, you will get the wrong size.

   class uu : public xx { }

   xx ∗ xxp = new uu; // use the uu ∗ as a base-class pointer

   delete uu; // dsz gets the size of xx, not uu !

2. The base class has a virtual destructor that has been redefined for the derived class. For example:

```
class vv {
    //...
public:
    // ...
    void operator delete(void * dp, long dsz);
    virtual ~vv( ) { }
}
class ww : public vv {
public:
    //..


    ~ww( ) { }
};
vv * vvp = new ww;
delete vvp; // dsz gets the right size
```

Global new *and* delete

The global **operator new** and **operator delete** are used when no user-defined **operator new** or **operator delete** can be found for the class being created or destroyed, or any of its base classes. Global **new** and **delete** are also used for built-in types and for arrays of objects (which must have a constructor that takes no arguments or a constructor with all default arguments). When deleting an array of objects, you must still specify the number of objects in the array.

```
class yy;

yy * yp = new yy[10];

delete[10] yp;
```

(In C++ release 2.1, you do not need to specify the array size for delete.)

The Placement Specifier
For operator new

Assignment to **this** allowed the programmer to specify the placement of objects in selected areas of memory, rather than just taking the next piece of free store that became available. This can be very useful, especially if you have external constraints that give special significance to certain areas of memory, or if you are programming a system that cannot support a free store (an embedded system, for instance), but still requires the creation of objects with arbitrary lifetime.

To specify placement when using **new**, put the starting address in parentheses, where you want the object to be, preceded by the keyword **new** and followed by the type of object you are creating.

class foo { /* ... */ };

foo *fp = new(starting_address) foo;

This code places an object of type **foo** beginning at the address **starting_address**.

When you create an object and place it at a specified address, you cannot call **delete** to destroy the object. The reason is that **delete** expects an address that was created on the free store (with the attendant bookkeeping) and will try to deallocate that memory after calling the destructor for the object. When you have created an object using the address specifier and later want to destroy that object, you *don't* want to deallocate the memory—you just want to call the destructor for that object. This is accomplished by explicitly calling the destructor for the object. As an example, here's a piece of code that places an object in a global data area and later destroys it:

```
//PLACEMNT.CPP : The placement specifier for operator new,

// and explicit calls to the destructor.

#include <stdio.h>

#include <stdlib.h>
```

```
void* operator new(size_t, void* p) { return p;}


class mo {
  int i,j;
public:
   mo(int x = 0) { i = j = x; }
   ~mo( ) { puts("bye!"); }
};


unsigned char global_data[sizeof(mo)];


main( ) {
   mo * mp = new(global_data) mo(47);
   // Sometime later:
   mp->mo::~mo( ); // explicit destructor call
   // ...
}
```

You can only explicitly call the destructor through a pointer; a call to the destructor using the member selection operator (the **.**) is not allowed. You only need to call a destructor explicitly like this when you create the object using **new** with the placement specifier.

New Operators Can Be Overloaded

Release 2.0 adds the ability to overload two new operators: the comma operator, which is used for sequential evaluation, and the member selection operator,**->**, sometimes called a "smart pointer." You can also overload **->*** (see "Pointers to Members").

Overloading the Comma Operator

In a sequence of expressions separated by commas, the expressions are evaluated (including the side effects) from left to right (except in function argument lists, where the order is implementation-dependent). All the values resulting from the evaluation of the expressions are discarded except for the final value, which is the result of the entire comma-separated sequence. Thus, all the expressions except for the last one are only used for their side effects.

When the expression to the left of the comma is an object or produces an object, the comma operator can be overloaded to generate a user-defined side effect appropriate for that object. Here is a simple example:

```
// CRISPY.CPP : overloading the comma operator
    #include <stdio.h>

class crispy {

    static int i;

public:

  crispy operator,(crispy &);

};


crispy crispy::operator,(crispy & c) {

    switch(c.i) {

        case 0 : i++; puts("snap!"); break;

        case 1 : i++; puts("crackle!"); break;

        case 2 : puts("pop!"); break;

        default : i = 2; break;

    }

    return c;

}
```

```
main( ) {
    crispy rice1, rice2, rice3, rice4;
    // rice4 gets the value of rice3 (with i = 2) :
    rice4 = (rice1, rice2, rice3, rice3);
}
```

The parentheses are necessary because the = operator has higher precedence than the comma operator.

Smart Pointers

You can only define the unary **operator->( )** as a member function for a class. The use of a smart pointer is a little counterintuitive, because the pointer is used on an *object* of the class, and not a *pointer* to an object, which is what you normally use the **->** operator for. For example, if **C** is a class with an **operator->( )** member function, and **el** is a member of that class or some other class, **struct** or **union**, then

C cobj;

cobj->el;

evaluates as

(cobj.operator->( ))->el;

which means that **operator->( )** must return either

- A pointer to a class object containing the element **el**. The "normal" dereferencing using the **->** operator is performed to select **el**.

- An object of another class. This other class must contain a definition for **operator->( )**. In this case, the **operator->( )** is called again for the new object. This process is repeated recursively until the result is a pointer to a class object containing the element **el**.

Here's an example that uses the recursive-dereferencing property of the smart pointer:

```
// SMART.CPP : "smart pointer" example

#include <stdio.h>

struct str {
 char * s;
 str(char* si) : s(si) {}
 const char * operator->() { return s; }
};


class str_holder {
    str * m;
public:
    str_holder(str * si) : m(shi) { }
    str* operator->() { return m; }
};


main( ) {
    str x("hello, world!\n");
    str_holder X(&x);
    printf("%s", X->s);
};
```

Pointers to Members

Although pointers to class members were actually introduced in release 1.1, release 2.0 clarifies their use and adds some new operators specifically designed for pointers to members.

A class is just a template for creating new objects and has no physical embodiment until objects of that class are created. Similarly, a pointer to a class member represents not an address of a physical element but instead the "place where that element will be" for any particular object. Because of this, you cannot dereference a pointer to a member by itself—it must always be associated with an object.

When you define a pointer to a member, it must be given the exact type of the member it will point to, as well as the class name. Here is an example showing the syntax of pointers to members:

```
class I {
    int i;
public:
    int v;
    I(int ii = 0) { i = v = ii; }
    int mul(int x) { return i * x; }
};
int I::* ptr_mem_int; // pointer to an int member
int (I::* ptr_mem_funct)(int); // pointer to a function member
ptr_mem_int = &I::v; // assign to an int member
ptr_mem_funct = &I::mul; // assign to a function member
```

To use a pointer to a member, you must first create an object of the class associated with that pointer, and then dereference the pointer using the object. For example:

```
I a(4);
a.*ptr_mem_int = 12; // sets a.v to 12
int b = (a.*ptr_mem_funct)(47); // same as int b = a.mul(47);
```

The .* operator dereferences a pointer to a member. You can also use pointers to objects with pointers to members using the ->* operator.

```
I * c = new I(11);

c->*ptr_mem_int = 44; // same as c->v = 44

int d = (c->*ptr_mem_funct)(9); // same as int d = c- >mul(99);
```

Note that release 2.0 allows **operator –>*** to be overloaded.

Pointers to members are useful if you want, for example, to create a function that will apply an operation to all the elements in a list. For instance, suppose you have a class that has three member functions with identical arguments and return values.

Now suppose you have some sort of dynamically sized array (like **DynArray**, from Chapter 6) or linked list (see the **controlr** example from Chapter 11) called **dweeblist**, which is filled with **dweeb** objects; a pointer to the current **dweeb** object is produced with a member function **current( )**. You can define a function that applies a member function (which is passed as an argument) to all the **dweeb** objects in **dweeblist**.

```cpp
//DWEEB.CPP : pointers to members: the "apply" function

#include <stdio.h>


class dweeb {
public:
  dweeb() {}
  void spin() { puts("spinning!");}
  void dodge() { puts("dodging!");}
  void feint() { puts("feinting!");}
};


class dweeblist {
  dweeb ** list;
  int cursor;
  const sz;
  public:
```

```
    dweeblist(int size) : sz(size) {
      list = new dweeb*[sz]; // make an array of dweeb pointers
      for(int i = 0; i  sz; i++)
        list[i] = new dweeb;
    }
    ~dweeblist() {
     for(int i = 0; i  sz; i++)
       delete list[i];
       delete list;
    }
    void reset() { cursor = 0; }
    dweeb * current() { return list[cursor]; }
    void next() { cursor++; }
    int end() { return cursor  >= sz; }
    void apply(void (dweeb::* df)()) {
      reset();
      while(!end()) {
        (current()->*df)();
        next();
      }
    }
};
main() {
  dweeblist dl(7);
  dl.apply(&dweeb::spin);
  dl.apply(&dweeb::dodge);
  dl.apply(&dweeb::feint);
```

}

A pointer to a member of a base class can be converted to a pointer to a member of a class derived from that base if the base class is **public** in the derived class and the conversion is not ambiguous.

New Qualifiers
For Member Functions

Release 2.0 has introduced new ways to control the creation and use of class member functions. Member functions can now be **const**, **volatile**, or **static**.

const *Member Functions*

A **const** member function doesn't modify the member data of an object, and is the only type of member function that may be called for a **const** object. A **const** member function may also be called for non-**const** objects. You cannot qualify a function definition with **const** and then attempt to modify data members (this will generate an error). To create a **const** member function, you place the **const** qualifier after the argument list and before the opening brace of the function definition. This example shows the correct and incorrect creation and use of **const** member functions:

```
class T {
    int i;
public:
    int value( ) const { return i; } // OK: doesn't modify member
    void change( ) const { i++;} // ERROR: modifies member
    void chng2( ) { i++; } // ordinary (non-const) member function
};
main( ) {
```

```
    const T a;

    a.value( ); // OK: const function called for const object

    a.chng2( ); // ERROR: non-const function called for const object
}
```

const member functions can only call other **const** member functions. Constructors and destructors do not need to be declared **const** member functions to be invoked for **const** objects.

volatile *Member Functions*

volatile member functions are the analogue of **const** member functions, and are created in the same fashion, by placing the **volatile** qualifier after the argument list and before the function body. Only **volatile** member functions can be called for **volatile** objects, and **volatile** member functions can only call other **volatile** member functions. Unlike **const** member functions, **volatile** member functions can modify the data members in an object.

Constructors and destructors do not need to be declared **volatile** member functions to be invoked for **volatile** objects. A member function can be both **const** and **volatile**.

static *Member Functions*

A **static** member function is analogous to a **static** data member in that it "belongs to the class" rather than belonging to a particular instance of a class. A **static** member function can be called for the class as a whole, that is, without specifying a particular object. It can only affect data that is shared by all objects in the class (**static** data members or global data). Ordinary (non-**static**) member functions always have the starting address (**this**) of the structure of the object they were called for; usually **this** is secretly passed by the compiler as an argument to the member function. **static** member functions have no **this**.

static member functions are in the same scope as non-**static** member functions, so they have the same access rights. Because there is no **this** in a **static** member function, however, you cannot call non-**static** member functions and you cannot manipulate non-**static** data members. The effect of a **static** member function is the same as if you were to use a global function and declare it a **friend** of the class, but a global function "pollutes" the name space with an identifier that might be used in someone else's library. Member functions must be called for an object even when it makes no sense to do so, and the superfluous **this** must be passed as an additional argument.

Here's an example of a **static** member function that manipulates a **static** data member:

```
class joe {
    static int i;
public:
    //...
    static void set(int x) { i = x; }
};
main( ) {
    joe::set(47); // how to call a static member function
}
```

You can also call a **static** member function in the "regular" way, associated with an object.

As a good example of a place where **static** member functions are useful, **class storable** in Chapter 7 must initialize **static** data members whenever a file is opened. To do this, you must either have an instance of the class lying about, or you must make a dummy instance to use when calling the function. This is tedious—and confusing for anyone reading the code. If the example is recompiled with an implementation of C++ release 2.0, and the functions that modify the **static** data members are themselves made **static**, those functions can be called without associating them with an (arbitrarily selected) object, and the code will make more sense to the reader.

New Forms of Initialization

Release 2.0 has removed some limitations of previous versions by allowing nonconstant expressions for initialization of static objects and new ways to initialize aggregates. Static member objects are now more fully supported, with a special way to initialize them before **main( )** is entered. The = sign now performs new kinds of initialization.

Initialization of Static Objects

Before release 2.0, all objects declared at file scope (*static objects*) could only be initialized with an expression that could be evaluated at compile time (a *constant expression*). Release 2.0 removes this restriction, so you can initialize static objects with any general expression. For example, assume all the following are at file scope:

extern int foo(int);

extern int bar(int);

int x = foo(12);

int y = bar(x);

Note that static objects also include objects that are declared **static** inside a function or class.

Initialization of Static Member Objects

Release 2.0 adds full support for static member objects inside classes by specifying a syntax for initializing those objects before **main( )** is entered. Static data members are initialized by default to zero and static class object members are initialized by default by calling the constructor with no arguments. If you want to perform other than the default initialization, you must do it explicitly. Initializing a static member object is just like defining and initializing a global object, except that you add the class name and the scope resolution operator; for example:

```
// VALVE.CPP : initialization of static member objects


struct Reynolds_number {
 Reynolds_number(double, char *, int);
};


struct Turbulence {
 Turbulence(Reynolds_number, float);
};


class valve {
    static Reynolds_number R;
    static float scale_factor;
    static Turbulence * turb;
public:
    static float open( );
    static float close( );
    // ...
};


Reynolds_number valve::R(1.2,"valve", 3);
float valve::scale_factor = 4.2;
Turbulence * valve::turb =
 new Turbulence(valve::R, valve::scale_factor);
```

As you can see, you can refer to static members independently of any object, and you can gain access to normally **private** static members for the purpose of initialization. Static members exist even if no instances of the class containing the static members have been created. You can also refer to static members using the **.** and **->** member access operators.

Note that if a class is declared local to some function, its static members are also local (that is, they have "no linkage") and cannot be initialized.

Initialization of Aggregates

An *aggregate* is an array, or an object of a **class, struct,** or **union** (collectively referred to as a class). If a class has no constructors or nonpublic members, it may be initialized with an *initializer list,* which is a list enclosed in braces with the individual elements of the list separated by commas. If the aggregate is an array, the elements of the list will be placed into an array in order of increasing subscripts. If the aggregate is a class object, the elements of the list will be placed into the object in the order in which members are declared. For example, here's an array:

float f[4] = { 1.1, 2.2, 3.3, 4.4 };

You don't have to specify the number of elements in the array if you don't want to; the compiler will count them for you.

float f[ ] = { 1.1, 2.2, 3.3, 4.4 };

Here's a class with no constructor or nonpublic members:

class X {

    public:

    int i, j;

    float ff;

};

X xx = { 1, 2, 3.3 }; // xx.i = 1, xx.j = 2, xx.ff = 3.3

If an aggregate contains other aggregates, the initialization is applied recursively. For a two-dimensional array ("an array of one-dimensional arrays") initialization works like this:

```
int twoD[3][4] = {
    { 1, 4, 7, 10 },
    { 2, 5, 8, 11 },
    { 3, 6, 9, 12 },
};
```

This is an array of three rows by four columns. The first (vertical) column is 1, 2, 3, the second is 4, 5, 6, and so on. The same effect is achieved by

```
int twoD[3][4] = { 1, 4, 7, 10 , 2, 5, 8, 11, 3, 6, 9, 12 };
```

An array of class objects is also an aggregate containing other aggregates. For example:

```
class Y { public: int a; float b; };
Y yy[3] = {
    { 1, 1.1 },
    { 2, 2.2 },
    { 3, 3.3 },
};
```

Or, equivalently,

```
Y yy[3] = { 1, 1.1, 2, 2.2, 3, 3.3 };
```

If you don't include enough initializers in the list to fill all the members of the aggregate, the remaining members are padded with 0. In a simple array, for instance,

```
int uu[4] = { 1, 2 };
```

uu[2] and uu[3] are zero. In a multi-dimensional array or an array of class objects, braces determine how the sub-aggregates are filled. For example:

```
int vv[2][3] = {
    { 1, 3 },
    { 2, 4 },
};
```

Here, the last column is initialized to zero. For an array of class objects, the syntax looks like this:

```
class Z { public: int i, j; };

Z zz[ ] = {
    { 1 },
    { 2 },
    { 3 },
};
```

This creates an array of three **Z** objects: **zz[0].i = 1**, **zz[1].i = 2**, and **zz[2].i = 3**. All of the **j** elements are zero.

If a class has a constructor, the constructor is used when initializing an aggregate. If the class has constructors that take only one argument, then the initializer list doesn't have to explicitly call the constructor. If a constructor takes more than one argument it must be called explicitly. For example:

```
class Q {
    int i;
    float f;
    char c;
public:
    Q(int);
    Q(float);
    Q(int, float, char);
```

```
// ...
};
```

Q q1 = { 1 }; // calls Q(int)

Q q2 = { 2.2 }; // calls Q(float)

Q q3 = { 'a' }; // error!

Q q4 = { Q(1, 2.2, 'a') }; // explicit constructor call

Aggregate initialization as shown here, used to initialize only one object at a time, isn't very useful. It is valuable, however, for arrays of objects.

Q qq1[ ] = { 1, 2, 3, 4.4, 5.5, 6.6, Q(7, 8.8, 'b'), Q(9, 8.8, 'c') };

If there aren't enough initializers for all the elements in the array, the default initializer (the constructor with no arguments or the constructor with all default arguments) is used for the trailing elements. If there is no default constructor, you must have an initializer for each element. For example:

Q qq2[3] = { 1.1, 2.2 }; // qq2[2] initialized with Q( )

A union that has no constructor can be initialized with another union, or with an initializer , enclosed in braces, for the first member of the union. You cannot initialize anything but the first member of the union this way. For instance:

union UU { int i; float f; char c; }; // no constructor

UU uu1 = { 47 }; // you can only init the first element this way

UU uu2 = uu1; // initializing one union from another is OK.

UU uu3 = 47; // error—braces required

UU uu4 = { 3.14159 }; // error—only first element allowed

UU uu5 = { 'x' }; // error—only first element allowed

If you want more involved initialization for unions, simply provide a constructor and use the rules for classes that have constructors.

AUTO-INITIALIZATION OF AGGREGATES EXPLICITLY SUPPORTED
Although versions of C++ prior to release 2.0 did not exclude support for
aggregate initialization of automatic variables (local variables), most implementations did not support it. Release 2.0 explicitly states that an
initializer for a variable may be an initializer-list enclosed in braces, which
means that aggregates can be initialized locally, although this feature may
not be universally implemented.

Parameterized Types

When you want to create a new type of class from an old one, inheritance
is usually the solution. However, it has its limitations. One problem in
particular occurs when you create a class that uses some other type, either
built-in or user-defined. For example, consider a matrix class similar to
the one described in Chapter 9 or Appendix B. You could define your matrix
like this:

```
class mat {
    float ** data;
    int rows, cols;
public:
    // ...
    float determinant( );
    float minvalue( );
    float maxvalue( );
    float mean( );
    // ...
};
```

But suppose you need the greater precision in your matrices gained by
using **double** values instead of **float** values, or you want to create integer

matrices, or matrices of a user-defined type, such as a complex number type? Inheritance doesn't work here. What you really need in a case like this is some sort of template that allows you to change all the **float** keywords to some other data type. You can't just use an editor and do a global search and replace, because some calculations in function bodies may truly require **float** types.

As a second example, consider the idea of a container class—a class designed to contain other classes. A good case is a linked list. A linked list is a general-purpose tool and is used repeatedly in many different situations, but for each case you must (at best) copy some general piece of code to implement a linked list and then modify it to handle your particular type of data. Of course, your list can use **void** pointers and then you can cast the result to the desired type, but this removes a level of type checking and so is not a very good solution.

The traditional solution to this problem in C++ has been to use the preprocessor to create a kind of template, and then allow the user to create a new version of the class by calling a preprocessor macro. In the preceding **mat** class, for example, the template would look like this:

```
#define mat_declare(type) \
class mat ## type { /* concatenate mat & the type name */ \
    type ** data; \
    int rows, cols; \
public: \
    // ... \
    type determinant( ); \
    type minvalue( ); \
    type maxvalue( ); \
    type mean( ); \
    // ... \
}; \
// All the definitions here ... \
// ...
```

This is most useful when the class definitions can all be **inline**, or are at least small, because the template must include all the member function definitions as well as the class definition. (In fact, that is where most of the work is done.) In a class as large as **class matrix** in Appendix B, it is hard to see it as practical.

At the time this book was written, no description for parameterized types was available (it was described as "experimental"), but the keyword **template** has been reserved for this purpose. For further information about the proposed design, see Bjarne Stroustrup, "Parameterized Types for C++," Proceedings USENIX C++ Conference, Denver, October 1988.

Exception Handling

An *exception* can be thought of as a "disastrous" error condition that makes the normal flow of a program impractical or illogical. When an exception is encountered, the system must respond by escaping to some "known good" state. For example, many operating systems can respond to a "divide-by-zero" condition by printing a message and aborting the program.

A traditional method of handling errors is for a function to return an error value to the caller, or to set a global error variable that must be checked by the caller. From a design and maintenance standpoint, this is undesirable because the error handling is outside the scope of control of the function. That is, there is no way to ensure that the caller will check and properly handle error conditions. The error condition must be tested at every call of the function, which is tedious and repetitive. Maintenance is painful because, if a new possibility for error is discovered or created through modification of the function, a new error value must be returned. The programmer must find every place the function is called and change the code to check for and handle the new error condition. Because this is such a time-consuming and tedious way to handle errors, the whole problem is often ignored, to the detriment of the system.

An ideal error-handling system would be, in a sense, orthogonal to the normal operation of a program. It would act as a separate process, watching the execution of the program. If an exception occurred, the error-handling system would step in and move the system out to a known-good state. This would allow the checking and handling of errors to be localized, and the addition of a new type of error would be easy to manage. Of course, it can never be so simple that the person calling the function that can generate exceptions is completely uninvolved. For instance, the caller must inform the error-handling system what the "good" states are.

ANSI C provides one solution to the exception-handling problem with the *nonlocal goto* library functions **setjmp( )** and **longjmp( )**, demonstrated in the **controlr** example in Chapter 10. **setjmp( )** stores information about the current state of the program (the stack frame, and so on) in a special buffer called a **jmp_buf**. At any point later in the program, you can return to the state where **setjmp( )** was called by calling **longjmp( )** with the same **jmp_buf**. It doesn't matter how far down on the stack you are or how deep you are into function calls. You can establish numerous "known good" points by calling **setjmp( )** with different **jmp_buf**s.

You can easily use the nonlocal goto functions to perform exception handling in C since the data types are quite simple and local variables are always on the stack (unless the programmer is building **struct**s with pointers in them). "Cleaning up" local variables after an exception can thus be accomplished by simply moving the stack pointer up; effectively all you have to do is forget about the variables. C++ user-defined data types are much more sophisticated—they often have destructors that must be called to clean up the variables. The simple act of moving the stack pointer up is not satisfactory. When an exception is generated in C++, the stack must be "unwound," calling all the appropriate destructors until the known-good state is reached.

A programmer can achieve a "pseudo-unwinding" of the stack by writing a function that adds to a list the **this** and the type of all user-defined types that require a destructor call to clean them up into a list. The function would be called inside the destructor of all such user-defined types; and the **setjmp( )** function would be used to set a known-good state. When an exception was generated, the **longjmp( )** function would be used to return to the known-good state, and all the destructors in the list would be explicitly called. While this may be a workable solution, it is still somewhat tricky to implement and doesn't solve the general-purpose need.

At the time this book was written, exception handling was considered an "experimental" feature in release 2.0, and no syntax had been established. The keywords **catch** and throw have been reserved for use with exception handling in future releases of C++.

Miscellaneous Changes

Release 2.0 has introduced a group of small changes designed to either clarify a previously ambiguous or unclear point of the language, or to make programming a little easier. These changes are grouped together in this section.

Enumerations Are Local to Classes And May Be private or protected

One problem with using enumerations in programming is that the programmer must be careful not to use a name more than once, to prevent conflicts with other enumeration names. This restriction may prevent some programmers from using enumerations at all, especially in library packages that are intended to be used by others who may want to create their own enumerations. Release 2.0 has reduced this restriction greatly by making the elements of an enumeration local to the class in which they are declared. In addition, you can control the access to an enumeration using the **private** and **protected** keywords. Here's an example:

```
class baby {
protected:
    enum diaper { fresh, soiled, questionable };
private:
    float length, width;
    diaper smell;
public:
    // ...
    friend check(baby &);
};
```

Now the elements of **diaper** are available to all the member functions of **class baby**, and to any class that publicly inherits **baby**. The **friend** function **check( )** may also access **protected** members; to use the **protected** members of the **enum** it must use the scope resolution operator and the class name.

```
check(baby & bb) {

if(bb.smell == baby::soiled | | bb.smell == baby::questionable)

    return 1;

return 0;

}
```

The name of the enumeration is not local to a class. Only its members must be qualified with the class name when used outside the scope of the class.

When you inherit a base class containing an **enum**, you can modify the access to the **enum** just as you would for any other member.

```
class boy : private baby {

protected:

    baby::diaper; // makes a normally private member protected

public:

    // ...

};
```

Anonymous Unions at File Scope Must Be Static

Release 2.0 requires that an anonymous union declared at file scope must be made **static** (visible only in that file).

An *anonymous union* is a union that has no tag or instances. You can create an ordinary union with a tag and no instances,

```
union u1 { int a; float b;};
```

in which case no space is reserved for the union until you use the tag to define one or more instances.

u1 x1;

Then you must refer to elements of the union using the object identifier.

x1.b = 3.14;

You can also create an untagged union with no tag, but with instances,

union { int a; float b; } x2, x3;

in which case you must also refer to elements of the union using the object identifier.

x3.a = 1;

When you create an anonymous union, however, the declaration of the union is also a definition. Only one space is reserved and the element identifiers are all that is needed to access them.

union { int i; double d; }; // anonymous union—space is created
d = 1.159;

In release 1.2 and earlier, this definition at file scope (outside any function definitions) made the identifiers **i** and **d** global, which means that any global use in another file will cause a multiple-definition error at link time. To avoid name clashes between members of anonymous unions, release 2.0 forces you to explicitly make the identifiers local to the file with the **static** keyword. The preceding definition is thus illegal at file scope. You must say instead

static union { int i; double d; };

or

static union u1 { int a; float b;};

or

static union { int a; float b; } x2, x3;

Default Arguments Cannot Be Specified More than Once

Before release 2.0, you could specify default arguments in both the class declaration and the function definition, like this:

```
class cat {
    float purr_volume;
    int purring;
public:
    cat(float purr_vol = 1.0); // one default argument
    void pet(int times);
    int is_purring( ) { return purring; }};
// ...
cat::cat(float purr_vol = 2.0) { // another default argument
    purr_volume = purr_vol;
    purring = 0;
}
```

The default arguments could be different, and no checking was performed. This could cause subtle problems, depending on the cleverness of the compile-time evaluation. In release 2.0, you cannot specify default arguments more than once, not even if you give the same default values. In addition, default arguments can now be arbitrary expressions that use constants, variables, and functions (which have been previously declared). This means you can say

```
int floor(float);
float x = 1.41;
float foo(int arg = floor(x));
```

```
main( ) {
  x = 3.25;
  // ...
  {
    float x = 5.5; // not the x used in the default argument !!
    foo( ); // same as foo(floor(3.25));
  }
};
```

Although you cannot redefine default arguments, you *can* add new ones in a later declaration. For instance:

```
foo1(int x = 1, int y = 2, int z);
// ...
foo1(int x, int y, int z = 3);
```

virtual *Functions*

Before release 2.0, if a function was declared **virtual** in a base class and you redefined it with a different prototype in a derived class, it was an error because the interface must remain the same for all implementations of a virtual function. For instance:

```
class base {
  //...
public:
  virtual func(int, int, float);
  // ...
};
```

```
class derived : public base {
    // ...
    public:
    func(int, int); // this is an error in release 1.2 and before
    // ...
};
```

In release 2.0, it is allowed to create a new definition for a function that has been declared **virtual** in a base class. However, that new function is not treated as a virtual function.

It is an error if a function in a derived class differs only by the return type from a virtual function in a base class.

Local and Nested Classes

Class declarations can be nested inside other class declarations. This, however, is only a syntactic freedom—the class is not hidden, as you might expect. The declaration is exactly as if you had declared the class outside of the enclosing function. Thus it can be deceiving to the reader of the code.

Classes can also be defined as local to a function definition. Here, the meaning changes subtly. In particular, static members of such a class are local to the function (they have "no linkage") and they cannot be initialized.

The Order of Initialization Of Static Objects

The sometimes thorny problem of the order of initialization of static objects was not addressed in release 2.0. The only guarantee you have is that global objects will be initialized in the order they appear in a single file. However, you have no control over the order of initialization across several files (no general way of specifying such order is known). The solution presented in Chapter 7 must suffice until the problem merits a further improvement to the language.

A MicroCAD

This appendix presents a program called MicroCAD that uses the full feature set of C++, including **virtual** functions. The program uses a mouse and graphics package to draw, move, and erase small shapes on the screen. You can easily add to the possible shapes by deriving a new subclass of shape.

MicroCAD diverges from the "ANSI C library functions only" rule followed by the rest of the book, and uses the mouse package and graphics package that comes with the Zortech C++ compiler. However, the use of these packages are hidden in the methods of the classes—the program structure will not be affected if you use a different mouse or graphics package. Portions of this program were originally published in *Micro Cornucopia*.

The MicroCAD Code

MicroCAD consists of many files, each of which is logically separate from the others. This appendix gives you an example of how to manage a project with many files. This is, however, a relatively small number of files compared to what a truly big project would use.

A class *to Manage the Mouse*

The first class controls the mouse and makes a selection menu. The menu is created in graphics mode. The function **get_selection( )** draws the menu, changes the mouse cursor to the appropriate arrow for that menu, and returns a value based on your selection. You can also change the shape of the cursor yourself.

Here is the **class** definition:

```
// MSMENU.HXX
// A mouse control class with a menu to choose from.  This is
// an example of data encapsulation, since it wouldn't make any
// sense to declare more than one instance of an msmenu (you
// only have one mouse!).

#ifndef MSMENU_HXX
#define MSMENU_HXX

#define LINESIZE 11
#define CHARWIDTH 10
#define BUFFER 10  // buffer zone for bounds checking
struct menu_s { // to hold the a user menu
    char * name; // displayed on screen
    int  item_number;
};

class msmenu {
    // pointer to the user's menu:
    struct menu_s * m;
    // char size of the menu:
    int height, width;
    // graphic size of the menu:
    int xsize, ysize;
    // graphic areas used by the menu:
    int msize;
    fg_color_t *color_p,
                // graphic storage area:
                *blank_p;
                // graphic box:
                fg_box_t   sizing_box;

    int count;  // for messages
```

```
      // private function — can only be called
      // by member functions:
      void drawmenu(int x, int y);
   public:
      // constructor called for a new object:
      msmenu(struct menu_s *);
      // destructor called when object goes out
      // of scope or delete is used:
      ~msmenu( );
      // bring up the menu and get user's choice:
      int get_selection(unsigned x, unsigned y);
      // translate mouse to flash graphics coords:
      void translate_coords(unsigned * x, unsigned * y) {
         *y *= -1;
         *y += fg_displaybox[FG_Y2];
      }
      void boundary_check(unsigned * x, unsigned * y) {
         if (*y >= fg_displaybox[FG_Y2] - BUFFER)
            *y = fg_displaybox[FG_Y2] - BUFFER;
         if (*x >= fg_displaybox[FG_X2] - BUFFER)
            *x = fg_displaybox[FG_X2] - BUFFER;
         if (*y <= fg_displaybox[FG_Y1] + BUFFER)
            *y = fg_displaybox[FG_Y1] + BUFFER;
         if (*x <= fg_displaybox[FG_X1] + BUFFER)
            *x = fg_displaybox[FG_X1] + BUFFER;
      }
      // different types of cursors:
      void default_cursor( ); // arrow
      void menu_cursor( ); // horizontal arrow
      void cross_cursor( ); // crosshair
      // wait for buttons to be pressed:
      void wait_left_pressed(unsigned *x, unsigned *y) {
         while (!(msm_getstatus(x,y) & 1))
            ;
      }
      void wait_right_pressed(unsigned *x, unsigned *y) {
         while (!(msm_getstatus(x,y) & 2))
            ;
      }
      // wait for buttons to be released:
      void wait_left_released(unsigned *x, unsigned *y) {
         while (msm_getstatus(x,y) & 1)
```

```
          ;
      }
      void wait_right_released(unsigned *x, unsigned *y) {
        while (msm_getstatus(x,y) & 2)
            ;
      }
};
#endif MSMENU_HXX
```

And here are the methods for **class msmenu**:

```
// MSMENU.CXX
#include <stdio.h>
#include <stdlib.h>
#include <conio.h>
#include <msmouse.h>
// flash graphics declarations:
#include <fg.h>
#include <string.h>
#include "msmenu.hxx"

msmenu::msmenu(struct menu_s * mp) {
    char buf[15];
    count = 0;
    // attach the menu pointer to this object:
    m = mp;
    // Store the size of the menu:
    height = 0;
    struct menu_s * mm = m;
    // look for end marker:
    while ( mm->item_number != -1) {
        height++;
        mm++;
    }
    int ss, i;
    for(i = 0, width = 0; i < height; i++)
        if ((ss = strlen(mp[i].name)) > width)
            // find the largest element:
            width = ss;


    // graphic width:
```

```
    xsize = width * CHARWIDTH;
    // graphic height:
    ysize = height * LINESIZE;

    sizing_box[FG_X1] = 0;
    sizing_box[FG_Y1] = 0;
    sizing_box[FG_X2] = xsize + LINESIZE;
    sizing_box[FG_Y2] = ysize + LINESIZE;
    msize = sizing_box[FG_X2] - sizing_box[FG_X1] + 1;
    msize *= sizing_box[FG_Y2] - sizing_box[FG_Y1] + 1;
    msize *= sizeof(fg_color_t);
    // allocate memory for graphics storage:
    color_p = new fg_color_t[msize];
    blank_p = new fg_color_t[msize];
    // save blank image of menu size:
    fg_readbox(sizing_box, blank_p);
    // initialize mouse:
    msm_init( );
    // turn mouse cursor on:
    msm_showcursor( );
}

msmenu::~msmenu( ) {
    delete color_p;
    delete blank_p;
    // turn mouse cursor off:
    msm_hidecursor( );
    // terminate use of mouse:
    msm_term( );
}

void msmenu::drawmenu(int x,int y) {
    struct menu_s * elem = m;
    for (int i = 0; i < height; i++) {
        fg_puts(FG_WHITE, FG_MODE_SET, ~0, FG_ROT0,
                    x,y, elem->name, fg_displaybox);
        elem++;
        y -= LINESIZE;
    }
}

/* The following patterns were created from the
```

commented block of ones and zeros using the
tool MSCURSOR.CXX */

```
static int default_cur[] = {
0xffff,        /* 0000000000000000 */
0xdfff,        /* 0010000000000000 */
0xcfff,        /* 0011000000000000 */
0xc7ff,        /* 0011100000000000 */
0xc3ff,        /* 0011110000000000 */
0xc1ff,        /* 0011111000000000 */
0xc0ff,        /* 0011111100000000 */
0xc07f,        /* 0011111110000000 */
0xc03f,        /* 0011111111000000 */
0xc01f,        /* 0011111111100000 */
0xc1ff,        /* 0011111000000000 */
0xdcff,        /* 0010001100000000 */
0xfcff,        /* 0000001100000000 */
0xfe7f,        /* 0000000110000000 */
0xfe7f,        /* 0000000110000000 */
0xffff,        /* 0000000000000000 */
0x0, 0x2000, 0x3000, 0x3800, 0x3c00, 0x3e00,
0x3f00, 0x3f80, 0x3fc0, 0x3fe0, 0x3e00,
0x2300, 0x300, 0x180, 0x180, 0x0,
};

static int menu_cur[] = {
0xffff,        /* 0000000000000000 */
0xffff,        /* 0000000000000000 */
0xffff,        /* 0000000000000000 */
0xffff,        /* 0000000000000000 */
0xffef,        /* 0000000000010000 */
0xdfe7,        /* 0010000000011000 */
0x6fe3,        /* 1001000000011100 */
0xb7e1,        /* 0100100000011110 */
0xc000,        /* 0011111111111111 */
0xb7e1,        /* 0100100000011110 */
0x6fe3,        /* 1001000000011100 */
0xdfe7,        /* 0010000000011000 */
0xffef,        /* 0000000000010000 */
0xffff,        /* 0000000000000000 */
0xffff,        /* 0000000000000000 */
0xffff,        /* 0000000000000000 */
0x0, 0x0, 0x0, 0x0, 0x10, 0x2018,
```

```
0x901c, 0x481e, 0x3fff, 0x481e,
0x901c, 0x2018, 0x10, 0x0, 0x0, 0x0,
};

static int cross_cur[] = {
0xffff,        /* 0000000000000000 */
0xffff,        /* 0000000000000000 */
0xffff,        /* 0000000000000000 */
0xfeff,        /* 0000000100000000 */
0xfeff,        /* 0000000100000000 */
0xfeff,        /* 0000000100000000 */
0xfeff,        /* 0000000100000000 */
0xfeff,        /* 0000000100000000 */
0x0,           /* 1111111111111111 */
0xfeff,        /* 0000000100000000 */
0xfeff,        /* 0000000100000000 */
0xfeff,        /* 0000000100000000 */
0xfeff,        /* 0000000100000000 */
0xffff,        /* 0000000000000000 */
0xffff,        /* 0000000000000000 */
0xffff,        /* 0000000000000000 */
0x0, 0x0, 0x0, 0x100, 0x100, 0x100,
0x100, 0x100, 0xffff, 0x100, 0x100,
0x100, 0x100, 0x0, 0x0, 0x0,
};

// the first two numbers are the x and y
// coordinates of the "hot spot", with the
// upper left corner = 0,0:

void msmenu::default_cursor( ) {
    msm_setgraphcur(-1,-1,default_cur);
}

void msmenu::menu_cursor( ) {
    msm_setgraphcur(-16,-8,menu_cur);
}

void msmenu::cross_cursor( ) {
    msm_setgraphcur(-8,-8,cross_cur);
}

int msmenu::get_selection(unsigned x, unsigned yy) {
```

```
unsigned int u,v, startv;
unsigned y = yy;
fg_box_t   read_box;
translate_coords(&x,&y);
read_box[FG_X1] = x;
read_box[FG_Y1] = y - ysize + LINESIZE;
read_box[FG_X2] = x + xsize;
read_box[FG_Y2] = y + LINESIZE;

msm_hidecursor( );
// use special cursor:
menu_cursor( );
fg_readbox(read_box, color_p);
// blank section out:
fg_writebox(read_box, blank_p);
// call a private function:
drawmenu(x,y);
// trial-and-error:
msm_setcurpos(x - 35 , yy -22);
msm_showcursor( );
msm_setareax(x -35, x - 35);
msm_setareay(yy - 22, yy - 22 + ysize - LINESIZE );
startv = yy - 22;
wait_left_pressed(&u,&v);
wait_left_released(&u,&v);

// put everything back the way it was:
msm_setareax(fg_displaybox[FG_X1], fg_displaybox[FG_X2]);
msm_setareay(fg_displaybox[FG_Y1], fg_displaybox[FG_Y2]);
msm_hidecursor( );
// Restore old cursor:
default_cursor( );
// restore original position:
msm_setcurpos(x, yy);
// restore screen:
fg_writebox(read_box, color_p);
msm_showcursor( );
// calculate which item was selected:
return m[(v - startv)/LINESIZE].item_number;
}
```

The mouse cursors are created from ASCII text files (the commented bitmaps shown above, without the comment marks) with the following tool:

```
// MSCURSOR.CXX
// Given a bitmap of ASCII ones and zeros,
// mscursor < bitmap > outfile.cur
// generates a structure for a new mouse cursor, with the bitmap
// as a comment block.  This shows how useful streams can be.
#include <stream.hxx>

main( ) {
    char binary[20]; // holds the source pattern
    unsigned int positive[16];
    unsigned int j; int x = 0;
    cout << "int NAME[] = {\n";
    while(cin.good( )) {
        cin >> binary;
        j = 0;
        // note the '<<' operator has a different
        // meaning depending on what context it is
        // being used in:
        for (int i = 0, k = 15; i < 16; i++, k— )
            j |= (binary[i] == '1') ? (1 << k) : 0;
        // streams allow easy writing of hex:
        cout << "0x" << hex(~j) <<
            ",\t\t/* " << binary << "*/ \n";
        positive[x++] = j;
        if (x > 15) break;
    }
    for (int i = 0; i < 16; i++) {
        cout << "0x" << hex(positive[i]) << ", ";
        if ( i == 8) cout << "\n";
    }
    cout << "\n};\n\n";
}
```

A Polymorphic Base class

The **cadshape** class is a base class for all the shapes used in the MicroCAD program. Notice that almost all the functions are defined using the **virtual** keyword. Any function can be defined in a base class and redefined in an inherited class. An object of an inherited class can be treated as an object of the base class—if you use a pointer to an inherited class object for calling a function in the base class everything works fine, except you can only call the base class function this way. A **virtual** function, on the other hand, allows you to call the proper function for an inherited class via a pointer of the base class type.

In the MicroCAD program, there is a **virtual** function called **draw( )** in the **cadshape** base class. **Cadshape** is inherited into **class circle, class square** and **class line**, each of which has a different way of drawing itself. What you want to do is manipulate a list, and not have to worry about how to draw, erase, or alter individual shapes. **virtual** functions allow this— they call the correct **draw( )** function at run time regardless of whether the shape is a **circle, square, line**, or some new type of shape you've added to the program.

Notice that a **virtual** destructor is used in **cadshape**—the destructor from the derived class is used, not the base class. The derived class may have special initializations or other side effects that need to be cleaned up.

The cadshape code follows.

```
// CADSHAPE.HXX
// A polymorphic base class for all shapes. Almost all
// functions are virtual, so they can be redefined in derived
// classes. Then you can make a list of shapes and draw( )
// each shape in the list without knowing exactly what it is.
#ifndef CADSHAPE_HXX
#define CADSHAPE_HXX
class cadshape {
protected:  // so derived classes have access
  unsigned x_center, y_center;
public:
  // virtual functions must have SOME
  // definition in the base class, even
  // if it's just empty:
  virtual ~cadshape( ) {}
  virtual void draw( ) {}
  virtual void erase( ) {}
  void
  move(unsigned new_x, unsigned new_y ) {
    x_center = new_x;
    y_center = new_y;
    draw( ); // call proper virtual function
  }
  unsigned long range( unsigned xr, unsigned yr ) {
    // a measure of distance between a
```

```
        // selected point and this object's center
        unsigned long xx =
          xr > x_center ?
          xr - x_center : x_center - xr;
          // (ternary if-then-else)
        unsigned long yy =
          yr > y_center ?
          yr - y_center : y_center - yr;
        xx *= xx;
        yy *= yy;
        // delta x squared + delta y squared:
        return xx + yy;
    }
};
#endif CADSHAPE_HXX
```

Deriving New Shapes from cadshape

Each time you want to add a new kind of shape to MicroCAD, you must derive a new subclass from **cadshape** and redefine the **virtual** functions for that specific shape. MicroCAD has three shapes, but you can easily add others.

Square   This listing shows **class square** being derived from **cadshape**.

```
// SQUARE.HXX
#ifndef SQUARE_HXX
#define SQUARE_HXX
#include <fg.h>
#include "cadshape.hxx"

class square : public cadshape {
   fg_box_t small_box;
public:
   void draw( );
   square(unsigned x, unsigned y) : ( ) {
      x_center = x; y_center = y;
      draw( );
   }
   void erase( );
   ~square( ) { erase( ); }
```

```
   ~square( ) { erase( ); }
};
#endif // SQUARE_HXX
```

The methods for **square** are

```
// SQUARE.CXX
#include "square.hxx"
#include <fg.h>
#inculde <msmouse.h>

void square::draw( ) {
   msm_hidecursor( );
   small_box [FG_X1] = x_center;
   small_box [FG_X2] = x_center + 20;
   small_box [FG_Y1] = y_center;
   small_box [FG_Y2] = y_center + 20;
   fg_drawbox (FG_WHITE, FG_MODE_SET, ~0, FG_LINE_SOLID,
                  small_box, fg_displaybox);
   msm_showcursor( );
}

void square::erase( ) {
   msm_hidecursor( );
   fg_drawbox (FG_BLACK, FG_MODE_SET, ~0, FG_LINE_SOLID,
                  small_box, fg_displaybox);
   msm_showcursor( );
}
```

Circle

The following listing shows **class circle** being derived from **cadshape**.

```
// CIRCLE.HXX
#ifndef CIRCLE_HXX
#define CIRCLE_HXX
#include "cadshape.hxx"

#define x_radius 10
#define y_radius 10
class circle : public cadshape {
public:
```

```
    void draw( );
    circle(unsigned x, unsigned y) : ( )
       { x_center = x; y_center = y; draw( ); }
    void erase( );
    ~circle( ) { erase( ); }
};
#endif // CIRCLE_HXX
```

The methods for **circle** are

```
// CIRCLE.CXX
#include "circle.hxx"
#include <fg.h>
#include <msmouse.h>

void circle::draw( ) {
    msm_hidecursor( );
    fg_drawellipse (FG_WHITE, FG_MODE_SET,
       ~0, x_center, y_center, x_radius,
       y_radius, 0, 3600, fg_displaybox);
    msm_showcursor( );
}

void circle::erase( ) {
    msm_hidecursor( );
    fg_drawellipse (FG_BLACK, FG_MODE_SET,
       ~0, x_center, y_center, x_radius,
       y_radius, 0, 3600, fg_displaybox);
    msm_showcursor( );
}
```

Line

The next listing shows **class line** being derived from **cadshape**.

```
// LINE.HXX
#ifndef LINE_HXX
#define LINE_HXX
#include <fg.h>
#include "cadshape.hxx"

class line : public cadshape {
    fg_line_t line_data;
```

```
      fg_line_t line_data;
public:
   void draw( );
   line(unsigned x, unsigned y): ( ) {
      x_center = x; y_center = y;
      draw( );
   }
   void erase( );
   ~line( ) { erase( ); }
};
#endif // LINE_HXX
```

The methods for **line** are

```
// LINE.CXX
#include "line.hxx"
#include <msmouse.h>
#include <fg.h>

void line::draw( ) {
   msm_hidecursor( );
   line_data [FG_X1] = x_center;
   line_data [FG_X2] = x_center + 30;
   line_data [FG_Y1] = y_center;
   line_data [FG_Y2] = y_center + 30;
   fg_drawlineclip(FG_WHITE, FG_MODE_SET, ~0,
                   FG_LINE_SOLID, line_data);
   msm_showcursor( );
}

void line::erase( ) {
   msm_hidecursor( );
   fg_drawlineclip(FG_BLACK, FG_MODE_SET, ~0,
                   FG_LINE_SOLID, line_data);
   msm_showcursor( );
}
```

Linked Lists

The MicroCAD program is really just managing a linked list of **cadshape**s. This linked list is a container **class** called **shapelist**, which manipulates the list, and hunt for the shape nearest a set of coordinates. (See Chapter 10 for a cleaner implementation of a linked list.)

```
// SHAPELST.HXX
// Two classes to manage a list of cadshapes. A shapelist
// contains a list of (what else?) shapelist_elements, which
// simply hold a cadshape and a link to the next element.  The
// usual linked list stuff: you can insert, step through, etc.
#ifndef SHAPELST_HXX
#define SHAPELST_HXX
#include "cadshape.hxx"

// tell the compiler the class exists:
class shapelist;

class shapelist_element {
    cadshape * shp;
    shapelist_element * next;
public:
    // allow shapelist access to the
    // private elements of this class:
    friend shapelist;
    shapelist_element(cadshape * s, shapelist_element * hd) {
        shp = s;
        next = hd;
    }
};

class shapelist {
    shapelist_element * head, * current;
public:
    shapelist( ) { current = head =
        new shapelist_element((cadshape*)0, (shapelist_element*)0);
    } // end of list marked by null pointers
    void insert(cadshape * s) {
        shapelist_element * p = new shapelist_element(s, head);
        head = p;
    }
    void reset( ) { current = head; }
    cadshape * next( );
    void remove(cadshape * s);
    // hunt through the list and find the
    // nearest element to x,y:
```

```
      cadshape * nearest(unsigned x, unsigned y);
};

#endif SHAPELST_HXX
```

The following are the **shapelist** methods.

```
// SHAPELST.CXX
#include "shapelst.hxx"

cadshape * shapelist::next( ) {
   cadshape * r = current->shp;
   if ( r != (cadshape *)0 )
      current = current->next;
   return r;
}

void shapelist::remove(cadshape * s) {
   shapelist_element * pp = head, * qq;
   if ( pp->shp == s) {  // check head
      head = pp->next;
      delete pp;
   } else
   while ( pp->next->shp != 0 ) {
      // (the next element isn't the last)
      if ( pp->next->shp == s) {
         // unlink the matching element:
         qq = pp->next;
         pp->next = pp->next->next;
         delete qq;
         return;
      }
      pp++;
   }
}

// Find the nearest shape to co-ordinates (x,y) :
cadshape * shapelist::nearest(unsigned x, unsigned y) {
   cadshape * kk;
   cadshape * cshape;
   unsigned long distance;
   reset( );  // start at beginning of list
```

```
      cshape = next( ); // test the first element
      distance = cshape->range(x,y);
      while ((kk = next( )) != 0)
         if ( kk->range(x,y) < distance ) {
            cshape = kk;
            distance = cshape->range(x,y);
         }
      return cshape;
}
```

The main( ) *program*

The main driver for MicroCAD simply uses the other classes. After initialization, it checks for menu requests and executes them using a **case** statement. You can see examples of the use of **virtual** functions in the MOVE and DELETE cases.

```
// MICROCAD.CXX
// The main driver program for the CAD system.  This includes
// all the other types, declares some instances, and makes them
// dance around.
#include <stdio.h>
#include <stdlib.h>
#include <conio.h>
#include <msmouse.h>
// flash graphics declarations:
#include <fg.h>
// (All items starting with "fg" are from
// the flash graphics library)
#include <string.h>
#include "msmenu.hxx"
#include "circle.hxx"
#include "square.hxx"
#include "line.hxx"
#include "shapelst.hxx"

// associate unique integers with the following:
enum { CIRCLE, SQUARE, LINE, MOVE, DELETE, EXIT};

struct menu_s my_menu[] = {
   " circle",    CIRCLE,
```

```
            " square",  SQUARE,
            " line",    LINE,
            " move",    MOVE,
            " delete",  DELETE,
            " exit",    EXIT,
            "", -1              /* end marker */
        };


    main( ) {
        unsigned x, y;
        int quit = 0;  // flag
        int result;
        shapelist list;
        if (fg_init_all ( ) == FG_NULL) {
            fputs ("Unable to open graphics device.\n", stderr);
            exit (1);
        }
        // create an msmenu and attach our menu:
        msmenu mouse(my_menu);
        while (!quit) {
            // look for right button press:
            if (msm_getstatus(&x,&y) & 2) {
                // get a menu selection:
                result = mouse.get_selection(x,y);
                // change from mouse to fg coords:
                mouse.translate_coords(&x,&y);
                mouse.boundary_check(&x,&y);
                switch(result) {
                    case CIRCLE:
                        // create an object on the free
                        // store via "new" and add it
                        // to the list:
                        list.insert(new circle(x,y));
                        break;
                    case SQUARE:
                        list.insert(new square(x,y));
                        break;
                    case LINE:
                        list.insert(new line(x,y));
                        break;
```

```
            case MOVE:
                mouse.cross_cursor( );
                mouse.wait_left_pressed(&x,&y);
                mouse.translate_coords(&x,&y);
                // you can declare a variable at
                // the point of use:
                cadshape * mv = list.nearest(x,y);
                // object pointers use arrows
                // for de-referencing members:
                mv->erase( ); // pick it up
                mouse.wait_left_released(&x,&y);
                mouse.translate_coords(&x,&y);
                mouse.boundary_check(&x,&y);
                mv->move(x,y); // put it down
                mouse.default_cursor( );
                break;
            case DELETE:
                mouse.cross_cursor( );
                mouse.wait_left_pressed(&x,&y);
                mouse.translate_coords(&x,&y);
                cadshape * rm = list.nearest(x,y);
                rm->erase( );
                list.remove(rm);
                // free the memory created w/ new:
                delete rm;
                mouse.default_cursor( );
                break;
            case EXIT:
                quit++;
                break;
            default:
                break;
        }
    }
}
fg_term( ); // back to text mode
}
```

Features to Add as an Exercise

Here are some features you might want to add:

- Create a class to hold coordinates. This could then be passed around instead of the X,Y pair used here. Create member functions to convert coordinate objects from mouse coordinates to flash graphics coordinates and back.

- Create stretchable objects, with dashed lines to indicate size.

- Add dashed outlines when an object is being moved.

- Create a supershape that holds any number of other shapes to enable the user to create new composite shapes. Include storage and retrieval of these shape libraries.

- Add a method to translate a shape outline into some independent graphics representation, which can then be sent through filters to generate output for PostScript, Epson, or other printers.

- The mouse menu should be created as a simple graphics block and simply painted onto the screen, instead of drawing it character by character, as was done here. It would be much faster.

Makefile for MicroCAD

The makefile will build MicroCAD from scratch. If you want to build MicroCAD on a different machine or use a translator other than Zortech, you must modify the source code and this **makefile**.

```
# makefile for MicroCAD in Appendix A
# Only works with Zortech C++ on a PC

.cxx.obj:
        ztc -c $*.cxx
```

```
microcad.exe: msmenu.obj microcad.obj circle.obj square.obj \
        line.obj shapelst.obj
    ztc -omicrocad.exe $** fgs.lib

mscursor.exe : mscursor.cxx
    ztc mscursor

msmenu.obj: msmenu.cxx msmenu.hxx

microcad.obj: microcad.cxx cadshape.hxx shapelst.hxx

circle.obj: circle.cxx circle.hxx cadshape.hxx

square.obj: square.cxx square.hxx cadshape.hxx

line.obj: line.cxx line.hxx cadshape.hxx

shapelst.obj: shapelst.cxx shapelst.hxx cadshape.hxx
```

Standard Matrix Files

For ease of testing, one of the matrix constructors will read from an ASCII text file following a "standard" format (this is shown in the ANALYZE.CXX program). Comments in this file begin with # and continue to the end of the line. The file must contain a header block and a data block. The two blocks are separated by three colons (:::). At this point, the header block only needs to contain information about the number of rows and columns in the matrix. The constructor only searches for **r**, **c**, and = so you can say

r = 3 c = 3

or

rows=3 columns=3

You must list rows before columns. This can be changed by modifying the constructor.

In the data block, data are separated by spaces. All data are treated as floating point numbers, whether or not they contain decimal points and exponents. New lines are ignored in the data block.

The member function **write_standard( )** writes a matrix to a file in the standard format, adding date and time information and a message, if you desire. (You can also add information about the path the matrix is located in if you use platform-specific function calls.)

Other constructors create different types of matrices. For example:

matrix ID('T',10); // a 10 x 10 identity matrix

matrix F(10,10,3.14); // init each element of a 10 x 10 matrix to 3.14

You can also create a matrix from an array of doubles:

double dd[] = { 1.1, 2.2, 3.3, 4.4, 5.5, 6.6, 7.7, 8.8, 9.9 };

// the above definition should be global or static

matrix A(3,3,dd);

B *The Matrix Class*

This appendix contains the full source code for a **class** to create and manipulate mathematical matrices. The structure of this **class** was introduced in Chapter 9; this appendix fleshes it out with a full set of operations including **inverse( )** and **determinant( )**. The **matrix** class follows strict portability guidelines, so you can use it on any system with an ANSI C library.

Using matrices, you can easily construct matrix equations like

A = B.determinant( ) * C + D;

An equation like this allows you to focus on the mathematical problem instead of the programming problem.

The algorithms for the **inverse( )** and **determinant( )** (using LU decomposition) are translated from *Numerical Recipes,* by William H. Press and Brian P.Flannery (Cambridge University Press, 1987), which used Fortran. If you want further information on matrix manipulation and numerical methods in general, consult their later book *Numerical Recipes in C* (Cambridge University Press, 1988). Since the algorithms were not developed by this author, they may not work correctly in all situations— you should not trust the results until you verify them with an independent test. The test shown here simply multiplies a matrix by its inverse to check for the identity matrix (a matrix with 1's along its diagonal, and 0's everywhere else), which should always be produced.

Standard Matrix Files

For ease of testing, one of the matrix constructors will read from an ASCII text file following a "standard" format (this is shown in the ANALYZE.CXX program). Comments in this file begin with **#** and continue to the end of the line. The file must contain a header block and a data block. The two blocks are separated by three colons (**:::**). At this point, the header block only needs to contain information about the number of rows and columns in the matrix. The constructor only searches for **r**, **c**, and **=** so you can say

r = 3 c = 3

or

rows=3 columns=3

You must list rows before columns. This can be changed by modifying the constructor.

In the data block, data are separated by spaces. All data are treated as floating point numbers, whether or not they contain decimal points and exponents. New lines are ignored in the data block.

The member function **write_standard( )** writes a matrix to a file in the standard format, adding date and time information and a message, if you desire. (You can also add information about the path the matrix is located in if you use platform-specific function calls.)

Other constructors create different types of matrices. For example:

matrix ID('T',10); // a 10 x 10 identity matrix

matrix F(10,10,3.14); // init each element of a 10 x 10 matrix to 3.14

You can also create a matrix from an array of doubles:

double dd[] = { 1.1, 2.2, 3.3, 4.4, 5.5, 6.6, 7.7, 8.8, 9.9 };

// the above definition should be global or static

matrix A(3,3,dd);

A column vector is a matrix with one column. Because default arguments are used, a vector definition looks quite sensible, as in

matrix vec(3); // vector with 3 elements

You can multiply a matrix by a column vector in the usual way.

matrix result = A * vec;

Row vectors are not quite as obvious (but they are not used as often, either).

matrix rowvec(1,3); // row vector with 3 elements
matrix rowresult = rowvec * A;

Speed Improvements

Since **double** values are twice as large as **float** values, calculations on **double**smax take significantly longer (depending on the implementation). For most problems, the use of **double** is overkill; you will never need that level of precision. You should see speed improvements by changing all the **double** declarations to **float**.

An obvious way to speed things up is to add a hardware floating point coprocessor to your system and recompile the code using the proper flag to force in-line generation of calls to the floating point coprocessor.

Code for the matrix class

This appendix is provided to give you an example of the structure of a larger **class**. Other than the description of the design in Chapter 9, a thorough explanation of the code will not be given.

Matrix Definition

The header file must be included in all programs that create and use matrices. Notice that the header file includes no other header files—this will make compilation of programs using the matrix class much faster. Although the definition for **struct matrep** is actually public, it is placed inside the **private** section of **class matrix** to emphasize that it is only used with the **matrix class**. (In Chapter 9 it was defined separately.)

```
// MATRIX.HXX: fully functional matrix class based on
// design in chapter 9.
#ifndef MATRIX_HXX
#define MATRIX_HXX

class matrix {
    struct matrep {
        double **m; // pointer to the matrix
        int r,c;       // number of rows and columns
        int n;         // reference count
    } *p;
    void error(char * msg1, char * msg2 = ""); // private function
public:
    matrix(int mrows = 1, int columns = 1, double initval = 0);
    matrix(int mrows, int columns, double* initvalues);
    matrix(char * flag, int dimension); // create an ident matrix
    matrix(char * matfile); // read from a "standard" matrix file
    matrix(matrix& x); // copy-initializer
    ~matrix();
    int rows() const {  return p->r; }; // rows in matrix
    int cols() const {  return p->c; };  // cols in matrix
    matrix operator=(const matrix& rval); // matrix assignment
    // Write a "standard" matrix file:
    void write_standard(char * filename, char * msg = "");
    matrix operator+(const matrix& rval); // matrix addition
    matrix operator+(const double rval); // scalar addition
    matrix operator-(const matrix& rval); // matrix subtraction
    matrix operator-(const double rval); // scalar subtraction
    matrix operator-(); // unary minus
    matrix operator*(const matrix& rval); // matrix multiplication
    matrix operator*(const double rval); // scalar multiplication
    double & val(int row, int col); // element selection;
    // can be used to read or write an element.
    matrix transpose(); // transpose a square matrix
    double determinant();
    matrix inverse();
    double mmin(); // find minimum element in the matrix
```

```
    double mmax();  // find maximum element in the matrix
    double mean(); // average all the elements of the matrix
    double variance(); // statistical variance of all elements
    void print(char * msg = ""); // print matrix with a message

    private: // functions used by inverse() and determinant()
    void switch_columns(int col1, int col2);
    void copy_column(matrix& m, int from_col, int to_col);
    matrix scale(); // Scale a matrix (used in L-U decomposition)
    void deepcopy(matrix& from, matrix& to); // make an image
    matrix lu_decompose(matrix& indx, int& d );
        // Returns the L-U decomposition of a matrix
    void lu_back_subst(matrix& indx, matrix& b);
        // Uses L-U decomposition for matrix inverse
    double & mval(int row, int col) {
        return (p->m[row][col]);
    } // used by matrix functions which KNOW they aren't
    // exceeding the boundaries
};

#endif // MATRIX_HXX
```

Matrix Methods

Your system limitations may not allow the entire file to be compiled without running out of memory; this is particularly true with a C code generator on the PC. If this is the case, break the code into several files. The **streams class** was purposely not used here because it adds extra overhead to the compiler, as well as slowing the compiler down. The code was compiled on both Zortech C++ and Glockenspiel C++.

```
// MATRIX.CXX: fully functional matrix class based on
// design in chapter 9.

#define TINY 1e-20

#include <stdlib.h>
#include <stdio.h>
#include <string.h>
#include <math.h>
#include <time.h>
#include "matrix.hxx"

void matrix::error(char * msg1, char * msg2) {
    fprintf(stderr,"matrix error: %s  %s\n", msg1, msg2);
```

```
        exit(1);
    }

matrix::matrix(int mrows, int columns, double initval)
{
    // create the structure:
    p = new matrep;
    p->r = mrows;
    p->c = columns;
    // allocate memory for the actual matrix:
    p->m = new double *[mrows];
    for (int x = 0; x < mrows; x++)
        p->m[x] = new double[columns];
    p->n = 1;  // so far, there's one reference to this data
    for (int i=0; i< mrows; i++)
        for (int j = 0; j < columns; j++) {
            mval(i,j) = initval;
            }
}

matrix::matrix(int mrows, int columns, double* initvalues)
{
    //printf("mrows = %d, columns = %d\n",mrows,columns);
    // create the structure:
    p = new matrep;
    p->r= mrows;
    p->c = columns;
    // allocate memory for the actual matrix:
    p->m = new double *[mrows];
    for (int x = 0; x < mrows; x++)
        p->m[x] = new double[columns];
    p->n = 1;  // so far, there's one reference to this data
    int c = 0;
    for (int i=0; i< mrows; i++) {
        for (int j = 0; j < columns; j++) {
            mval(i,j) = initvalues[c++];
        }
    }
}

// create an identity matrix:
matrix::matrix(char * flag, int dimension)
{
    if (flag[0] != 'I')
        error("to create an identity matrix: "
                "matrix(\"I\",dimension)");
    p = new matrep;
    p->r = dimension;
    p->c = dimension;
```

```
            p->m = new double *[dimension];
            for (int x = 0; x < dimension; x++)
               p->m[x] = new double[dimension];
            p->n = 1;
            for (int i=0; i< dimension; i++) {
               for (int j = 0; j < dimension; j++)
                  mval(i,j) = (i == j ? 1 : 0);
                  }
         }

         // error message when trying to read a "standard"
         // matrix file:
         static char nonstandard[] =
         " is a 'non-standard' file. A 'standard' matrix file must\n"
         "start with the dimensions of the matrix, i.e.:\n"
         "\t rows=12 columns=14\n or abbreviated:\n\t r=12 c=14\n"
         "Notice rows appear before columns, and chars are lowercase\n"
         "comments follow '#' signs to end of line, data follows :::\n";

         // read from "standard" matrix file:
         matrix::matrix(char * initfile)
         {
            const int BSIZE = 120;
            FILE * from;
            if ((from = fopen(initfile,"r")) == 0)
               error("cannot open matrix initializer file",initfile);
            char buf[BSIZE], *cp, *cp2;
            int rfound = 0, cfound = 0, colonsfound = 0;
            p = new matrep;
                  /* Parse file initialization header */
            while(fgets(buf, BSIZE, from)) { // for each header line
               // Remove comments with ANSI C library function "strpbrk()":
               if( ( cp = strpbrk(buf,"#")) != NULL ) // look for comments
                  *cp = '\0';  // terminate string at comment
               if( ( cp = strpbrk(buf,"r") ) != NULL )
                  if ( ( cp2 = strpbrk(cp, "=")) != NULL )
                     if ( ( cp = strpbrk(cp2, "0123456789")) != NULL ) {
                        p->r = atoi(cp);
                        rfound++;  // flag to say rows were found
                     }
               if( ( cp = strpbrk(buf,"c") ) != NULL )
                  if ( ( cp2 = strpbrk(cp, "=")) != NULL )
                     if ( ( cp = strpbrk(cp2, "0123456789")) != NULL ) {
                        p->c = atoi(cp);
                        cfound++;  // flag to say cols were found
                     }
               if ( strstr(buf,":::") != NULL ) {
                  colonsfound++;
                  break; // ... out of "while" loop
```

```
         }
       }
       if ( !rfound || !cfound || !colonsfound ) {
           fprintf(stderr, "%s%s", initfile, nonstandard);
           exit(1);
       }
       p->m = new double *[p->r];
       for (int x = 0; x < p->r; x++)
           p->m[x] = new double[p->c];
       p->n = 1;  // so far, there's one reference to this data
       for (int row = 0; row < p->r; row++)  {
           for(int col = 0; col < p->c; col++){
               char nb[20];
               fscanf(from,"%s", nb); // scan for space-delimited string
               mval(row,col) = atof(nb); // convert it to a double
               if(ferror(from))
                   error("problem with matrix initializer file",initfile);
           }
       }
   }

   matrix::matrix(matrix& x) {
       x.p->n++; // we're adding another reference.
       p = x.p;  // point to the new matrep.
   }

   matrix::~matrix() {
       if (—p->n == 0) { // if reference count goes to 0
           for (int x = 0; x < rows(); x++)
               delete p->m[x];
           delete p->m; // delete data
           delete p;
       }
   }

   matrix matrix::operator=(const matrix& rval) {
       // clean up current value:
       if(—p->n == 0) {  // If nobody else is referencing us...
           for (int x = 0; x < rows(); x++)
               delete p->m[x];
           delete p->m; // ...nobody else can clean us up...
           delete p;
       }
       // connect to new value:
       rval.p->n++; // tell the rval it has another reference
       p = rval.p; // point at the rval matrep
       return *this;
   }
```

```
void matrix::write_standard(char * filename, char * msg) {
    FILE * to;
    if ((to = fopen(filename,"w")) == NULL)
        error("cannot open or create matrix output file",filename);
    fprintf(to,
        "# %s: matrix file written in \"standard\" format\n",
        filename);
    time_t clock;
    time(&clock);
    fprintf(to, "# %s", asctime(localtime(&clock)));
    fprintf(to, "# %s\n", msg);
    fprintf(to,"rows= %d columns= %d\n", rows(), cols());
    fprintf(to, ":::\n");
    for (int row = 0; row < rows(); row++){
        for(int col = 0; col < cols(); col++){
            fprintf(to,"%6.6g  ",mval(row,col));
            if(ferror(to))
                error("problem with matrix output file",filename);
        }
        fprintf(to, "\n");
    }
}

matrix matrix::operator+(const matrix& arg) {
    if(( rows() != arg.rows()) || ( cols() != arg.cols()))
        error("must have equal dimensions for addition!");
    matrix sum(rows(),cols());
    for (int i=0; i< rows(); i++)  {
        for (int j = 0; j < cols(); j++)
            sum.mval(i,j) = mval(i,j) + arg.mval(i,j);
        }
    return sum; // see note for operator*()
}

matrix matrix::operator+(const double arg) {
    matrix sum(rows(),cols());
    for (int i=0; i< rows(); i++)  {
        for (int j = 0; j < cols(); j++)
            sum.mval(i,j) = mval(i,j) + arg;
        }
    return sum; // see note for operator*()
}

matrix matrix::operator-(const matrix& arg) {
    if(( rows() != arg.rows()) || ( cols() != arg.cols()))
        error("must have equal dimensions for subtaction!");
    matrix sum(rows(),cols());
    for (int i=0; i< rows(); i++)  {
        for (int j = 0; j < cols(); j++)
```

```
        sum.mval(i,j) = mval(i,j) - arg.p->m[i][j];
        }
    return sum; // see note for operator*()
}


matrix matrix::operator-(const double arg) {
    matrix sum(rows(),cols());
    for (int i=0; i< rows(); i++)  {
      for (int j = 0; j < cols(); j++)
        sum.mval(i,j) = mval(i,j) - arg;
        }
    return sum; // see note for operator*()
}


matrix matrix::operator-() {
    matrix unaryminus(rows(),cols());
    for (int i=0; i< rows(); i++)  {
      for (int j = 0; j < cols(); j++)
        unaryminus.mval(i,j) = -mval(i,j);
        }
    return unaryminus;
}


matrix matrix::operator*(const matrix& arg) {
    if( cols() != arg.rows())
      error("# rows of second mat must equal "
            "# cols of first for multiply!");
    matrix result(rows(),arg.cols());
    for(int row = 0; row < rows(); row++)  {
      for(int col = 0; col < arg.cols(); col++){
        double sum = 0;
        for(int i = 0; i < cols(); i++)
          sum += mval(row,i) * arg.p->m[i][col];
        result.mval(row,col) = sum;
       }
     }
    return result; // Returning a local variable?
    // copy-initializer happens before the destructor,
    // so reference count is 2 when destructor is called,
    // thus destructor doesn't free the memory.
}


matrix matrix::operator*(const double arg) {
    matrix result(rows(),cols());
    for (int i=0; i< rows(); i++)  {
      for (int j = 0; j < cols(); j++)
        result.mval(i,j) = mval(i,j) * arg;
        }
    return result;
```

```
    }

    double & matrix::val(int row, int col) {
        if (row > 0 && row < rows() && col > 0 && col < cols())
            return (mval(row,col));
        else
            error("index out of range");
    }

    matrix matrix::transpose() {
        if(rows() != cols())
            error("matrix must be square to transpose!\n");
        matrix trans(rows(),cols());
        for (int row = 0; row < rows(); row++) {
            for(int col = 0; col < cols(); col++)
                trans.mval(col,row) = mval(row,col);
                }
        return trans;
    }

    double matrix::mmin() {
        double temp;
        if(rows() <= 0 || cols() <= 0)
            error("bad matrix size for min()");
        double minimum = mval(0,0);
        for (int row = 0; row < rows(); row++)  {
            for(int col = 0; col < cols(); col++)
                if ((temp = mval(row,col)) < minimum)
                    minimum = temp;
                }
        return minimum;
    }

    double matrix::mmax() {
        double temp;
        if(rows() <= 0 || cols() <= 0)
            error("bad matrix size for max()");
        double maximum = mval(0,0);
        for (int row = 0; row < rows(); row++) {
            for(int col = 0; col < cols(); col++){
                if ((temp = mval(row,col)) > maximum)
                    maximum = temp;
            }
            }
        return maximum;
    }

    double matrix::mean() {
    int row, col;
```

```
    double sum = 0;
      for (row = 0; row < rows(); row++)
        for(col = 0; col < cols(); col++)
          sum += fabs(mval(row,col));
      return sum/(row * col);
    }

    double matrix::variance() {
       int row, col;
       double s_squared = 0;
       double mn = mean();
       for (row = 0; row < rows(); row++)  {
         for(col = 0; col < cols(); col++){
           double temp = mval(row,col) - mn;
           temp *= temp;
           s_squared += temp;
         }
        }
       s_squared /= row * col -1; // number of elements minus one
       return s_squared;
    }


    double matrix::determinant() {
       if(rows() != cols())
         error("matrix must be square for determinant()");
       matrix indx(cols()); // create the "index vector"
       matrix B(cols()); // see pp 38. in Numerical Recipes
       int d;
       // perform the decomposition once:
       matrix decomp = lu_decompose(indx,d);
       double determinant = d;
       for(int i=0; i < cols() ; i++)
         determinant *= decomp.mval(i,i);
       return determinant;
    }

    matrix matrix::inverse() {
       if(rows() != cols())
         error("matrix must be square for inverse()");
       matrix Y("I",rows()); // create an identity matrix
       matrix indx(cols()); // create the "index vector"
       matrix B(cols()); // see Press & Flannery
       int d;
       // perform the decomposition once:
       matrix decomp = lu_decompose(indx,d);
       for(int col = 0; col < cols(); col++){
         B.copy_column(Y,col,0);
         decomp.lu_back_subst(indx,B);
         Y.copy_column(B,0,col);
```

```
      }
   return Y.transpose();
}

void matrix::print(char *msg) {
   if (*msg) printf("%s:\n",msg);
   for (int row=0; row< rows(); row++){
      for (int col = 0; col < cols(); col++)
            printf("%6.6f  ", mval(row,col));
      printf("\n");
   }
}
```

```
/******************************************************************
The private support functions for determinant & inverse.
******************************************************************/
```

```
// copy the from_col of mm to the to_col of "this"
void matrix::copy_column(matrix& mm, int from_col, int to_col) {
   if(rows() != mm.rows())
      error("number of rows must be equal for copy_column()");
   for(int row=0; row < rows(); row++)
      mval(row,to_col) = mm.mval(row,from_col);
}
```

```
void matrix::switch_columns(int col1, int col2) {
   matrix temp(rows());
   for(int row = 0; row < rows(); row++)
      // temporarily store col 1:
      temp.mval(row,0) = mval(row,col1);
   for(row = 0; row < rows(); row++)
      mval(row,col1) = mval(row,col2); // move col2 to col1
   for(row = 0; row < rows(); row++)
      mval(row,col2) = temp.mval(row,0); // move temp to col2
}
```

```
// make an image of a matrix (used in L-U decomposition)
void matrix::deepcopy(matrix& from, matrix& to) {
   if(from.rows() != to.rows() || from.cols() != to.cols())
      error("matrices must be equal dimensions for deepcopy()");
   for(int row = 0; row < from.rows(); row++) {
      for(int col = 0; col < from.cols(); col++)
         to.mval(row,col) = from.mval(row,col);
         }
}
```

```
// scale a matrix (used in L-U decomposition)
matrix matrix::scale() {
   double temp;
```

```
      if(rows() <= 0 || cols() <= 0)
          error("bad matrix size for scale()");
      if(rows() != cols())
          error("matrix must be square for scale()");
      matrix scale_vector(rows());
      for (int col = 0; col < cols(); col++){
        double maximum = 0;
        for(int row = 0; row < rows(); row++)
          if ((temp = (double)fabs(mval(row,col))) > maximum)
            maximum = temp;  // find max column magnitude in this row
        if(maximum == 0)
            error("singular matrix in scale()");
        scale_vector.mval(col,0) = 1/maximum; // save the scaling
      }
      return scale_vector;
}
matrix matrix::lu_decompose(matrix& indx, int& d ) {
/*
    Returns the L-U decomposition of a matrix. indx is an output
    vector that records the row permutation effected by the
    partial pivoting, d is output as +-1 depending on whether the
    number of row interchanges was even or odd, respectively.
    This routine is used in combination with lu_back_subst to
    solve linear equations or invert a matrix.
*/
      if(rows() != cols())
          error("Matrix must be square to L-U decompose!\n");
      d = 1; // parity check
      int row,col,k,col_max; // counters
      double dum; // from the book — I don't know significance
      double sum;
      double maximum;
      matrix lu_decomp(rows(),cols());
      // make a direct copy of the original matrix:
      deepcopy(*this,lu_decomp);
      matrix scale_vector = lu_decomp.scale(); // scale the matrix
      // The loop over columns of Crout's method:
      for(row = 0; row < rows(); row++){
        if (row > 0) {
          // eqn 2.3.12 except for row=col:
          for (col = 0; col <= row-1; col++) {
          sum = lu_decomp.mval(row,col);
          if(col > 0) {
            for(k = 0; k <= col-1; k++)
              sum -= lu_decomp.mval(row,k)•lu_decomp.mval(k,col);
            lu_decomp.mval(row,col) = sum;
          }
          }
        }
```

```
    // Initialize for the search for the largest pivot element:
    maximum = 0;
    // i=j of eq 2.3.12 & i=j+1..N of 2.3.13:
    for(col=row; col <= cols()-1; col++){
       sum = lu_decomp.mval(row,col);
       if(row > 0){
       for(k=0; k <= row-1; k++)
          sum -= lu_decomp.mval(k,col) * lu_decomp.mval(row,k);
       lu_decomp.mval(row,col) = sum;
       }
       // figure of merit for pivot:
       dum = scale_vector.mval(col,0) * fabs(sum);
       if (dum >= maximum){ // is it better than the best so far?
       col_max = col;
       maximum = dum;
       }
    }
    // Do we need to interchange rows?
    if(row != col_max) {
       lu_decomp.switch_columns(col_max,row); // Yes, do so...
       d *= -1; // ... and change the parity of d
       // also interchange the scale factor:
       dum = scale_vector.mval(col_max,0);
       scale_vector.mval(col_max,0) = scale_vector.mval(col,0);
       scale_vector.mval(row,0) = dum;
    }
    indx.mval(row,0) = col_max;
    // Now, finally, divide by the pivot element:
    if(row != rows() -1){
       if(lu_decomp.mval(row,row) == 0)
          lu_decomp.mval(row,row) = TINY;
       // If the pivot element is zero the matrix is
       // singular (at least to the precision of the
       // algorithm).  For some applications on singular
       // matrices, it is desirable to substitute TINY for zero
       dum = 1/lu_decomp.mval(row,row);
       for(col=row+1; col <= cols()-1; col++)
       lu_decomp.mval(row,col) *= dum;
    }
 }
 if(lu_decomp.mval(rows()-1,cols()-1) == 0)
    lu_decomp.mval(rows()-1,cols()-1) = TINY;
 return lu_decomp;
}


void matrix::lu_back_subst(matrix& indx, matrix& b) {
/*
Solves the set of N linear equations A•X = B.  Here "this"
 is the LU-decomposition of the matrix A, determined by the
```

routine lu_decompose(). Indx is input as the permutation
vector returned by lu_decompose(). B is input as the
right-hand side vector B, and returns with the solution
vector X. This routine takes into account the possibility
that B will begin with many zero elements, so it is efficient
for use in matrix inversion.   See pp 36-37 in
Press & Flannery.

```
*/
   if(rows() != cols())
      error ("non-square lu_decomp matrix in lu_back_subst()");
   if(rows() != b.rows())
      error("wrong size B vector passed to lu_back_subst()");
   if(rows() != indx.rows())
      error("wrong size indx vector passed to lu_back_subst()");
   int row,col,ll;
   int ii = 0;
   double sum;
   for(col=0;col < cols(); col++){
     ll= (int)indx.mval(col,0);
     sum = b.mval(ll,0);
     b.mval(ll,0) = b.mval(col,0);
     if (ii >= 0)
        for(row = ii; row <= col-1; row++)
        sum -= mval(row,col) * b.mval(row,0);
     else if(sum != 0)
        ii = col;
     b.mval(col,0) = sum;
   }
   for(col = cols() -1; col >= 0; col—){
     sum = b.mval(col,0);
     if (col < cols() -1)
        for (row = col + 1; row <= rows()-1; row++)
        sum -= mval(row,col) * b.mval(row,0);
     // store a component of the soln vector X:
     b.mval(col,0) = sum/mval(col,col);
   }
}
```

Testing the Matrix Class

This program exercises some of the features of **class matrix**. You can get
much more sophisticated, as in the matrix equation at the beginning of
this appendix.

```
// ANALYZE.CXX: Exercise some of the features of the
// matrix class.
#include <stdio.h>
```

```
#include "matrix.hxx"
#include <stdlib.h>

main(int argc, char * argv[])
{
    if (argc != 2) {
        puts("usage: analyze matrix_file_name");
        exit(1);
    }
    matrix  m(argv[1]);
    m.print("m is");
    matrix minv = m.inverse();
    minv.print("inverse of m is");
    (m * minv).print("m * m.inverse()");
    printf("determinant = %6.6f\n",m.determinant());
    printf("min = %6.6f\n",m.mmin());
    printf("max = %6.6f\n",m.mmax());
    printf("mean = %6.6f\n",m.mean());
    printf("variance = %6.6f\n",m.variance());
    m.write_standard("test.$$$", "this is a test");
}
```

The following file is an example in standard matrix format that was used for testing. To use it, type **analyze test.std**.

```
# TEST.STD: a file in "standard" matrix format
# A large matrix for testing the inverse function
r = 7 c = 7
# (elements must be separated by at least one white space)
:::
3      - 5      6       4      -2      -3       8
1        1     -9      15       1      -9       2
2      - 1      7       5      -1       6      11
- 1      1      3       2       7      -1      -2
4        3      1      -7       2       1       1
2        9     -8      11      -1      -4      -1
7        2     - 1      2       7      -1       9
```

Makefile for matrix class

Here is the makefile for the examples in this appendix.

```
# makefile for Appendix B
```

```
# Zortech C++:
CPP = ztc
# Glockenspiel C++:
#CPP = ccxx

.cxx.obj:
        $(CPP) -c $*.cxx

all : analyze.exe

analyze.exe : analyze.obj matrix.obj
        $(CPP) $**

matrix.obj: matrix.cxx matrix.hxx

analyze.obj: analyze.cxx matrix.hxx
```

C Windows

Like Appendix A, this is a PC-only project. It is a small text windowing package developed with the Zortech C++ **disp** display package. Since the **disp** package performs direct screen writes, it should be possible to use this package with TSRs (terminate-and-stay-resident programs), but it hasn't been tested.

When you define a new window, the area under the window is saved, then the window is drawn, boxed, and given a title. The WINDEMO.CXX program gives an example of how to use windows. It also shows how you can use **new** and **delete** to create windows that are not subject to normal scoping rules, so they can be created at run time or managed in a linked list. (See Appendix A and Chapter 10 for examples of a linked-list class.) When a window goes out of scope, it is cleared from the screen and the previous screen contents are restored.

The window class is a good example of the C++ "data encapsulation and hiding" feature. As you can see, it is much easier for the window to create its own structure and carry it around than for you to create a global structure and explicitly pass it to each window function (which is normally necessary for these types of systems in plain C).

To create a window, enter

```
window  foobar(left_x, top_y, right_x, bottom_y,
               WHITE_CHAR I BLACK_BACK,
               "A window called foobar");
```

To write into **foobar**, enter

foobar.puts("A string to be written into the foobar window");

The window will automatically clean itself up when it goes out of scope.

Code for Class Window

As you will see in the demonstration program, building a window into a class is helpful not only because it encapsulates and hides the data for the window. Since any object can be created dynamically (by using **new**) as easily as it is created at compile time, the class adds great programming flexibility.

Control of Screen Colors

Each text character displayed on the IBM PC has an accompanying *attribute* that determines how the character will be displayed. Bits in the attribute byte control various aspects of the character, for instance color or underline. This header file allows you to give the foreground and background colors by name, instead of by some bit pattern. Since the operations are performed at compile time, these definitions do not add any run time overhead.

```
// COLORS.HXX: definitions for CGA screen
// characteristics and colors.
// base address of CGA (and EGA in color graphics mode):
#define SCREEN_BASE 0xb800
#define SCREEN_HEIGHT 25
#define SCREEN_WIDTH 80
// number of chars and attributes in a screen:
#define SCREEN_CHARS (SCREEN_WIDTH * SCREEN_HEIGHT * 2)

#define BIT0 0x01    // bit masks
#define BIT1 0x02
#define BIT2 0x04
#define BIT3 0x08
#define BIT4 0x10
#define BIT5 0x20
```

```
#define BIT6 0x40
#define BIT7 0x80

// Make a complete attribute by ORing a
// CHARacter type with a BACKground type:
#define BLUE_CHAR        BIT0
#define GREEN_CHAR       BIT1
#define RED_CHAR         BIT2
#define INTENSE          BIT3
#define BLUE_BACK        BIT4
#define GREEN_BACK       BIT5
#define RED_BACK         BIT6
#define BLINKING         BIT7


#define BLACK_CHAR 0
#define CYAN_CHAR (GREEN_CHAR | BLUE_CHAR)
#define MAGENTA_CHAR (RED_CHAR | BLUE_CHAR)
#define BROWN_CHAR (RED_CHAR | GREEN_CHAR)
#define WHITE_CHAR (RED_CHAR | GREEN_CHAR | BLUE_CHAR)
#define GRAY_CHAR (INTENSE | BLACK_CHAR)
#define LIGHT_BLUE_CHAR (INTENSE | BLUE_CHAR)
#define LIGHT_GREEN_CHAR (INTENSE | GREEN_CHAR)
#define LIGHT_CYAN_CHAR (INTENSE | CYAN_CHAR)
#define LIGHT_RED_CHAR (INTENSE | RED_CHAR)
#define LIGHT_MAGENTA_CHAR (INTENSE | MAGENTA_CHAR)
#define YELLOW_CHAR (INTENSE | BROWN_CHAR)
#define BRIGHT_WHITE_CHAR ( INTENSE | WHITE_CHAR)


#define BLACK_BACK 0
#define CYAN_BACK (GREEN_BACK | BLUE_BACK)
#define MAGENTA_BACK (RED_BACK | BLUE_BACK)
#define BROWN_BACK (RED_BACK | GREEN_BACK)
#define WHITE_BACK (RED_BACK | GREEN_BACK | BLUE_BACK)
#define GRAY_BACK (INTENSE | BLACK_BACK)
#define LIGHT_BLUE_BACK (INTENSE | BLUE_BACK)
#define LIGHT_GREEN_BACK (INTENSE | GREEN_BACK)
#define LIGHT_CYAN_BACK (INTENSE | CYAN_BACK)
#define LIGHT_RED_BACK (INTENSE | RED_CHAR)
#define LIGHT_MAGENTA_BACK (INTENSE | MAGENTA_CHAR)
#define YELLOW_BACK (INTENSE | BROWN_BACK)
#define BRIGHT_WHITE_BACK ( INTENSE | WHITE_BACK)
```

Window Class Definition

Here is the header file for **class window**.

```
// WINDOWS.HXX: A text Windowing system for the IBM PC
#ifndef WINDOWS_HXX
#define WINDOWS_HXX
#include "colors.hxx" // CGA color #defines

class window {    // coordinates start at upper left corner as 0,0
    int left_x;      // left-most extent of window
    int top_y;       // upper limit of window
    int right_x;     // right-most extent of window
    int bottom_y;  // lower limit of window
    unsigned char attributes;   // default char & background colors
    int cursor_x; // for functions that need a window cursor
    int cursor_y;
    long screen_chars;   // number of chars in the patch of window
    // place to save the screen so it can be restored:
    unsigned * save_buf;
public:
    window(int left, int top, int right, int bottom,
             unsigned char attrib = WHITE_CHAR | BLACK_BACK,
             char * window_title = "");
    ~window();
    void clear(); // clean the text from a window
    // Write text to a window:
    void puts(char *string, unsigned char attrib);
    void puts(char *string) { puts(string, attributes); }
    // create the frame around the window:
    void make_box();
    // Puts window up if it isn't already; clears it if it is:
    void draw() { clear(); make_box(); }
    // Center the title at the top of the window:
    void title(char *msg, unsigned char attrib);
    void title(char *msg) { title(msg, attributes); }
    // Move the cursor in the window, respecting boundaries:
    void gotoXY(int X, int Y);
    void dump(); // for debugging
};

#endif WINDOWS_HXX
```

Window Methods

The tiny class called **_display**, and the single global instance of it called **_automatic_disp**, will automatically call the **disp_open( )** function from the **disp** display package upon start up, and the **disp_close( )** function when the program exits, so you don't have to worry about calling these functions.

```
// WINDOWS.CXX: Text windows for the IBM PC
#include <stdio.h>
#include <stdlib.h>
#include <disp.h>
#include "windows.hxx"

//*********************************************************************
// By creating a single global instance of _display, you insure
// the disp_open() function is called once at start-up, and
// disp_close() is called once at exit.  This class is created
// solely for the use of the constructor and the destructor.

class _display {
public:
   _display() { disp_open(); }
   ~_display() { disp_close(); }
};

_display _automatic_disp;

//*********************************************************************
// Constructor for a window

window::window(int left, int top, int right,
            int bottom, unsigned char attrib, char * window_title) {
   left_x = left; // establish global window values
   top_y = top;
   right_x = right;
   bottom_y = bottom;
   attributes = attrib;
   cursor_x = left_x + 1; // put cursor inside box
   cursor_y = top_y + 1;
   screen_chars = ((right_x - left_x) * 2) *
                       (bottom_y - top_y + 2) *
                       sizeof(unsigned);
   save_buf = new unsigned[screen_chars];
   // Now save the screen we interrupted:
   disp_peekbox(save_buf,top_y,left_x,bottom_y,right_x);
   draw();
   title(window_title,attributes);
}

//*********************************************************************
// Destructor for a window.  This function is called
// automatically when a window goes out of scope (or when
// "delete" is used on a dynamically-allocated object).
window::~window() {
   // restore the screen to what it was before this window:
   disp_pokebox(save_buf,top_y,left_x,bottom_y,right_x);
}
```

```
//*********************************************************************
// Clears a window (including the border), retaining the
// attributes.
void window::clear() {
    for (unsigned y = top_y; y <= bottom_y ; y++)
        for (unsigned x = left_x; x <= right_x; x++)
            disp_pokew(y,x,(attributes << 8) + ' ');
}


//*********************************************************************
// Puts a string in a window, wrapping if it hits a border and
// refusing to go past the lower right corner.
void window::puts(char *string, unsigned char attribute) {
    if (!*string) return; // empty string
    do {
        if (*string == 10) { // check for newline
            cursor_x = left_x + 1;
            cursor_y += 1;
            if (cursor_y > bottom_y - 1)
                cursor_y -= 1; // just bump against the bottom
        } else {
            disp_pokew(cursor_y, cursor_x, (attribute<<8) + *string);
            // Move cursor ahead, but keep it inside window
            if (++cursor_x > right_x -1) {
                cursor_x = left_x + 1;
                if (++cursor_y > bottom_y -1)
                    cursor_y—;
            }
        }
    } while (*++string); // stops at the string's null terminator
}


//*********************************************************************
// Puts a box of double bars around the window, using the
// window's pre-defined character and background colors.
void window::make_box() {
    int x,y;
    for (x=left_x, y=top_y; x++ < right_x; )       // top bar
        disp_pokew(y,x,(attributes << 8) +  0xCD);
    for (x=left_x, y=bottom_y; x++ < right_x; ) // bottom bar
        disp_pokew(y,x,(attributes << 8) + 0xCD);
    for (x=left_x, y=top_y; y++ < bottom_y; )     // left bar
        disp_pokew(y,x,(attributes << 8) + 0xBA);
    for (x=right_x, y=top_y; y++ < bottom_y; )   // right bar
        disp_pokew(y,x,(attributes << 8) + 0xBA);

        // bottom left corner:
    disp_pokew( bottom_y, left_x, (attributes << 8) + 0xC8);
        // top left corner:
    disp_pokew(top_y, left_x, (attributes << 8) + 0xC9);
        // top right corner:
```

```
    disp_pokew(top_y, right_x,  (attributes << 8) + 0xBB);
      // bottom right corner:
    disp_pokew(bottom_y, right_x,  (attributes << 8) + 0xBC);
}

//*******************************************************************
// Centers a title with foreground and background colors of
// your choice.  Title is placed in the top bar of the window.
void window::title(char *title, unsigned char attribute) {
    char *title_ptr;
    int title_count, x;
    make_box(); // redraw box if new title is smaller than old one
    for (title_ptr = title, title_count = 1; *++title_ptr;
            title_count++)
        ; // count number of chars in string
          // (stops when *title_ptr == '\0')
    // starting x value to center the title
    x = (right_x - left_x - title_count)/2 + left_x + 1;
    while (*title)  // stops when *title == '\0'
        disp_pokew(top_y,x++,(attribute<<8) + *title++);
}


//*******************************************************************
// Move the window cursor within the window, respecting the
// boundaries.
void window::gotoXY(int X, int Y) {
    // If X isn't outside of the window bounds, set cursor
    // to X, else set it to just inside the window bounds
    if (X > left_x && X < right_x )
        cursor_x = X;
    else
        if (X <= left_x)
            cursor_x = left_x +1;
        else
            cursor_x = right_x -1;

    // same for y
    if (Y > top_y && Y < bottom_y )
        cursor_y = Y;
    else
        if (Y <= top_y)
            cursor_y = top_y +1;
        else
            cursor_y = bottom_y -1;
}
```

```
void window::dump() {
    // print some information for debugging
    printf("left_x = %d\n",left_x);
    printf("top_y = %d\n",top_y);
    printf("right_x = %d\n",right_x);
    printf("bottom_y = %d\n",bottom_y);
    printf("attributes = %d\n",attributes);
    printf("cursor_x = %d\n",cursor_x);
    printf("cursor_y = %d\n",cursor_y);
}
```

Demonstration of the Window Class

The following program creates several windows, gives them titles, and displays text. A window is also created, using **new**, and destroyed, using **delete**.

```
// WINDEMO.CXX: demonstration of windows class
#include "windows.hxx"

main() {
    int x = 0, y = 0, ch;
    window foo(20,10,70,24,WHITE_CHAR | BLUE_BACK,
                "A Test of A window Object");
    foo.puts("This string starts at 1,1");
    getch();  // pause so we can see the effect...
    // The following window "tiny" is created on the heap via
    // dynamic memory allocation (the "new" operator).  It is
    // immune to scoping rules, and only goes away when we use
    // "delete" later in the program.  Thus, you could create a
    // list of windows at run time and manipulate them via a
    // linked-list (see appendix A).
    window * tiny = new window(0,20,6,24, RED_CHAR | WHITE_BACK,
                                "Tiny");
    tiny->puts("scoping demo");
    { // "bar" is a window in it's own scope, so we get to see it
        // disappear when it goes out of scope.
        window bar(0,0,30,10, BLUE_CHAR | RED_BACK,
                    "A window called Bar");
        bar.gotoXY(2,2);
        bar.puts("This is another string which probably won't fit "
                    "into the window on a single line, so we'll make "
                    "sure it wraps properly");
        getch();
    }
    window tall(40,0, 75,20, GREEN_CHAR | YELLOW_BACK,
```

```
                    "A Tall Window");
        tall.puts("With nothing very significant in it...");
        getch();
        delete tiny;
        getch();
        window bye(20, 8,60,16);
        bye.gotoXY(8,4);
        bye.puts("That's all, folks!!");
        getch();
}
```

Improvements You Could Add

This class is only set up to display text in pop-up windows. There is no capability to accept user input, but it should be easy to add. You could also create subclasses for dialog or yes and no answers. You may also want to pop the active cursor from window to window and bring the active window to the front.

The mouse will also work in text mode, as well as in graphics mode as shown in Appendix A. You can add mouse control of window selection, text selection within a window, text menus for the mouse, or cut and paste between windows, among other things.

Makefile for Appendix C

Here is the **makefile** to compile the examples in this appendix.

```
# Appendix C: Text Windows for the IBM PC

.cxx.obj :
        ztc -c $*.cxx

windemo.exe : windows.obj windemo.obj
        ztc -owindemo $**

windows.obj : windows.cxx windows.hxx colors.hxx

windemo.obj : windemo.cxx windows.hxx colors.hxx
```

Trademarks

Epson®	Seiko Epson Corp.
FORTH®	FORTH, Inc.
HP LaserJet™	Hewlett-Packard Company
IBM® PC®	International Business Machines, Corp.
Macintosh®	Apple Computer Inc.
MicroCAD™	Imagimedia Technologies, Inc.
MS-DOS®	Microsoft Corporation
Oregon Software C++™	Oregon Software
PostScript®	Adobe Systems, Inc.
Quick C™	Microsoft Corporation
Topspeed®	Jensen & Partners International
Turbo C®	Borland International, Inc.
Turbo Pascal	Borland International, Inc.
UNIX®	AT&T
Zortech C++ Compiler™	Zortech Inc.

Index